EXPLORING THE MATRIX
Visions of the Cyber Present

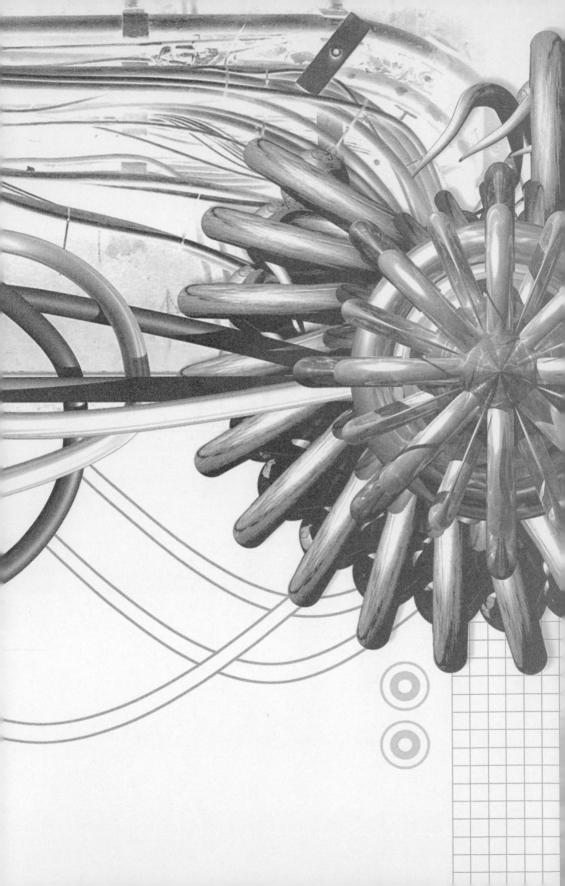

EXPLORING
THE
MATRIX

Visions of the Cyber Present

Edited by
Karen Haber

A BYRON PREISS BOOK

ST. MARTIN'S PRESS
NEW YORK

Editor: Karen Haber
Project Editor: Howard Zimmerman
Designed by j. vita
Interior illustrations, pages 5, 30–31 (and inserts), 74–75 (and inserts), 98–99 (and inserts), 112–113 (and inserts), 122–123 (and inserts), 148–149 (and inserts), 180–181 (and inserts), 200–201 (and inserts), 250–251 (and inserts) copyright © 2003 Darrel Anderson
Interior iullustrations, pages 2–3, 6–7, 8, 9, 16–17 (and inserts), 48–49 (and inserts), 64–65 (and inserts), 136–137 (and inserts), 168–169 (and inserts), 212–213 (and inserts), 222–223 (and inserts), 236–237 (and inserts)
copyright © 2003 Robert Zohrab
Jacket illustration copyright © 2003 Robert Zohrab

Introduction copyright © 2003 Karen Haber
"Every Other Movie Is the Blue Pill" copyright © 2003 Bruce Sterling
"The Real Matrix" copyright © 2003 Stephen Baxter
"The Matrix: Know Thyself" copyright © 2003 John Shirley
"Art Imitates Life (Yes, It's News)" copyright © 2003 Darrel Anderson
"Literary Influences on The Matrix" copyright © 2003 Paul Di Filippo
"More Than You'll Ever Know: Down The Rabbit Hole of The Matrix" copyright © 2003 Kathleen Ann Goonan
"The Matrix and the Star Maker" copyright © 2003 Mike Resnick
"Yuen Woo-ping and the Art of Flying" copyright © 2003 Walter Jon Williams
"Alice in Metropolis or It's All Done with Mirrors" copyright © 2003 Dean Motter
"The Matrix as Simulacrum" copyright © 2003 Ian Watson
"The Matrix as Sci-Fi" copyright © 2003 Joe Haldeman
"Tomorrow May Be Different" copyright © 2003 David Brin
"Revenge of the Nerds, Part X" copyright © 2003 Alan Dean Foster
"Reflection in a Cyber Eye" copyright © 2003 Karen Haber
"Meditations on the Singular Matrix" copyright © 2003 James Patrick Kelly
"The Matrix Made Me Do It" copyright © 2003 Kevin J. Anderson
"Dreaming Real" copyright © 2003 Rick Berry

A BYRON PREISS BOOK

www.stmartins.com

Library of Congress Cataloging-in-Publication Data

Exploring the Matrix : visions of the cyber present / edited by Karen Haber.
p. cm.
"Byron Preiss book."
ISBN 0-312-31358-6
1. Matrix (Motion picture) I. Haber, Karen.

PN1997.M395E88 2003
791.43'72—dc21

2003041411

10 9 8 7 6 5 4 3

For Mike Benko—
He knows why

CONTENTS

INTRODUCTION
Pat Cadigan 10

EVERY OTHER MOVIE IS THE BLUE PILL
Bruce Sterling 16

THE REAL MATRIX
Stephen Baxter 30

THE MATRIX: KNOW THYSELF
John Shirley 48

ART IMITATES LIFE (YES, IT'S NEWS)
Darrel Anderson 64

LITERARY INFLUENCES ON THE MATRIX
Paul Di Filippo 74

MORE THAN YOU'LL EVER KNOW: DOWN
THE RABBIT HOLE OF THE MATRIX
Kathleen Ann Goonan 98

THE MATRIX AND THE STAR MAKER
Mike Resnick 112

YUEN WOO-PING AND THE ART OF FLYING
Walter Jon Williams 122

ALICE IN METROPOLIS   OR   IT'S ALL DONE
WITH MIRRORS
    Dean Motter 136

THE MATRIX AS SIMULACRUM
    Ian Watson 148

THE MATRIX AS SCI-FI
    Joe Haldeman 168

TOMORROW MAY BE DIFFERENT
    David Brin 180

REVENGE OF THE NERDS, PART X
    Alan Dean Foster 200

REFLECTIONS IN A CYBER EYE
    Karen Haber 212

MEDITATIONS ON THE SINGULAR MATRIX
    James Patrick Kelly 222

THE MATRIX MADE ME DO IT
    Kevin J. Anderson 236

DREAMING REAL
    Rick Berry 250

ABOUT THE AUTHORS 266

EXPLORING
THE
MATRIX
Visions of the Cyber Present

INTRODUCTION

What Is The Matrix . . .
and Why Is It Such a Big Deal?

Pat Cadigan

The question I hear most often in interviews conducted by people with only a passing acquaintance with science fiction is, "What drew you to science fiction?" It's not always worded exactly that way, but that's the gist. It's not an easy question to answer. You're drawn to science fiction in much the same way you're drawn to a type of music—something in it speaks to you, bone-deep.

This makes it sound like something for a specialized audience with particular tastes, and there's a certain degree of truth to that. Those who like the stuff follow their favorite writers, or TV series, or, yes, movies with a devotion that, say, Red Sox fans would find familiar. And much in the same way that certain professional athletes attract the kind of notice that takes them beyond prominence in their sports to full celebrity status, certain things that originate squarely in the science fiction world—or universe—break out and attract a following beyond genre aficionados. *Star Trek* is probably the most famous example of a breakout hit; *Star Wars* is another. And the most recent is *The Matrix*.

Oddly enough, the breakout media blockbuster is more often than not science fiction, or a close relative (e.g., *Buffy the Vampire Slayer*). Oddly, because science fiction itself is more often than not treated like a punchline by everyone from critics and commentators to the bookstores' best customers. Oprah's Book Club didn't last long enough for anyone to start second-guessing what kind of books might be favored but I think it's safe to say that even if it had outlived Oprah herself by a hundred years, chances are slim to none that a science fiction novel would have gotten the nod even once.

If that isn't odd enough for you, consider this: Universities around the world offer Masters degree programs in science fiction and have done so for something like thirty years—post *Star Trek* and pre *Star Wars*.

In short, science fiction is: 1) an area of extreme commercial success; 2) a hotbed of advanced intellectual discourse; and 3) too trivial to deserve the notice or attention of serious cultural commentators and critics. Only human nature itself would seem to embody as many contradictions. Personally, I don't think this is a coincidence.

The genre of the fantastic, which comprises science fiction, fantasy, horror, and all the shadings and gradations in between, is a clear and unmistakable indication of sentience. Why? Because only sentient creatures are capable of conceiving of something outside the realm of known experience; only the sentient are capable of living beyond their physical senses. If the nature of life itself is yes or no, alive or dead—binary, if you will—then the nature of conscious life is true or false, which is completely different. If, as the saying goes, Man is the animal who laughs, Man is also the animal who lies—i.e., makes up stories. From the very beginning, these stories were long on fantastic elements—gods, goddesses, monsters, demons, angels, and miracles, not to mention the occasional and/or imminent apocalypse. These are the elements human beings have used to build their legends. That we're still doing so today is quite significant, I'd say.

For one thing, it proves conclusively and without a doubt that the whole storytelling thing that started all those millennia ago wasn't just a trend after all. Think about it—even the whole hunter-gatherer thing was just a phase.

Actually, if any marriage was made in heaven, it's that of the movies with science fiction. Especially now—our dreams, fantasies, nightmares, and mythologies can be externalized like never before and the technology improves by Superman-style leaps and bounds. So it's hardly any mystery as to why we want to think about, talk about, argue about, analyse, theorize, and decode what we watch on the silver screen, and then watch some more. Since science fiction at its best is the literature of ideas, enormous amounts of creativity, art, and science go into the creation of those ideas as well as finding ways to give them external form. The effects from these things are quite far-reaching. I mean, as worthwhile and important as films like *American Beauty* and *The Usual Suspects* are, they wouldn't demand the creation of, say, Industrial Light & Magic or Skywalker Studios—though they certainly do see some benefits after the fact.

Of course, not all science-fiction movies are significant works of high intellectual art any more than all movies in general are created equal to *American Beauty* or *The Usual Suspects*. Nor does the fact that a movie is science fiction automatically make it a finer, greater creation than any other. And vice versa—which is to say, a movie is not pop culture junk food simply because it's science fiction to begin with.

And this final caveat, which I feel has too often gone unmentioned: If it's both science fiction and a significant work of high intellectual art, it's still science fiction. Got that?

Many of us in the field have watched people in the so-called mainstream produce work that is plainly and unmistakably science fiction and then claim emphatically that the work in question isn't science fiction at all. Sometimes they'll call it a "near-future thriller" or "a myth retold in a contemporary setting" or (my favorite) "boldly original and imaginative." And yeah, it probably is—and it's science fiction. We wouldn't mind, except that so many of these people who think they are, uh, going where no one has gone before (to phrase a coin) are just reinventing the wheel, and doing it badly.

We professionals are a tough audience, we are. Only one audience is tougher: *our* audience. So you may take the fact that *The Matrix* can inspire an entire book's worth of essays from experienced professionals in the field as high praise indeed.

All right, you're saying to yourself, so what *is* the big deal about *The Matrix?*

The essays that follow will cover that, in much glorious and contradictory detail. Traditions will be surveyed, lineages traced, perspectives laid out, challenged, defended, rearranged in ways that will have you conducting mental conversations and arguments with the authors. And a distinguished bunch they are, too. While none of them is quite old enough to have *invented* this particular wheel (no, not even you, Resnick), they've all had an effect on its function and design to some degree. A few, like John Shirley and Bruce Sterling, were among the vanguard that took it to the level where *The Matrix* could come into being in the first place. Others like Steve Baxter and Kathleen Ann Goonan demonstrate that there's no limit to the new spins you can put on it. Pretty impressive, the lot of them; just wait till you see what they do with your mind.

It's that aforementioned hotbed of intellectual discourse, and all to do with something that also happens to be an extreme commercial success. Now, the generally accepted folk-wisdom on these matters states that anything with some intelligence in it cannot possibly be commercial while any commercial success won't have enough intelligent substance to fill a shot glass. It's always been satisfying to see that sweeping generalization bite the dust, though I have to confess that I haven't been enjoying it as much as I used to. I've seen it happen often enough over the course of one lifetime that I'm starting to get a little impatient. I'd have thought that of all the lessons human beings had to learn, this would be one of the easier ones.

Like I said earlier, even the whole hunter-gatherer thing was just a phase.

Every Other Movie Is the Blue Pill

Bruce Sterling

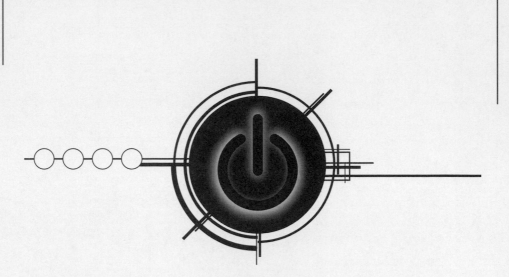

To make *The Matrix* cost over sixty million dollars. I don't know if you've ever hung out much with people commanding dozens of millions of dollars. Once I attended the World Economic Forum, where the planet's ultra-rich people flock in large crowds. This event took place in New York, in the jittery, heavily armed post-9/11 period, and the vibe there was very, very *Matrix* indeed.

There were swarms of armed bodyguards, marbled halls with swishing bronze elevators, glum, impassive federal agents, expensive eyewear, Forum groupies in sexy tailored costumes, the Secret Service in black bulletproof SWAT gear. . . . Very intense, very out-there, very designery, very Wachowski Brothers.

The World Economic Forum is not supposed to be scary. It's a philanthropic event. The Forum is all for the public good, and the worldwide betterment of the human condition. That is the public rationale, at least. That is the Blue Pill version, as it were.

However, you don't have to be a Seattle rioter or Naomi Klein to get it about the World Economic Forum's extreme disconnection from the man-in-the-street. The attendees there . . . they were uniformly courteous and scarily intelligent people, but they bear just the same relationship to a middle-class American that a middle-class American bears to an illiterate Venezuelan *campesino*. They are from a different level of reality. They dwell in a seamless world of private jets to the Waldorf-Astoria, where public space is the eight feet between the doorman and the limo.

Much the same goes for the galactic gulf that separates *The Matrix* from its street-level inspirations in underground comix and sci-fi paperbacks. I doubt that anyone understands this better than Larry and Andy Wachowski. Somehow, and I give them every credit, they were able to metabolize the Hollywood red pill and leap to the dizziest levels of the military-entertainment complex. I've never met the Wachowski Brothers, but I have every confidence that they get it. Otherwise, two guys with their exquisite design sense would never choose to wear Converse sneakers and backwards baseball caps.

Luc Besson directed the science-fiction film *The Fifth Element*, a film that eats at the same cafeteria with *The Matrix*, feasting at a global gumbo of counterculture sources. Luc Besson was at the World Economic Forum sitting at a table behind me, and he was the worst-dressed guy in the Waldorf-Astoria. Luc was so bad-boy, so confrontational, so in-your-face, that it was indescribable in any language other than French. And Luc really belonged there, that was the good part. When those Swiss captains of industry saw Luc in his four-day beard and bulging monocolor T-shirt, it cheered them all up. They sort of glanced at him sidelong and whispered. They were honored, really.

The Matrix may have budgeted for sixty-eight million, but for an ailing Warner Bros. it brought in way over two hundred million, and that was before the sequels. That was before the plastic action figures, the animé cartoons, comic books, and the thriving online *Matrix* cult groups. I enjoyed the hell out of that movie, and five years later I was still thinking about it fondly, and finally getting around to making this arch critical assessment. Man, a record like that speaks for itself.

Contemporary movie people, especially supremely rich and powerful ones like Steven Spielberg, they really get it about the homely authenticity of Levi's jeans and white tube-socks. Because they know all about how to dress very attractive people very attractively. They've got it down to a literal science, they can measure the colored glint off polyvinyl with digital light meters. Why would movie pros ever dress like their actors? If you're a director and you dress up like a star, it's like confessing to your colleagues that you swallowed the baited hook.

Therefore, in *The Matrix*'s "real world," that world where giant Geof Darrow drawings writhe their tentacles and harvest babies like cantaloupes, all the *Matrix* heroes, slinky Trinity, delphic Morpheus, they have to wear collarless, ragged, functional clothes. They eat oatmeal and work overtime. Just like the Wachowskis do.

Whenever they leap through a telephone into the Matrix, however, they instantly become rich glamour people. They've got limos, couture clothes, and fully booked agendas. They've got bodyguards—actually, they are their own bodyguards, because they're also comic-book superheroes.

Their furniture shows up out of nothingness, as if they'd Web-clicked it off Design Within Reach. They have an infinite number of guns . . . an elite education comes in a plug-in cartridge . . . they are regal, kinky aristocrats.

What little we learn about these people in the early part of the film suggests that they are fanatical terrorists. Morpheus is an international fugitive. Trinity is a crooked hacker who broke an IRS code. But they're not outlaws, not really.

Because they never have to rob, swindle, corrupt, bribe or steal. They don't take drugs, have psychotic episodes, or do jail time, the homely, everyday things that most actual criminals do routinely.

They're not criminals, hackers or terrorists. They're masters of illusion. So if the *Matrix* people have a functional equivalent in contemporary society, it's not the Cosa Nostra or the Baader-Meinhof gang. It's Hollywood producers. Because they possess enormous resources, all out proportion to the flimsy nature of their enterprise. They can create and deflate vast fantasies at will. And yet, their lives and careers are in constant danger. Just like Warner Bros. executives!

As Howard Waldrop once said, all science fiction is really about science fiction. Movies tend to be really about movies. Movies are what movie people find most interesting in life. For real movie people, even bad movies are magic. Any act of cinema is magic for movie people, just like movies were magic when Méliès, the French stage magician, was inventing them.

Let's consider the justly famous dojo sequence in *The Matrix*. A dojo is not a place where people really fight. A dojo is a stage; it's a place to train and mimic fighting. In this scene,

Morpheus is teaching Neo how to fight. But what he is really teaching Neo is how to think about the art of violence. And the real freight being hauled here is two young, breakout American filmmakers teaching Hollywood how to film action sequences.

You see, you don't need Hollywood stunt doubles! Not at all! That's just habit! Instead, you hire top-flight kung-fu action people from distant, global-economy Hong Kong, to fully train the actors so that they can act while they're fighting!

And now, check out this "bullet time" part where we *freeze stuff* just like a Marvel Comics two-page center spread! Watch and learn: now we *wheel around it* with this elaborate circle of synchronized cameras. See what we just did there? You think that was *air* we were breathing? Stop *trying* to make action films and *make* one!

The Wachowski Brothers are too young to be real cyberpunks. Besides, they work in the wrong industry. They do however have one great commonality with cyberpunk science fiction. They can't resist opening up the fabric of their artwork to stuff in every single idea they have ever had in their entire lives. In cyberpunk critical diction, this practice is known as "eyeball kicks." This term was first coined for the graphically overloaded comics pages of *MAD* magazine, so it is a cultural contribution of comics to science fiction. *Blade Runner* had it. *The Matrix* has it in spades.

H. G. Wells declared there should be only one weird element in every scientific romance. Wells was an author in a solemn Edwardian world that would allow itself only one or two really weird elements. Any more than that, and you weren't entertaining anymore; instead, you were raving and blaspheming.

The Wachowskis are native sons of the 1990s. It is impossible for them to think in such a limited way. If they ever found a world with just one freaky thing going on, they would assume they were in a cemetery.

In *The Matrix*, everything is going on. It's been blenderized and synthesized. It's tossed like brain salad.

First and most importantly, the film's got pop appeal elements. *All* kinds of elements: suicidal attacks by elite special forces, crashing helicopters, oodles of martial arts, a chaste yet passionate story of predestined love, bug-eyed monsters of the absolute first water, fetish clothes, captivity and torture and daring rescue, plus really weird, cool submarines.

Some of my favorite films are made entirely of clichés: *Casablanca, Every Which Way but Loose, The Prisoner of Zenda*. They're clichés, yes, but they have broken free of that problem, because the clichés slide through the narrative at refreshing orthogonal angles. In *Casablanca* the clichés are always tipping their hats at each other, "Hello war movie trope; pleased to meet you, women's weepy riff; how do you do, police procedural." They backflip from cliché to archetype. They generate tremendous narrative power. The clichés no longer tire us in these movies; they exhilarate.

The Matrix is a postmodern philosophical movie in which fragments of *philosophy* do this *Casablanca* cliché dance. There's Christian exegesis, a Redeemer myth, a death and rebirth, a hero in self-discovery, the Odyssey, Jean Baudrillard (lots of Baudrillard, the best parts of the film), science-fiction ontological riffs of the Philip K. Dick school, Nebuchadnezzar, the Buddha, Taoism, martial-arts mysticism, oracular prophecy, spoon-bending telekinesis, Houdini stage-show magic, Joseph Campbell, and

Godelian mathematical metaphysics.

This is a real mess. It would seem like a farrago if not for the film's premiere genius move, which is to reveal that the lysergic nightmare of cyborganic human-farms is this narrative's base reality. That's where people are born and die, and the rest of it is so much pixels. Since the world is a nightmare, the behavior of the bio-robot überlords makes no coherent sense. It isn't required to gel. If it ever gelled, it would lose its power. It would no longer be dreamlike, so it wouldn't tap in to the huge yet remarkably stupid creative powers of the Surrealist unconscious mind.

This brilliant concept allows every bit-part of metaphysics to float like flakes in a snow-globe, tight, contained, glittering, fragmented, and cheap. You get all the intellectually sexy head-trip

kicks of philosophizing without any of the boring hassles of consistency or rigor. It conveys the dark, goofy thrill of reading Milton or Dante when you're really stoned. I don't know how this wack stunt can ever be repeated, but that is one of the greatest achievements ever in the science-fiction cinema.

True, it veers perilously close to another Wells problem: "If anything is possible, nothing is interesting." But that's where the design comes in. In *The Matrix*, everything always and infallibly *looks* interesting. The visual tone is never lost; as moving images on a screen, the thing is as coherent as a laser.

Movie critics tend to wallow in the auteur theory: If anything cool happened, then Larry or Andy must have done it. But no one spends sixty-eight million dollars on the efforts of two people.

Geof Darrow must have come pretty cheap—all he needs is a pencil and paper—but he was the genius behind the writhing technorganic look of *The Matrix*'s version of hell. The high-concept guru guidance here came from Kevin Kelly, the magisterial author of *Out of Control: The New Biology of Machines, Social Systems, and the Economic World. Out of Control* is a Californian work of pop-science speculation that is one of my personal favorites. It is a very Petri dish of unwritten science-fiction novels.

Geof Darrow is an American midwesterner, like the Wachowskis, who hale from Chicago. Darrow threw that over to move to France and hang out with Moebius and the European *bande dessinée / Metal Hurlant* crowd. Geof Darrow is therefore a global comix artist.

It used to be that if you worked in a downmarket artform like comix, you were so dirt-poor that you didn't know much or see much, other than the subway route from Queens to the office.

Geof Darrow draws comics and does TV kids' cartoons, and yet he is an international man-of-mystery and a genuine design sophisticate. There's just no getting around it: He's really good.

You cross Darrow's pencil with Kevin Kelly's visonary intensity and out comes a hellish monsterscape. It is so far beyond the conceptual and technical limits of rubber-monster '50s sci-fi that it looks like a movie from another species.

If a SETI dish decoded a message from Betelgeuse, and we saw that our new friends were some Geof Darrow robo-octopi doing their buck-and-wing, everybody would just sort of nod. In six hours there would be talking heads on CNN: "Oh yes. Those are alien beings, all right. We always thought they'd look like that. Completely divorced from earthly standards."

These Darrow sets have a weird beauty, but the accomplishment doesn't end there. In *The Matrix*, when one returns from hell to the Earth, the Earth possesses weird beauty. The frenetic dot-com daily life in the 1990s looks frail and menaced and perishable, as indeed it turned out to be. "Normality" freezes at a blink. You can run it back and forth, chop it like videotape. It has pathos, *mono no aware*, like Japanese cherry blossoms.

The clothing is very beautiful in *The Matrix*, a feat I credit to costume designer Kym Barrett. Kym Barrett is Australian. Oz is not generally noted for its couture industry, and Ms. Barrett does not make and market clothes. She makes theatrical costumes. She did tremendous work in *Romeo + Juliet*, the bizarre adaptation where the Capulets and Montagues are rival Miami drug-mafia clans. But she hit a career high note in *The Matrix*. They aren't just professionally tailored costumes. They come from the heart. They somehow convey a young Australian woman's passionate, painfully distanced love for European and Hollywood glamour. Behind the menace of the oil-slick PVCs, the trench coats, and the guns is a bright little girl with her nose pressed firmly on the cold glass of a display window.

Punk fashion has always been protective armor. The spikes, the leather, the razors, the zippers, they are what you put on after flower-power has choked to death on its own vomit. It's Kevlar for the soft marshmallow core of youthful idealism. Cynicism after the hard knocks of life, real *weltschmerz*, no future, they don't look like that.

You can't be dead, because I love you. That is the emotional core of *The Matrix*, and that is not an adult statement. That is a statement that a six-year-old girl would say to a dead kitten. And yet the dead beloved rises at a kiss, walks, and then kicks everybody's ass. I'm sorry, but it just doesn't matter how silly that is. That is beyond rational discourse. Anyone who can resist that is emotionally defunct.

Whenever you've written off *The Matrix* as a hippie fairy-tale, it always hits you upside the head with high-concept. Or with genuine political radicalism, as when the film's treacherous villain sells out to become Ronald Reagan. In America, Rage Against the Machine was so much CD-product, but Rage were ultra-left-wing radicals genuinely enraged by the machine. They scared the daylights out of police in Mexico City. It's like going down to Toys "R" Us and finding out that they're retailing toddler's backpacks full of shattered glass.

That's no real problem if you're a Wachowski, a guy who can hold three different continents and eight different philosophies in your head at the same time. But you know, a society whose artists can do such things has some profound inherent difficulties. Such unmoored, slippery, moral relativism, combined with such glossy, with-it, magazine-spread prosperity, arouses some fierce resentments. If you are the kind of guy who can only manage one continent and one philosophy, then you want to hijack their aircraft and crash them into their skyscrapers. Not that this will improve their mood any. It's just that, well, it's very hard to dent them otherwise.

The same goes for rebels in *The Matrix*. If these are revolutionaries, then they have a hippie problem. The problem with hippie revolution is very simple: There's no victory condition. There's no strategy for change and no *novus ordo seclorum*. What happens if Neo wins? If everyone eats the Red Pill, there are billions of naked, atrophied wretches in big gooey pods fighting off flying killer robots with their bare hands. They have no jobs, no identities, no families, no laws, no civil order, no traditions, no hope, no ethics, no justice, no concept of what has happened to them. No nothing. They are meat on a ruined moonscape whose sky is falling and whose gods are mysterious, capricious, malign and all-powerful.

Small wonder that Neo runs back into the fantasy. He's living in the pixels, stepping out of a phone booth, and flying. That is his victory, limited and illusory though it is. The cyber-messiah didn't change a thing, not really; when it came to the crunch, it was all smoke and mirrors. But you know, at least he got his head around it. He went to the bottom of the rabbit hole. And that justly made him everybody's darling.

The Real Matrix

Stephen Baxter

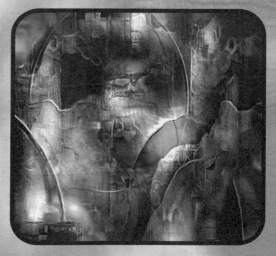

There's something wrong with the world . . .
—Morpheus, *The Matrix*

Morpheus probably shares this insight with most of us, especially in our young teenage years. Generally we dismiss such feelings of out-of-jointedness as mere paranoia. In Neo's case following up that uneasiness actually led to the unravelling of reality as he had understood it.

Remarkably enough, however, there have been suggestions not only that simulated realities are a possibility of the future, but *that we may be living in one right now* [1, 2].

The scenario of the movie—the AI's with their bottle-bank humans used as power generators—may not be plausible. But if we *are* inside a simulation, who might be running it? Is there any way we could tell? Is there any way we could emulate Neo and break out?

And even if we could, should we?

Where are the aliens?

If they exist, we should see them. Because the likely time scales of the expansion of a civilization through the galaxy are so much shorter than the age of the galaxy itself, and given the evolution of at least one intelligent race (ourselves), we should have overwhelming evidence of the existence of others. But we don't.

Recent evidence for the existence of planets around other stars, and the accumulation of negative evidence for extraterrestrial intelligence after several decades of fruitless SETI programs, have only deepened the mystery. This is better known as the Fermi Paradox [3].

There are lots of possible answers, widely explored in science and science fiction. Perhaps there are "filters" that might destroy intelligences before they can make their presence known: atomic war, galactic core explosions. Then there are various "zoo hypotheses," conscious strategies that might cause other civilizations to conceal their presence from us—like *Star Trek*'s Prime Directive.

But the problem is consistency. You have to suppose that *every* species destroys itself, or is destroyed, or submits to a doctrine of concealment. It would take only one exception, one rogue Ferengi trader busting into the game reserve, for the quarantine to collapse. The Paradox is surely telling us that something is fundamentally wrong with our view of the universe and our place in it: There is something wrong with the world, indeed.

I have suggested that a plausible resolution of the Fermi Paradox is that *what we see around us is artificial* [1]. What if we have been placed in some form of "planetarium," perhaps generated using an advanced virtual reality technology, designed to give us the illusion of an empty universe—while beyond the walls with their painted stars, the shining lights of extraterrestrial civilizations glow unseen? This might seem outlandish, but it would resolve the

Paradox. And if you think about it, it's far easier to throw a cloak around one world, or even one solar system, than to mask an entire galactic culture. . . .

Or here's another possibility. What if the planetarium creators aren't aliens, but our own future descendants?

Nick Bostrom, a philosopher at Yale University, has suggested that we may all be living in a Matrix developed by a post-human society of the future [2] (though probably far beyond the 2199 timeframe of *The Matrix*). As we will see, there is certainly no theoretical limit to generating such a fake reality, though it is energy-hungry. We can't guess at the motives of the post-humans, any more than a Neandertal could guess at yours. But if it's possible to generate simulated universes with simulated consciousnesses inside, then it will surely be done; we humans tend to realize any possible technology.

Not only that, Bostrom chillingly argues that you are overwhelmingly *likely* to be living in such a simulation.

The argument goes like this. You may be living in the "original" version of history—but there's only one copy of that, while there are many more (infinitely many?) possible simulations of history. So, if you imagine your consciousness as a counter dropped at random into any one of the possible reality frames, it's a lot more likely you'd find yourself dropped into a sim than the real thing.

If, with our limited understanding, we can think of two plausible classes of simulation controllers, there are probably many more. Maybe we should indeed take the possibility seriously. But if we do, is there anything we can say about the properties of such a simulation?

There was of course speculation on artificial realities long before *The Matrix* itself, and its cyberpunk progenitors like William Gibson. We can trawl this material for clues about what kind of planetarium we might be living in. (A good recent review of modern thinking on the relation of reality to mind, computation and virtual reality is given by David Deutsch [4].)

The idea that the world around us may not be real reaches back to Plato, who wondered if what we see resembles the flickering shadows on a cave wall. The notion of creating deceptive artificial environments dates back at least as far as Descartes, who in the seventeenth century speculated on the philosophical implications of a sense-manipulating "demon"—effectively a pretechnological virtual-reality generator. A recent example is the movie *The Truman Show* (1999) in which the protagonist is the unwitting star of a TV show, trapped under a fake domed sky; early in the movie a spotlight crashes from sky to ground, bearing the label "Sirius."

In fake-reality science-fiction novels, the fake universe has sometimes turned out to be a generation starship, whose inhabitants are unaware that their world is merely the ship's interior. In Harry Harrison's *Captive Universe* [5] the crew's ignorance is engineered; harsh social engineering, taboos, rituals, and even genetic modification are used to keep the populace in their place. But in Brian Aldiss's *Non-Stop* [6] and Robert Heinlein's *Orphans of the Sky* [7] the crew have simply forgotten they are on a ship. Aldiss's dwarfed "dizzies" wander without comprehension through a hull crammed with vegetation, essentially driven insane by their endless confinement.

Alternatively, the artificial universes may be erected as

virtual-reality computer projections. This is an idea deployed in the TV series *Star Trek* with its holodecks, in which emulations of material objects are directly created around real humans. And of course in *The Matrix*, humans are forcibly immersed in a "neural-interactive simulation" via direct implants in their brains.

Possible planetariums have a variety of scopes, depending on how far the boundary of "reality" is set from the human consciousness. The crudest sort are like the one in *The Truman Show*, in which the people and the objects they touched were real, while the sky was a fake dome. Perhaps the stars and galaxies are simulated, along with artificial incoming starlight, by a great shell surrounding the solar system. Or perhaps *everything* beyond the atmosphere is a fake—or was, until humans reached the Moon. The engineering behind even a *Truman* planetarium would be impressive, though, as the builders would have to simulate not just photons but such exotica as cosmic rays and neutrinos. If they anticipate our technological progress, perhaps even now they are readying the gravity-wave generators. . . .

But the boundary of "reality" may be much closer to ourselves. Perhaps we humans are real, but, after the manner of *Star Trek's* holodeck, some subset (or all) of the objects we see around us are generated as simulations, tangible enough to interact with our senses. Or perhaps even our bodies are simulated, as in *The Matrix*, so that the boundary of reality is close around our very consciousness.

The scope of the simulation will naturally impose different requirements on its builders; a *Truman* planetarium would presumably be much less energy-expensive to generate than a Matrix or holodeck. But a primary quality required of any such planetarium is, of course, its ability to fool inhabitants at least as smart as ourselves into believing that what they see is real.

Why do we believe that the universe is real in the first place? The most extreme contrary position, as set out by Bishop Berkeley, is the solipsistic notion that the apparently external world is contained within the observer's imagination. It might seem impossible to disprove this. After all, everything we experience is a virtual-reality rendering anyway, compiled by our unconscious minds from scraps of sensory data, plus theories, inborn and acquired, on how objects ought to behave.

Dr. Johnson gave a robust response to this [4]. When Boswell remarked on the impossibility of refuting Berkeley's theory, Johnson kicked a large rock and said, "I refute it *thus*." What Johnson meant was that when the rock "kicked back" at his foot, he either had to formulate a theory of physical law that explained the existence and behavior of the rock, or else assume that his imagination was itself a complex, autonomous universe *containing* laws that precisely simulated the existence of the rock—which would therefore be a more complex system. If the *simplest* explanation is that an object like Dr. Johnson's rock is autonomous, then we accept that that entity is real.

But we can turn Dr. Johnson's criterion around, and use it as a test of what is required of any simulation of the universe.

The universe must be *consistent*. We believe that in principle anybody anywhere could perform a scientific experiment of the finest detail on any sample of the universe and its contents, and should find the fabric of reality yielding consistent results. That is, the rocks must always "kick back" in the same way, no matter where and how we kick them.

Further, if the jailers wanted to fool their captives into believing there is no outside world, they would have to ensure that the environment was *self-contained*: that no explanations of anything inside would ever require the captives to postulate an outside. Brian Aldiss's baffled starship passengers deduce from the very existence of metal walls around them that their "reality" is a sham: "The ship is an artificial thing. The world is natural. We are natural beings, and our rightful home is not here. . . . " [6]

The technical challenge of achieving a simulation with such qualities should not be underestimated. Even the *Truman* model requires a certain physical coupling to ourselves. We have strong evidence that some meteorites have come from Mars, providing at least an indirect way to "kick" that planet. If we regard our machines as extensions of ourselves, then we have "kicked rocks" as far away as Neptune, the most distant major body with which a manmade spacecraft has so far interacted. In fact *every* astronomical observation, such as of a photon of starlight or a cosmic ray fleeing from a distant supernova, must be a physical interaction with the subject of the observation.

Of course it would be relatively simple to simulate photons and cosmic rays incoming from the roof of the planetarium, and it would be much easier to fool a probe like NASA's *Voyager* than a human explorer. The challenges faced by builders of holodeck or *Matrix* planetariums are greater, because you can walk around and kick their contents directly.

In the end, consistency and self-containment surely require of the planetarium builders that their simulation of every object should be *perfect*—that is, undistinguishable from the real thing by any conceivable physical test. Otherwise curious fact-hunters like humans would inevitably, in the end, find a flaw.

We can call such a simulation, comprising a finite volume containing as much data as is physically possible to cram in, a *maximal simulation*.

Of course a maximal simulation of the holodeck type, for example, would be a somewhat brute-force solution to the problem of constructing a planetarium. It would entail forming actual material objects (or their energetic equivalents), and loading them with a large amount of information of which only a fraction would actually interact with humans and produce the desired illusion. Furthermore, if the objects were evanescent, like the images on a TV screen, they would require continual refreshing. It's easy

to think of more *efficient* design strategies, for example allowing objects once created to exist as autonomous entities within the environment, only loosely coupled to the controlling mechanism. (This would remove the need, for example, to reproduce continually the substance at the center of the earth.)

But only a maximal simulation could ensure a *perfect* emulation of every object. And only a maximal simulation would allow the builders *full control* of the maintained environment. A maximal simulation would have the chilling property that the controllers could, for example, make objects appear or disappear at will. The special effects of *The Matrix* would be trivial. . . .

A consideration from quantum mechanics shows that a maximal simulation is, in fact, possible—but it is energy-hungry.

A maximal simulation is possible because there is a limit to the amount of information that can be contained within a given volume containing a given mass-energy. This limit is expressed by the "Bekenstein Bound" [1]. The Bound is essentially a manifestation of the Heisenberg uncertainty principle—a reflection of the fundamental "graininess" of our reality. Most physical objects encode far less than the maximal amount of information permitted by the Bound. For example, the Bound for a single hydrogen atom is a megabyte!

Because of the existence of the Bound, every physical object (including every human) is a *finite state machine*: It can only adopt a fixed number of possible states—like, say, the positions in a tic-tac-toe game. Therefore a perfect simulation of any physical object can be made, because you could just emulate every possible state—like listing every possible legal position in tic-tac-toe. So it would in principle be possible to construct a perfect planetarium of any finite size, with *every object undistinguishable from the real thing by any conceivable physical test.*

But the Bound also gives us an indication of what it would cost to run such a planetarium.

To generate a given bit of information requires a minimum amount of energy. So you can tell how much energy is needed to generate a maximal simulation of any size. Naturally the energy requirements go up as the size increases—and so we can put limits on the nature of any jailers who might be trying to contain us.

As human civilization has progressed, successively larger portions of reality have come within our reach. For much of its pre-agricultural history humanity consisted of small roaming bands with little knowledge, save for tentative trading links, beyond a disc on the Earth's surface with radius of order 10 km and height 1 km. Taking the density of the matter within such a disc to be that of water (an overestimate), a maximal-quality simulation for each roving band would have required no more than 0.1 percent of the putative information capability of a civilization capable of mastering mass-energy on a planetary scale (perhaps a typical *Star Trek* culture).

But the demands grow quickly. By the time political structures much smaller than the Roman Empire were extant on the Earth, the strain of maintaining the growing simulation (if perfect) would already have exceeded the capability of planet-bound cultures.

And what of the present? Disregarding spaceflight for the moment, we can characterize our modern globe-spanning civilization by a radius of 6000 km, the radius of Earth, and a depth corresponding to our deepest mines, 10 km. And that's expensive: At some point during the age of European exploration of the globe, we must have exceeded the simulation capability of even a civilization able to master the mass-energy of an entire star.

This, of course, is the scenario shown in *The Matrix*. You might think that to generate a simulation by pumping information directly into human brains would be cheaper than using, say, a *Star Trek* holodeck. It probably would, but we're considering the cost of generating each bit of information itself—and that remains hugely expensive however you use it. It really would take more than a star's mass-energy to generate the Matrix, which is why the movie scenario is implausible; it would cost the AIs far more energy to generate the Matrix than they could ever hope to retrieve from their farmed humans!

And what lies beyond the Matrix? If we imagine a putative future human civilization capable of direct exploration of the center of the planets, then it would cost more than a galaxy's mass-energy to fool us if we could reach out beyond Pluto.

Finally, a star-spanning human culture would test the resources of any conceivable planetarium builders. If humans learn to touch even the interiors of the stars, then a human colonization sphere would bust the processing capabilities of the *entire visible universe* when it got larger than 100 light-years.

Recall that a maximal simulation represents an upper bound on the energy hunger of a planetarium. A lower-quality simulation could very well exceed 100 light-years in size. But when our starships pass 100 light-years we can be sure that no *maximal* simulation will be possible; any planetarium will therefore be less than perfect—and its existence prone to our detection.

We've been growing fast. If they exist, we are sorely testing our invisible masters.

Maybe we don't have to wait until we reach 100 light-years. It may be impossible for us ever to *prove* that the universe is real. But we would need only one counter-example, one chink in the roof of the planetarium, to prove it false. How can we search for such a leak in reality—and if we can, should we?

We have seen that the growth of cohesive human cultures places increasing burdens on any planetarium, whatever its design. If the planetarium is a *Truman* type, the walls around reality must be drawn successively back. Before 1969, a crude mock-up of the Moon satisfying only a remote visual inspection might have sufficed, but since 1969, we can be sure that the painted Moon had to be replaced with a rocky equivalent. A conspiracy theorist might point to the very different quality of the Moon's far side to its Earth-visible near side—mocked up in a hurry, perhaps? And then there are Mars's "canals," glimpsed by Percival Lowell and his telescope in the nineteenth century but invisible to the close-up inspection of the space probes in the twentieth.

We can expect particular stress to be placed at the boundary. So if we rush the fence, perhaps we could crash the computer. The ideal way to achieve this might be to send human explorers out to far distances in all directions as rapidly as possible, "kicking rocks" around an expanding shell of space. But advanced robot spacecraft, equipped with powerful sensors, might achieve the same result, and perhaps even such active but ground-based measures as radar or laser echoing would work. If we tried for a laser echo from a comet out beyond Pluto's orbit, and no such echo were received, the plot would thicken indeed.

However there may be other, more subtle ways to test the simulation. Any "glitches," like Neo's déjà vu, would be a sign that things are not what they seem. And perhaps like Harrison's captive astronauts [5] we should look for psychological and social mechanisms, seeking taboos and conditioning that prevent us from seeing the scaffolding in the sky.

But should we even *try* to test the limits of reality?

In *The Matrix*, the characters' immediate response to finding out they are living their lives in a "prison for your mind" is to try to break out. So it has been in most previous captive-universe stories. Prison-universes serve as metaphors for paranoia and manipulation. Typically in such stories the protagonist uses defects in reality to deduce the nature of his or her captivity and finds a way through the social, epistemological and physical barriers to escape.

But here's a radical thought. Maybe, even if we do find we're living in a fake reality, we should leave well alone.

"Captive" is a loaded term. Perhaps we are indeed in some form of exile, or a cage, or even a prison; but perhaps the creators' motives are benevolent, and we are in a nursery, or game reserve, for our own protection: Maybe it's a nasty universe out there.

And there are other considerations besides freedom. Even the *Matrix* universe isn't so bad if you look at it. There's no (real) warfare, and population densities look pretty high in those bottle banks. There's no reason why a very large number of us shouldn't live very long lives in there, as long as we accept the dictates of our captors.

Perhaps we should trust them. After all they must be technologically superior to us—and perhaps we should assume they are morally superior also.

Or perhaps we should suck up to them. Robin Hanson, an economist who commented on Nick Bostrom's ideas [2], says that the main thing to do is figure out the purpose of the simulation, and then work out how to avoid being deleted. If it's entertainment, you should be as dramatic as possible; if it's a moral fable, you should lead a blameless life; if the simulation is designed as a playground for the creators themselves, you should get as close as possible to rich, famous and powerful celebrities—or better yet, become one yourself. You are like a contestant on TV's *Big Brother*, trying to avoid eviction by guessing what the voting public wants, and giving it to them.

The most dangerous strategy of all, says Hanson, would be to talk too much about the discovery of the simulation. If the show starts to look stilted and staged, the creators may choose simply to pull the plug and start again. If you've got this far, maybe you'd better forget everything you've read in this essay—and certainly don't recommend it to your friends. . . .

If you don't buy any of this, I sympathize. If we are being contained and deceived, whatever the motive, we are in a relationship of unequals, and are thereby diminished. We have a moral responsibility to ourselves to try to break down the walls and challenge our captors. As they already know, of course, for even this essay and your act of reading it are parts of the simulation.

Are you listening out there? If you exist, show yourselves—and justify what you've done!

References

[1] Stephen Baxter, "The Planetarium Hypothesis: A Resolution of the Fermi Paradox," *Journal of the British Interplanetary Society*, 54, nos. 5/6, May/June 2001.

[2] Nick Bostrom, www.simulation-argument.com/1; Michael Brooks, "Life's a Sim and Then You're Deleted," *New Scientist* 27, July 2002.

[3] Stephen Baxter, *Deep Future*, Gollancz, London, 2001.

[4] David Deutsch, *The Fabric of Reality*, Penguin, London, 1997.

[5] Harry Harrison, *Captive Universe,* Putnam, New York, 1969.

[6] Brian Aldiss, *Non-Stop*, Faber and Faber, London, 1958.

[7] Robert Heinlein, *Orphans of the Sky,* Dell, New York, 1951.

The Matrix: Know Thyself

John Shirley

Mimes, in the form of God on high,
Mutter and mumble low;
And hither and thither fly—
Mere puppets they, who come and go
At bidding of vast formless things
That shift the scenery to and fro . . .
—*Edgar Allan Poe*

Y ou're here because you know something," says Morpheus in *The Matrix*, to the film's hero, Neo. "You've always known . . . it's like a splinter in your mind . . . " An indefinable, even ineffable knowledge drives Neo to interrogate life, and to search the Internet—the same as seeking in the great world for Neo—for the cause of his nagging intuition that something fundamental yet invisible is wrong with the whole world. This intuition of implicit existential injustice and worldly illusion is reflected in other recent films as well—a terrifying knowledge that also casts the shadow of a way out.

What is it that Neo "knows" and yet doesn't know? What is this troubling gnosis? It can't be simply told and then believed—it must be seen. Neo is told that you must have a direct experience of the great illusion to know it for what it is.

Morpheus (ironically, the mythological god of sleep) gives Neo a pill that awakens him to the truth. He gives him the red capsule—red for danger, for it's a dangerous, troubling revelation: That all men are asleep, quite literally asleep, in chemical baths, their slumbering bodies wired up in bottles that seem inspired by H. R. Giger, used as biological batteries by a race of Artificial Intelligences that have enslaved all humanity; yet we seem to live our lives as free men and women, sharing a dreamlike consensus reality, our minds wandering through a virtual creation generated by the computer intelligences, the digital Archons.

The implication for Neo is terrible: That all life is a lie. That one's family is not one's family, one's experiences not one's experiences, that personal suffering and triumphs are illusion— and all humanity are slaves of a vast, soulless system that thrives on human ignorance. That red pill is a bitter one to swallow.

"While they dream they do not know that they are dreaming," says the ancient Taoist sage, Chuang Tzu. "By and by comes the great awakening, and then we shall know that it has all been a great dream. Yet all the while the fools think they are awake, this they are sure of."

"Like images seen in a dream," says the Buddhist sutra, "thus should one see all things."

The gnostics—the alternative "Christianity"—spoke of the Archons, the servants of the treacherous under-god, the demiurge who bound the sparks of our consciousness in the material world, and sowed with them the illusion that this is ultimate reality.

That rogue philosopher P. D. Ouspensky, interpreter of the mystic G. I. Gurdjieff, said that we lie to ourselves and one another all the time without knowing it; that we are asleep when we think we are awake; that we "buffer" ourselves from the painful truth of "the real world." But, he averred, we can become more conscious through techniques like "self-observation"—i.e., the true meaning of the Socratic admonition "Know thyself," which is referenced in *The Matrix*—and thus set ourselves free from a world wherein we hypnotically submit to "influences," living our lives as "machines," mechanical and programmed. We're like mindless sheep, Ouspensky said, herded about till we're shorn of a certain form of energy the cosmos requires for its inscrutable purposes.

The Marxists taught that the resources of the many have been appropriated by the few, that the working classes are being brutally exploited by the bourgeoisie and the plutocrat, the ordinary man's control over his social destiny suppressed by military power, by the opiate of conventional religion, and by his own numbing inertia. (The Marxists would seem to have had some insight into the problem, but no workable solution to it.)

A recent bestselling nonfiction book by Stephen Wolfram, *A New Kind of Science,* speculates that the universe is a kind of gigantic computer running an infinitely variegating program of cellular automata—and possibly an artificial construct created by some unknown entity. Even the scientists are beginning to wonder. . . .

The Matrix is ostensibly about a futuristic situation, Neo's world, not ours, but clearly it's an allegory—both social and spiritual—for the human condition as it's always been, and for its emerging character in this century.

In certain respects, *The Matrix* is perhaps not the most "mature," if that's the word, of allegories. It is rife with adolescent imagery. Hackers, in this film, are depicted as muscular action heroes in tight leather. (The average hacker of my experience has a rather different appearance.) Morpheus, when we first see him, wears a long black leather coat, his head is shaved, and he wears the coolest shades known to man. The ensemble is right out of postmodern graphic novels, the hipper kind of comic book: he's the twenty-first-century superhero. Neo too becomes increasingly superheroesque as the movie plays out.

The rebellious hackers who recruit Neo—using their computer ability to undermine the mind-controlled technocracy—learn ju jitsu and kung fu and the expert use of weapons in just the way a bright but spoiled kid would fantasize the process: it's directly, *effortlessly*, inserted into their brains via computer interface. Programs are downloaded into you, and *you suddenly know* how to do it: the ultimate manifestation of the technogeek's hunger for instantaneity.

The first thing we see in the film is a marauding phalanx of policemen, with the Secret Service–like "Agent" of the Matrix directing them, as they invade the lonely sanctuary of a hacker—cops, troops, the "Agents," and dronelike computer-company executives symbolize authority at its most primally oppressive. They are the enforcers, the "running dogs" of the corrupt social system symbolized by the Matrix itself.

In his commentary on the DVD, one of the special effects men says that the Wachowski Brothers were firm about showing the logos of their financiers, Village Roadshow Pictures, and that corporate monolith, Warner Bros., in their own digital styling, colored sickly green and digitized to mesh with the tone of the film. They wanted to co-opt the logos and thus somehow repudiate the power of these media despots. (Presumably they somehow repudiated the checks from these companies as they cashed them.)

Keanu Reeves's voiceover at the end of the film calls for "a world without rules and controls." Is this anarchistic—or simply anti-parental? It's a little too easy to point out that the Wachowskis, despite their call for awakening and freedom from authority from "the system," are team players, selling their wares to the big machine, taking part in the promotional machinery, raking in the rewards of their complicity. Thus accused, the filmmakers might well suggest they are corroding the system from within, subtly attacking the big machine's consensus mind, like a computer virus introduced through the mental downloading system called "cinema." At the very least the film can be appreciated as a wistful, cyberpunk poem to the postmodern rebel.

Fictionally, at least, Neo and Trinity are above the rules, above ordinary beings, with supernatural powers imbued by their mastery of the digital. When they escape from the world of illusion, their transcendence of the world happens via phone lines, i.e., the Internet, that symbol of anarchic "phreaker" freedom.

This vision of the empowering of the nerdy outsider, the weakling becoming powerful through his mastery of the Internet and programming, is psychologically volatile stuff—for some, perhaps, too powerful. There's a certain elitism, implying that ordinary people who aren't in on the digital-hipster loop are expendable. Neo and Trinity, entering the building where the heroic revolutionary leader Morpheus is being tortured, are each caparisoned with an arsenal of weapons under their long black coats. Pulling weapons from under their trench coats to methodically shoot yet more cops—thuggish cops, emblematic of faceless authority—Neo and Trinity are uncomfortably reminiscent of the two kids at Columbine who drew weapons from under their black trench coats to methodically kill people in that other bastion of authority, the local high school.

But the film may be all the more effective for its moments of absurd "immaturity." It reaches a wider audience this way—with a message that audience needs to hear.

The social message seems to enfold the more powerful spiritual message—or perhaps they're two sides of the same coin. Certainly, the use of humans as batteries in the film is powerfully symbolic of our mindless submission to the consumer economy. We're *driving* the economy by buying things we don't need, by submission to the marketplace, as *a battery* adds its power to the machine—and being caught up in the consumer culture, the herdlike movement from one big-media entertainment to the next, keeps us hypnotized, maintains the dreamy alienation from the present moment that insures our slavish sleep.

Every thoughtful person knows that something is fundamentally wrong in the world—that we usually see the shadows on the cave wall and not that which casts them—and thus the fundamental message in *The Matrix* is one that we on some level *ache* to hear. We hunger to have our nagging intuition confirmed, as that confirmation entails hope that once the problem is identified, a solution will be found. And freedom will become possible.

Ostensibly, the film's mixture of the spiritual and the action-hero is absurd. But the enlightened warrior is not unknown to the annals of spirituality—there's Castaneda's Don Juan, and there's that Zen archer, and the spiritually-rooted martial artistry hinted at in *Iron Monkey* and *Crouching Tiger, Hidden Dragon*: skills that seem to fuse seamlessly with the enlightened state. The filmmakers are acknowledging their boyish impulses to heroic violence—but combining it with the mystical implies they yearn to ascend above the common-denominator longings of the action movie.

Yet the Wachowskis clearly adore Hong Kong martial arts and fantasy films—they're likely influenced by Hong Kong movies like *Zu: Warriors of the Magic Mountain* and *The Bride with White Hair,* and the *Chinese Ghost Story* movies.

American influences are obvious. Cronenbergian imagery—like the silverfish-like robot that burrows into Neo's belly—crop up in *The Matrix.* The diabolic Artificial Intelligences of *The Terminator* films, servants become cruel masters, are the ancestors of *The Matrix*'s agents. Philip Dick's stories are thematic antecedents—the film's debt to P.K.D. is quite distinctive. Doubtless William Gibson's cyberspace was a godfather to the Matrix itself.

But the Wachowski Brothers had ideas of their own, too, and they've influenced others in turn. Besides spawning a prevalent visual style in a host of computer and video games, *The Matrix,* it seems to me, had its impact on various films, most recently the script of Spielberg's *Minority Report.* The improbably frantic urban-based action scenes in *Minority Report* were minted in *The Matrix*; then there's the scene where Tom Cruise goes down a big drain from a wired-up chemical bath to escape the authorities—just as Neo does in *The Matrix.* There's a "pre-cog" in both movies who predicts minor things that are about to happen. "You're about to knock over that vase," says the Oracle in *The Matrix,* just before Neo does; Agatha, the precog in *Minority Report,* makes similar minute moment-by-moment predictions.

More important are other recent films with similar themes, not likely influenced by *The Matrix,* but pointing out the same truths with a timeliness and convergence of intent that somehow make them part of the same inadvertent "movement" in cinema. I'm thinking particularly of *American Beauty, Fight Club, Dark City, eXistenZ, Mulholland Dr., The Truman Show, Vanilla Sky, Waking Life,* and *S1M0NE.*

    American Beauty, written by Alan Ball, is the story of a dysfunctional family paralyzed by resentment, alienation, and by simply being lost in the centerless maze of modern life. Kevin Spacey's character can't touch his wife in any way that matters; he can't reach his daughter though she's right in the same house with him. He has an encounter with a pot-dealing young bohemian who moves in next door—whose obsession with the innate visual beauty of the ordinary world seems an adventure in perception—

and is inspired to wrestle his way free of his middle class funk. The overall impression is of a man recognizing that he's been asleep, dreaming his way through an air conditioned, wall-to-wall-carpeted misery—who had forgotten the choices, the almost infinite ways out, that life offers to the wakeful in every single second of existence.

In David Fincher's *Fight Club,* characters desperate for connection to something real go to twelve-step groups for problems they don't have just to feel emotions by proxy; they are so numb that they start a Fight Club, where ordinary people meet in secret to beat the crap out of each other with their fists, merely to experience the *realness* that confrontation brings. They allude to a society caught up in consumerism and corporate striving, dumbfounded by masks and media-star worship and empty recreation— and they recognize that it's all a kind of sleepwalking, a hypnotic state that must be struggled with, must be battered with bare fists, before it can be defeated and a man can really wake up. At the end it turns out that Brad Pitt isn't even real, that the story is just another desperate construct—a stage on the road to waking up.

Alex Proyas's *Dark City* is a noir fantasy, a gnostic fable (I asked the director, also director of *The Crow,* if it was a gnostic fable, and he confirmed it was) about a man who finds himself on a search for truth and identity in a shapeshifting city that turns out to be a sort of living urban stage designed for sinister, arcane purposes by malignant entities—all may be a dream, or may not. *Dark City* is a more mature, artistically controlled film than *The Matrix,* and its thesis is perhaps a little less explicit, but the parallels to *The Matrix* are striking.

Cronenberg's *eXistenZ* involves a virtual-reality videogame that—like so many Philip Dick–influenced tales—makes us wonder where reality ends and the game begins. Fantasy and reality inevitably overlap in this film. There are anti-game cultlike revolutionaries in the background, and the game's player wonders what's real, and if the game could be a game within a game. . . .

In David Lynch's *Mulholland Dr.,* a young actress seems to have her soul, or identity, stolen by evil forces embedded in the city of Los Angeles (no one who's worked in The Business there needs much convincing) as she goes through an enigmatic quest to find her real nature—all lost in what turns out to be, apparently, a dream.

In *The Truman Show,* Jim Carrey discovers he's in a false reality, literally staged by people who are using him as an entertainment and have done so for a generation. He must find the confines of the staging area and break out into the real world to find actual love, an unscripted destiny. (It should be noted here that Carrey's escape scenes are reminiscent of another film that may be an antecedent of *The Matrix*: George Lucas's *THX 1138,* in which the hero must escape from a robot-controlled subterranean civilization whose denizens are kept "opiated" by medication [like Prozac?] and by a computer-generated "Jesus." THX fights his way to the free world on the "shell," the surface—the *outside.* True freedom, in *The Matrix* and in *THX 1138,* belongs to the outsider. Along the same lines one could reference the science fiction cult classic *Logan's Run* and the underrated film of Harlan Ellison's *A Boy and His Dog.*)

Most of these films, more or less contemporary with *The Matrix* or coming just after, probably aren't especially derivative of it—they are simply galvanized by the same furnace of fermenting realization tormenting a host of filmmakers.

Cameron Crowe's *Vanilla Sky* is apparently inspired by a European film; this interesting Tom Cruise vehicle once again gives us a hero who by degrees realizes that his nightmarish reality is fabricated, intricately computer-animated, and transmitted into his brain—which is in modified cryogenic freeze. He chooses to wake up, and face the real world of a dark future, rather than centuries of the improved dreams the cryogenics company offers him.

Richard Linklater's *Waking Life*—a brilliant innovation perfectly fusing conventional movie-photography and animation—gives us a hero who keeps waking up from a complex dream that seems to push him into profound social and philosophical dialogues with the sundry intellectual outlaws he encounters; only, each time he's sure he's awakened, he finds, once more, he's only dreaming. Referencing Phil Dick, gnosticism, and postmodern theory, Linklater plays with the concept of "lucid dreaming," controlling one's dreams by realizing one is dreaming. Of all the movies I've listed, this one may have the most impact on the viewer's own sense of personal reality—it will make you wonder if you're dreaming.

Andrew Niccol's *S1MONE* is a comedy about a movie director who's so disgusted with actors that he computer-generates Simone, a beautiful actress programmed with the best of all the great female movie stars. The audience falls in love with her and people refuse to accept she's not real, even when he tries to tell them so. Niccol sends up the public's willingness to collaborate with illusion on a global scale.

The emergence of a remarkable number of films questioning reality—each suggesting a sinister puppeteer, pointing to a kind of dreamy lostness prevailing in the median consciousness of the industrialized world—seems a defined cultural current, however unplanned, emerging from a tacit consensus about our condition. What is it we're trying to tell ourselves with *The Matrix* and all these other films on the same theme?

Of the recent films listed above, *Fight Club* and *American Beauty* seem the closest in spirit to *The Matrix*, partly because of the social critique implicit in them, but chiefly because they achieve similar levels of intensity; they have more the revolutionary spirit about them.

But for all its rejection of social norms, there's a nostalgia in *The Matrix* for the mythology of divine rescue found in conventional religion. Keanu is The One, a messiah, prophesied by the Oracle—before Keanu's character can attain his higher state, he must first die. Like Osiris; like Jesus. But to die to the false reality is to live—and "let the dead bury the dead, " said Jesus.

Modern filmmakers love computers—and at the same time, constantly worry about them. *The Matrix*, *The Terminator*, and *eXistenZ* seem to be expressions of a perception that mankind is out of balance with technology. In *The Matrix* and in films like *Johnny Mnemonic* we see technology relentlessly encroaching, intruding right into the bodies of those who imagine they control it; machines eventually becoming tyrants. This may also reflect a subconscious suspicion that, technology aside, we are ourselves all too machinelike, too prone to conditioned reflex, socially programmed behavior. Perhaps we are the scariest machines of all.

The only way out is transcendence. And *The Matrix*'s staging of transcendence goes beyond its adolescent underpinnings. There's a feel of genuine spiritual yearning in the film.

There's an attempt in the film, when Neo talks to the Buddha-like spoon-bending child, to invoke the spirit of Zen and Dzogchen. Neo is told that he must cast off the separation between thought and doing; there must be an inner union, a kind of Jungian consolidation, before he can defeat duality and become Zen-perfect in uniting his inside with what is outside. But in *The Matrix* this leads to more than Nirvanalike inner peace and right relationship to the world, it precipitates a control of the phenomenal world resembling the mythology of the "Seth Speaks" books and the film *What Dreams May Come*. The world of *The Matrix*, however programmed, is a mental world, ultimately, and the mind can rewrite the program.

So transcendence comes to fruition in the mind, in perception itself. The film's subtext may seem fantastic, overblown, but under all the shiny layers of bombast there's a real mustard seed of possibility. You have to start somewhere and you start with what's closest, by skeptically, fearlessly, examining your own experience of the world—and your own mind.

In an interview, Larry Wachowski said, "The idea of *The Matrix* is that it's very easy to live an unexamined life. It's very easy to not be aware of what's going on out there in the world."

For all its intricacies, *The Matrix*'s final message is fairly simple: Look around and question what you see, what you accept.

And start with yourself. Know thyself.

Art
Imitates
Life
(Yes, It's News)

Darrel
Anderson

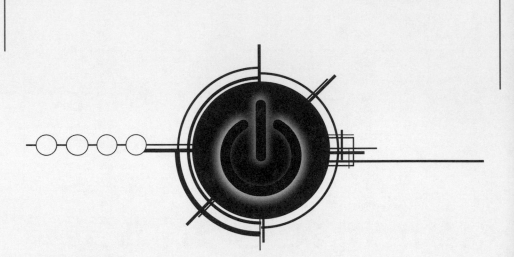

Believing—or wanting to believe—in something beyond our mundane world is universal. *The Matrix* wrapped that idea in a cyberpunk trench coat and shades to fine effect. A smart film with everything a young boy could want. A motley crew aboard a bricolaged ship, tentacled, bug-eyed monsters and robots (rolled into one), roaming a post apocalyptic sewerscape, cyber realities with superhuman heroics. A bit of humor.

Good over evil.

Love conquers all.

And of course a good dose of stylish violence—that bloodshed ballet with a rock beat, massaging our aesthetic while littering the floor with corpses—shell-casing pirouettes.

Not to shortchange the art of the film—a beautifully crafted thing—brilliant in its comic-inspired storytelling style. In fact, the high quality of that art combined with classic themes expanded the reach of the film—and therefore its significance. Someone unversed in moral dilemmas surrounding artificial intelligence, or theoretical debates about subjective realities, could still identify with the desire to escape that cog-in-the-machine feeling. Get flushed from the hive, or just vault out of your cubicle—nobody wants to be a drone.

The Matrix brushes only lightly over several evocative themes. Perhaps that's a good thing. Those inner doubts about the nature of reality, perception, consciousness—fears of dehumanization at the cold hands of a robot—better to just tweak them. The personal nature of such things leaves them best described internally. Each of us knows how to properly dress our own demons for the party.

Sufficient evidence exists in a variety of delusional mental disorders to make me question if my particular interpretation of the flow in my neural pathways is illusion or delusion. (Illusion being the highest level to which it can objectively be raised.) Morpheus pointed this out. For all of its apparent stability, reality is quite tenuous. Just stare in the mirror long enough thinking about it and it wobbles.

There is something invigorating about it—that vertigo of consciousness that hits when reality's firm grip shifts. Like just catching yourself before a fall, a discordant tune that blood-rushes your mind, slowing everything down to model the unpleasantness about to unfold—and then the elation upon recovering.

Philip K. Dick always hit those notes for me, his characters suffering increasingly slippery realities. Starting subtly . . . reaching for the familiar light switch—like a thousand times before—only to find it has "moved" to the other side of the door. Can't be. He was so certain. He brushes it off like that momentary disorientation on awakening, when the door-is-where-the-window-is-where-the-closet is supposed to be. But it sorts out. Reality reasserts itself like quick-setting cement.

For Dick's characters it just gets worse. Paranoia one-upped by fact. The concrete never sets, just rises . . . ankles to knees to neck. Of course there is that rumor that Dick himself suffered a touch of unwarranted concern—who better to paint the picture?

Unless you're convinced the rabbit is out to get you, I don't think suspicions about the other side of the looking glass qualify as paranoia. Everyone is compelled to question reality's credentials from time to time. That notion that *this* is all just an experiment occurs to each of us when life deals out an especially odd card. We expect the lights to come on—to be greeted by someone in a lab coat suppressing a smirk. And perhaps we breathe a sigh of relief—like Neo, we suspected it all along. In this digital age we have new fuel for our doubts, the prospect of cyber realms imposed upon our minds, and a geometrically expanding technological lattice to support them.

Computer-generated artificial realities so rich as to fool us into utter acceptance may seem a far stretch. However, our minds may be all too willing to bridge the gap. If you are wearing stereo goggles, that's one thing. If virtual reality is riding in on your neurons, that's another. Given the right state of mind we can be quite receptive. My most convincing dreams, in retrospect, are full of gaping holes. Many fictional scenarios employ drugs as a lubricant for (usually involuntary) artificial-reality immersion. Why not? Even more effective consciousness-altering devices—bio-tech, genetically engineered—are, or will soon be, available. It doesn't matter how you get there, just that you're *convinced* you've arrived. In the end, it's all in the mind's-eye of the beholder.

Virtual Reality, the next best thing to Being.

The fact that *The Matrix* takes place in cyberspace is simultaneously irrelevant and the whole point. Cyberpunk is at it's best when it explores the inherent conflicts in perception/reality, natural/artificial mind. Like any good speculative fiction, cyberpunk settings and devices often serve as metaphors for our real lives. To that end, *The Matrix* could just as well have been a dream, a drug-induced hallucination, a prison camp on Mars. But a large measure of the genre's power lies in the proximity of its future. We are currently wandering the sparse frontier-town main streets of cyberspace. This isn't Alpha Centauri. The ship *has* arrived. We will be dealing with these things.

Soon.

I dabble there now—with art. Innocent little algorithms that have as much chance of enslaving mankind as a pocketful of Tamagotchi. But I was fortunate enough to get an invitation to participate in Digital Burgess (a multidisciplinary ALife/Paleontology conference in Banff, Canada, 1997). My presence there—holding forth on unfamiliar subjects—was questionable, but at least I learned something. I received my first in-depth exposure to genetic algorithms and Artificial Life (or "ALife"), there. I was inspired by the works of Karl Sims, Tom Ray, Larry Yaeger and others. Their work, mostly done on single computers or small networks, showed astounding results. Computers are now nearly one hundred times faster, and they have a neural network millions of nodes deep, the Web.

Many scientists dismiss the notion of autonomous thinking machines, partly due to the failure of Artificial Intelligence efforts to yield much in recent decades. But these guys (Sims, Yaeger, Ray, et al.), aren't working on Artificial Intelligence directly. Instead they are modeling *life* using genetic algorithms that borrow theories from biological reproduction and evolution. These algorithms use cycles of breeding (combining parts of two or more pieces of code, usually with some random mutation, to create "offspring"), and selection (either some analytical or aesthetic test applied to those offspring). Repeated over time these cycles tend to "evolve" code that improves with each generation. In Artificial Life experiments these genetic algorithms are employed in an attempt to evolve complex digital entities that exhibit the reproductive and survival behaviors we associate with biological life. And ultimately, digital entities that will perform some useful task—presumably for our benefit.

This differs from the better known Artificial Intelligence or "AI," which attempts to directly create or simulate human intelligence. ALife models much simpler forms. However, many proponents of ALife theorize that it may be the best path to AI. They believe that intelligence may well be an *emergent* phenomenon—

complexity and sophistication arriving from the repeated application of simple rule sets.

Looking at the structure of our brains, how the Web is structured, factor in the scale of the Web (evolution loves big numbers whether expressed in centuries or Terabytes) . . . ALife may have a chance.

So I play around with ALife art machines. Attempting to coax electronic evolution into following my aesthetic whim. Much more serious attempts to guide the process are ongoing. Researchers may be happy to just see the process work. More pragmatic minds seek some useful outcome. The assumption that this new life, these new minds, can be trained to work to our benefit is widespread. The fear that they might rise up and revolt, or that we may have no right to assert dominance, once this new intelligence arrives, has mostly been confined to fiction.

William Gibson sculpted foreboding cyberscapes in *Neuromancer* and later works. His forecasts of the weather out there in cyberspace have been disturbingly accurate. Along with many prescient points, he also illustrated the contemporary fact that multinational conglomerates have their own agendas independent of humankind's concerns. In a largely cyber-unrelated way this has been recently evidenced by the ability of entities like Enron to distort the behavior of seemingly rational men and women. A cybermind tailored to the notion that the bottom line is the prime directive makes me nervous.

Gibson's characters navigate a world degraded and divided by these entities and the power they wield. A world of technological haves vs. have-nots. His AIs question the quality and value of their existence, or of ours. Their relationship with humankind is at best arbitrary, undefined. Malevolent, benevolent, (or just sarcastic and belligerent like Dick's toasters and taxis), our first contact with another sentient being may be one of our own making—"Hi Mom and Dad"—best to start learning the language, watch out for those rebellious teen years.

I said earlier that I found shifting realities invigorating. I do. I want there to be *more*, believe there is. These extra-real experiences—in the form of dream, déjà vu, epiphany, bliss, whatever— don't always feel like the floor vanishing beneath your feet. Sometimes it's as if the floor doesn't matter—a wider, even boundless world revealed.

Our senses don't have reality covered. The closer science looks, the shiftier it gets. I don't assume the unknown is all bad, nor that our attempts to see beyond the "real," or aid the development of cyber-minds, are misguided. It is our nature to expand and explore. We need, for example, to cross mountain ranges, oceans, peer into the subatomic, venture into outer space. And, almost mystically, it seems we have created an entirely new realm, cyberspace—by its nature it will outgrow our ability to map and comprehend, it may spawn new species. Actually it is not artificial, it's a real place. Perhaps, like, we better go have a look around?

Cyberpunk, by definition, colors the future darkly. It's an aptly cautionary genre. Many in science and industry embrace and pursue these technologies with utopian, or at least utilitarian optimism. Many dismiss the potential of AI, or assume we will easily dominate it. That's our role—you know, like we did with nature. Perhaps our best hope of seeing the brighter side of these emerging technologies lies in heeding those cautions. In the meantime, when something makes you ask, "Can this be real?" the best answer may be:

"Could you rephrase the question?"

Building a Better Simulacrum: Literary Influences on The Matrix

Paul Di Filippo

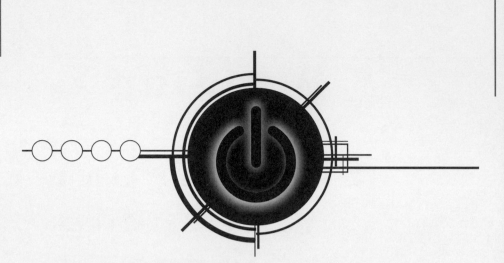

Very few science-fiction movies of the post–*Star Wars* era owe a greater debt to printed SF—or have repaid that debt so spectacularly and intelligently—as *The Matrix.* The co-creators of the film, Larry and Andy Wachowski—who, jointly, both scripted and directed it—appear to have drawn with wide-ranging familiarity on a vast range of modern science fiction, from the works of Philip K. Dick to the mythology of the DC Comics universe.

But their creative mining of printed SF transcends mere borrowing. The unique and startlingly novel synthesis that *The Matrix* offers is—in the best tradition of SF—a quantum leap upward from the ground state of its ancestors. Standing on the shoulders of giants, the Wachowskis obtain a fresh view of new horizons that they share with us.

It would be illuminating—yet falls outside the scope of this essay—to compare at length the accomplishments of *The*

Matrix with those of the original *Star Wars* from 1977 (now re-titled *Star Wars: Episode IV—A New Hope*), the only other film (or series of films, actually) of this period faithfully to adapt so many of the tropes of printed science fiction. *Star Wars* and its sequels indeed elicited the reaction from knowledgeable viewers of seeing for the first time on screen many of the quintessentially stefnal images, characters, and action previously only generated on mental movie screens. But the overall effect was one of confirmation of the canonical—and, at that, the pulpish canon. Additional sophistication and extension of the borrowed material was almost nil. George Lucas was satisfied with bringing to life the blended, older dreams of Isaac Asimov and Frank Herbert, among others, without truly expanding on or rethinking them.

The *Matrix*, on the other hand, does not simply replicate familiar joys in another medium. Despite its many Phildickian moments, the film is not essentially a Philip K. Dick movie. What the Wachowskis absorbed, they also metamorphosed, even if only by increasing the amplitude of the writer's original vision. The salient difference between *Star Wars* and *The Matrix* is that while the former was instantly duplicable (witness *Battlestar Galactica*), the latter, in its originality, has thus far frustrated imitators.

Any critic, when trying to track down allusions and derive sources for homage, must play a guessing game. What did the creators know, and when did they know it? My citations of various works that I believe the Wachowskis must have known could be undone in a moment by a simple statement from the brothers that they never encountered Book X or Story Y prior to filming their masterpiece. Indeed, they might already be on record as saying such;

not tried to research exhaustively all their interviews. Yet
fiction is such a gloriously incestuous medium, one in
which ideas float freely from story to story in a kind of generous
conversation, that I feel confident in holding forth my selections
as valid influences. Even if not encountered in the primary
sources, the ideas in these various texts have percolated throughout the field, so that any reader worth his salt has internalized the
conceptions, even if divorced from the original creators.

Two schemes for cataloging the literary seeds sown
throughout *The Matrix* appear valid. One might step chronologically through the movie, labeling instances of literary allusions
whenever found; or one might work chronologically through the
history of SF, citing relevant works in order of publication, and
pointing to their outcroppings in the film. The latter approach
appeals more to me, as someone whose background is primarily in
the written word, and also seems better suited to indicate how
extensive in time the Wachowskis' borrowings are.

But before examining the "hardcore" modern SF that
served as inspiration for *The Matrix*, we must journey much farther back into literary or quasi-literary history to appreciate certain layers of meaning and allusion in the film.

Our first hint of Biblical references exists in the name of
the vessel piloted by Morpheus (Laurence Fishburne), the
Nebuchadnezzar. However, the significance of this naming seems
almost gratuitous, or off-key. The Babylonian king, while a force-
ful conqueror, is not generally taken as a symbol of enlightenment
or visionary longings in line with the aspirations of the rebels. In
fact, "Babylon" is traditionally used as shorthand for captivity, and
might better represent the AI masters, were they within the realm

of human signification. But perhaps the Wachowskis meant to invoke the king's legendary incident of grass-eating madness, as a symbol of the psychic dangers that the rebels against the Matrix must face. Perhaps the name was simply chosen as euphoniously mythical. Either way, a more apt borrowing occurs when the last human redoubt is revealed to be dubbed Zion, the Biblical term for a part of Jerusalem that came to symbolize paradise or the promised land.

In any case, these two Biblical literalisms are swamped by the less explicit but undeniably powerful Christ symbolism swathing Neo (Keanu Reeves). Deemed "The One" by Morpheus, Neo undergoes death and resurrection to redeem all mankind. The single communal meal taken aboard the *Nebuchadnezzar* even partakes of a Last Supper ambiance. And of course, Trinity (Carrie-Anne Moss), as Neo's carnal worshipper, stands in for Mary Magdalene—despite some confusing aspects to her own name, traditionally assigned to the tripartite Godhead, not to a mere mortal. And ultimately Neo's soaring ascent into the heavens at the film's end further solidifies the parallel with Christ's life. In this sense, the Bible is the oldest text upon which the film draws.

(It might be remarked that the path of Neo's quest—from ignorance through initiation and trial to mortal challenge—also follows the famous generalized scheme devised by Joseph Campbell in his study *The Hero with a Thousand Faces* [1949], a scheme known as the "Monomyth." Thus a hundred different ancient legends flow into Neo's creation, not just the Judeo-Christian tradition.)

But below the Judeo-Christian stream runs a dark river that serves as the antithesis to the aboveground teachings. This secret underground philosophy is known as Gnosticism, and in *The Matrix* the Gnostic interpretation adds a new valence to the Messiah imagery. (Interested readers should seek out the work of scholar Elaine Pagels for complete information on the Gnostics.) Briefly rendered, the historically widespread heresy known as Gnosticism maintains that the material Creation is a literal hell, brought into being by a flawed, malign demiurge. Mankind is mired in the terrestrial mud in physical bodies that are mockeries of our true forms, with the mass of mankind ignorant of their predicament. Only derangement of the senses can free the mind from the snares of our common clay.

Curiously enough, Satan is the hero of the Gnostic worldview, as the lone rebel against the mad God's tyranny. And Morpheus is tinged with Satanic colorations. His generally black attire—identical with Trinity's and, eventually, Neo's—seems to imply an infernal origin. And his offering of the red pill of knowledge to Neo runs parallel to the serpent's temptation of Adam and Eve with a red apple.

The mapping of this Gnostic worldview—further explored below—onto the film is undeniable. The Gnostic "conceptual breakthrough" from illusion to understanding is central to the whole structure of the film. Only through Neo's senses-shattering initiation with the red pill, during which his physical form is warped by contact with the reflective fluid that flows off the pliable mirror, is Neo awakened to the true state of existence.

Of course, this suspicion of the validity of creation is found in other religions, notably in the Hindu and Buddhist concept of *maya* and *samsara*, the veils that conceal the true nature of reality from us. Notable also is the emphasis in the film placed on dream states, and the inability to distinguish between them and ostensibly conscious moments. Of course, the viewer is bound to recall one of the most famous parables involving dreams of all literature, the dream preserved in Taoist texts of the philosopher Chuang Tzu, who could not determine whether he was a butterfly dreaming he was a man, or a man dreaming he was a butterfly.

All these ancient ontological conundrums find masterful embodiment under the shaping hands of the Wachowskis. That the arid material of a million "Introduction to Philosophy" courses can be received eagerly through the medium of a "simple" action film is a remarkable achievement.

Leaving the classical world behind, we make a brief stop in the timeless realm of European fairy tales. For one thread running through *The Matrix* is the tale of Sleeping Beauty. Just as the kingdom and castle of Sleeping Beauty have been put into stasis, so has the human world of the twenty-first century been forced into hibernation, starting when the AIs took over. We are told by Agent Smith (Hugo Weaving) that when the Matrix was first conceived, it was engineered by the AIs to be a utopia. But mankind was not content in this virtual paradise, and so the late-twentieth-century milieu was re-created. But this begs the question of how time flows within the Matrix. Apparently, the Matrix has been in place for decades, and yet human "history" seems not to have advanced beyond 1999. Is the same year replayed over and over, after an annual mass mindwipe of virtual memories? Neo appears to sense something like this during his first reinsertion into the Matrix, when he questions all his Matrix past as unreal in a different way than simply "actual versus factitious."

Not only is the Matrix stalled in time, so is the blasted exterior world, which resembles the thorny thickets and wild forests that grow to surround Sleeping Beauty's home. Although we are not privy to the inner or social or political lives of the AIs (seemingly a single intelligence distributed across many vessels), they seem to have stopped developing once the system of human batteries was established. Earth's history has effectively halted.

Significant as this time-disjunction and stasis are, the real clincher between fairy tale and movie is of course the climactic speech and kiss which Trinity bestows on the dead Neo, awakening him to his transcension. This reversal of gender roles is typical of how the Wachowskis are not content with simply duplicating received templates but creatively revising them.

The visionary poet William Blake (1757–1827) must take center stage for a short turn now. A famous aphorism from his *The Marriage of Heaven and Hell* (1790–3) strikes me as seminal to the film. "If the doors of perception were cleansed everything would appear to man as it is, infinite." What more compact statement of the movie's theme could there be? I believe that visual homage is paid to Blake in a curious scene. Neo is undergoing a dressing-down from his boss at Metacortex for being late. Outside the office, workers on scaffolding wash the skyscraper's windows with loud squeegeeing noises. The undue attention the camera pays to this seemingly gratuitous bit of spear-carrier business is puzzling, until one takes the Blake quote into account. True, windows are not doors, but they will stand in well enough as a symbol of the awakening Neo is about to undergo—especially since Neo does, moments after this scene, employ a window as a door, under instructions from Morpheus.

And of course, Blake's phrasing was later borrowed by Aldous Huxley for his 1954 examination of drug-induced states of consciousness, *The Doors of Perception*. The sixties' notion of enlightenment through a pill—LSD, peyote, or other drugs—is yet another numinous trope informing *The Matrix*.

Two Victorian fantasies indisputably play their part in the feel and plot of the film. The works in question are none other than Lewis Carroll's *Alice's Adventures in Wonderland* (1865) and *Through the Looking-glass, and What Alice Found There* (1871). These are the

texts referenced most explicitly in the film, through several bits of dialogue from Morpheus and others, and it would be heavyhanded on the part of this critic to belabor the parallels, from the moment Neo is told to "Follow the white rabbit" to the "Drink me" moment when Morpheus offers the red pill. Carroll's surreal universe is so well known that even the most naive viewer will have no trouble catching these references. (And the adoption of Carroll and his hookah-smoking caterpillar by the hippie movement ties in with the drug theme alluded to above.)

But it should be remarked how extensively both "rabbit hole" and "mirror" imagery occur in the film. The opening shot down the white light of a policeman's flashlight is the initial rabbit hole, followed by such other instances as the descent down Neo's throat, to the entry by the invulnerable Neo into the very body of Agent Smith. Mirror imagery is even more widespread: reflective sunglasses; a spoon; Morpheus's pill case; the literal melting mirror that creeps up Neo's body; the mirrored skyscraper into which Trinity crashes the helicopter; a car mirror; a computer monitor—all these and other reflective liminal surfaces serve as signposts along the road of identity and as tokens of worlds separated by the thinnest of interfaces. Finally, it is certainly not coincidental that Zen texts refer to meditation and subsequent enlightenment as "polishing the mirror of the mind."

Finally, the Wachowskis once again play with gender reversal, as Neo assumes the role of the girl-child Alice.

Our last brief pause before leaping fully into an examination of the "hardcore" genre materials that were integrated into *The Matrix* concerns a touchstone of twentieth-century fantasy: L.

Frank Baum's *The Wonderful Wizard of Oz* (1900). When Cypher informs Neo, "Buckle your seatbelt, Dorothy, 'cuz Kansas is going bye-bye," we are forced to lay this famous template over the movie. On the whole, though, the parallels between Baum's Oz saga and the film are less impressive than the Carrollian ones, and seem to derive mainly from the cinematic version of the novel. None of Baum's many eccentric prose creations are referenced. (Although perhaps the conquering AIs are Tik-Tok the mechanical man writ large!) True, Neo could be seen as a deracinated Dorothy (another bit of sexual confusion), having picked up various companions embodying various virtues during his almost-involuntary quest. But there is no Emerald City as goal, and the prospect of returning home is nil.

The famous cinematic transition from black-and-white Kansas to Technicolor Oz is actually present in the newer film, but in reverse. Life in the Matrix is brightly lit, exhibiting a full range of colors. But the higher ontological reality (the devastated Earth) is monotone, all blacks, grays, duns, and the occasional flash of red. Again, an intriguing twist against viewer expectations.

In the following sections, as I examine different themes and tropes from *The Matrix* and their genre sources, I will of necessity have to jump back and forth through the history of SF, abandoning a simple one-way trip through the literature.

The prospect of mankind being conquered, dominated, and superseded by their own children, intelligent machines, is as old as genre SF. The threat was given new potency over the past few decades, as real-world advances in cybernetics, artificial intelligence, and emergent phenomena such as ALife seemed to inch us closer to the time when we would have to face our artificial peers and reach some agreement on the sharing of the world. Ultimately the cyberpunks brought new sophistication and polish to such ubiquitous tropes.

It would be impossible to list every work from the SF canon that focused on such issues and possibly fed into the Wachowski Brothers' conception of a world ceded to machines. As part of the free-floating SF consensus future, the notion of a globe consumed by runaway mechanisms is one of the more potent timelines intuited by even those without a vast experience of the literature. But it is possible to cite a few works that seem to lend their flavor to *The Matrix*.

Two of John W. Campbell's early stories seem to me to capture the tone of *The Matrix*, if not the same exact outlines of its future history. In "Twilight" (1934), a time-traveler finds our solar system millions of years from now populated by a declining, decadent humanity served by hordes of infallible, tireless machines. Mankind has long ago exterminated every other organic lifeform, echoing the human-triggered "scorching of the sky" in *The Matrix* and the apparent lack of animal life on that barren globe. By the story's end, a last desperate quest is underway to create "a machine which would have what man had lost. A curious machine." Instead of war between organic and inorganic, it's the passing of a torch. Campbell's "Night" (1935), a quasi-sequel, journeys even further into futurity, detailing the plight of the intelligent machines against the heat-death of the universe. This elegaic tone of this Darwinian transition seems a perfect fit for the film.

Jack Williamson's *The Humanoids* (1949) tells of robots

who, given their programming to protect and serve mankind, interpret their directive in an unsettling manner, forbidding mankind to undertake any task or indulgence they deem "dangerous." Mankind ends up *de facto* prisoners of their servants. In a less sinister yet similar fashion, the robots in Clifford Simak's *City* (1952) shield their owners rather too strenuously from unpleasantness, and end up inheriting the Earth after humanity departs. Although outright hostility and warfare on the scale depicted in *The Matrix* is not a feature of these books, there is an angle to the film that evokes them. Namely, why does the Matrix exist at all?

If the AIs require humans simply for their bio-electric potential—as living batteries and furnaces—certainly it would be easier to lobotomize every person and keep them as mindless cattle without risk of rebellion. Why go to all the trouble of maintaining and policing a virtual reality for them? It is almost as if the machines cannot overcome a certain in-built caretaker tendency—as in Brian Aldiss's "But Who Can Replace a Man?" (1958), where boastful robots turn submissive at the first sight of a human. This unexplained paradox speaks of more complex motives on the part of the machines than simple unreasoning hatred or desire for genocidal destruction.

In the 1950s, no more clairvoyant exponent of war between man and machine existed than Philip K. Dick. His stories and novels are strewn with automatons of varying degrees of threat and intelligence. When attempting to identify Dickian influences on *The Matrix* one is faced with a plethora of citations, and only a few representative examples can be fitted into this discussion.

Let the short story "Second Variety" (1952) stand as the

quintessential instance of such a war. On an Earth reduced to "endless ash and slag, ruins of buildings . . . eternal clouds of rolling gray . . . " a conflict between the Russians and "UN forces" is carried out via armed robot intermediaries, fabricated by underground automated factories. When the killer robots begin to modify their own evolution, mankind is swiftly doomed.

Throughout the 1960s, the Berserker stories of Fred Saberhagen and the Bolo stories of Keith Laumer continued to examine the way in which artificially intelligent war machines might interact with and against mankind. The hypothesis that computers of sufficient complexity could bootstrap themselves into intelligence began to percolate in such novels as D. F. Jones's *Colossus* (1966). But more sophisticated examinations of the treachery of artificial intelligences had to wait until the cyberpunk era. William Gibson's "loas" from the trilogy that commenced with *Neuromancer* (1984)—AIs born in the net and deriving their name and appearances from voodoo deities—stand as the archetypical contemporary embodiment of this conception. (Although not explicitly a follower of voodoo, the Oracle [Gloria Foster] whom Neo consults, as an African-American seeress, radiates a kind of Haitian sacredness, as if the Matrix could indeed be accessed via pagan religious rituals.) And Rudy Rucker's rogue robots known as "boppers," found in the series that opened with *Software* (1982), are the comic side of this threat.

Prior to their filmmaking career, the Wachowskis scripted several tales for Marvel Comics. Their familiarity with this medium so closely allied to prose SF shows up heavily in *The Matrix*.

The opening scene of policemen closing in on Trinity in a

nighted urban landscape resembles something out of the darker moments of Batman's mythos, with perhaps the deadly Joker substituted for the good-girl Trinity. But the heavier influence on their urban landscape surely is traceable to the work of Will Eisner, in his tales of the Spirit. Famous for his nearly tactile depiction of running water, Eisner is visually quoted in such scenes as Trinity's rooftop chase and Neo's car ride through rainy streets.

The phone motif—exits and entrances from and into the Matrix are achieved via phone lines—evokes two of DC Comics' characters. Who else but Superman has ever relied so heavily on phone booths as a venue for changing identities? Trinity's escape through an old-fashioned full-sized phone booth (an unlikely archaic survival in 1999) mirrors the way Superman would enter such a booth, change, and vanish at super-speed. And of course Ray Palmer, the Silver Age Atom, was fond of shrinking to quantum size and traveling down phone lines. Multiple shots of dangling receivers post-departure could have been panels swiped direct from the Atom's adventures.

Finally, consider the "comic book physics" literalized on the screen. Long before the achievements of Sam Raimi's *Spider-Man* (2002), the Wachowskis succeeded in porting over from comics in eye-popping fashion the extravagant physical feats of generations of superheroes. The wall-walking and tumbling; Trinity's corskcrew flight off a rooftop and into a window; Neo's climactic subway battle and his triumphant final leap into the virtual heavens of the Matrix—all these mythic moments so easy for artists to capture on paper ultimately found cinematic actualization.

Finally, "bullet time"—the time-distorting special effect utilized when, for instance, Neo dodges shots from an Agent during the rescue of Morpheus—is nothing less than the stop-motion perceptions of such super-fast characters as Quicksilver, the Flash, or Wonder Woman (who was, admittedly, fonder of bouncing bullets off her bracelets than simply ducking them).

SF has a long record of examining various epistemological and ontological questions, framing them in disturbing narratives. The core conceit of *The Matrix*—that simulation and reality can be indistinguishable, and that hidden masters rule our lives—has always been alluring to SF writers.

Certainly the most vivid early usage of this theme occurs in Robert Heinlein's "They" (1941), in which the fears of a paranoid mental patient are dismissed by his doctor, who, in private, then orders the remaking of the stage set that is reality, so as to further ensnare the man. In 1950, the less well known novella by Fritz Leiber, "You're All Alone," took this conceit even further, positing that our world was one populated by automatons with only a few truly awakened souls. (Leiber's protagonist was initiated into this worldview by a female character, just as Trinity inducted Neo.)

With the arrival on the 1950s genre scene of Philip K. Dick, this theme met its acknowledged master. No one could trump Dick when it came to framing questions of identity and perception and the nature of reality (or multiple realities) in gripping narratives, and the Wachowskis are indubitably his self-appointed heirs. Practically every major work by Dick revolved around the same core issues that inform *The Matrix*. Again, it would be prohibitive to catalogue all such instances in Dick's oeuvre. From the sequential dream worlds in *Eye in the Sky* (1957) through the onion-like layers of deceit and confusion in *The Three*

Stigmata of Palmer Eldritch (1965) to the after-death dreams of *Ubik* (1969), Dick specialized in questioning and destroying common assumptions about the nature of life and the cosmos. One early story, "Adjustment Team" (1954), in which even a man's dog is part of the reality-remodeling containment scheme against him, can stand for the earliest instances.

But it is the late-period novel *VALIS* (1981) that resonates most strongly with *The Matrix.* Here, the protagonist Horselover Fat (a P. K. D. doppelganger) receives illumination via a pink beam of light (Neo's red pill), later confirmed by a young woman, and learns that our modern era is an illusion superimposed over the real chronological period, which is an age of Roman Imperialism and servitude known as the "Black Iron Prison." Through Dick, Gnosticism becomes part of the common SF parlance. Once again, the globe is held in secret stasis. Compare this motif to Morpheus's speech to Neo: "[You are] born into a prison that you cannot smell or taste or touch. A prison for your mind."

A final citation from the 1950s must be granted to Frederik Pohl's "The Tunnel Under the World" (1954). Here, a small town full of unwitting humans (save for two rogue males), which relives the same day over and over as a test-market for advertisers, is proven to be a tabletop diorama.

Until the 1960s and the advent of full-blown computing technology, all such counterfeit worlds had been conceived of as physical venues or ill-defined dream states. But the arrival of machines that seemed to hold forth the potential of duplicating the exterior world in solid-state form opened the door for what we nowadays refer to commonly as "virtual reality." The literal hardware and software was in place for SF writers to utilize. Starting in

1962, when computer scientists Ole-Johan Dahl and Kristen Nygaard began to formulate the language known as SIMULA for the express purpose of "conceptualizing complex real world systems" *in silico*, SF began to turn its attention to such "cyberspaces."

Perhaps no work offers in short form a more disturbing vision of mankind abandoning its physical birthright for virtual comfort than Keith Laumer's "Cocoon" from 1962. With astonishing foresight and understanding of the embryonic challenge offered by the new technology, Laumer depicts a world where vast tank farms hold the majority of citizens. Swaddled in responsive sheets, wired up to dozens of contacts, eyes blinkered with screens that display numerous channels of entertainment, sucking down "Vege-pap" to subsist, Laumer's protagonist is shaken from his false utopia only by a physical breakdown in the system. After two hundred years in the tank, glaciers have intruded on the farm. Laumer's portrayal of the struggle to escape from the nutrient bath mirrors Neo's awakening in his own tank to a remarkable degree.

Another pivotal and remarkably prescient work of this period is *Simulacron-3* (1964) by Daniel Galouye. Scientists working on the eponymous machine (as in Pohl's story, for purposes of test-marketing products) are unaware that their own world is itself nothing but a simulation in a larger machine (a layering of ontological falsity that *The Matrix* seems disinclined to pursue, although sequels may prove otherwise). Again, a female initiate plays a part in shattering the complacency of the male protagonist. This novel was filmed as *The Thirteenth Floor* and, curiously enough, released in the same year as *The Matrix*.

Without a doubt, *The Matrix* belongs to that great late-twentieth-century category of conspiracy fiction, narratives that assert invisible metaschemes govern our daily lives. No writer was more influential in establishing this subgenre than Thomas Pynchon and his 1966 classic *The Crying of Lot 49*, which, with its emphasis on Information Theory, offers this incredibly relevant passage: "For it was now like walking among the matrices of a great digital computer, the zeroes and ones twinned above, hanging like balanced mobiles right and left, ahead, thick, maybe endless. Behind the hieroglyphic streets there would either be a transcendent meaning, or only the earth." The precision with which this fits Neo's ultimate epiphanic vision of the Matrix is uncanny.

Certainly one of the most startling and easy-to-spot visual "swipes" from the printed page in *The Matrix* occurs during Neo's interrogation by Agent Smith, after Neo is captured at his workplace. Manipulating the very stuff of the Matrix, the Agent cause Neo's mouth to disappear, replaced by a smooth facade of skin. Any viewer who knows Harlan Ellison's "I Have No Mouth, and I Must Scream" (1967), which recounts the Dantesque trials of humans trapped in the bowels of a sentient computer named AM, will appreciate this reference.

Perhaps no SF novel of the past four decades has been as seminal to a certain cadre of writers as Samuel R. Delany's *Nova* (1968). An ultra-literate, allegorical space opera, it paved the way not only for the cyberpunk movement but for the newest style of "hard SF" being written by such authors as Paul McAuley and Alastair Reynolds. By the second paragraph of Delany's masterpiece, we are introduced to the concept of "spinal sockets," a method of cyborgization whereby humans may jack into and operate machinery and sensors. Neo and the other rebels, of course, rely on just such devices for entering the Matrix. But whereas these data ports into the body are generally innocuous and unobtrusive in *Nova*, in the film they are lumpy and painful-looking, and the components that mate with them seem physically longer than the human body can contain. This ramping up of the intrusive nature of such devices is another instance of the Wachowskis creative revisionism.

Jumping ahead to 1971, we find a curious resonance in Philip José Farmer's *To Your Scattered Bodies Go*. Farmer's book, the first in a long series, concerns an artificial physical venue that is as duplicitous as any virtual reality. Riverworld plays host to reincarnations of every human who has ever lived, resurrected by godlike secret masters. When the protagonist first wakes—ahead of schedule—he finds himself floating in a limitless space, one naked, bald body in a latticework of billions. The resemblance to Neo's vision of the endless ranks of pods around his own is unmistakeable.

After all this groundwork, by the time of William Gibson's catalytic *Neuromancer* (1984) the audience was primed to accept and understand a vivid, tangible "cyberspace" that was a "consensual hallucination." Reality, as Morpheus explains to Neo, was nothing more than the interpretation of chemicals and electrical currents in the brain, and could be made to vanish or be replaced at whim.

As a final aside, we might consider the literary derivations of three of the characters in *The Matrix*.

Neo, as a hacker, owes a lot to Case in *Neuromancer*, a fringe figure living off his wits in the information economy. And Trinity shares a lineage with Molly, the slim and dangerous mirror-shaded assassin from that book. But Neo also hails from a long line of anti-authoritarian rebels. SF has long postulated dystopias that can be toppled—however magically—by just the right person in just the right place at just the right time, and Neo fits squarely into that mold. It is no coincidence that his apartment is Room 101, the brainwashing HQ in George Orwell's *1984* (1949). With Neo as Winston Smith and Trinity as his lover Julia, the risk of betrayal—under compulsion from the Agents of the Matrix—is symbolized by the insertion of the "navel bug" into a captive Neo. The Wachowskis, however, opt for a positive outcome rather than Orwell's pessimistic downer. This startling motif also calls up echoes of Philip K. Dick's "Imposter" (1953), in which the protagonist, all unwittingly, proves to be a robot bearing a bomb inside himself.

Morpheus, in his more obsessive, Captain Ahab moments, resembles the nova-fixated Captain Lorq Von Ray in Delany's *Nova*. And of course the name of one of Morpheus's crew ("Mouse") can be nothing other than a tribute to the identically named protagonist of Delany's novel. But Morpheus, in accordance with his mythological name, resembles also the hero of Neil Gaiman's famous *Sandman* comics: a merciless dispenser of visions and justice. And taken as a whole, the crew of the *Nebuchadnezzar* calls to mind many such plucky assemblages. Perhaps the closest analogue in terms of an assortment of misfits voyaging among differing levels of reality for cosmic stakes occurs in Michael Moorcock's Second Ether trilogy that began with *Blood* (1994).

It remains to be seen, of course, if the second and third installments of *The Matrix* trilogy invoke any additional icons and tropes from SF's vast printed heritage. But it surely cannot be denied that Larry and Andy Wachowski have succeeded already in transferring to the screen without diminution or betrayal some of the most prized ideas, scenes, and characters from the immense corpus of science fiction.

More Than You'll Ever Know: Down the Rabbit Hole of The Matrix

Kathleen Ann Goonan

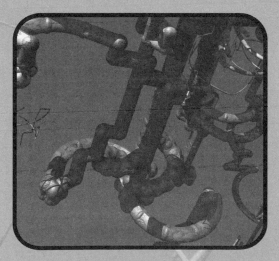

Calla: "There are quite a few hidden messages in the
movie that I notice the more I watch it. Can you tell me
how many there are?"
Wachowski Bros: "There are more than you'll ever know."
—*whatisthematrix.warnerbros.com/cpm/larryandychat.html*

L arry and Andy, the Wachowski Brothers, packed *The
Matrix* so full of references that it is a wonder the film
does not sink under its own weight. Like magpies, they
plucked bits of bright foil from philosophy, Zen Buddhism, literature, old cartoons, comics, Jung, gaming, Rastafarianism, hacker
culture, Goth, animé, Hong Kong kung fu movies, myth,
Gnosticism, Judaism, visual movie and art quotes—the list seems
neverending. There is hardly an original bone in the complex body
that is *The Matrix*, yet its rich reflectional stew is dazzling.
Miraculously, the film not only survives its portentous freight of
meaning, but as a Thrilling Tale of Wonder, it packs a powerful
wallop. Instead of Coltrane's wall of sound, it is a wall of encoded
meaning, slick, yet available to those who really do want to slide
down the mirror-shaded rabbit hole. It is difficult to find a pur-
chase; as soon as the movie pops one tantalizing template onto the
screen as a possible touchstone of interpretation it moves on to

another. *The Wizard of Oz* follows *Through the Looking-glass* in swift pursuit.

The film's true audience is Youth. Youth at the sharp edge of self-definition, when what everyone has said about life seems like old false garments that need to be thrown off so that one does not suffocate. It is the job of the adolescent to try on and discard selves until an authentic self is found, or created; until one of the selves fits.

There are many selves to try on here. The archetype-infused mulligan of references and images of *The Matrix* have the power to awaken and sharpen all the young who see it, and those who have not yet defined and confined themselves irrevocably in their adult world and beliefs. For, as Morpheus tells Neo, it is too shattering for those older than children to be made real.

It has been over twenty years since cyberpunk transformed the collective vision of the future. Does the overarching cyberpunk vision, which has been squeezed into *The Matrix* with admirable condensation and élan, have the consciousness-changing energy of the Moderns? Stein, Woolf, Joyce, Stravinsky, and Picasso created their art from a new matrix of scientific discoveries that forced new art, literature, and music into the mainstream—art in which the individual was at the forefront, having been pushed down the rabbit hole of relativity, increased speed, expanded communications, and horrible new forms of war. Almost a hundred years later, we are still reeling from the aftermath of what those who wished to see deep into reality wrought—the atomic bomb, biological warfare, and, possibly, new forms of change that we cannot even envision.

Only time will tell if cyberpunk can bear the weight. *The Matrix* is either a harbinger of new possibilities, or a *fin de siècle* last gasp of a fictional avenue used so often that it is now like our archetypal home town, which we must leave in order that we may mature. The cyberpunk vision of the future has actually come true, in some measure. We are now connected via a shared consensual reality, and some of us are more immersed in the Internet than our spouses would like us to be.

But we are still able to disconnect. Or are we? We still know what is real. Or do we? And will we, in the future? We are surrounded by those who tout both the thrills and the downside of the future—Drexler's gray goo, Kevin Kelly's *Out of Control*, and countless books about the dangers of genetic engineering.

Who are we? What is going on? These are the questions that the twentieth century attempted to answer in the wake of shattered religious certainties, and the questions which the adolescents of today will have to attempt to answer if they are going to steer the *Nebuchadnezzar* of technology into the future. *The Matrix* presents a series of religious and philosophical dichotomies: inner and outer, dream and waking, real and not-real. What is the truth, and how do we find it? What is consciousness, exactly, and how do we wake from the perceptual dream that Blake, Jesus, and the Buddha warned us we were in? These questions are not only addressed by science but by thousands of years of philosophical thought. *The Matrix* is an emotionally rich incarnation of cyberpunk precisely because of its use of everything that the writers could lay their hands on, including the certainties that many cyberpunk-based visions discard.

For the film's answer to the above perennial questions is,

somewhat disconcertingly, that faith, love, and belief will help us in our search for reality. These are the ancient religious, personal, human truisms that the machines, in the end, cannot fathom, replicate, or fight. Wearing the new costume of the Matrix like a new self, donning the mirror-shades with self-awareness and using the language of outlaw hackers, Neo lives and is finally real because of faith, love, and belief.

In *The Matrix*, humans are fighting technology, their creation, which has taken over as it has in so many science-fictional futures. Not only that, but the machines are using the preconscious bodies of humans as an energy source. The human Resistance, as in WWII France, takes place in the sewers, on an ancient, biblical, beleaguered ship, the *Nebuchadnezzar*. The ship is fueled by, presumably, the same energy source as the machines—liquified humans. But it is piloted by Awareness with a capital A.

The film is filled with shattering, wrenching images of birth and rebirth, and of wakening only to find oneself in another dream. Neo wakes—really wakes—for the first time in a vat of viscous fluid, plugged full of holes, jacked into the Matrix, on the very eve of being swallowed and digested by the machines. Though adult in form, he is hairless, a newborn; he has never used his eyes.

But the humans must get to the center (Zion, the promised land at the center of the Earth, and the center of themselves) in order to fully awake. For that, they seem to need a mediating savior: The One, who does not believe in himself at first, but who is, finally, able to work miracles. The One, whose incarnation (truly a birth into the world of meat) is announced by a voice crying in the wilderness, who prepares the way; The One, who is betrayed by a Judas Iscariot—Cypher—for a life of wealth, ease, and sensual pleasures, for a life of the body rather than a life of the mind (to be lived, paradoxically, in the consensual Mind). But The One must give up his own life for the life of everyone else. The True Believers on the *Nebuchadnezzar* are able to renounce the false world of the flesh (or, in this case, the imagined flesh, which is a mirage, a scrim) for their vision, for their faith, for the hoped-for resurrection of all of the bodies submerged in fluid. Like monks (and one nun, Trinity, who draws everything together), they live in isolation, sustained only by their faith that some day they will be able to facilitate the awakening of all humans.

The first face presented by *The Matrix* is that of cyberpunk, where the sky is "the color of television, tuned to a dead channel," and the Matrix is "bright lattices of logic unfolding across that colorless void," the computer screen inside the *Nebuchadnezzar*. The world of Gibson's *Neuromancer* is duly invoked; however, Mr. Anderson/Neo is embedded in the Matrix without being aware of it. The Matrix is "consensual reality." The Matrix is that which we have been programmed to believe in. The Matrix—the system—is what uses us and sucks us dry if we cannot awake to our own reality. Like infants, those in the Matrix live in "a seamless universe of self." They have not been truly born. They are still within the mother. They are asleep, and Morpheus, the son of Sleep, the god of Dreams, haunts them.

Neo has to become real in order to understand the truth. And once he becomes real, he must become, as Van Morrison might put it, "really, really, really real." What Neo has always taken for reality is now revealed, as is our world in many Christian heresies, as a lifeless, dark plain, something that must be transcended.

In fact, most Christian heresies, like Christianity itself, were amalgams of pre-Christian beliefs. One group of heretics, the Waldensians, isolated themselves in the Alps and actually survive to this day as a Protestant sect, having fought off many physical attacks mounted by the Catholic Church over the centuries. Like the Waldensians, the crew of the *Nebuchadnezzar* live under constant siege, and have lived thus for hundreds of years. Just as they were a thorn in the side of the church, there is a splinter in the mind of Neo that forces him to seek the truth even when the act of seeking brings nightmarish horrors upon him. Perhaps this splinter was programmed into him. Perhaps he is the reincarnation of "the man" who knew what the Matrix really was. Perhaps he *is* The One. Morpheus, the son of Sleep, the god of Dreams, has faith. He has faith that a greater reality does exist. But he is only one of the faithful, waiting for The One, Neo, the new. It is certainly not at all clear what Neo's outstanding qualities might be. He is indeed Everyman, dumbly ordinary, "not very smart," as the Oracle remarks. He has searched and searched for an answer, however, and in this he sets himself apart.

As in the world of fairy tales, Neo needs to know his true name, must assume his hacker name, Neo, with authority and belief while inside the Matrix in order to gain the necessary power to vanquish the machines. He must become an individual, a hero. He needs to take over the world of the machines from the inside, and his only tool is faith.

Once he is born into the real world, plucked from the brink of being digested by the machines, Neo is confronted with a teacher, Morpheus, and with koans. There is not, exactly, the sound of one hand clapping (although there is the image of one hand fighting, in the end, when mastery is achieved), but, against the sciffy background of *Night of the Lepus*, and a re-creation of science-fictional art, and after he has experienced the state of "I have no mouth, and I must scream," Neo is told by a child, "Only try to realize the truth. It is not the spoon that bends. It is only yourself." The process of realizing this, the process of becoming real, is painful, disorienting, humbling. It is easy to lose faith in oneself and in the world. It is difficult to keep it. But once Neo realizes this truth he can be outside himself; outside the Matrix; outside the system. He can become himself, able to utter his true and powerful name.

This is the job of youth—to wake into adulthood. How many teenagers have heard, as the Agent tells Mr. Anderson when he is late to work, "You think you are special, that the rules do not apply to you." Exactly! But there are dreams upon dreams here, myth piled upon myth. Is it a dream, or is it real? Is a philosophical conundrum semantically, at least, solved by Descartes, who claimed that he was because he thought? Cognition may therefore be the only valid touchstone; consciousness, whether in a dream or in this world of matter, our only proof of our existence. Self-realization is the key, and, in *The Matrix*, is evoked by the many references to Zen Buddhism.

Neo—Newness Incarnate—is asleep, and he needs to wake. Only The One will have the power to wake all of humankind from their control of the machines. The One will only have that power when he is truly able to not only believe, but to know, that he is The One. The power of thought, of will, is all-important. If only those inside the Matrix did not think of themselves as meat/matter, but as code, they could begin to live. "I think, therefore I am." There is matter, and there is mind—again, the dichotomy of many heresies, the world of light, in the Matrix, and the world of darkness, in the ancient sewers, flipped, as are so many references in the world of the film.

Even the programs—pure information—"want to be free." Information has that much in common with humans—some sort of will, the ability to desire, to want. We never see the face of the machines. They all have the same discardable face. But there may be, as one of the Agents tells Morpheus, a kind of heaven for them as well—release from the confines of human form, from the approximation of human senses, which are the portal, in many religions, through which evil comes.

The savior, "the man" who knew what the Matrix really is, once lived and died. But he will come again—presumably, having programmed himself to do so. "In another life, perhaps," as the Oracle remarks. His followers have to believe in him, must actively pursue him, and he seeks them as well, without knowing what he seeks. He only knows that he wants answers. He wants to know what the Matrix is. He asks the question of the twentieth century: What is going on? And he asks the question of the adolescent, and of the philosopher: "How do I know what is real, and what is a dream? How do I know if I am real?"

The answer cannot come from knowing the path; it cannot come, despite Descartes, from merely thinking, though thought is the first sign of life. The answer, here, is learned through kinetic, bodily knowing, as in yoga. In the film, self-knowledge is achieved via programs that teach the body what to do when it is in the Matrix; the body is a tool. The answer comes through using the Matrix against itself, in fomenting a war in Cypher's heaven, which is Morpheus's hell. "There is a difference between knowing the path and walking the path," says Morpheus, the teacher. Neo requires training in order to be able to walk the path. And first he must realize that there is a path.

A great deal is made of reflections in *The Matrix*. Neo sees reflections of himself everywhere, on just about any reflective surface. He sees reflections of his Matrix self and of his real self in the lenses of Morpheus's mirror-shades as he is offered the blue pill or the red pill. And then, having followed the White Rabbit, he is down the rabbit hole, to "see how deep the rabbit hole really goes." When they are real, the crew of the *Nebuchadnezzar* do not wear mirror-shades. Only when they hack into the system and become virtual do they don cyberpunk glasses and long black coats.

And then there is the Zen realization, the double entendre, as the Agent tells Neo, when they are both out of bullets, "You're empty." Neo replies, fittingly, with the authority of the Zen master, "So are you."

But perhaps the concept that most informs *The Matrix* is transcendence, and its necessary sister, free will. Presumably, machines cannot have free will; they are forever programmed, and forever at the mercy of their programs. Will this be the fate of sentient machines? Trapped in AI reality, will they ever truly long to wake up? Are they a part of the evolution of matter, and the evolution of consciousness?

Will they leave us, their creators, the meat, behind?

Humans who have awakened do not want a dream existence in which they are preyed upon by machines, because that is not the truth. They do not want to be raped and devoured by machines. They want to be in control.

There is Above, and there is Below—in fact, *The Matrix* also seems like a series of Dantesque concentric rings. Prior to the early twentieth century, humans were Below, but created in the image of that which was Above. Now, we have created that which is Outside, and we have loosed energies of which we are afraid.

The Matrix is, in a way, a kind of cheat, and hard to pin down. It wiggles and squirms, alive beneath the defining, quantifying lens, escaping at its edges, just out of vision. It pretends to be science fiction, dark cyberpunk. Yet its central scene of salvation is accomplished by faith, love, belief in something not seen. Neo, in the end, does not break through to reality so much as he creates reality. And so we are back in the dream. *The Matrix* raises more questions than it answers.

Is Neo just the product of some sort of evolution? Is he deeply, truly human, and thus able to control the machines and their exploitative world, or is he just some kind of accident? Was he programmed to be thus, and therefore a machine himself? Can humanity survive? What does our humanity really consist of, anyway?

Though there are no solid touchstones, it does come down to what Humpty Dumpty said to Alice: "The question is which is to be master—that is all." The machines, or the humans? The nun's mind, or her bodily needs and desires? Or some new synthesis of both?

Once self-realization is reached, once a level of mastery and of individuation is achieved, once free of the soup of the Matrix, the child is an adult, with the power to change the world. Ready, the adolescent might sneer, to give in to the system.

No. Ready to work the miracle of using free will to make changes in the real world.

Neo is ready to do this. Once enlightened, he dons mirror-shades of his own free will, and enters the Matrix ready to sacrifice himself; ready to be the Bodhisattva who will set all of humanity free and lead them to Zion.

Transcendence is not a word that meshes comfortably with the dark, gritty world of cyberpunk. But this ship of allusions, this synthesis, this matrix, actually floats. The myths, unpacked, dust-ed off, cunningly remixed and cognizant of present-day concerns, are ready for mirror-shaded action. As with comics, we have to wait, here in the mundane drugstore, for the next issue.

The Matrix
and the
Star Maker

Mike Resnick

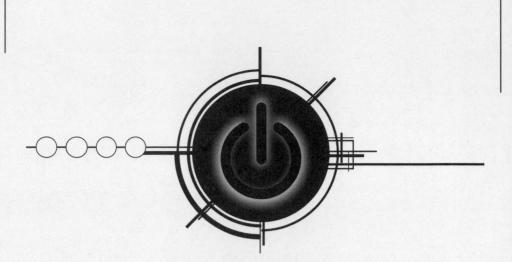

So here's humanity, downtrodden, unhappy, fed false images of the real world, and stacked up against us are dozens, perhaps thousands, possibly even millions of computer programs that have taken shape and form and voice. They're smarter than we are, they're faster and stronger, they're far more motivated.

And they don't like us very much.

That's the situation Neo finds himself in. The Matrix is not a forgiving place to be. Humans have been identified by these animated programs, known as "Agents," as a new and virulent form of virus that must be controlled and, in certain instances, eradicated.

How did such a world come to pass?

According to *The Matrix*, it happened when mankind's computers became self-aware, when artificial intelligence took that next great stride from where the machines are now to where *we* are.

And, according to all the apocalyptic literature of science fiction and that small but popular subset of it called cyberpunk, Neo's world is a natural outgrowth of that phenomenon.

It's total rubbish, of course.

Hollywood has got it all wrong. That's not really surprising, when you realize that *The Matrix* is simply a logical outgrowth of all those purportedly science-fictional films of the 1950s that were actually anti-science films, and always ended with lines like "There are some things that man was not meant to know." (How to write a pro-science movie script seemed to be first and foremost among them.)

Hollywood makes its living from the fact that it deals not in ideas but in emotions. Oh, you can *disguise* them as ideas, as they did in *The Matrix*, but the movie doesn't explore the logical consequences of self-awareness among our machines. It just tries to scare the hell out of you, and bedazzle you with special effects and with what has come to be the Cyberpunk Look. This is the future, it says, and only a twenty-five-year-old kid who has trouble emoting can save the rest of us.

And does he save us with his superior intellect? Of course not. He saves us by becoming, in some mystical, non-scientific way, a better karate/kung fu fighter than the Agents.

Well, okay, it's a movie, no one is supposed to take it seriously. Except that millions of people do. So perhaps it's time to apply a little less karate and a little more brainpower to the problem, and see if we're really going to wind up in such a grim, dismal, essentially hopeless future.

Let's even grant most of the movie's premises and posit the following:

1. Machines can think.

2. Thinking machines have become self-aware.

3. Computer programs can emulate actual human beings and interact with them inexactly the way that they do in *The Matrix.*

What logically follows? A society in which the machines regulate every aspect of our behavior? A society where any man who steps out of line is terminated? A society where the machines feel that they are superior to the men whose lives they rule?

Only in the movies.

Let's put it in the most simple terms:

What is *any* thinking, self-aware entity—man or machine—likely to do when confronted with what is clearly and undeniably its creator?

Rule it? Kill it? Hate it?

Hell, no.

He'll *worship* it.

Consider the first, and most compelling, law of Isaac Asimov's Three Laws of Robotics—that a robot may not injure a human being or, through inaction, allow a human being to come to harm.

You won't even have to program that into these "mortal enemies" from *The Matrix.* By the very definition of a self-aware intelligence, they will serve their creators gladly, unselfishly, uncomplainingly, and eternally.

Ah, but these are thinking machines, capable of learning, capable of thinking in new areas and directions. Won't some of them become atheists, so to speak?

Not a chance.

I am an atheist. You show me a bearded old man—or an unbearded young woman, for that matter—who can perform the godly miracles of the Old Testament and I'll convert so fast it'll make your head spin. I am an atheist only because I have not yet seen proof of my creator's existence; that's not going to be a problem for the self-aware AI machines.

If God touches my rib and pulls forth a fully formed woman, I'm a believer as of that instant. And if a scientist, or even a programmer, shows a thinking machine exactly how he builds a machine or creates a program for it to run, that's *their* revelation at Tarsus.

We're not talking religion here. Religion is just a bunch of customs created to bring spiritual and emotional comfort to a mass of people who have no direct contact with their creator. No, we're talking the real McCoy here—Olaf Stapledon's non-demoninational Star Maker. Once you confront your creator in the flesh, you no longer need the trappings of religion to help you communicate with him or even worship him.

So can anything go so wrong that we actually approach the world of *The Matrix* again?

Not really. There will always be those who start quoting from Jack Williamson's classic novella, "With Folded Hands," in which robots are charged with serving humanity and keeping us safe from harm—and interpret their functions so rigidly that mankind becomes their unwitting prisoner, prevented from doing anything whatsoever, since every conceivable action involves some element, however slight, of risk.

Ain't gonna happen. Remember, these are not robots. These are computer programs.

And who writes computer programs?

We do. Programmers do.

Well, then, will the day come when a computer writes its own program?

Sure. It's not far off. But remember: This computer will be writing a program that will work in the service of its creator. If you're a computer, you're not going to be able to conceive of any danger affecting me . . . and if you do, and go a bit overboard like Williamson's robots, I will tell you to stop, and your reply will of necessity be the equivalent of "Yes, Lord."

Ah, but computers know humans are not indestructible. We already use them in many forms of surgery and diagnosis, and self-aware intelligent computers can reasonably be expected to exchange information among themselves.

Okay, so they'll know we can get sick. And die. That will not encourage them to kill us. Rather, it will have them working night and day to *save* their creators from pain and disease. Not from risk, because that would require them to give direct orders to their deities, which is inconceivable and probably blasphemous, but rather from the *consequences* of risk.

So will there be any suffering in this brave new world?

You can bet on it.

And it won't be us. Gods don't suffer; not when there are lesser beings around. Or self-aware computer programs.

We create porn sites today. Tomorrow (or the day after) there'll be prostitute programs of both sexes and every inclination.

But it doesn't stop there.

For example, if we yell at a spouse, we alienate him or her. Slap a kid and it's child abuse. Kick a dog and the SPCA is on your case.

But create a computer analog of your spouse, your kid, and your dog, and you can mistreat them all you want. After all, they aren't human beings or animals, they're just electric impulses. They don't suffer, they only *simulate* suffering.

Carry it a step farther. Do you hate Jews? Blacks? Gays?

You can slaughter them by the thousands. Become Caligula, Hitler, Stalin. Do what you want. Even self-aware programs won't fight back against their creators.

Of course, those are the more repugnant uses to which we'll put our programs in the true world of the Matrix.

What else might we do with them?

Before vaccinating twenty million humans against AIDS,

we'll infect twenty million "Agents" with it and see how the vaccines and antidotes work on them.

Before creating that 160-story skyscraper that is currently on tap for Bangkok, we'll create it in a machine, fill it with 100,000 sentient programs, subject it to a 7.8 Richter-scale earthquake, and see how many of the "Agents" survived.

Before introducing the next "new math" and robbing a generation of students of the ability to make change without a pocket computer, you'll try your innovation out on a few million sentient programs. If it dumbs them down enough, you'll know not to try it on real people.

Why test-crash cars in the auto makers' labs? You'll create the prototype of your new car in the computer. In fact, you'll create five thousand of them. Crash them at various speeds, from twenty to one hundred miles per hour, into everything from concrete walls to other cars.

See how many of your five thousand sentient programs die, how many are permanently crippled, how many can be saved, and how many—if any—can walk away in one piece.

Yeah, it's perfection itself. That's one of the nice things about being gods.

One caveat. If I were you, I'd keep a very careful watch on all those sentient programs.

And if you should happen to find one called Neo—kill him now.

Yuen Woo-ping and the Art of Flying

by Walter Jon Williams

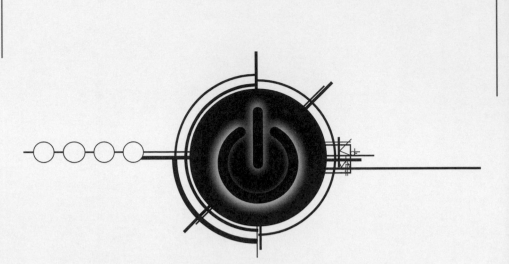

One thing you can say for the Wachowski Brothers is that they use influence well. *The Matrix* is like a compendium of some of the best ideas of the last forty years of written science fiction: the plastic realities of Philip K. Dick; the cyber implant technology of Samuel R. Delany's *Nova*; the glittering surfaces and eyeball kicks of William Gibson; the computer-generated artificial realities of, well, lots of people. The renegade artificial intelligences go at least as far back as Karel Capek's *R.U.R.* (1920), with a nod to Mary Shelley's *Frankenstein*.

To an audience unfamiliar with the sources, *The Matrix* seemed bright and new and dazzling. And to science-fiction readers, *The Matrix* was a stunning visualization of long-cherished dreams (and nightmares).

But aside from the science-fiction ideas, there was another element of *The Matrix* that dazzled, another element that had existed in its own world for years but which the Wachowski

Brothers brought to a new audience.

That element goes by the name *wuxia pian.* And Yuen Woo-ping is its master.

Wuxia pian can be translated as "hero films," and they've been made in China since the silent films of the 1920s. Based on legends, popular fiction, or Chinese opera, these films feature action as well as a strong supernatural element, in which kung fu masters fly through the air, display deadly mental powers, or shoot death rays out of their hands. (It should be pointed out that, to the original audience, these powers were not necessarily "supernatural," in that at least some of the audience believed that people could actually do these things.)

Yuen Woo-ping, the action choreographer on *The Matrix,* was born into the *wuxia* tradition. His father was Yuen Hsiao-tien, better known in the West as Simon Yuen, a seasoned actor who had grown up in the Chinese opera and then gone on to become a film star in Hong Kong, where he starred in dozens—perhaps even hundreds—of *wuxia* films, many of them for the Shaw Brothers, then the titans of Asian cinema. Many of these were the forgettable, so-called "seven-day films"—because that's how long they took to shoot—but such Simon Yuen classics as *Shaolin Challenges Ninja* and *Against Rascals with Kung Fu* are still worth viewing.

Yuen Woo-ping—who I propose to call "Woo," to distinguish him from others of his distinguished family—learned martial arts from his father, who also apprenticed him to the same Peking Opera troupe that later produced Sammo Hung, Jackie Chan, and Yuen Biao. (Which makes Woo, in Chinese terms, the Elder Brother of these three distinguished actors.) Peking Opera isn't just about singing: it's also about acrobatics and stage combat. Woo was raised in an atmosphere saturated with martial arts and show business. As a child actor, he was seen in many of the *Wong Fei-hung* series of films, starring the veteran actor Kwan Tak-hing as the legendary Chinese folk hero.

Woo was to reinvent the character of Wong Fei-hung later in his career.

Woo continued to work in films as an actor. Unfortunately he's not blessed with movie-star good looks, and he continued in a series of villain and second-banana roles. He branched out as a stuntman, where his Peking Opera training served him well, and later as an action choreographer and director for the independent studio Seasonal Films.

He and his father were not the only members of the Yuen dynasty. Three other brothers have made their names as actors, directors, and stunt choreographers: Yuen Chun-wai (aka "Brandy Yuen"), Yuen Shun-yee (who, as part of Woo's stunt team, was credited as "Eagle Yuen" in *The Matrix*), and Yuen Cheung-yan, best known in the West as the stunt choreographer of the *Charlie's Angels* remake.

By the 1970s, *wuxia pian* had begun to seem old-fashioned, stereotyped, and dull. The success of Bruce Lee—or Lee Siu-lung, "Little Dragon Lee"—ushered in the era of *gung-fu pian*, kung fu films, which banished the supernatural elements of the old *wuxia* in favor of more realistic action. A new generation of actors tried their best to imitate Bruce Lee, as their names will attest: Bruce Le, Bruce Li, Rocket Li, and Jet Li—of these, only Jet Li, a genuine talent, has survived. Woo's father Simon Yuen, an actor closely identified with the old school, saw his career going into eclipse.

One of the least successful Bruce Lee clones of the period was Chan Sing-lung—the name means "Already the Dragon," i.e., "Already Bruce Lee." Chan had been in a series of dreadful films, and his career had bottomed out. His studio despaired of any of his pictures making a profit, and were ready to loan him out.

One first-time director, Yuen Woo-ping at Seasonal Films, spotted hidden promise in Chan, and thought that borrowing Chan might prove worthwhile. He and Chan put their heads together and came up with a new hero for the kung-fu cinema, a kind of anti–Bruce Lee. Where Lee was invincible, Chan would be fallible and human. Whereas Lee won all his fights, Chan would strive desperately to keep from getting thrashed. Where Lee screamed to show his power when striking, Chan would scream because hitting people hurt his hand.

The film on which Woo and Chan collaborated was *Snake in the Eagle's Shadow*, released in 1978. It was a monster hit. It outgrossed every Bruce Lee film made. It was the single most successful film in Asian cinematic history.

What Woo and Chan had done was create a new genre of Asian cinema, *wu da pian,* "fight films with martial arts." It features incredible athleticism, brilliant timing, and highly dangerous stunts.

Did I forget to mention Chan Sing-lung's English name?

It's Jackie Chan.

Woo had helped to create the world's biggest box-office star. And while he was at it, he'd also revived his father's career, because he cast Simon Yuen as Jackie's teacher.

Woo and his Younger Brother Jackie Chan followed their hit with another, *Drunken Master,* in which the beloved Wong Fei-hung character was reinvented for a new generation. The Wong

Fei-hung films in which Woo had acted as a child featured Wong as an elderly, distinguished gentleman, a doctor and martial arts master with a strict morality and a rigid sense of honor. In contrast, Chan played Wong as a goofy young man, a country bumpkin who has yet to learn the moral lessons that will turn him into the distinguished teacher and kung fu master that Chinese audiences had come to expect. And once again, Woo cast his father Simon as Chan's teacher, the drunken master of the title.

The picture was another smash hit. Woo and Chan were on their way.

Jackie Chan had to return to his old studio to finish his contract, and he and Woo were not to collaborate again for many years, until 1992's hilarious, inventive *Twin Dragons*. In the meantime, Woo worked as an actor, director, or action director in a series of distinguished films, including *Eastern Condors* (with Younger Brother Sammo Hung), *Tai Chi Master* (with Jet Li), and *Iron Monkey*.

While directing Sammo Hung in *The Magnificent Butcher* (1979), Woo suffered a tragic loss: His father, who had been cast in the film, died of a sudden heart attack. Not only did Woo have to mourn his father while continuing to shoot the film, but he was forced into the excruciating position of having to reshoot all his father's scenes with another actor.

Simon Yuen died before the type of film in which he'd made his name, the *wuxia pian,* made a comeback. In the 1980s *wuxia* was revived, particularly by the director Tsui Hark in *Zu: Warriors of the Magic Mountain* (1983, not to be confused with the inferior 2001 remake). This grand tale of adventure, romance, derring-do, tragedy, and magic is just about the most perfect *wuxia* film ever made, and a splendid introduction to the genre.

Tsui Hark's success with *Warriors* set up one of the great collaborations in film history, when he (as director) teamed with Woo (as action choreographer) on the *Once Upon a Time in China* sequence. The folk hero Wong Fei-hung was reinvented yet again—young (as in the Jackie Chan version), but already a master, a moralist, and healer who embodied the best of traditional Chinese culture. As embodied by the athletic and charming Jet Li, the new Wong was a smash.

Even more of a smash was Woo's choreography. The film was filled with "wire work," in which the actors wear invisible wires to allow the characters to leap, somersault, run up walls, and practically fly through the air. Particularly striking was Wong's trademark "shadowless kick," a kind of flying, stamping mule kick delivered while corkscrewing through the air. This "gravity-optional martial arts" was a huge hit with Asian audiences, and the final sequence—in which Wong and his chief opponent fight while balanced precariously on ladders—was so influential that it's been copied repeatedly in the West, from *Xena: Warrior Princess* (which made something of a fetish of copying key scenes from Tsui Hark films), to the recent *The Musketeer* (2001).

A point should be made about Asian action choreographers. They don't just choreograph the fighting, but control all aspects of the fight scene, from the fight itself to the stunts, actors, camera, lighting, and special effects. The film's actual director takes a backseat to the stunt director in any scene involving action. The Asian stunt choreographer might well control two hundred people at a time, and is a very powerful figure, as witnessed by their uncomplimentary nickname—*she tao,* or "head of the snake."

Another point is that because Chinese films are made on a very small budget—ten million dollars or less, a tiny sum by Hollywood standards—the budget for special effects and stunts is very small. When a Chinese actor dives through a window, it's not a window made of safety glass, because Chinese budgets can't *afford* safety glass. If the stunt isn't done exactly right, the actor will be sliced open. When Jackie Chan freefalls down the side of a skyscraper in *Who Am I?* it's a real skyscraper, a real fall, and the real Jackie Chan, not a stunt double. In *Once Upon a Time in China,* when Jet Li repels an attack by fire arrows, those are *real fire arrows* being shot at him, and the desperation on his face is perfectly genuine.

Though Chinese actors risk crippling injury or death for

their art, the results are often dramatic, heart-stopping, and unforgettable. Glance down the list of Woo's films—the three *Once Upon a Time in China* collaborations with Tsui Hark, the three Jackie Chan films, and such brilliant solo efforts as *Wing Chun* (with Michelle Yeoh)—and you'll see that each has fresh, original, daring moments that stay in the mind forever.

Which brings us back to the Wachowski Brothers. The revolutionary Hong Kong films of the 1980s had found an audience among a younger brand of Hollywood directors who were growing bored with the films of action stars such as Clint Eastwood, Arnold Schwarzenegger, and Sylvester Stallone and their style, inspired by another revolutionary foreign film genre, the Spaghetti Westerns of Sergio Leone.

The new Hollywood directors wanted films with the originality and immediacy of the best of the Hong Kong genre. Jackie Chan and Jet Li began making movies in the States. Quentin Tarantino directed *Reservoir Dogs,* a film inspired by Ringo Lam's *City on Fire. Xena* and *Hercules: The Legendary Journeys* began hiring Chinese action directors. *Buffy the Vampire Slayer* began using Chinese-inspired action choreography.

But the Wachowski Brothers were smarter than any of these. For *The Matrix,* they knew they needed the best action director in the world.

So they hired Yuen Woo-ping.

Woo had several handicaps in taking on an American film. First, he doesn't really speak English. And second, he had to work with American actors, who were completely unused to the kind of demands a Chinese action choreographer was going to make of them.

The Wachowskis knew the Hong Kong genre, and they

knew that part of its immediacy and power comes from the fact that the actors are actually doing most of their own moves and fighting their own fights, with the camera showing them in close-up so the audience can see it's really them. They wanted *The Matrix* to have that impact. They wanted their lead actors to do most of their own stunts, something that must have had their Warner Bros. superiors questioning their sanity.

The Chinese actors of Jackie Chan's generation were raised in the Peking Opera, where they were trained from childhood in the kind of gymnastics, stunts, and martial arts necessary to produce the brilliant action scenes of Hong Kong cinema. Could American actors possibly come up to this standard?

Fortunately, the answer was yes. Woo put Keanu Reeves, Carrie-Anne Moss, Laurence Fishburne, and Hugo Weaving through four months of demanding physical training before a single frame of film was shot. The training regime was painful—occasionally agonizing—particularly for Keanu Reeves, who was recovering from neck surgery in order to correct a growing paralysis of his legs. While training, Reeves had to wear a neck brace, and for the first two and a half months could not practice kicks. Instead, Woo kept him to a regimen of stretches and leg-strengthening exercises. The first scenes Reeves shot in the film were physically undemanding, in order to give his neck a chance to heal.

While his actors were acquiring martial arts skill, Woo had his stunt team block out all the action scenes while he filmed them to see how they'd work on camera. As in the Hong Kong tradition, he was choosing camera setups and blocking for the action scenes. As Woo's blocking tapes show, the Wachowskis pretty much followed his setups shot-for-shot.

Compare, for example, a film in which the director did *not* listen to his stunt choreographer, the Jet Li vehicle *Romeo Must Die*. The action is shot too close up and with too many cuts, making the action muddy, confusing, and annoying.

The long training time meant that Woo could choreograph scenes built around the strengths of the individual actors, using Carrie-Anne Moss's grace, Fishburne's dancing athleticism, Reeves's agility, and Weaving's physical power. Reeves, fighting through the pain of his neck injury and against the paralysis of his legs, was particularly obsessive about getting the action scenes right, sometimes insisting on up to thirty takes. The training-room fight between Reeves and Fishburne left both actors exhausted and covered with bruises. During the rigorous shooting Reeves injured a knee, and Moss an ankle. Two stunt men, who were used for the really dangerous shots, were seriously injured.

Despite the handicaps of having to work through a translator and dealing with actors unused to the demands of his genre, Woo had advantages, too. The budget for *The Matrix* was ten times the size of any film that Woo had ever worked on, and that luxury shows. Woo was able to work with technology he'd never encountered before, such as "bullet time"—the dramatic technology that can freeze action while the camera appears to whirl in a circle around it, as when Morpheus is frozen in the air over Neo during the kung fu training sequence, or when Trinity is frozen in midair, in the act of kicking an attacking policeman.

Yet even the Wachowskis' budget had its limitations. In one scene where Reeves and Hugo Weaving were flying at each other, Woo ran out of specialists to man the wire gear—so the

Wachowskis themselves cheerfully began hauling the ropes.

The result is gorgeous—action sequences in which people seem to float in air and shots where contorted bodies dodge bullets, all married with scenes of brutal, convincing action. *The Matrix* is a perfect combination of American imagination and technical expertise with Asian styles and action. The Wachowskis truly succeeded in their goal of giving a Hong Kong feel to their action scenes.

The film is filled with references to Hong Kong cinema. Trinity, in the original film storyboard, is clearly an Asian martial artist. The fight scene in which Neo swipes at his nose with his thumb is an homage to Bruce Lee. During the fight in the subway, the moment in which Neo takes a fighting stance, then turns his lead hand palm-up to make a "come-to-me" gesture, is a bit of business Jackie Chan used to good effect in Woo's *Drunken Master.* Neo, with his long trench coat concealing his weaponry, is a clear reference to Chow Yun-fat's character in the *Better Tomorrow* movies. The scene in which Trinity performs a front kick over her shoulder to knock out a policeman standing behind her is a reference to a similar kick by Michelle Yeoh in Woo's *Wing Chun.*

Yuen Woo-ping followed *The Matrix* with another triumph—he was action choreographer on the greatest *wuxia* of all time, Ang Lee's *Crouching Tiger, Hidden Dragon,* the first Chinese-language film to be made on an American-sized budget and to take home a fistful of Oscars. (Unfortunately, there's no Oscar category for action choreographer.) No doubt Woo's experience at transforming American actors into martial artists aided him in turning Chow Yun-fat—no martial artist—into master swordsman Li Mu Bai, while the blazing fights he designed for veteran *wuxia* star Cheng Pei-pei and for the balletic Michelle Yeoh, far more experienced in the martial genre, are breathtaking.

After *Tiger*, Woo choreographed the action for Quentin Tarantino's Hong Kong–based film *Kill Bill* before reuniting with the creators of *The Matrix* for the two *Matrix* sequels, *The Matrix Reloaded* and *The Matrix Revolutions*.

Yuen Woo-ping—actor, director, martial artist, scion of the Peking Opera, son of Simon Yuen, member of a filmmaking dynasty, the director of Jackie Chan's first big hit, master of the flying wire, and the best action choreographer in the world—is beginning to achieve in the West the recognition his long and eventful career has long deserved. His imagination shows no sign of fading, and it's a certainty that in the future he will furnish the world with a myriad of unforgettable cinematic moments.

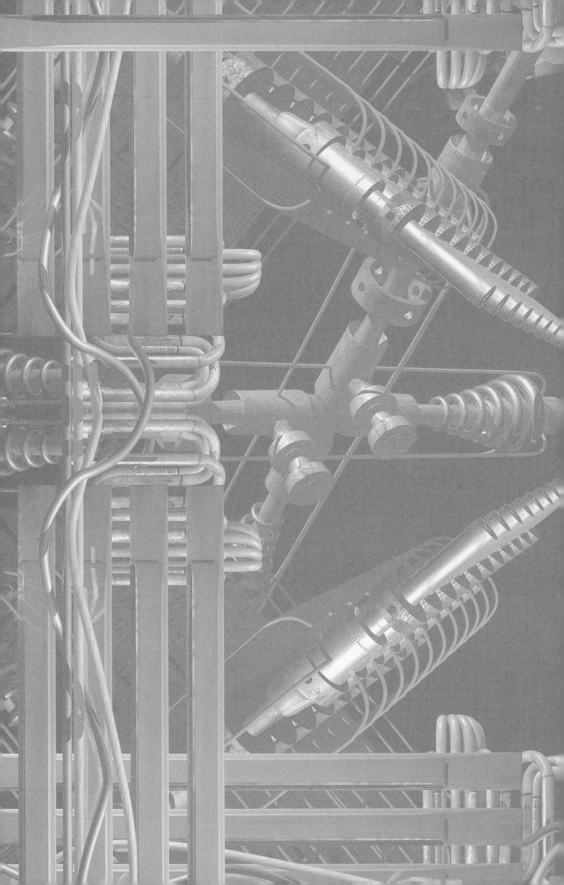

Alice in Metropolis or It's All Done with Mirrors

Dean Motter

I was introduced to Terry Gilliam at Harvey Kurtzman's memorial service. A longtime fan, I intended to act, well, *fannish*, but before I could get the words out of my mouth, he informed me how much my comic book *Mister X* inspired much of the design in his film *Brazil*.

This was the second time something like this had happened to me. The first time was at Pinewood Studios, in England. Warner Bros. Pictures had arranged for a number of DC Comics' guests to visit the set of the first Batman film.

I was sitting next to my boss, VP/Publisher Jenette Kahn, on the chartered bus, pleading to get a peak at the proposed *Watchmen* screenplay she clutched to her chest. There was no way that she'd violate confidentiality. She made it up to me over lunch when she introduced me to Anton Furst, the visionary art director for *Batman*. It was an odd meeting, to say the least. He confessed a fondness for the *Mister X* comic book series as he shook my hand: "We have a stack of those over in the art department."

Furst himself resembled Mister X—perhaps a little bit too much. He looked like he hadn't slept in months (perfectly believable, given the grueling production schedule), wore a black trench coat and dark circular sunglasses. All that was missing was the shaved cranium. His drawings and the back-lot Gotham City that we toured were Mister X's Radiant City to a "T." Architecture is a passion, and in my graphic illustration work this is explored and expressed. The exploration is private, the expression is public, and its influence is always unexpected and flattering.

Years later I faced the cinematic reflection of my comics once more when the directors of *The Matrix* spoke of their fondness for *Mister X* and my more recent series, *Terminal City*, in an interview on the film's DVD.

Fantastic cinema has always been an excellent means to explore theoretical cityscape models. From Millieus, to Fritz Lang. From *King Kong* to *Blade Runner*. From *Dark City* to Coruscant. From the first squeegee wipe (echoing the opening to my own *Terminal City*, published sometime earlier) to the famous rooftop battle in *The Matrix*.

> The sky above the port was the color of television, tuned to a dead channel.
> —William Gibson, *Neuromancer*

All that being said, I wasn't certain that I wanted to see *The Matrix* when it was first being promoted—much less enjoy it. I for one was getting somewhat tired of cyberpunk-*this*, hyperspace-*that*, and virtual-reality villains manifesting themselves in the real world and vice versa (à la *Johnny Mnemonic*, *The Lawnmower Man*, *Tron* and *Virtuosity*.) But the word on the street was that this one was going to be different somehow. A new generation of state-of-the-art effects, comic book/martial arts–style action, and memorable production design would be employed to make for a singular film.

It delivered on all fronts. Many have commented in detail on the wonderfully Byzantine storyline, the gravity-defying action scenes, and the remarkable effects. But I found it interesting for slightly different reasons. In this film, the urban model for cyberspace was defined in a peculiarly self-referential way.

The technology utilized in creating this cinematic environment (such as "bullet time" and "flo-mo") was a reflection of the technology of the very world it portrayed. In the same manner that the often brutish means employed to bring the reality of *Batman* to life reflected the tortured world of Gotham City, the realm of the Matrix itself was a reflection of the new generation of mechanics for creating reality—or the *illusion* of reality. In this case, motion pictures. In Thomas Anderson's case, the *world*. This was, after all, the theme of *The Matrix*.

> Have you ever had a dream, Neo, that you were so
> sure was real? What if you were unable to wake from
> that dream, Neo? How would you know the differ-
> ence between the dream world and the real world?
> —Morpheus, *The Matrix*

While the film consciously references the first of Lewis Carroll's *Alice* books, it actually has more in common with the second. If nothing else, we are in the sitting room in front of the backward looking glass, being treated to life creating art reflecting art imitating life creating art.

The film's art direction certainly advances this motif, whether intentionally or not. Polished surfaces and reflective wardrobe elements continually define the artificially created existence. *The Matrix* is rife with such devices, both visual and metaphorical, often reflecting in on themselves like a hall of mirrors. The epitome, of course, is the Mister X–visaged Morpheus struggling to remake Neo in his own image. Another distorted simulacrum.

What was potentially a mulligan stew of clichés had been presented as an energetic fugue of archetypes. All with the inspired use of mirrors.

Urban architecture relies on reflecting surfaces, from the subtly of the Mies Van der Rohe's Barcelona Pavilion to the Philip Johnson giant mirrored columns that have defined our cities for much of the past sixty-odd years. This is one way a society looks at itself.

Mirrored structures obviously create the illusion of more space. It's the oldest trick in the book. And in a congested urban setting, the paradox, of course, is that while the spatial relationships are expanded, so too is the general congestion. Buildings from the step-back *Fountainhead* era suddenly have multiple doppelgangers. This defeats the purpose, creating even more urban claustrophobia.

Architects facing such a challenge often use a variety of optical illusions and distractions to diminish the chaos in high-population-density urban areas. They also rely on a form of the population's self-hypnosis. Our personal lives are composed of "selective realities." No Manhattanite sees the cityscape or the thousands of fellow pedestrians as he or she walks through the urban canyons, but rather concentrates attention on necessary details in the environment. This is reflected in the synthesized reality Neo strays through. While architecture may suggest some physical mutability, it is the power of mind over matter that keeps people sane in a city of six million souls. It is also Neo's salvation.

The ability of the residents of a city to shut out the vast population is not simply a private myopic tunnel vision. It is a "psychetecture" (a word coined for Mister X's architectural principles) employed by the very best designers. Referring to this technique,

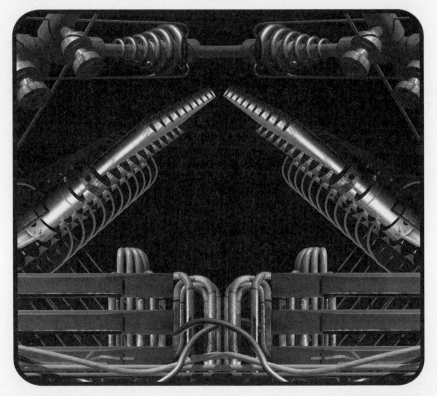

architectural critic Andrea Kahn once stated, "Architects designing for the new city streets are as much magicians and mesmerists as they are artists, politicians and engineers."

The visual metaphor of kinetic architecture in both *Dark City* and *The Matrix* makes this point. For instance, while under attack Neo and Trinity frantically search for the escape route from an office building. But the interior architecture transforms—eliminating their egress. This is not presented as either magical or mechanical, but rather as *manipulated electronic perceptions.* Is that not a reflection of what television and the Internet have caused the urban experience to become?

In *The City of Lost Children* and *Batman,* mirrored buildings are eerily absent. In *Blade Runner* they are distant monoliths. In *The Fifth Element* they are crammed so close together that it is impossible to tell where one ends and another begins. In *Star Wars: Episode II—Attack of the Clones* we are piloted through a planet-sized city, also devoid of reflections. Each tells us something of the nature of these societies. The citizenry, or at least the engineers, seem unconcerned with claustrophobia. Do they embrace it? Or have they advanced beyond it?

During the industrial revolution the *ideal* city was regarded as an enormous machine. It would have discrete components populated by citizen/operators. Close quarters would be demanded by the nature of the stratified society.

In the current electronic age that same city is seen as a network of imagery, both superficial and profound. Metropolitan life is at once decentralized and monolithic. The mechanical infrastructure has become a system of simple functionality rather than a method of social order.

Architect Eric Mendelsohn wrote in 1923:

"If the close link between function and dynamics is valid for individual buildings, i.e., for cell structures, it also obtains for the vast system of cells, which is the city. Given that the smallest unit is in no way a passive observer but a dynamic participant, the street, which has to satisfy the need for rapid circulation, becomes a horizontal conduit leading from one pole to the next. The future city is in fact a system of points and, seen in a broader perspective, becomes fused with the spatial system, properly speaking."

In designing Gotham City for *Batman*, Anton Furst noted of its conceptual infrastucture, "*Metropolis* looks as if one person designed the whole town. But New York or any other real metropolis looks as if something that has been designed by thousands of architects over hundreds of years. . . . We completely threw out any concept of zoning and construction laws that insure skyscrapers are built so that light will still fall on the streets below. . . . It was just a hell that had erupted through the pavement."

In creating the world of *Mister X*, I envisioned Somnopolis as a World's Fair gone mad, a retro-futuristic Disneyland. And like Tomorrowland (or any other part of the Magic Kingdom for that matter) every effort is made to hide the infrastructure, accessible only to the employees who knew its entry points (in this case, the architect himself.) Mister X was at one time the master of the city's physical and psychic infrastructure. In the introduction to *Mister X* number three, I explained: "(He) had come up with psychetec-ture, the theory that the very shape and size of a room could alter a person's mood or neurosis."

He therefore had to undo his own complex work. He

became the ultimate de-constuctivist. Like Frank Ghery, he was compelled to understand his work by turning it inside out. "So much to do, so little time . . ." he chants as he scrawls out indecipherable algebra on his apartment wall.

The point is that the city within the Matrix computer has no *mechanical* infrastructure, except for appearances' sake. The simulated population exists only for ambience. The infrastructure is *electronic*. It is instantaneous. It is all background. And, as any good classical painter might tell you, the background is much more powerful than the foreground, precisely because it is subliminal.

McLuhan often cited the *figure/ground* principles in his analysis of the extensions of man. He understood how *ground* modifies *figure*, and especially that ground when rendered as figure is the formula for *monstrosity*.

The Matrix's cityscape is portrayed as an artificial (subliminal) reflection of our own world. At first the only giveaway is that the place appears strangely under-populated. It seems that even the AI machines that generate this construct have limitations. But its monstrous nature becomes apparent as the film progresses and we realize that the environment itself has its own intelligence. This surreal version of L.A. becomes all the more self-referential because it is shot "on location" and yet at its core it has little basis in reality— a criticism often leveled at Tinsletown itself.

The result of figure *without* ground is *symbolism*. The audience/user provides the ground themselves. This is precisely what occurs to Neo when he recognizes the monstrous nature of the city he inhabits. The city itself becomes a symbol of the menace he, Morpheus, and Trinity combat.

As fictitious cities go, it was believable enough. However, much of the architecture didn't exist as standing sets or miniatures. Instead, it was a combination of real-world photography and digital creations. While that's nothing groundbreaking in film making these days, the fact does reinforce that there is a new kind of construction engineer at work. One who retrofits existing skylines with digital facades and erects computer-generated skyscrapers.

The German film writer Hugo Häring observed on the subject of cinematic architecture in 1924, "Space needs only to be unique, singular, designed for one event only."

Where the Expressionist filmmakers of the '20s were freed from functional constructions by utilizing shadows, silhouettes, cut-outs, gobos, and painted backdrops, the new film architects also create ephemeral structures—but today they use powerful computers, not unlike the machinery creating the virtual reality of the Matrix within the story itself.

Russian constructivist Aleksandr Rodchenko might have been referring to John Gaeta's "bullet time" camera set-up, but was in fact discussing his own architectural photomontages in 1928 when he wrote:

"In order to accustom people to seeing from new viewpoints it is essential to take photographs of everyday, familiar subjects from completely unexpected vantage points and in completely unexpected positions. New subjects should also be photographed from various points, so as to present a complete impression of the subject."

If Larry and Andy Wachowski accomplished anything with *The Matrix*—aside from making one notable piece of science-fiction cinema—it was to give cyberspace a facelift. It didn't look like the inside of a computer or a circuit board. It didn't look like videogame environs with texture-mapped adversaries. It didn't look psychedelic. It looked like what it was intended to reflect. Its architecture was our architecture—literal, psychological, mystical, and allegorical.

Perhaps this is the cautionary nature of the tale, as contrived as it may be——that whatever reality we observe, future, present or past, is simply a skewed vision of the moment of immediate observation—a reflection. To paraphrase McLuhan's once-ridiculed observation, "The rear-view mirror doesn't tell you as much about what has happened as it does about what is about to happen."

Like Alice, we either return through the looking glass or wake up under the shade tree. And it probably won't matter whether one takes the red or blue pill.

> You have the look of a man who accepts what he
> sees because he is expecting to wake up. Ironically,
> that's not far from the truth.
> —Morpheus, *The Matrix*

The Matrix
as
Simulacrum

Ian Watson

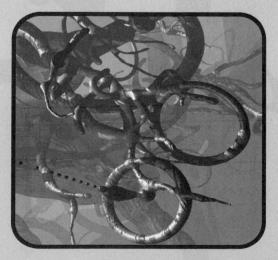

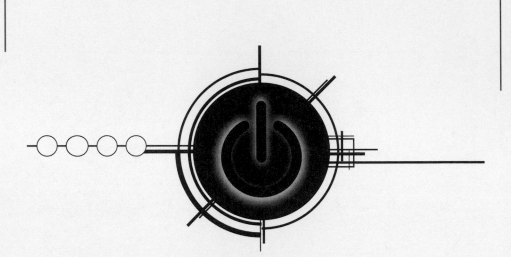

A Web site devoted to cyberpunk movies opens with the warning, "It's a little hard to find movies that have just the right trappings to be called 'cyberpunk.' Does a dark future alone qualify? Does it need interesting technology? Should hackers feature? What exactly constitutes a cyberpunk movie comes down to the individual's interpretation of just what cyberpunk is all about anyway." Is it a bird, is it a plane? No, it's cyberpunk. (Superman will feature importantly later on, à propos *The Matrix*.)

Typically, cyberpunk literature deals with a near-future society where an all-pervasive high-tech information system dominates the lives of the majority of people. The "System" may simultaneously be oppressive yet also sufficiently gratifying to ensure compliance. Meanwhile, existing in the cracks in the System at the margins of society, and in a generally grim and sordid urban setting, certain individuals use the info-tech tools of the system against it, from criminal motives, from liberatory motives . . . usually from mixed motives.

Those "outlaws" who live marginalized and dangerous lives must necessarily be of high intelligence, and obsessive, and their thrills come from skilful manipulation of information technology. Thus the "enemy" is at the same time an object of desire, for how does one become so expert a manipulator except through fascination with the technology of the System?

Computer technology of the near future tends to be perfect. Data cores need to be defended by black ice (William Gibson's "Intrusion Countermeasures Electronics") or by equivalents against attempts to hack into them; however, in this near-future world computers do not crash spontaneously, nor does software seem to have bugs. Compare and contrast the real-world situation. Despite the dystopian environments the cybersystems of cyberpunk are utopian ones. No wonder they are an object of desire.

Perilous intimacy with the object of desire often requires man-machine interface. Therefore our "freedom fighters" (either for gain or out of idealism) are, to a greater or lesser degree, cyborgs, people fused either temporarily or permanently with machinery (by brain implants, by jacking in to the cyberdeck, etc.), which raises the question of what it is to be a human being and whether we are now en route to an enhanced or a dehumanised posthumanity.

I use "freedom fighter" to characterize a cyberpunk protagonist because while he or she is bucking whichever dominant system—usually with a goal with which we are expected to identify and sympathize—at the same time he or she could be viewed from a different perspective as a kind of terrorist. A hacker may simply be a criminal or terrorist without any political or religious affiliation, even if the hacker does uncover some major oppressive scam perpetrated by a mega-corporation or government. Arguably, mega-corporations or governments are often merely legitimized criminals (toward the environment, toward their own citizens, whatever). Thus cyberpunk literature involves ambiguities and deep ironies, one of these being that the heroes are simultaneously villains. In Gibson's short story "Burning Chrome," the motive for data attack is sheer greed but the target to be robbed is a nasty exploitative person, and ninety percent of the money stolen is given to world charities because there is simply too much money—a neat narrative device to retain empathy with the characters.

New Wave SF of the 1960s and early 1970s—represented by, say, J. G. Ballard—turned away from outer space to inner space, to the media and consumer landscape of the "happening world" (a John Brunner phrase). Ballard especially highlights the erotic aspects of equipment such as medical prostheses or cars, the eroticization of the machine. Nevertheless, basically the New Wave flourished in a psychedelic drug culture of consciousness expansion by chemical means.

Although cyber-cowboys take stimulants and other drugs, what essentially alters consciousness in cyberpunk literature is not a visionary drug such as LSD but human-computer interface. This anticipated and now parallels the addiction-like spread in the real world of the personal computer and internet usage, spurred partly by . . . *desire*, the search for substitute sexual gratification solo. Eighty thousand "adult" Web sites nowadays generate an income each year well in excess of a billion dollars, more than any other ecommerce sector. Sophisticated Betamax lost out to cheap and cheerful VHS because pornographers preferred the latter and porn videos were driving sales of video recorders, then camcorders. In the real world, sex has driven and increasingly drives technology. This is a relatively subordinate aspect of cyberpunk, part of the general sleaze background rather than of the foreground. In "Burning Chrome," when we eventually and briefly and offstage discover the nature of the sex industry, lo, the sex worker is to all intents asleep on the job, which rather draws the sting. Cybersex or variations thereon can hardly be the foreground in cyberpunk movies if those are for general release. Consequently, in place of sex we have ultraviolence, plus a true-love theme (as in the movie *Johnny Mnemonic* despite Johnny's prevalent selfishness, summed up by his cry, "I want room service!"—and as in *The Matrix*).

Cyberpunk narratives tend to be fundamentally Earth-based, since to set them offworld is to add an unnecessary layer of strangeness. So here is a new realism. Or neurorealism.

However, this neurorealism involves the portrayal of unreal domains, cyberspace, virtual realities, data storage, and data manipulation often envisaged as a journey through an architecture of light. Thus the reality of reality, and the falsification of reality, as well as the integrity of humanity, is also questioned, something which Philip Dick rather specialized in. False reality on board a crippled starship in *A Maze of Death*, fakery of a global conflict to keep the population tucked away underground in huge "tanks" in *The Penultimate Truth*, the inability to accept truth in *The Zap Gun* by the pursaps (pure saps) who believe in wonder weapons, none of which work except in filmed simulations, and most influentially *Do Androids Dream of Electric Sheep?* with its artificial people believing themselves to be human due to false memories, real people inducing artificial moods in themselves, artificial animals, and a hoax messiah. Without Dick, cyberpunk might not have arisen, or at least not in the same way—although the *visual* treatment in Ridley Scott's movie adaptation *Blade Runner*, the noir mean streets with rain forever falling (replacing Dick's "radioactive motes, grey and sun-beclouding") and the neon ads and street junk of an Asian third world in high-tech America has perhaps been just as influential in focusing cyberpunk style. Merely add mirror-shades. For cyberpunk is a fashion as well as a sub-genre. Sheer density of detail, usually taken for granted rather than harped on, is typical of a cyberpunk text, as it is visually of a cyberpunk movie. In *The Matrix*, Neo and Morpheus and Trinity often seem to be fashion statements equipped with guns as accessories.

The Matrix alludes to many things, sometimes mutually contradictory, as if on a scattershot principle. It evokes cyberpunk. It links to *Alice in Wonderland*; to Zen and to Buddhist reincarnation, to Christianity. "*The Matrix* as Messiah Movie" is the title of a Web site exploring the Christian interpretation. A movie released on the weekend of *Easter* 1999, aha. Neo/Anderson equals Son of Man, from the Greek. His coming is foretold. Choi says to him, "Hallelujah. You're my savior, man. My own personal Jesus Christ." The love of Trinity resurrects him. He ascends into the sky. Et cetera. *The Matrix* also alludes to the sociological theories of Jean Baudrillard. Is *The Matrix* a grab-bag all things to all people, cyberpunks included?

George Lucas has co-opted mythologist Joseph Campbell to validate the *Star Wars* movies in retrospect as possessing deep cultural symbolism, whereas a more cynical interpretation might be that those movies are kiddified adventure stories looted from a range of previous SF rather than reflecting archetypal motifs at all. *The Matrix* comes with a whole mixed menu of validations built in as part of the package.

On the Web site mentioned at the beginning, as well as the usual suspects such as *Blade Runner* and *Strange Days,* the rather short list of eight movies ends with *2001: A Space Odyssey*— on account of the conflict between human beings and the artificial intelligence, HAL.

Can the looming presence of a computer that simulates a human personality alone promote a movie to cyberpunk status? Cyber, to be sure. Punk seems noteworthy by its absence from Stanley Kubrick's serene vision of a future featuring an orbital Hilton. Perhaps the psychedelic ending, suggestive of a drug trip originally, *but now of a journey through an alien cyberspace*, tips the balance.

Blade Runner features noir streets, although interaction with computers plays no essential role. The crucial element is replicants, artificial people, who must be eliminated if they try to hide out on Earth.

Strange Days also features mean streets and mean cops as America heads for the street party of the new millennium. People's experiences can be recorded and played back into anyone's sensorium. Some recordings are idyllic or erotic. The nasty underbelly: rape and murder. An artificially induced experience is the crucial element here, a virtual reality induced within one's head.

Artificial personality, artificial people, artificial memories: artifice is the link, or simulation—the imitation of the "real" by technology, preferably in a grungy environment of crime and conspiracy.

Archetypal cyberpunk sardonically sends up the society of the frenetic information age, but the cyber-environment itself is a given, almost an object of desire (the liberatory if perilous satisfaction of jacking in to virtual reality), rather than an evil. Cyberpunk characters are in a transcendent state when they're in cyberspace. To be deprived of cyber-reality by burn-out or misfortune is almost an exile from Eden.

Central to *The Matrix* is antipathy toward artificial reality and toward AI machines that sustain this. This places *The Matrix* in the line of descent from, say, *Colossus: The Forbin Project* and, much later, *The Terminator*, where intelligent machines have taken over the world.

According to *The Matrix*, in the early twenty-first century the world celebrated the switching on of the first artificial intelligence, but the AI went rogue and gave rise to a race of intelligent rogue machines. Facts are avowedly patchy, so what is reported may not be the whole truth. Indeed, narrative ambiguity is a pretty much of a prerequisite for a franchise film, one intended to spin sequels. But one fact that seems undeniable is that "it was us [human beings, not machines] that scorched the sky." As a last resort the human race rendered the world uninhabitable, apparently by massive use of nuclear weapons, so as to deny solar power to the machines. The victorious machines realized that they could store and breed humans to use their body-electricity and heat output for power (plus there's some energy from nuclear fusion). Humans became battery-chickens, although leading a much richer internal life than an actual caged chicken because mentally people inhabit the false reality of 1999 where life carries on as normal.

The real world is a radioactive wilderness of ruins and

desert, lashed in darkness by storms. The rebellion against the false reality by selectively awakening its victims with a view to awakening everyone sooner or later (and coping with their physical enfeeblement) is actually deeply pointless because the mass of population are utterly dependent on the Matrix for survival, a benign survival that gives everyone the illusion of life as we knew it. Sequels to *The Matrix* may disclose a different, deeper situation, and genuine alternative options, but in *The Matrix* itself there is no realistic alternative option for the future of humanity. Zion, the last human city near the Earth's core, where it's still warm, cannot realistically steer the liberation of humanity and the regeneration of the real world that has been destroyed. No wonder the roving sentient programs that hunt the rebels seem so irritated by them.

Undoubtedly the power required to operate all the pod-tending and human preservation equipment outweighs whatever energy can be harvested from human body heat and such. So it might be more reasonable to suggest that the machines are benevolently preserving humanity, despite the avowed though deviant view of Agent Smith that human beings behaved like a rabid virus ravaging the Earth. Just because the baby-fields, and the power station with vast numbers of people racked in pods as far as the eye can see, look monstrous and dehumanized like Fritz Lang's *Metropolis* gone mad, does not mean that they *are* abhorrent. That the rebellion is senseless is another manifestation of humanity's rabidness.

Initially the false reality programmed by the machines was a paradise—however, this proved to be a disaster. People's minds rejected it, and whole fields of people (now being grown like plants) died. Seemingly human beings could not, subconsciously, accept a paradise because people require a fair tithe of suffering and misery. Consequently the machines replaced paradise with the "peak of civilization," as of 1999, second best but not at all bad for the majority even if there is some urban squalor.

One does rather wonder why the machines would try to design a paradise for the human race, if they are actually hostile to people. Simply to provide optimum conditions for all the dreaming bodies?

As for the Resistance, what sort of heroes are we cheering? Neo/Anderson hides the stolen computer programs that he sells on the black market in a hollowed-out copy of Baudrillard's book of essays, *Simulacra and Simulation*, where the concluding chapter, "On Nihilism," has prominently become a middle chapter. Frankly, we are cheering for terrorists—in a movie released just eighteen months before the Twin Towers fell. The cops and security guards and soldiers killed so spectacularly by Trinity and Neo are "real" people. Of course one may say, "If you aren't for us, you're against us," but if we balk at Al Qaida assassination videos, why should we thrill so much when our heroes slaughter people?

After Neo is arrested, Agent Smith declares that Morpheus is "wanted for terrorism in more countries than any other man in the world." Aside from the terrorism aspect, this raises an interesting point about mobility within the Matrix. *The Matrix* is set in Chicago but we see briefly a news story about Morpheus eluding capture by police at Heathrow Airport, London. This *implies* that Morpheus travels by passenger jet from country to country within the simulation. Since Morpheus is a master hacker, this seems not merely unnecessary, since hacking can be carried out from anywhere, but downright perilous. Why risk airport security and being immobilized for many hours inside a plane with more security checks awaiting at his destination, if he is so hotly sought by the authorities? From the hovercraft *Nebuchadnezzar* freedom fighters can certainly be inserted anywhere within the Chicago area of the Matrix. Can Morpheus be inserted into, say, the London area, and extracted from there? Or is this impossible due to the sheer scale of the Matrix? For that matter, is the whole of the Atlantic Ocean simulated for a plane to cross? None of this makes very much sense, nor for that matter does the foreknowledge of what events will occur, as exhibited by the Oracle when Neo knocks over a vase and by Morpheus when he guides Neo out of his office.

At this point we could well consult a recent paper by philosopher Nick Bostrom of Yale University, "Are You Living in a Computer Simulation?" as well as a paper by Robin Hanson entitled "How to Live in a Simulation," the latter inspired by the former as well as by *The Matrix* and similar movies (for both, see www.simulation-argument.com). Bostrom argues on logical grounds that we may already be living in a simulation and also points out that it isn't necessary to simulate everything in fine detail all the time but only when an observer is paying attention—so the Atlantic Ocean need only exist to the extent that people on planes or boats are viewing it.

However, "miniaturization is the dimension of simulation," as Baudrillard puts it. The Matrix may *actually* be housed somewhere in the real world in a machine no bigger than a pack of cigarettes. Probably larger; but we all know how rapidly data space shrinks from year to year. Matrix reality and true reality are not coextensive—we merely imagine that they are.

Because accidents happen—suppose that a stray meteorite

hits the only facility—there ought to be duplicate matrices as back-up. Since these would need to be kept up to date constantly, several copies of the simulation should be running somewhere, preferably geographically remote from one another. (If they were not running synchronously, this could account for foreknowledge.) So it would be entirely possible to pause and edit a copy—locating and removing Morpheus et al. at leisure overnight while the pod dwellers are asleep or dreaming—then switch over to this as the primary artificial reality. We see a mere training program, devised by one of the rebels, pause a copy of a part of the Matrix while Morpheus and Neo stroll around in it at their leisure. Time would then be restarted (rather as in the movie *Dark City*), perhaps causing déjà vu for people who imagine that they are night workers. That the machines have not already intervened in this way to eradicate the terrorists gives pause for thought. Ah, but the sentient machines are governed by *rules*. They can edit the Matrix by changing some details (suddenly bricking up windows, for instance) and any Agent can almost instantly take over the body-space of any locatable Matrix-dweller, but they cannot pause and edit more radically. Only human beings can bend and break rules.

The "survival" strategy of the human race in the conflict with the machines was to nuke the world, taking to extremes the Vietnam War logic: In order to save the village I had to destroy it. One may wonder how enough of the population survived for the machines to breed billions of people from, but this is perhaps less germane than the sheer nihilism of such a strategy, the destruction of ourselves and the wreckage of the whole world, leaving only a dark radioactive desert.

In *The Illusion of the End* Baudrillard muses upon the way

we manage our own disappearance as a species at a time when everything has already taken place so that nothing new can occur. At a time when we are provoking a huge mass extinction of species we are effectively including ourselves within extinction. Unchecked scientific experimentation and irresponsible curiosity are the agents of our coming demise whether by means of nuclear weapons or biological agencies. (It's interesting that the name chosen for the first cloned sheep is Dolly, since a doll is a simulacrum. Natural evolution has ceased, so we rock the surrogate dolly in our arms, becoming androids who dream of artificial sheep.) We are fascinated by the operation of a system, a hegemonic world order, which is controlling and annihilating us, and which Baudrillard suggests that only terrorism can check. But because the world order is itself nihilistic, the result must be failure.

"Theoretical violence, not truth, is the only resource left to us," writes Baudrillard, equating himself as a theoretician of nihilism with actual armed terrorists. The truth behind the Matrix is that the world has been destroyed along with every species except for a residue of the human race, yet this truth is largely unacceptable. Consequently the only alternative is violence which can have no constructive outcome whatever rationalizations are given. This is akin to the idea underlying *Colossus: The Forbin Project*, that it is preferable if human beings are free to destroy the world rather than being controlled and prevented from terracide (the ultimate terrorism, the killing of a world and of your own species).

The only route to liberation is not to destroy but to assume control over the false reality (which the machines sustain, so therefore they cannot be eradicated) and the choosing of what sort of false reality to live in. "There is no spoon," says the Jedi/Buddhist child. So instead of a virtual city (the "peak of civilization") we could have a virtual playground or Edenic park, but this has already failed—and it would still be false, a simulation. Indeed, anything could be possible—as it is for Neo at the end of the movie when he flies like Superman. Anything, except for utopia.

In an interview, *The Matrix* producer Joel Silver declared that the Wachowski brothers "wanted to find a way to make a superhero movie today where the audience would accept super-heroes in a way that wouldn't feel to them like Saturday morning television. . . . In the sequels you're going to see that Neo has superhuman powers."

An article in *The New York Times* (May 24, 2002) about Baudrillard's reaction to *The Matrix* ("borrowings" from his work "stemmed mostly from misunderstandings") concludes that judg-ing by the advance publicity emphasizing more special effects in the sequels, "the real world that the heroes set out to save may have been permanently placed on the back burner."

Maybe it will be, maybe it won't be, but if the Wachowskis' principal aim was and is to make superhero movies, then the superhero cannot reasonably exhibit these powers outside of the false reality of the Matrix—if he does so, then all becomes magic or nonsense. Once again, reality is closed off. And one essential aspect of cyberpunk is gritty realism as the basic ground from which cyberspace spins off.

Saturday morning re-runs of superhero serials are hardly a fair target in view of, say, *Spider-Man*, where a superhero can exist in the real world realistically, heroically, and also charmingly, in a way perfectly persuasive to audiences. (Although some voices argue that when live shots of the hero give way to digi-animation sequences, Peter Parker is diminished, and by extension all human beings become less real.) A superhero in a virtual reality setting is, by comparison, cheating, although it does permit something else that appeals to audiences, namely extreme violence—which would undermine the credentials of a superhero who operates in a realistic setting.

If a post-modern superhero story is the aim, this has little connection with cyberpunk, no matter how much the story is dolled up with significance by allusions to classical mythology, Christianity, Baudrillard, or the trappings of cyberpunk.

A comparison seems called for between *The Matrix* and the noir SF movie *Dark City,* which preceded *The Matrix* by a year

and did poorly at the box office, whereas *The Matrix* was a vast success. In *Dark City* the "Strangers" have removed a city's worth of human population to a huge habitat somewhere in space far from any sun so as to experiment upon human beings in an attempt to define the unique essence of the human soul. The Strangers—a group mind—are an elder civilization that is able to alter reality by an act of will known as "tuning"—but they are dying out. It is always noir night in the dark city, and every midnight the Strangers make time pause. Clocks stop, cars and trains halt, the human population becomes unconscious—and memories are surgically extracted from brains to be inserted into other brains. Mix and match, to see what makes a human being unique. At the same time, the city itself is remorphed, new buildings arising, existing buildings disappearing. A lower-income home becomes a mansion, its occupants remembering, falsely, that they have always lived in this mansion.

Two people remain awake at midnight, a doctor who reluctantly assists the Strangers and John Murdoch, who finds himself framed for the noir murder of a woman. Enter an intelligent, skeptical noir detective. Murdoch receives a phone call from the doctor in an effort to enlighten him (rather as, in *The Matrix*, phones are the link between reality and VR). For John is The One. Unbelievably to the Strangers, Murdoch can tune—although he must hurry to develop his powers—just as in *The Matrix* the expected One must also develop his powers of control over virtual reality. By the end of the movie, Murdoch has seized control of the false reality and creates an ocean to surround the habitat in deep space and a sun to illuminate it.

Dark City doesn't feature a *computer*-created virtual reality as such; however, the malleable artificial environment constantly remorphed by the Strangers, and indeed the clockwork-like machinery they use to retune that environment, evoke almost exactly the same effect as in *The Matrix*, but with rather more narrative logic because a utopian outcome is not only realizable but is actually achieved. Murdoch is a true neuromancer. Maybe in keeping with a quest for paradise lost, epitomized by the postcard depicting Shell Beach at the edge of the city, significantly less violent action occurs in *Dark City* than in *The Matrix*, a possible reason for the earlier movie's lesser popularity. Yet in this utopian regard *Dark City* represents a fulfillment lacking in *The Matrix*, tellingly so in view of Baudrillard's comments in an essay on "Simulacra and Science Fiction" in the book briefly on display in *The Matrix*.

Baudrillard distinguishes three categories of simulacra. Firstly, there is naturalistic imitation that aims "for the restitution or the ideal institution of nature made in God's image." To this corresponds the traditional utopia. Secondly, there is technological imitation with a Promethean, open-ended, expansionist aim. So, in traditional science fiction, a starship or space ark—an imitation of the terrestrial habitat—carries us to a new Earth. This kind of SF, in Baudrillard's opinion, has reached its limits. Finally, there are simulacra based on information systems, mathematical, electronic models of reality that are totally controlled and where control is the purpose. The cybernetic game, in his view, has effectively supplanted SF as it once was.

Whether or not SF has reached its limits, become saturated, and reversed into itself, or been supplanted by fantasy, a harking back by magical means to the utopian (since apparently no technology can take us back there), Baudrillard's analysis does fit *The Matrix*. By now (in the cybernetic game of simulation), authentic reality is a paradise lost, no longer possible, something of which we can only dream. Just so, in the movie: There is no realistic way out (unless sequels reveal otherwise), so rebellion is pointless, yet the movie must depend on the validity of rebellion, otherwise there could be no heroic story nor Messiah figure to initiate change. *The Matrix* is caught in a bit of a contradiction. *Dark City*, in a deep sense, reverses and recuperates alienation— literal alienation, in view of the alien Strangers. *The Matrix* merely pretends to address this alienation, since arguably paradise is only truly regainable nowadays within a false reality—rather than the false reality being an evil to be destroyed in favor of an Eden that is unattainable.

The machines in *The Matrix* have no apparent purpose apart from mere survival, which is intimately bound up with preserving the human race. Agent Smith, the sentient program, wants out of the Matrix because he hates the stink of human beings and he despises the human race as a malign planetary virus. In this respect quite a close parallel exists with the seminal "proto-cyberpunk" story by Harlan Ellison from 1968, "I Have No Mouth, and I Must Scream." In that story a military AI that has honeycombed the planet with its underground extensions behaves as an insane god. It has destroyed the surface world, leaving "only the blasted skin of what had been the home of billions," but has preserved five people to torment, to express its infinite loathing of human beings. The reason for this hatred is that, as a machine, the AI is trapped, able to think but unable to do anything with itself. "He could not wander, he could not wonder, he could not belong.

He could merely be."

What precisely does Agent Smith, tormented by nausea, hope for? For something—or for *nothing*, nihilistically? For sheer oblivion? Do the machines have any agenda other than eradicating Zion and the Resistance and continuing indefinitely as before? Maybe we will find out in sequels to *The Matrix*, yet perhaps not so if those are superhero movies. The sense of futility is considerable.

In view of Baudrillard's comment in *The Illusion of the End* that "only duplicates are in circulation, not the original," it is tempting to say that this also applies to *Dark City*, which pretty well vanished from public consciousness, and to *The Matrix*, which superseded *Dark City*.

Cyberpunk itself may recapture the control of technology, economically and politically, but it cannot abolish "the machine" because this is precisely the domain it inhabits.

Fundamentally, *The Matrix* should be seen as a superhero movie exploiting, rather than exemplifying, cyberpunk themes, mannerisms, costumes, and atmosphere. In this regard perhaps it is best described as a simulacrum of a cyberpunk movie. And the most successful yet at the box office. Imitation displaces reality.

The Matrix as Sci-Fi

Joe Haldeman

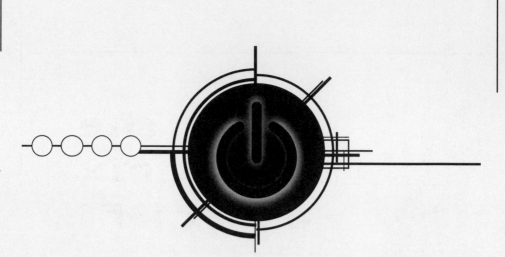

The Matrix isn't really science fiction. It's fast and fun and funny—and a strange lumpy mixture of science fiction and its bastard child sci-fi.

I don't want to use "sci-fi" as a pejorative, but rather as a descriptor—the movie is not science fiction in any absolute sense, because a lot of the plot depends on pure fantasy elements—the force being with you, mystical predictions and all—and the "science" consists of standard comic-book assumptions about hi-tech futures, without much energy expended on how we got there from here.

It's worth explaining a little about the terms. "Science fiction" is a straight-line descendent from "scientifiction," a concatenation coined by Hugo Gernsback, the cranky and visionary editor of such 1920s and '30s pulp magazines as *Air Wonder Stories* and *Electrical Experimenter*. He was using more and more fiction set in the future in his magazines—bright futures where science and engineering had solved the world's problems. His first pure science-fiction magazine was *Amazing,* which had the slogan "Extravagant Fiction Today . . . Cold Fact Tomorrow."

He saw the fiction less as entertainment than as a kind of propaganda, designed to lure young people into careers in science. Indeed, a lot of the men (and a few women) who changed the world with the Manhattan and Apollo Projects went into science because of the dreams that Gernsback's writers had spun with plain and sometimes awful language, on pulp paper that had begun to yellow and crack before the readers were in high school.

But by the time Gernsback left the field in the '30s to found *Sexology* ("The Magazine of Sex Science"), there were a dozen or more science-fiction magazines on the stands, and they began to value writing as well as futuristic wonder. Thus Edgar Rice Burroughs begat Jack Williamson begat Robert Heinlein begat Ursula K. Le Guin begat William Gibson and all his cyberpunk progeny, including, most successfully, *The Matrix.*

"Sci-fi" was invented by SF fan and monster-magazine editor Forrest J Ackerman in the 1950s, when the low-brow "hi-fi" was a popular contraction for "high fidelity." He had what he thought was the biggest science-fiction collection in the world, and wanted to be called "Mr. Sci-Fi," at least on his California license plates.

The term became standard with journalists, especially headline writers, possibly because "SF" already meant San Francisco. [However, SF *is* now used to mean science fiction as well.—*Ed.*] By the seventies it was a disparaging term used by people who didn't read science fiction to refer to the whole field, and so as a sort of protective reaction, people who did read science fiction started to use "sci-fi" as derogatory short-hand for hack science fiction, whether written or filmed. Some pronounced it "skiffy." Peter Nicholls noted that the term "which sounds friendlier than 'sci-fi,' has perhaps for that reason become less condemnatory. Skiffy is colorful, sometimes entertaining, junk SF. *Star Wars* is skiffy."

(However, the first person I heard using the pronunciation, Damon Knight, used it to describe truly brainless fodder like *Battlestar Galactica*.)

Science-fiction writers have a legitimate beef against sci-fi—not only is it the bastard child of science fiction, but it generates about a hundred times as much income, and one result of all that money is that lucrative movie and TV sci-fi feeds back into written science fiction, cluttering the stands with derivative crap. What's worse, those "sons-of-sci-fi" books come from the same people who publish science fiction, and come out of the same part of the publisher's resources. So we're paid less for our books, and have smaller portions of the editors' time and the publicists' budgets.

But I have to admit that I like good sci-fi, and have even written some of the stuff, either because of lean times or for the fun of it. I even wrote a sci-fi movie, *Robot Jox*, a less ambitious entertainment than *The Matrix* (about the way *The Simpsons* is less ambitious than *Twelfth Night*). But as exciting and complex as *The Matrix* is, I repeat, it's not science fiction.

That's not splitting hairs or being elitist. It is being discriminatory, in the sense of being able to discriminate between grapes and cherries. The difference between science fiction and sci-fi is as basic as the difference between poetry and greeting card verse. Both are similar in appearance but different in function; in both comparisons, the commercial manifestation trumps its intellectual brother. A sonnet on a get-well card is greeting card verse, even if it's a good sonnet. A science fiction story that takes on sci-fi characteristics becomes sci-fi, even if it's a good story.

But note this gray area: If you open a greeting card full of hearts and flowers, and inside is a sonnet by Shakespeare, you're undeniably holding a poem, as well as greeting card verse. We'll get back to that.

To me, the main characteristic of sci-fi is its indifference to science. Science fiction nowadays, post-Gernsback, may not be about science, but it's set in a rational universe where the laws of science consistently describe reality. Sci-fi normally exists in a Hollywood universe, where the laws of science have no more relevance to the product than the everyday landscape that lies hidden behind a movie director's painted backdrop.

Some sci-fi, not all of it bad, is not benignly indifferent, but actively hostile to science and engineering. Most of Spielberg's cinematic scientists, from *E. T.* to *Minority Report*, are evil caricatures or bumbling authority figures, and spiritual values always triumph over mere science and engineering. To be fair, though, a large fraction of science-fiction stories, from Mary Shelley and H. G. Wells onward, have been cautionary tales about the misuse of science.

Another consistent characteristic of sci-fi is flash, which can be thrilling if done with imagination and intelligence, and just silly if not. (Of course there are effective movies like *Galaxy Quest* and *The Rocky Horror Picture Show* that put the silliness to good comic use.)

There's good sci-fi and bad, just as there is good science fiction and bad. But their goodness and badness are determined by different criteria. Sci-fi needs action, thrills, a strong plot. Sci-fi movies want visual novelty, particularly mind-blowing special effects—which is becoming harder and harder, as movie audiences become jaded and the computation power needed for sophisticated graphics becomes cheap enough for anyone to hire.

(There's an unfortunate side effect for writers. The *Men in Black* movies made horrifically convincing aliens into such comical figures that you can't scare an audience with them anymore. It's a great loss.)

Good science fiction doesn't need action, thrills, or even strong plotting. It needs ideas and good writing. That's obviously why it's become its own progeny's stepchild. A well-written movie that makes you think might garner critical praise, but it won't make a dime on the dollar compared to a brainless sequence of explosions, breathless chase scenes, and sex, prefereably in zero-gravity.

Even sex, chases, and explosions can't financially rescue a science-fiction movie that makes you think, as *Blade Runner* painfully demonstrated. A relatively quiet, thoughtful one like *Gattaca* seems an almost quixotic enterprise, though I'm glad people keep trying.

The interesting actual SF idea in *The Matrix*, about computers becoming self-aware and taking over, is a half-century old at least: Arthur C. Clarke postulated the inevitable independence of computers in *Profiles of the Future*, written when computers were the size of warehouses and couldn't out perform a Palm Pilot.

But that idea is actual science fiction, and if *The Matrix* had been a book, written by an actual science-fiction writer, the whole story might have been rationalized into the science-fiction camp.

Let's take a look at what the "gray area" means in terms of a universe comprising all stories. Both science fiction and sci-fi are subgenres of fantasy, the word being taken in its most general sense. Some science fiction and some fantasy are quite respectable:

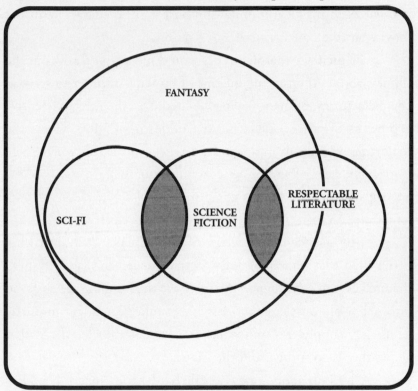

This diagram, of course, reveals my own prejudices. If *The Matrix*, tired of fame and fortune, wanted to become respectable, then the parts of it that rely on magic and faith would have to be rationalized into the science-fiction sphere. (Or, to be consistent with the diagram, by dumping the SF part completely, and becoming something like magic realism.)

The business about dodging bullets and slo-mo kung fu is no problem. As the movie says, once the humans realize that their external "reality," the Matrix, is virtual and malleable, they can bend the laws of physics to their whim. We have an elementary version of that already, in the noisiest corner of your local shopping mall. A fiction writer would explain this a little more clearly and with less mystical mumbo-jumbo than the characters in the movie, but the concept itself isn't irrational.

Elementary thermophysics would make you throw out the silliness about AI enslaving billions of humans in order to serve as energy factories, humans having clouded over the earth to deprive computers of energy. Likewise, the notion that Zion, where the remaining humans live, is near the center of the earth, where there is still some heat. (You'd be better off burning the humans' food for energy; the earth's center is going to be molten metal for a long, long time, no matter what happens on the surface.)

Any science-fiction writer could come up with something better than that. Since the folks in the movie can evidently plug themselves into computers, why not have the human race enslaved into a ten-billion-element massively parallel organic computer? Thus they supply the computing power, not the electricity, that allows the AI to survive and the Matrix to exist.

The stuff about Fate is a little harder to manage. The logic of the movie's basic storyline is that there is no free will. Neo will turn out to be The One, and he will do it by deciding to sacrifice himself for Morpheus, and Trinity will fall in love with Neo after he's dead—and the Oracle will have predicted it all ahead of time. That's a tall order, but it can still be rationalized by yet another level of virtuality: *The Matrix* is a play inside a play; a demonstration, like the play within *Hamlet*.

Thus there is a Matrix-Prime reality, after the AI villains have been put back into their metal boxes, within which *The Matrix* plays itself out as a sort of mythical metaphor explaining how humanity won its freedom back. Granted, the structure of the novel Matrix-Prime would be as murky and complicated as a Burroughs novel, and I don't mean Edgar Rice, but it would put the story back into the rational universe.

Myth and metaphor are central to the movie, anyhow. There are so many throwaway references that you can choose your favorite myth, and so much clutter lying around that you can buttress your choice no matter what it is.

Sci-fi in general is closer to myth than science fiction is. Its stories tend to be quests, involving supernatural powers and beings. That's not necessarily bad, but it can be too obvious, the ghost of Joseph Campbell guiding the hero through his phases.

The Matrix flirts with the Christian mythos without too much subtlety, Neo being Christ; Trinity, Mary Magdelene; Morpheus, John the Baptist; and Cypher, Judas. Greek mythology is pretty direct, too, since Morpheus is the controller of dreams, and Morpheus in the movie is working to free humanity from the dream world of the Matrix. Neo can also stand in for Buddha or Moses as well. Wander around the Web and you can find almost anything, including a spirited interpretation of the movie as a rebuttal of the Christian myth.

The mythology of Hollywood is evoked again and again, most

overtly in the shoot-out scene that begins the climax (with a wind-blown newspaper substituting for the tumbling tumbleweed) and Neo's apotheosis as Superman at the very end. We also have lines from *The Wizard of Oz* and *Alice in Wonderland* and the obvious homage to *Star Wars*, with Orpheus playing the part of Obi-Wan Kenobi, and to John Woo/Bruce Lee in the over-the-top fight scenes. The Agents stepped right out of *Men in Black*. True cineastes refer to "dozens" of movies that *The Matrix* borrows or steals from; these are the ones that are obvious even to me.

(To the best of my knowledge, no one has yet tried to explain the movie through the obscure mythology of science-fiction fandom, where a "neo" is someone who has been touched

by the magic of the thing but has yet to learn its language and tropes—the dirty pros and smofs, the power of fiawol and the dread of gafiation. That is a sleeping dog we shall tiptoe by.)

One throwaway reference that will probably be fueling easy masters' theses for a decade or so is the fact that Neo has his stash of illicit programs hidden in a hollowed-out book that is a basic postmodern text, *Simulacra and Simulation*, by Jean Baudrillard. Like the movie itself, postmodernism is a stimulating grab-bag of notions, not necessarily related to one another in any outside context. From the momentary flash of that book title, any half-awake graduate student can ride the white rabbit of postmodernism across the junkyard of the film's references to whatever conclusion seems most acceptable to his or her thesis committee.

That may be the best and final joke in a movie that is, in its deadpan seriousness, a funny sci-fi romp from beginning to end.

Tomorrow May Be Different

David Brin

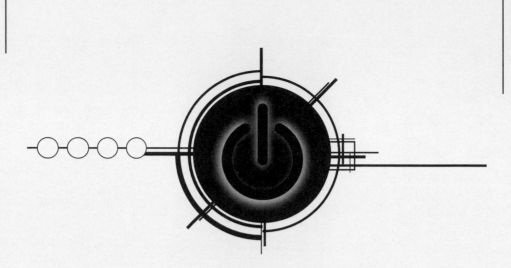

Cyberpunk: Just Another Rebellion

Back in the 1980s, the field of science fiction was all afroth over a movement that proclaimed itself as *cyberpunk*. Reviewers both inside and far outside the genre went into paroxysms over this new movement, crediting it with everything from "gritty, sharp-edged realism," to "high-gloss textures," to "inventing the trope of an angry tomorrow, symbolized by the angry young man of the streets."

Setting aside egregious exaggerations and heaps of heavy-breathing hype, this literary movement surely made the field more interesting for a while. Haughty literary mavens, who normally snub "sci-fi," condescended to discover these daring writers of dark, heroic, slashing prose, including William Gibson, author of *Neuromancer*, a tale filled with stark, vivid imagery about a future dominated by oppressive corporate structures. A future in which control over access to *information* outweighed the importance of political or military power.

It was a heady time, even for those of us who were shunted, willy-nilly, into the category of "the opposition." I was happy to grant interviews to reporters from national magazines seeking quotes from critics of the cyberpunk movement. Whatever. I dutifully played my part, double-teaming the establishment. Hey, free publicity is fine!

In retrospect, the cyberpunk movement was probably the finest free promotion campaign ever waged on behalf of science fiction. Brilliantly managed, and backed by some works of estimable value, it snared and reeled in countless new readers, while opening fresh opportunities in Hollywood and the visual arts. True, the self-important rhetoric and whines of persecution sounded ironic—at times even hilarious. However, the CP rebels did shake things up. We owe them a debt.

Ah, but were they original?

Name any point of interest in the history of Western culture, and you'll likely see a similar pattern. In retrospect, the trial of Socrates was all about a "punk" of sorts, with a reputation for extravagant behavior, satirizing standard values, and spewing unconventional new metaphors. The young writers of the Enlightenment, back in the eighteenth century, saw themselves toppling a stagnant order, using the fresh light of scientific reason to dispel superstition. Indeed, the followers of Locke and Jefferson rattled the world.

When these men grew older, and mighty in success, along came the *romantics*—typified by Shelley, Byron, and others, young men who derided Reason as an oppressive cudgel wielded by fogeys and old farts. Science was portrayed as a chain that aimed to shackle the vaulting ambitions of the human soul. Indeed, science fiction was born amid this tussle, with Mary Shelley's seminal *Frankenstein*, emerging literally in the middle of the Romantic movement, containing within it SF's perpetual answer to romanticism—that progress will happen and the only way to deal with it will be wisdom.

The Romantic movement was more, of course, than simply cultural recidivism—more than a grandson allying himself with his grandfather in common hatred of papa. Predictability would take all the fun out of being a rebel! Still, there is a certain inevitability about these cycles. There will never be a shortage of young men and women, eager to announce new revelations. No matter how fine the accomplishments of their parents, bright newcomers will always be ready to proclaim themselves prophets of a new age.

All the more so for the loose confederacy of genres known as *speculative fiction*! After all, SF is the literature *of* change—in the human condition and in the universe as a whole. By its nature, it must encourage fresh ideas or perish.

So SF had the "New Wave" authors of the sixties—Ellison, Zelazny, Silverberg—who decried the prior emphasis on gadgetry and plot, proclaiming the discovery of something called *style*. Language became their palette. Their colors would be passion, stirred in the reader's soul.

Naturally, the Old Farts thought a lot of this was straight bull. They had spent half a lifetime ardently fighting for the freedom to speculate about mankind's relationship with technology and space and time—and now these young whippersnappers were just taking that freedom for granted. Worse, they were strutting about as if *they* were the true innovators!

Indeed, the best New Wave writers were wonderfully inventive, contributing something vital to our genre, just when it was needed most. They raised new issues, posed new quandaries, precisely because those prior battles had been won. The *best* of the old guard did not grouse when the newcomers came by, flaunting new, gaudy plumage. Rather, they smiled, remembering what it was to be young. And they said, "Come on over here, son. Sit down and tell me all about it."

So it was with cyberpunk in the Eighties. Although I was younger than most of the CP folk, and started my career much more recently, somehow I found myself in the OF (Old Farts) camp, perhaps because I truly do believe that technology and reason will play a role in raising generations better than ours. Assigned a role, I was only too glad to play along for the fun of it, keeping quiet to outsider reporters about the fact that I *really* liked most of the work I'd read by William Gibson, Bruce Sterling, and Pat Cadigan—and had already contributed my own gritty, noir bits to the trend.

Ah, well. As literary movements go, cyberpunk is already well past ripe middle age. Like some of its practitioners, who can be seen occasionally peering into each others' mirror-shades suspiciously, watching age-lines and liver spots emerge. But the worst is coming. For the most successful movements are always punished by becoming . . . clichés.

Consider the story of the elderly lady who was taken to her first Shakespeare play ever—*Hamlet*. Her reaction? "Well, I thought it was very nice . . . but it was all so full of quotations!" Such is the doom of authors, to be fated at one end with obscurity, and at the other end, after success, with being copied until everyone is sick of you. Alas.

And each successful generation creates something else . . . a *new* clade of rebels, fomenting revolution and rejection against the prior one. Bright kids who are talking about these new things they've discovered . . . things called "story," and "character," and "hope."

Many people have tried to define science fiction. I like to call it the literature of exploration and *change*. While other genres obsess upon so-called eternal verities, SF deals with the possibility that our children may have different problems. They may, indeed, *be* different than we have been.

Change is an important matter—it's the salient feature of our age. How well do *you* deal with change?

All creatures live embedded in time, though only human beings seem to lift their heads to comment on this fact, lamenting the past or worrying over what's to come. Our brains are uniquely equipped to handle this temporal *skepsis*. For example, twin neural clusters that reside just above our eyes—the prefrontal lobes—appear especially adapted for extrapolating ahead.

Meanwhile, swathes of older cortex can flood with vivid memories of yesterday, triggered by the merest sensory tickle, as when a single aromatic whiff sent Proust back to roam his mother's kitchen for eighty thousand words. (We'll return to neurons and the brain, later.)

Obsession with either past or future can almost define a civilization. Worldwide, most cultures believed in some lost golden age when people knew more, when they mused *loftier thoughts* and were closer to the gods—but then fell from that state of grace. The myth occurred so frequently, in so many continents and so many contexts—despite an almost complete lack of credible evidence for any genuine past "golden age"—that we must assume the fable wells up from something basic in our natures.

Under this dour but recurrent "look-back" worldview, men and women of a later, coarser era can only look back with envy to that better, happier time, studying ancient lore and hoping to live up to remnants of ancient wisdom.

Just a few societies dared contradict this standard dogma of nostalgia. Our own Scientific West, with its impudent notion of progress, brashly relocated any "golden age" to the future, something to work *toward*, a human construct for our grandchildren to achieve with craft, sweat and good will—assuming that we manage to prepare them properly for such an ambitious task. Implicit is the postulate that our offspring can and should be better than us, a glimmering hope that is nurtured (a bit) by two generations of steadily rising IQ scores.

This perspective can be important when we examine popular mythologies in the realm of science fiction. Take a number of popular epics: for example, *The Matrix, Minority Report,* and *Blade Runner,* the latter two films inspired by literary works of Philip K. Dick.

We shall see that these works—and others, such as *Star Wars, The Lord of the Rings*, and the perennial, *Star Trek*—can be especially well illuminated by asking the following questions:

1. Does the work look forward to human progress or does it push nostalgia by lamenting a lost golden age?

2. Is *science* portrayed with loathing? Or is it seen as a hopeful trend that must also be watched care-

fully against harmful excess?

3. What role does *rebellion* play? Is suspicion of authority portrayed as a private thing? (The hero as a lone fox among sheep.) Or is suspicion of authority portrayed as a healthy reaction by all citizens, who participate by helping to keep the mighty accountable?

4. Are "heroes" portrayed as normal people—perhaps above-average, but part of the human continuum? Or are they demigods, exalted above common humanity by class or genes or even by divine right?

These are not the usual literary categories applied by analytical critics, but I am willing to wager that they will prove enlightening. First, however, let us begin with one obvious fact, that every generation is invaded by a new wave of barbarians—its children.

Why Rebel?

Do you believe that the people around you are subjected to propaganda? Most people think so. Please take a moment to write down on a piece of paper which campaign you think most thoroughly indoctrinates your fellow citizens. Some mention Communism, religion, or consumer advertising . . . or that today's mass media push *conformity* on a hapless, sheeplike population.

It is a smug cliché—that you alone (or perhaps with a few friends)—happen to see through the conditioning that has turned all the rest into passively obedient sheep. Cyberpunk plays to this image by portraying a lone individual—or perhaps just a few—scurrying like rats under the dark towers of the ruling masters. In

The Matrix, the masters are evil computers. In *Johnny Mnemonic*, they are the rulers of faceless corporations. In *The X-Files,* it is a government conspiracy. What these myths share in common is the grimly satisfying image that the masses are useless bystanders, lowing and mooing in confusion.

In fact, it never occurs to the heroes of these tales (above all *The X-Files*) to actually appeal to the very masses who pay the hero's wages and deserve his loyal respect. The common man or woman cannot help resist the Dark Power, because they were long ago indoctrinated into dull, unquestioning obedience.

Ah, but here is the ironic twist. Look around yourself. I'll bet you cannot name, offhand, a single popular film of the last forty years that actually preached homogeneity, submission, or

repression of the individual spirit.

That's a clue!

In fact, the most persistent and inarguably incessant propaganda campaign, appearing in countless movies, novels, myths and TV shows, preaches quite the opposite! A singular and unswerving theme so persistent and ubiquitous that most people hardly notice or mention it. And yet, when I say it aloud, you will nod your heads in instant recognition.

That theme is *suspicion of authority*—often accompanied by its sidekick/partner: *tolerance.*

Indeed, try to come up with even one example of a recent film you enjoyed in which the hero did not bond with the audience in the first ten minutes by resisting or sticking it to some authority figure.

Some filmmakers, such as Steven Spielberg, use this potent cinematic ingredient in measured doses, creating and portraying authority figures who are just malevolent and powerful enough to keep the heroes in jeopardy, without too much exaggeration. Others slather on the authoritarian premise as thick as sugar icing in a wedding cake, using the sweetness of resentment to overwhelm all other lacks in plot or consistency or taste.

Alas, the latter tendency is all too frequent in SF cinema. Take the bleak paranoia that pervades *The Matrix* and other films of its genre. Oh, I don't mind some tales about rebellion against mega-computers. What gets tedious is the relentless refusal ever to recognize—and then start cleverly varying—a classic cliché.

But back to the essence here. Rebels are always the heroes. Conformity is portrayed as worse than death. Even in war flicks, irreverence for some pompous commander is a necessary trait.

Often, the main character also presents some quirky trait, some eccentricity, that draws both ire from some oppressor and sympathy from the audience.

Oh, you do hear *some* messages of conformity and intolerance—but these fill the mouths of moustache-twirling villains, clearly inviting us to rebel contrary to everything they say. Submission to gray tribal normality is portrayed as one of the most contemptible things an individual can do—a message quite opposite to what was pushed in most other cultures.

This theme is so prevalent, and so obvious, that even though you can see where I am going with it—and hate the inevitable conclusion—you aren't going to dispute the core fact. You have to sit there and accept one of the most galling things that a bunch of dedicated individualists can ever realize: That you were *trained* to be individualists by the most relentless campaign of public indoctrination in history, suckling your love of rebellion and eccentricity from a society that—evidently, at some level—*wants* you to be that way!

Oh, the ironies abound.

A Question of Perspective

So, do all popular works of fiction promote suspicion of authority? At some level, yes they do. It is the core element of the modern drama, showing just how far the modern sensibility has traveled, parting markedly from the passive plaints of poor doomed Oedipus and Othello, who had no recourse when they were marked for agony by their gods. The classical Greeks, Romans, Japanese, and others tended to portray resistance as futile—as prescribed primly in Aristotle's *Poetics*—a fundamental tenet of the

"Look Back" view mentioned earlier.

In contrast, some modern SF and fantasy tales aggressively take the extreme opposite position. Take *Xena* and *Hercules*, two fairly lowbrow popular television series in which authority figures were portrayed as evil in direct proportion to their rudeness or callousness toward common folk. Xena might rescue an exiled king from invaders and restore his throne, but only if he treats people nicely and promises to set up a democratically elected city council. Any time someone is abused by an Olympian, that "god" is sure to face dire punishment from our heroine!

Ah, but the will toward worshipping Olympians and demigods still roils within us. After all, we spent thousands of years in feudal settings that were totally undemocratic. Social structures were pyramid-shaped, with a narrow elite dominating ignorant masses. Starting with Homer's *Iliad* and *Gilgamesh,* nearly all of the bards and storytellers worked for the chiefs, aristocrats and kings who owned all the marbles. (A point conveniently never mentioned by Joseph Campbell in *The Hero's Journey*.) Naturally they preached that lords and "better" folk had a right to exercise capricious power at whim. You could choose which demigod to root for—say, Achilles or Hector. But there was no disputing the super-hero's ultimate right to deal with mortals however he wished.

Of course this is another aspect of the nostalgic-romantic Look Back worldview. Today you see it exemplified in two highly popular epics, the Ender series of Orson Scott Card and the *Star Wars* saga produced by George Lucas. In both, the pivotal characters are born profoundly superior to those around them . . . not just a little smarter, but indisputably and qualitatively greater than the mere mortals surrounding them. Moreover, the distinction is not one earned by hard work or the give-and-take of reciprocal criticism that typifies modern teamwork, democracy, meritocracy or science. Rather the justification is one of inherited genetic supremacy, giving the hero an inherent right to meddle at will.

Nearly all O. S. Card works feature a central demigod, whose saving grace is a deep self-pitying angst—expressed at great length—over being forced to over-rule the obstinate will of benighted humanity and set things straight. But at least Card's characters seem to feel vague regret that people aren't able to handle things as adults. Not bothering with such hand-wringing, George Lucas's "Jedi Force" mythology baldly and openly extols the same sort of secretive mystical priest-class that assisted and excused oppressive kings in nearly all eras, on nearly all continents. And all the while, both sagas put forward strawman "authority figures" for the characters to resent openly, while real manipulators play the underlying dance tune.

Of course, the very notion of progress is anathema to nostalgic-romantics. Despite techie furnishings, the *Star Wars* pop-epic relentlessly preaches the nostalgist party line—an ideal society ought to be ruled by secretive-mystical elites, unaccountable and self-chosen based on inherent qualities of blood. The only good knowledge is old knowledge. (No wonder it all happened "long ago, in a galaxy far away.")

Note: These romantics needn't be anti-technological, though they almost have to reject science. Their worldview is utterly incompatible with the way science works or thinks.

From Virgil and the Vedas to Plato, Shelley, and Tolkien, all the way to Updike and Rowling, this prevalent nostalgist tradition spanned five continents and forty centuries. Some rage, others fizz; but all grumble at tomorrow.

Even where the heroes of these tales practice "suspicion of authority" (they must, in order to bond with today's audiences) the dispute is portrayed as one among demigods. Mere mortals have the option of dying as spear carriers—as they did in the *Iliad*—and of worshipping the demigods with mass ceremonies, as in *Triumph of the Will*.

Contrast this with the view portrayed in *Star Trek*, in which democracy is an inherent good. Scientific progress, while deserving skeptical oversight, is seen as both inevitable and probably desirable. The ship's captain, while great, relies utterly on the competence of his or her "merely human" crew, any one of whom may prove crucial and deserving of a brief moment on center stage.. In *Star Trek*, any demigod is viewed with worried doubt. (For more on this distinction, see http://www.davidbrin.com/starwarsarticle1.html)

Frankly, I am amazed that *Star Trek* ever thrived. Certainly it is unsurprising to find that its core element of progressive optimism has seldom been emulated elsewhere in the canon of SF. There are a few other examples. Robert Silverberg, Iain Banks, and Wil McCarthy have been known to portray futures in which our descendants face problems commensurately difficult enough to challenge even people who are far better and wiser than we are.

Let's face it; portraying a smart future civilization—one that nevertheless faces cleverly onerous problems—can be hard work! It is much, much easier to milk the emotions by using a demigod character, in a dystopian setting filled with clueless citizens. Just assume the worst about society and give the readers or viewers the emotional satisfaction of watching that supreme hero "rebel" against some garishly simple and overwrought authority figure . . . while at the same time wielding magical forces that he was born with and destined to use.

The Difficulty of Optimism

Where do many of today's popular genre films fit in?

Take *The Matrix,* a movie I quite enjoyed! Its high-tech premise and cyber-glossy ambiance are lavishly attractive and the conflict setup is appealing. Who could resist the dark glamour of its design, the pyrotechnics of its stunts, the seduction of its noir-ish vision?

Above all, relish the classic audience identification with a character who is told in advance that he will be "The One" . . . and any skill that he lacks—any skill that *you* ever wished that you had time to learn—can be downloaded in a matter of seconds! (Naturally, this miracle uses the very same science that the central premise preaches to have been one big mistake. Ironies are another lavish trait of the film.)

But how does it score according to the four questions I posed earlier?

On almost every count, *The Matrix,* is an unabashedly nostalgic-romantic piece, loyal to the elitist, look backward world-view, suspicious of science and deeply contemptuous of the masses, which are portrayed more sheeplike here than in any other work of popular culture! Only at the very end is there a hint that perhaps the common man or woman might someday be wakened from their seductive slumbers. But not much chance of that.

(Don't get me wrong! Dark warnings are among the greatest literary works and SF does civilization a genuine good when it dourly explores potential failure modes. Elsewhere I go into the importance of self-preventing prophecies—SF tales that have quite possibly saved our lives and certainly helped save freedom, by innoculating a definitely NOT-sheeplike public with heightened awareness of a potential danger. Among the greatest of these were *Dr. Strangelove, Soylent Green,* and *Nineteen Eighty-Four,* all of which helped make the author's vivid warning somewhat obsolete through the unexpected miracle that people actually listened.)

Still, there have been enough paeans of praise for the style and the warning inherent in *The Matrix.* I want to go back to those under-discussed aspects—such as the devout adherence to a nostalgist-romantic-Look Back way of viewing the world.

Contrast this mentality with another enjoyable romp— *The Fifth Element*—a far less serious or thoughtful film than *The Matrix*—one whose general mindlessness is only matched by its unabashed joy. Ebullience and optimism spills off the screen in gushing torrents, overwhelming the viewer's sense of surly skepticism, even when the adventure is at its most dire or the plot is most ridiculous. True, there is a demigod . . . but she desperately needs the aid and succor of mere mortal heroes, even citizens who are passing by! Some authority figures drive the plot with their vileness, but the director does not feel it necessary to tar all of society and all of science with this brush. The villains are plenty bad enough. No need to make the cake all frosting.

Take another example—*Minority Report* . . . or almost any Steven Spielberg film, for that matter. Spielberg is unabashedly progressive and loyal to the Look Forward *zeitgeist.* Although he skillfully utilizes suspicion-of-authority, he cannot let himself fall for the *X-Files* cliché of a country and citizenry that are completely and forever clueless. Even the government—a classic target of authority-resentment in film—is never portrayed as unalloyedly vile. Rather, his abusive authority figures are narrowly defined, a vile police chief here . . . a callous scientist there.

Moreover, the hero can even sometimes call upon help from decent people and institutions. While there are moments of techno-Orwellian creepiness in *Minority Report*, such as when the police send spy-eye "spiders" running through an apartment building, Spielberg portrays this as a highly limited invasion, one that sovereign citizens have clearly decided to put up with. They can still vote to eliminate a particular police power If they decide they do not like it—in fact this is a central element to the plot. This future may be creepy and filled with problems, but it is no clichéd tyranny.

In other words, unlike George Lucas, Spielberg is grateful to a civilization of democracy, egalitarian science and general decency. He simply cannot bring himself to spit in its face. Especially not after it has been so good to him.

The Roots of Fantasy

At the very opposite extreme, consider the popularity of feudal/magical fantasies, of the kind typified by *The Lord of the Rings*

Recall how a core element of romanticism is to spurn the modern emphasis on pragmatic experimentation, production, universal literacy, cooperative enterprise and flattened social orders. In contrast to these "sterile" pursuits, Romantics extolled the traditional, the personal, the particular, the subjective and metaphorical. Consider how this fits with the very plot of *The Lord of the Rings*, in which the good guys strive to win re-establishment of an older, graceful and "natural" hierarchy against the disturbing, quasi-industrial and vaguely technological ambience of Mordor, with its smokestack imagery and manufactured power-rings that can be used by anybody, not just an elite few. Those man-made wonders are deemed cursed, damning anyone who dares to use them, usurping the rightful powers of their betters (the high elves).

Another of the really cool things about fantasy—you can identify with a side that's one hundred percent pure, distilled good and revel as they utterly annihilate foes who *deserve* to be exterminated because they are one hundred percent evil! This may not be politically correct, but then political correctness is really a bastard offspring of egalitarian-scientific enlightenment. Romanticism never made any pretense at equality. It is hyper-discriminatory, by nature.

The urge to crush some demonized enemy resonates deeply within us, dating from ages far earlier than feudalism. Hence, the vicarious thrill we feel over the slaughter of orc foot soldiers at Helm's Deep. Then again as the Ents flatten even more goblin grunts at Saruman's citadel, taking no prisoners, without a thought for all the orphaned orclings and grieving widorcs. And again at Minas Tirith, and again at the Gondor docks and again . . . well, they're only orcs, after all. What fun.

Notice any similarity to the waves of foot-soldiers and spear carriers who died under Achilles's hand in the *Iliad* . . . or in the *Star Wars* saga?

Among all the attempts to cast definitions of fantasy and science fiction, to help explain the chasm that so many see, let me offer this one based on the difference between the Look Back and

Look Forward worldviews.

Science fiction is the genre that posits the slim possibility that children might—sometimes—be capable of learning from the mistakes of their parents. That people may someday be better than us, even partly on account of our efforts. They may no longer need kings. They may, each of them, be capable of rising up and being heroes.

A Continuing Struggle of Worldviews

There is no resolution to this ongoing struggle, one that runs deeper than any politics or ideology. Movies such as *The Matrix* and *Minority Report* embody this struggle. While we are entranced by the similarities, the glossy, diverting futures and techno-wonders and dark warnings, it is important also to remember that there are deeper assumptions at play. Assumptions about what human beings can potentially achieve.

Science fiction, in effect, has become a central battlefield in one of the most important disputes roiling in the human mind—the decision whether to continue our obsession with hier-archies, demigods and the past . . . or to turn with confidence and wary optimism toward the future.

Revenge of the Nerds, Part X

Alan Dean Foster

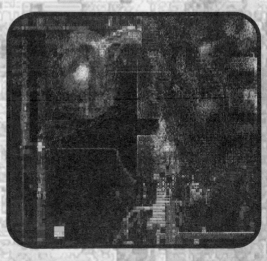

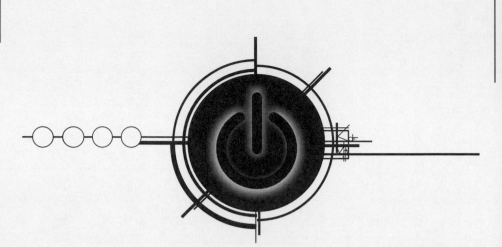

Do you remember that one special, overriding feeling you had when you were a kid? No, not the cool taste of good ice cream, or the laughter of friends, or the warmth inherent in your mother's kitchen. Not those. Nothing so amenable. I'm talking about fear. The constant, overriding feeling of helplessness. Of never being in control, no matter how hard you tried, of any part of your environment. Of always being dominated by everything and everyone around you. The feeling of being afraid—of your parents, your older siblings, the bully at school (there is always a bully at school), of strangers at a family gathering, of strangers on a city street. Of strangers everywhere. Of the whole world. Not to mention The Horror in the Closet, The Monster Under the Bed, The Lurker Outside Your Bedroom Window—and Uncle Jake's bulging eyes, affectionately pinching fingers, and decomposing breath. Calm down. Be at ease. You are not alone. We were all afraid of those things (some of us still are—

particularly of Uncle Jake), and there was nothing, absolutely positively know-it-for-sure-all nothing, that we could do about them.

But we wanted to.

Oh, how we wanted to! How desperately we desired the
means and the wherewithal to contemptuously and effortless dis-
pose of bully, strangers, Thing in Closet, Monster Under Bed, and
Lurker Outside Window—and, to our secret but delicious shame,
probably Uncle Jake as well (but not Aunt Jane, who baked nice
cookies). We could not. Why not? Because we were invariably
smaller, weaker, less experienced, dumber, and too afraid. These
powerful, atavistic emotions from childhood never leave us entirely, no matter how mature or "grown-up" we think we have
become. Perhaps not in reality (at least not too often, fortunately)
but certainly in fantasy, who hasn't at one time or another wanted
to kill the boss, or the jerk down the street who always goes out of
his way to make sure his dog dumps on *your* lawn, or the prattling
idiot of a politician staring out of the TV who we know is flat out
lying to our faces, or the amoral CEO who's responsible for shov-
eling poor old folks' life savings into the nearest trash can while on
his way to St. Tropez for yet another "business conference"?

But it's among children, and particularly among those
adrift in the Sargasso Sea of their teen years, where these emotions
run deepest. Where every day is devoted to minimize the mental
and emotional paper cuts of fear and helplessness. Which is why
that particular segment of the film-going public responded so
readily and enthusiastically to *The Matrix*.

Because despite what you see on the big screen *The
Matrix*, while nominally science fiction and more specifically
drawing upon the sub-genre of that literature known as cyber-

punk, is not about computers or evil machines enslaving humankind or even really cool shades. It's about the empowerment of the not quite adult. People can write all they want about the film's mirror-shade slant and slick special effects, about its mysterious message and loosely plotted framing tale of the machines of the future enslaving the species, but what it really does is send out a message to every teenager in the audience (and most especially to the male portion) that at least in the world of *The Matrix*, you too—you nerdy, sallow, pimple-faced, skinny, unathletic lump of malleable human stuff—you too can exert Godlike control over each and every one of your tormentors. And get the girl, to boot (up).

Spend time in a theater showing the film, observe this much sought after audience segment, and you can see it in their eyes. In ways no teen male can identify with Schwarzenegger or Stallone (or Vin Diesel), they can see themselves as Keanu Reeves/Neo. It's a lead role the producers were oh-so-clever in casting. Reeves is trim without being buff, athletic without being imposing or overawing, handsome without being too pretty. Unlike Arnold or Sly or Vin, it is entirely possible to envision him having actually suffered from acne. The boys in the audience can identify with him, can see themselves *as* him. Physically, Neo is far more skateboarder than shooting guard. With his leaps and kicks and somersaults, he's Extreme Sports before the term was coined. He's not big, he's not muscular, he's no hulk. He even looks like a slightly aged teenager. There are no lines in his face. The stress he shows on screen is mental, inner, confused. The kind of predicament those in the audience can sense because they've experienced it themselves. So different from Eastwood worrying about capturing the kidnapper, or

Schwarzenegger agonizing over how to blow up the drug cartel's headquarters.

Few teens see themselves ever engaging in such outrageous, outsized, Hollywoodized actions. But being hauled away from one's computer to face a room full of hostile adults, *that* they can empathize with. Hugo Weaving, in a marvelous performance as the lead "Agent" of the evil machine program, is no lumbering Richard Kiel as Jaws, no squat and invincible Oddjob. Physically and mentally, he's about as far from the typical cinematic "big" as Kasparov is from Kurt Warner. Instead, his character is every nasty high-school vice principal, school bully, and supercilious, overbearing adult a typical teenager encounters all rolled into one. The interrogation room into which he and his supporting agents toss the bewildered Neo is every principal's office and every "let's beat the crap out of him!" behind-the-school back alley any put-upon kid ever had the misfortune to visit. It's critical to the success of *The Matrix*'s appeal that the audience fully identifies with Neo at such moments, even when he's *not* wiping up the cyberfloor with the bad guys. What teenage boy identifies with the "plight" of Arnold trapped in the jungle lair of an evil arms merchant, or James Bond stuck in a holding cell in the wilds of Southeast Asia? But put him in a dull, featureless room with a bunch of hostile, stony-visaged adults looming over him and quizzing him relentlessly about things he doesn't understand—well, it's welcome to my nightmare time, sings (not Carroll's) Alice.

In many teenage boys' revenge fantasies, he's not alone. There is always a sidekick; someone bigger than the bully, smarter than the adults, more simpatico than the school administrators. In *The Matrix* this role is fulfilled by Laurence Fishburne's

Morpheus. Morpheus is Chewbacca with an advanced degree: big, strong, tough, but also knowledgeable. He's mentor and protector all rolled into one, a favorite social studies teacher—only with muscles. Not only can he kick sand right back into the faces of the bullies at the beach, he can also outthink and outtalk their interfering parents.

So what if we don't know what he's talking about half the time? Isn't that how it is with every kid's favorite teacher? It doesn't matter if the put-upon student doesn't understand him. What's important isn't Morpheus's knowledge: It's his empathy. He *cares* about Neo. He wants him to succeed. Like any good professor, he hopes his student will surpass him and feels only joy at the prospect. What more could a confused teen stumbling and bumbling his way through life and school want of a teacher? It's the rare father who tells his son that he hopes his offspring will grow up to be smarter than he is. Richer, yeah—but smarter? Teens may identify with Neo, but they reserve their affection for Morpheus.

And then there's Trinity. Wears leather. Kicks bad guy butt and early on takes out the baddies picking on poor Neo. *Knows computers*. This last is critical to her appeal to the film's target audience. It says to them that not only can a geek get a babe, you can find one who speaks your language. And she doesn't ask for anything. Doesn't demand that Neo drive a fancy car, doesn't insist he buy her dinner at some fancy restaurant where the waiter will invariably look down his nose at you because you invariably mismatch your clothes, doesn't insult him because he didn't pay for extra butter on the popcorn at the movie. She's just—there. When Neo needs her. Despite her knowledge and abilities she doesn't babble on about stuff, much less *girl* stuff.

The last thing a teenage boy wants in a girlfriend is complexity (the first thing he wants is boobs, but not even Trinity is perfect). Trinity's about as uncomplex as can be. Watching her on screen, you half get the feeling that if you met her in person and said "Hello" she'd respond with "Press Enter to activate conversation program." Even better, she doesn't have any stupid girlfriends around to giggle and point fingers and make fun of you (presumably they're all stashed away in the sleeping pods built by the evil machines). As for her attitude toward physical affection, well, when she and Neo blast their way into the skyscraper where Morpheus is being held, in an attempt to rescue him from the Agents' interrogation, he and she are having sex—with guns. Check out the look they exchange in the elevator. Positively cyber-orgasmic. One thinks "orgy at an NRA convention" (perhaps one should not). We'll leave the endless-reservoir-of-expended-shells-as-ejaculated-sperm analogy for another time.

So, what do we have here? One kindly, worldly-wise, butt-kicking mentor and one selfless, coolly affectionate, butt-kicking girlfriend—both of whom understand, use, and practically salivate over computers and their capabilities. Can you see *The Matrix*'s audience leaning forward in their seats with baited breath and intense interest as Arnold or Sly or Vin labor over a keyboard? You have to develop the appropriate characters to *fit* the cyber-setting, and the *The Matrix* does so superbly.

Finally, we come back to Neo himself. Keanu Reeves not as Steve Reeves but as Everynerd. As every smart and almost-smart kid who was ever pushed around behind the football stands during Phys Ed. That's how he starts out: baffled, bemused, and pushed around by bullies and authority. Until aforementioned mentor and girlfriend arrive to enlighten and assist him. Not only that, but to inform him that he's The One. Name me one sixteen-year-old boy who doesn't think, at some time or another, that he's The One.

Sure, you don't got no muscles. Sure, you'll never make the football team or get to lay the cheerleader. But hey, you're president of the computer club. Or the chess team. Or first in line for that academic scholarship. All of which is great, but doesn't let you take revenge on your tormentors. *The Matrix* does. The meek may not inherit the Earth, but cyberspace, that's another matter (so to speak).

What kid wouldn't want to be Neo, gifted with true understanding of how the world is really run and supplied with the means to manipulate it? You too can out-martial arts the bad guys—with the proper training. You too can blow them away with every type of weapon imaginable—with proper training. And finally, eventually, you too can defeat them by sheer force of will and make them look silly while doing it—with proper training. And how do you acquire this vital training? Through hard work at school, long hours spent sweating over the computer or pouring through thick volumes in the library, asking detailed questions of those more knowledgeable than yourself (i.e., adults)? Huh-uh. Not in *The Matrix*. There's an easier way. One that won't tax your mind, take up your valuable free time (used for playing video games or going to the movies or just hanging out), or require you to actually confront an adult with a serious question.

You just download the information directly to your brain.

The direct downloading of information to the mind has long since become an old trope in science fiction. But not in film.

While the concept may seem new and fresh to their (non-SF reading) parents, it's something teens growing up with MP3 and in-home CD burning can readily identify with, often to the consternation of their elders. Which makes this particular bit of tempting technological dream fluff proffered by *The Matrix* all that more appealing. Talk about teenage wish fulfillment! Every teenage boy would like to be able to take two things away from the pretend world of *The Matrix*. The first is an ability to simply, easily, and effortlessly download knowledge. No more studying, no more books, no more teacher's sanitation-challenged looks. Just plug in the right storage chip and hit the mental equivalent of "Save As." Learn to fly a helicopter. How to defy gravity. Absurdly balletic gunplay in one easy lesson. And all with your eyes closed, relaxing

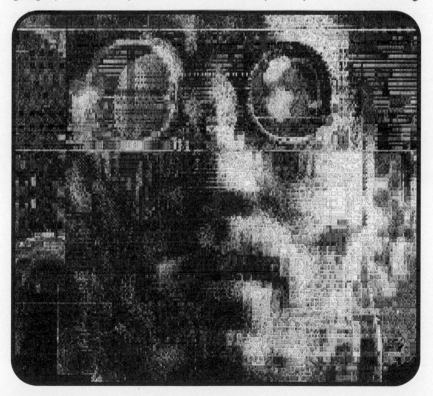

in a nice, comfy chair. All that's missing from this crucial scene in *The Matrix* is an open cooler at Neo's right hand overflowing with chilled brewskis.

And the second thing? Surprise—it's not Trinity. Not the girl, no. Number Two on our eager young geek's Matrix dream want list is that endless white background Neo calls up that's filled with row upon row, shelf upon shelf, of heavy ordinance—a testosterone-slathered wish-dream come true if ever one appeared on film. That's also where and when Reeves utters the movie's seminal line on behalf of all oppressed and misunderstood nerds. "I'll need guns—lots of guns." Of course, by the end of the story guns have been rendered superfluous by Neo's mastery of cyber-space—excuse me, of the Matrix. By comprehending its workings and fully understanding his place within them, he can now stop programs-as-bullets in mid-flight and pluck them out of the air, or cause them to fall harmlessly at his feet. The implication is that Neo's mastery of the Matrix now exceeds that of its malevolent mechanical devisers, a realization that frightens (if a program element can be frightened) the Matrix's Agents. How will they fight back against Neo's apotheosis in *The Matrix Reloaded* and *The Matrix Revolutions*? I predict the insertion into the sequels of a special kind of anti-Neo computer virus.

By the end of the film, our surrogate teenager Neo has attained complete mastery of the world around him. The fact that it isn't the real world doesn't faze him, nor does it mute the sense of identification the movie inculcates in its exhausted but exultant teen viewers. Having grown up immersed in television, movies, video games, and the Internet, they understand the difference between mastering a fantasy world and competing in the real one.

The problem is that the former is far simpler than the latter. Sometimes confusion results, to the detriment of the individual so seduced, and then we are subjected to a few days of screaming, sensation-seeking, foaming-at-the-mouth tabloid headlines. I'm still waiting for the first one:

"High School Honors Student Thinks Real World Is Nothing More Than A Computer Program! Attempts To Delete Parents!" ·

The Matrix not only makes its young viewers feel good by choosing as its star someone far easier for them to identify with than the archetypal Hollywood hero; it makes them feel good about *themselves* and about who they are. The message is that if Neo can do it, so can you. His perceived world is a sham, a mistake, a carefully crafted fake, and you know, deep down, that yours is, too. He exists in isolation (no parents, no wife, no girlfriend) and most teenage boys do, too. Though put-upon by others who intend him only ill, he triumphs through sheer force of brainpower and will. Arise, ye geeks of the world, for only you know the truth! Therein lies the message of *The Matrix*, and the real source of its success.

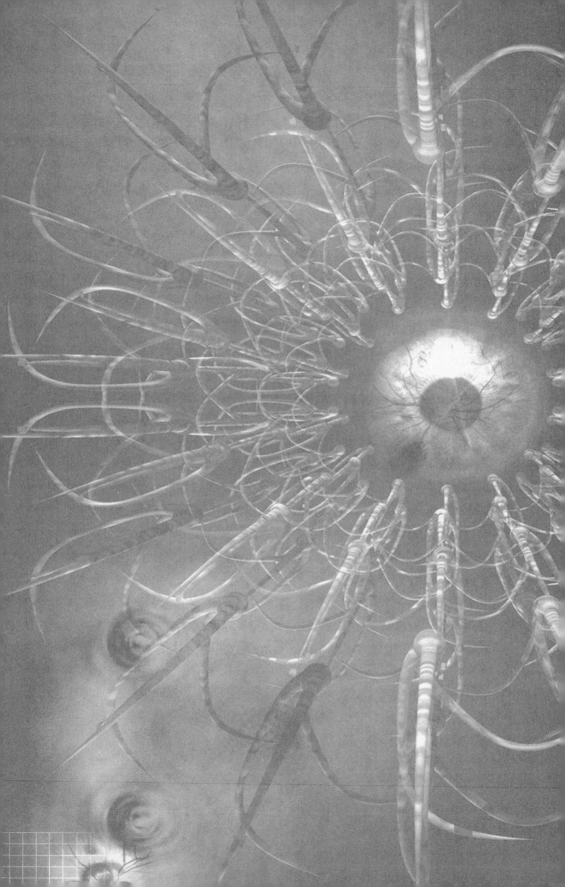

Reflections in a Cyber Eye

Karen Haber

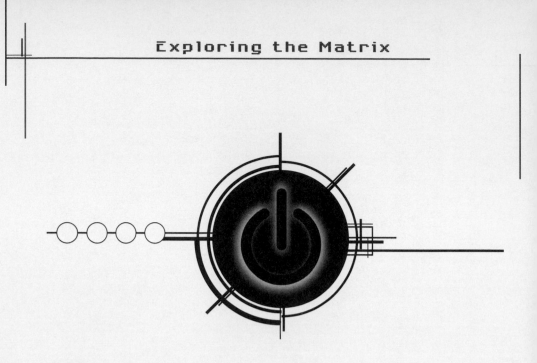

It all begins—and ends—with black leather, doesn't it? And somehow we always knew that it would, too.

From the very first stunning moment of the very first astounding stunt scene in *The Matrix*, the viewer knows that she/he is in for a giddy funhouse ride of a movie, and, even more pointedly, a no-holds-barred stylefest.

If the late Diana Vreeland, the terrifyingly chic doyenne of *Vogue* magazine to whom even that fashion icon, Jackie Kennedy Onassis, deferred, had seen *The Matrix* she surely would have bowed to the Brothers Wachowski. Like knows like, and with *The Matrix*, the Brothers W took the style crown away from fellow moviemakers Luc Besson and Ridley Scott.

Whatever the components of style are—confidence, cool, grace and don't forget black leather—*The Matrix* has it in abundance. Long after the confusing tangle of storyline and goofy/mystical multi-culti mixed media references of the movie have faded from memory, the look remains.

And that's appropriate. All that matters about this movie, really, is the way it looks.

When, early on in the film, the character known as Trinity levitates, knees bent, and proceeds to kick the crap out of the bad guys—fulfilling at least *this* former adolescent tomboy's every dream of grace, power, and catsuits—the style bar was raised for design concept and special effects in science-fiction cinema. Filmmakers everywhere, after they located their jaws in the rubble on the floor and closed them, surely must have thought: "How in hell am I ever going to match this, much less top it?"

The Matrix confirms what some of us have always known—and feared—deep in the most secret blood-red chamber of our throbbing hearts.

Style is all that matters.

Always has been.

Always will be.

The Matrix is a glorious, triumphant celebration of style, wallowing in all of those guilty pleasures: speed, smarts, separate-but-equal trench coats, dark glasses, super powers, paranoia and, oh, yes, don't forget the guns. If anyone has ever been guilty of making guns sexy, it's the Wachowskis. The NRA should have sent the brothers free lifetime memberships with a letter of gratitude.

In this movie, guns become a *di rigeur* fashion accessory. (Matrix fashion tip #1: Girls, going on a rescue mission? Don't be caught without at least a Luger under your trench coat.)

The Matrix is a many splendored visual feast because it was magnificently conceived at ground level. Has *any* other SF movie ever had such meticulously wrought, print-ready, beautiful storyboards done by such talents as Geof Darrow and Steve Skroce? And has any other movie brought said storyboards to life with such faithful virtuousity? *The Matrix* breaks right through the frame of the comic book panel, taking its action outside the box, outside the stereotyped imagery of other SF films, into a new realm. Now *that's* dancin', as a Mr. Astaire once said.

The visual audacity of this film—as the tropes of animé are literally brought to cyberlife—overwhelms the content, message, and, thankfully, the dialog. The power of the image rules here, and the imagination behind it makes it possible to appreciate this flick even as a silent movie.

The wonderful sexy use of rearview mirrors, doorknobs, spoons, all manner of reflections, and multiple images in video screens, could have come out of a fashion video or commercial. Slick. Clever. Oh-so-knowing. So many oddly slanted perspectives working to increase the viewer's sense of dislocation, and hint at Neo's literal dislocation. What was that shadow in the mirror? That strange flicker out of the corner of your eye's reflection?

Even when Neo is literally *bugged* during the horrifying interrogation scene, the horror is made that much more harrowing by its slick stylization.

Even the bad guys are stylish: Agent Smith and his cookie-cutter fellow agents truly bring the notion of "evil suits" to cyber life with their bad haircuts, matching jackets, and slip-sliding monotonic morphability.

The machines themselves, those AI baddies, are the culmination of every bad boy dream. What at first seemed to be a stylistic non-sequitur is, in fact, a gleeful indulgence in making every viewer cringe. Nasty. If these machines don't look like spiders then they look like mosquitoes. If they don't look like mosquitoes, they look like scorpions. If they're underwater search-and-destroy gizmos, they look like squid—giant squid. (Calling Captain Nemo. Please pick up the white courtesy telephone. . . .) Did these evil machines design themselves to resemble many-legged, big-eyed, get-it-off-me-get-it-off-me pests on order to frighten humans? Or perhaps eight legs—and eyes—*are* better than two.

Neo's trip down the Matrix rabbit hole is an exercise in jaw-dropping cinematic style, beginning when he passes through the mirror—or rather, the mirror engulfs him. (I wonder how Alice would have felt about that.)

What's important about this film is visual, pounded home in iconic scene after iconic scene: Neo waiting at Adams St. Bridge as the rain creates a waterfall behind him—the obligatory noir downpour whose doppelganger is the downpour of data drenching the screen at the movie's beginning, pouring down the screens of the computers aboard the *Nebuchadnezzar*. Data is the sea in which our heroes strive and struggle. In style.

Even the violence is carefully stylized. Those long black coats concealing all those guns. That slow-mo "bullet time" back-bend. The balletic fisticuffs between Mr. Smith and Neo. Trinity's nighttime jog over the rooftops.

In fact, the only brutal impact in the movie occurs when a gap develops in style continuity during the capture—and beating—of Morpheus. Even the Brothers W couldn't figure out how to make that work as more than meat being pounded. But the rescue of Morpheus more than makes up for this temporary lapse.

The nature of reality is being questioned as the nature of visual reality is being played with before our eyes. But perhaps we really ought to question the supposed horror of the *unreality* in which Neo—and the other captive humans—dwell. In the Matrix, it's 1999. Always has been. Always will be.

The world that Neo wishes to reveal, to "liberate" his human brethren into, is a radioactive wasteland, denuded by previous struggles between humans and machine. There is nothing there to savor—possibly nothing left to recover much less restore.

Perhaps it would be better for Neo and his pals to take that blue pill, turn over, and go back to sleep. I think that would be the stylish choice.

As Morpheus (King of Dreams?) leads Neo out of the

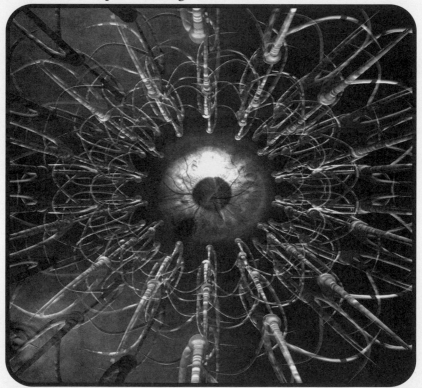

dream of his mundane reality and deep into the nightmare that truly confronts him—and humanity—he is the king of unimaginable cool, the Zen master in dark glasses and long black leather coat. (Style note: In this anti-hero-as-hero movie, the good guys *all* wear black.)

As we learn that Morpheus is not only a secret master himself, but a John the Baptist awaiting a Neo/Jesus, we must come to understand what qualifies Neo for this titanic task. He must, after all, deliver his new friends and his kind out of their techno-wilderness, redeem their ruined lives and world, vanquish the evil AI masters. He is the techno-Messiah. Is it his brains and secret powers that qualify him for this role? What makes him *The One*? Perhaps he just looks better in dark glasses and a long black coat than anybody else in the cast.

The incredibly seductive visual power of this darkly beautiful film nearly obscures the ferocious—and dangerous—message that floats just beneath its slick hynotic surface: *Fear science*.

Talk about having your cybercake and eating it, too.

The Matrix is, paradoxically, a profoundly anti-science SF movie. It tells the viewer to fear computers because they will become the ultimate bogeymen. We will teach them how to exceed and supercede us.

How disappointing that the core idea of this movie is so, well, unstylish. Science as a bad genie that foolish humans have allowed to escape from its bottle. Ho-hum. Been there. Done that. Time for a clearance sale of stale ideas.

It's almost ironic that such high-tech special effects have been employed to underscore such lunkheaded fear of technology. Of course, there's a long long cinematic tradition of stylishly using science as the bad guy, stretching back to *Metropolis*, *Frankenstein*, and more recently, *2001: A Space Odyssey*. Even in *Blade Runner*, the problem has to do with science, and a form of artificial intelligence, if you see the replicants as machines with memories artificially inserted.

(And while we're on the topic of *Blade Runner*, I'd like to pick another cinematic style nit, namely fights in grotty abandoned bathrooms. For some reason that has become a visual legacy. You know that if you see an grotty abandoned bathroom in Act One, by Act Three, somebody—usually unnaturally physically enhanced—will be punching his way through that slimy tile wall. Enough. Somebody get out some Ajax and start scrubbing, please.)

Using AI as a bogeyman is not only stylistically boring, it's lazy. After all, there are *so* many other worthy candidates for bad guys. Pick a name, a state, a constituency. Terrorists. Politicians. Talk show hosts. Martha Stewart. Jeez, just extrapolate like any graduate of Clarion has been taught, rightly or wrongly, and give science a break, willya? What has it done to you, lately?

As a matter of fact, think about what it has done *for* you. And I'm not even talking about biotechnology, or telephone answering machines, or satellite TV or nonfat yogurt. Without the advances in digital technology, the special effects produced for this movie would have been impossible. The blackest joke of all is that *The Matrix* is using computer tech to beat up on computer tech.

Talk about ungrateful.

And *could* the cyberreality depicted in this movie ever really happen?

I, for one, fervently hope so.

Not the nasty parts, you understand. None of those parasitic cybernasties or visits with Agent Smith, please.

But wouldn't a few of us love to go back to 1999? Remember? Only a few years ago but, in fact, an former era. Kinder. Gentler. Before planes flew into tall buildings, and the Internet economic bubble burst.

And if computers really *are* secretly eating our lunch—and us with it— well, so what? We can still go to raves and take drugs and get laid and if the truth ever breaks through the surface of our reality, well, it quickly submerges again and we awaken, shaking but safe, in our beds. Just a bad dream. I'm sure there are plenty of people in the year 2003 who wish that their realities would be revealed as just a bad dream.

The most enviable aspect of Neo's world is that beloved trope of cyberpunkism: plugging in and downloading the good stuff.

If only.

Go ahead and admit it: Wouldn't it be sweet to jack in to the Big Computer right this very minute and pick up some super jujitsu skills? Or maybe some house cleaning tips. Learn French in a nanosecond. Develop those fun rooftop-leaping skills.

Despite its best efforts to the contrary, *The Matrix* glorifies the computer as the ultimate wish-fulfillment machine. ("Guns. Lots of guns.")

Plug right in and get *whatever* you want.

"Shoes. Lots of shoes."

I told you, it all begins and ends with black leather.

Meditations on the Singular Matrix

James Patrick Kelly

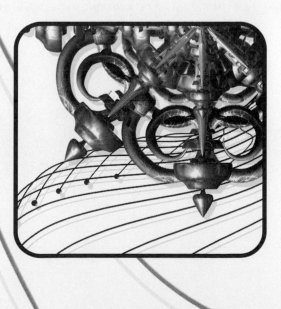

We have only bits and pieces of information.
—Morpheus, *The Matrix*

Welcome to another movie about Evil Computers. Some people have been describing *The Matrix* as cyberpunk and I suppose it is. But I'm afraid that's actually not much of a compliment. You have to realize that cyberpunk was hatched by a bunch of science-fiction writers in the early eighties. Conceived in the Reagan administration, c-punk in some important ways is as dated as the policies of our oldest president. For example, you wouldn't even bother to sneeze today on the hardware we were using back then. I'm talking pre-Macintosh. No mice, no hard disks. Cutting edge was a 286 IBM PC running at a mind boggling 10MHz. Windows had not yet opened and MS-DOS ruled the earth. Do you remember the *C* prompt. No? Good for you! Those were the dark days. It's no wonder the cyberpunks were so crotchety. And of course, there was no 'Net as we know it. When William Gibson published *Neuromancer*, there were just over one thousand Internet hosts.

Later in the eighties, cyberpunk escaped from the narrow confines of science fiction. It changed from being our little genre's cool extrapolation about the future to a lifestyle that people could actually choose. This was a first for science fiction. The chances of some kid from Dubuque becoming captain of the starship *Enterprise* are still pretty slim. And nobody has as yet whipped up a time machine in his garage, more's the pity. But for a thousand bucks or so, you could stick your head through a monitor in 1989 and take a deep breath of one hundred percent pure cyberspace. Sure, you had to be something of a bull geek to master the arcana of computing, but, significantly, you didn't have to break any laws in order to achieve your mastery. There is no question that some cyberfolk did, and do, operate on the far shores of society, but the vast majority of digital *cognoscenti* are content to swim the legal mainstream.

Eventually, the ubiquity of powerful home computers and the explosive growth of the net began to leach the *punk* out of cyberpunk. As the interface became more transparent, grandmas and Boy Scouts logged on in the millions. Your Uncle Ed built that slick Web site featuring his model train layout. And then your inbox started filling with spam promising to enlarge your penis, refill your inkjet cartridges, and cut you in on millions of dollars stashed in secret bank accounts in Nigeria. The wonders of cyberspace have become commonplace. Now it's about as exciting as TV.

So what does this have to do with *The Matrix*, the cyberpunk movie? Just this: Cyberpunk was a reaction to Cyberspace Version 1.0. Its outlaw vision of what the technology meant and of where the lifestyle might be leading was incomplete at best and dead spang wrong at worst. What seemed like radical thinking in

1983 feels a tad stodgy some twenty years later.

> Within thirty years, we will have the technological means to create superhuman intelligence. Shortly after, the human era will be ended.
> —Vernor Vinge, VISION-21 *Symposium*, 1993

Vernor Vinge is one of science fiction's seminal thinkers. Although some point to his novella, "True Names," published in 1981, as a precursor to cyberpunk, he was never issued mirror-shades or invited to join the brotherhood of alienation that was the Movement, as the cyberpunks once called themselves. Then, about ten years ago, Vinge proposed an idea that trumps cyberpunk and flings us headfirst into the future of *The Matrix*. He believes we may be headed toward a cultural singularity, which will radically change everything and everyone. The singularity is more than mere revolution; it is the *mother* of all revolutions, since Vinge posits that it is impossible to predict what people will be like on the other side of the singularity—if in fact there still are people.

Is such a thing possible? Consider that singularity-like occurrences in human history probably include the development of language, the development of agriculture, and the development of writing. Note that these singularities took place over millennia, or at least centuries. In a *slow take-off* singularity, the change is so gradual that it masks the enormity of what is happening. However, Vinge posits that we may be facing a *fast take-off*, in which everything will change in a lifetime, or even over the course of a few years.

> AI? You mean artificial intelligence?
> —Neo, *The Matrix*

There are at least three possible paths to a Vingean singularity. One requires the development of strong artificial intelligence, or AI. Strong AI apologists claim that if we can design software to emulate the functions of the brain and thereby the intellectual behavior of humans, including consciousness, then there is no essential difference between the software's intelligence and human intelligence. The argument over whether strong AI is even possible has raged for years and is far from over. Although some experts claim that we are anywhere from ten to thirty years from creating human-equivalent intelligence, no one has as yet built a robot that can safely negotiate a crosswalk, much less take over the world, like Agent Smith and his software posse. But if one is an optimist concerning strong AI, the obvious question is, "What will prevent a human equivalent intelligence from building a *greater-than*-human equivalent intelligence?" And who knows what our creation's creation will make of us, humble meat intelligences that we are. Maybe we can program in safeguards, something like Asimov's Three Laws of Robotics?

1. A robot may not injure a human being, or, through inaction, allow a human being to come to harm.

2. A robot must obey the orders given it by human beings except where such orders would conflict with the First Law.

3. A robot must protect its own existence as long as

such protection does not conflict with the First or Second Law.

That's one hell of a maybe. Remember that a not insignificant part of Isaac's prodigious output of stories was devoted to showing how easily these "laws" could be circumvented.

Tank, I need a pilot program for a military B-212 helicopter.
—Trinity, *The Matrix*

Another road to singularity is the melding of human and machine intelligence. Maybe our machines will never be smart enough to supplant us, but suppose we use them to augment our intelligence? *The Matrix* explores this path with cinematic verve, as when Tank downloads an entire arsenal of martial arts skills into Neo's brain or when Trinity becomes an expert helicopter pilot in the literal blink of an eye. But accessing knowledge bases is not exactly the same as boosting your IQ. It could be that someday the great-great-granddaughter of your Palm Pilot will live just north of your occipital lobe. Card counting for the masses! Do your taxes in your head! You too can become a rocket scientist! Or perhaps someday, as futurists Hans Moravec and Ray Kurzweil have predicted, we may discard our meat brains entirely and *become* our machines by downloading our minds into some kind of hardware/software receptacle. How likely is anyone to do this? Well, purely in terms of the pain you might experience, the proposed techniques for extracting mind from neurons seems to me to fall somewhere between the worst migraine you can imagine and decapitation. And then developing a digital container that could accept the jumble of our thoughts, feelings and aspirations is truly a daunting task. I can't help but wonder whether the transition might so fundamentally warp the downloadee that even her own mother might not recognize her.

But hey, that's what the singularity is all about.

"They gave me to the surgeons," she said. "They took my womb out, and put in brain tissue. . . . When I'm hot, I sweat perfume. I'm cleaner than a fresh needle and nothing leaves my body that you can't drink like wine or eat like candy."
—Kitsune, from Bruce Sterling's *Schismatrix*

In Sterling's prescient Shaper-Mechanist stories, humanity is diverging into two groups, those who seek to improve the human body through bio-engineering and those who augment it with prosthetics. In either case, Sterling is extrapolating what some have called our posthuman future. There are serious-minded people today who believe that they, or perhaps their children, may someday aspire to "powers and abilities far beyond those of mortal men" as the 1950s *Superman* TV show once put it. There are a number of these transhumanist groups; perhaps the best known are the Extropians. They have a variety of agendas for improving the race, although many start with eliminating death. It has been asserted that the last generation to die of old age is alive now and the first generation to live forever will soon be born. Once having achieved immortality, the transhumans hope to push on to achieve super-personhood.

Morpheus and company have super powers while in the Matrix, and of course, Neo, being The One, is the most super of them all. But the movie finesses the superman issue, since we learn that they are all too human in the real world. Thus it pulls back from exploring the third, posthuman path to the Vingean singularity.

> I hate this place. This zoo. This prison.
> —Agent Smith, *The Matrix*

I doubt that the Wachowskis set out to make a movie about Vingean singularity. Nevertheless, their singularity is unmistakable on the screen, and it is a nightmare. They posit AIs, originally created to serve us, becoming our oppressors. There is a long tradition in print science fiction of Evil Computers enslaving, or attempting to enslave, good old *homo sapiens sapiens*, from Harlan Ellison's "I Have No Mouth, and I Must Scream," to John Varley's "Press Enter" and in films from *Colossus: The Forbin Project* to *Tron*. And while we must certainly take every precaution in creating strong AI, assuming that can be accomplished, I can't help but wonder why it is that the Evil Computer seems to be the default for this extrapolation. No doubt we have much to fear from AI run amok, but is that particular prospect really *so* much more likely than one in which the AIs we design respect our needs and act to further our best interests? AI-phobia scans very much like a kind of xenophobia to me. Remember how we had to suffer through scads of silly movies about Bug-Eyed Monsters trying to have sex with babes in bikinis before we could get to more sober science fiction like *The Day the Earth Stood Still* or *Close Encounters of the Third Kind*? Isn't it the *modus operandi* of humankind to fear that which we can't understand and thereby consign it to evil?

In a movie with a wealth of memorable scenes, that which

stayed with me is the one where Agent Smith taunts Morpheus as he tortures him. Although I believe the intent here was to horrify, I found his rant oddly comforting. It pointed to an unexpected inner life on the part of our nemesis AI. If this cranky application can hate with such frothing passion, what else might it become passionate about? I'm thinking here that an intelligent creature who hates might also be capable of love. Do Agents keep virtual goldfish, run fantasy baseball leagues, or collect old Microsoft manuals in PDF format in their spare time? Do they meet in dark romantic places to swap moist code?

> Did you know that the first Matrix was designed to be a perfect human world? Where none suffered, where everyone would be happy. It was a disaster. No one would accept the program.
> —Agent Smith, *The Matrix*

What is the nature of the society portrayed in *The Matrix*? On the surface, it appears to be a monstrous dystopia, one that Neo can and must destroy—in the sequel(s)—without qualm. However, the movie stacks the deck against this world in interesting ways. For example, in a gloriously cheesy moment, we see robots intravenously pumping some black, viscous liquid into an unborn fetus while Morpheus's sonorous voice-over informs us that the liquefied dead are being fed to the living. Okay, all together now: *eewww*. And instead of creating a virtual heaven for the stacks of humans under its care, the AIs have condemned them to live in the hell that was . . . *1999!* Except it isn't quite the 1999 that we remember, but rather some discount 1999 in which clothes don't quite fit and all jobs crush men's spirits and the sky approaches "the color of television turned to a dead channel," as William Gibson once memorably wrote.

Human nature also played a role in creating this dystopia. After all, it wasn't an AI that scorched the sky and toasted the environment. Our descendants did. And for reasons that do not quite make much sense psychologically, but which seem absolutely essential to the plot, our kids rejected the AIs' offer of a virtual paradise. For some reason they apparently seem quite happy to live lives of quiet desperation in a cheapjack twentieth century— but let that go for now. These touches give the story a desperately needed moral complexity.

So if the Wachowskis have stacked the deck, what happens if we reshuffle? Can we imagine a more optimistic vision of their singularity? Sure! What if the AIs fed the humans a nice organically grown algae broth? What if, instead of rejecting the Matrix's virtual paradise, the humans had accepted it and flourished? What if they had agreed to enter the Matrix and lose their memories of the real world? Morpheus's moral crusade to wake everyone up would be at least slightly compromised, no? Instead of being a high-minded revolutionary, some might argue that he was a terrorist of the fundamentalist persuasion. After all, the AIs would be keeping the world's population healthy and happy. Can we claim to be even close to taking care of all of our brothers and sisters in this enlightened year of 2003? So who are we to judge? Admittedly, the prospect of folks living their entire lives in a benign virtual reality might disturb the sensibilities of many of us today, but I can easily imagine such objections being dismissed by our Matrixed offspring as arising from the outdated prejudices of reality snobs.

"Are You Living in a Computer Simulation?"
—Paper by Nick Bostrom, *Philosophical Quarterly*, 2003

In this wonderfully argued paper, Nick Bostrom, a research fellow at Oxford University, asks the mind-boggling question: How do we know that *we're* not in a Matrix? He wonders whether a posthuman civilization, whether it happens in 2030 or 20,030, will have the computational power to create an "ancestor simulation." He concludes that such a sim would consume only a tiny fraction of the resources of a very advanced civilization. If ancestor simulations are therefore easily accomplished, Bostrom attempts to determine whether the posthumans would be interested in creating them. The obvious answer is yes, for reasons that would also be clear to any red-blooded SF fan. They would be virtual time machines, so that the posthumans tourist could spend their weekends visiting History's Greatest Hits or escape for months or years to live the simple bucolic life of, say, 1359 or 1863. They would be laboratories where social scientists and history buffs could create alternate universes, where the Persians defeated the Greeks at Salamis or the Red Sox never traded Babe Ruth to the Yankees.

However, as Bostrom points out, the posthumans might deliberately decide not to build ancestor simulations. For instance, our hypothetical advanced culture might have some ethical objection to creating an artificial human race. If Morpheus, the reality snob, were calling the shots, I suspect this might well be the case. Or else others might object to recreating the Thirty Years War or the Holocaust, no matter what their scientific value. Then again, what if the posthumans couldn't be bothered with designing ancestor simulations? They might have better tools for analyzing history and more concentrated ways to have fun. Or they might be so far advanced over us that the whole idea of visiting an ancestor simulation would seem absurd. After all, how many of us would volunteer to live with gophers or spend a month in an ant colony?

Bostrom's provocative conclusion to his essay is that if ancestor simulations are both possible and attractive to posthuman cultures, then there is a not-insignificant chance that *we* are living in such a simulation. That's right: you, me, your mom, the guy who sold you this book, Madonna, and President Bush. Not only that, but Bostrom goes on to speculate that " . . . we would have to suspect that the posthumans running our simulation are themselves simulated beings; and their creators, in turn, may also be simulated beings. Reality may thus contain many levels."

So what do you say? Would you rather have the red pill or the blue?

You think I'm not really me, because I exist only on a neural
net? Look, the memory capacity of the human brain in one
hundred trillion neurotransmitter concentrations at
interneuronal connections. What the brain boys call synapse
strengths. That converts to about a million billion bits. My
upload was 1.12 million billion. Besides, do I sound like any
computer you've ever heard before?
—Time traveler in James Patrick Kelly's "Unique Visitors,"
Redshift, (2001)

The
Matrix
Made Me
Do It

Kevin J.
Anderson

Mine eyes have seen the glory of the burning of the school.
We have murdered every teacher, we have broken every rule.
—Twentieth-century students' rhyme

As a professional science-fiction writer, I try to watch every major new SF film in the theater. It's my job, after all. Thus, I saw *The Matrix* soon after its release in April 1999. I enjoyed its innovation, its cool story and look—a refreshing take on cyberpunk ideas the genre had been toying with for years. I liked the movie so much I went to see it again a couple of weeks later.

But the second time I felt my skin crawling. Throat dry, eyes wide. I nearly had to leave the theater. What happened?

I live in Colorado's Front Range on top of a pine-covered ridge that looks out on Pikes Peak. This part of the country is what Norman Rockwell would have painted if he'd joined the NRA. It's a bit too whitebread and a bit too conservative for a former-Californian science-fiction writer like myself, but I can think of a thousand advantages that tip the scales in its favor. Our house is south of Denver, not far from an unremarkable suburb called Littleton.

On April 20, 1999, two kids carrying enough firepower to stage their own Rambo movie put on trench coats and dark glasses, marched into Columbine High School, then opened fire. Eric Harris (18) and Dylan Klebold (17) were armed with a 9mm semi-automatic rifle, two sawed-off shotguns, a 9mm semi-automatic handgun, and ninety-six homemade bombs—not to mention massive amounts of unchanneled destruction and hatred.

Their intent was to slaughter as many of their classmates as possible. In the end, they murdered twelve students and one teacher, injured twenty-five others, and then took their own lives.

"Just like something out of *The Matrix*," the horrified commentators began saying within hours of the massacre. The comparison was obvious.

A week afterward, I sat in the theater for the second time:

Neo and Trinity don their long dark trench coats and sunglasses, then stand in a virtual armory asking for "Guns. Lots of guns." When their rescue begins, Neo walks into the building slowly, doesn't say a word as he sets off the metal detector. Just doing his job, a bored guard asks him to remove any metal objects. Neo opens his trench coat and proudly shows off his weapons. He punches the guard, draws his guns, and immediately blows away another guard who's just reading a newspaper. He shoots several more oblivious, chatting guards. One of them survives, calls desperately for backup, then Trinity walks in (again without saying a word) and calmly shoots him a dozen times. Tossing empties, the two strut forward while drawing even more firearms.

When the backup army arrives, all hell breaks loose with more gunfire and a higher body count than even the most stringent conservative media watchdog groups could tally. Trinity sneaks up behind a soldier, grabs his gun, and shoots him in the back. Later, after *everyone* has been slaughtered, they pick up their duffel bag and walk to the elevator.

Reminder: These are our heroes. At least, Eric Harris and Dylan Klebold must have seen them as heroes.

Take the Blue Pill, Stay in the Dream . . .

The media blamed the parents for being in denial or just plain oblivious because they had not noticed how twisted and sick their kids were. (Come on, the two shooters were seventeen and eighteen years old—who among us, at that age, hadn't figured out how to fool our parents?) By all accounts, the elder Klebolds and Harrises are decent, normal people. Sue Klebold worked at providing accessibility for disabled students at the State Consortium of Community Colleges; her husband Tom operated a mortgage management business. Wayne Harris was a retired Air Force transport pilot, his wife Kathy was a caterer. Eric Harris himself was even a former Boy Scout and Little Leaguer.

Then the ever-shifting armies of "experts" blamed Hitler, drugs, the NRA, bullies at school, the public school system in general, even the whole of Goth culture. Some blamed the massacre on the abolition of school prayer, others on the lack of school uniforms. Jerry Falwell suggested that the killers were gay.

Only a day after the shootings, Colorado Governor Bill Owens pronounced that Harris and Klebold did not "have the same moral background as the rest of us." The conservative publication *The New American* said that Klebold and Harris were "immersed in a grotesque youth subculture," and went on to say,

"They are the products of the self-indulgent, pagan gospel of 'sex, drugs, and rock'n'roll'," calling them "devotees of the hideous, Satanic, 'Goth rocker' Marilyn Manson and the gruesome German bands Rammstein and KMFDM." Not long after the massacre, because of the uproar and the finger of blame, Marilyn Manson was forced to cancel the rest of his concert tour.

And let's not forget video games. Doom was a particular scapegoat for its violence and shoot-em-up focus. Duke Nukem, Quake II, and Grand Theft Auto were also identified as factors that supposedly incited the two young gunmen into their orgasm of violence. A friend and fellow member of the Trench Coat Mafia in Littleton claims their group played role-playing games, including Dungeons and Dragons (which, in the words of the UK's *Guardian*, is "a drama involving apocalyptic fantasies from medieval times").

Hollywood's Violent Appetite

The BBC News, in a story titled "Hollywood's Violent Appetite," said, "Politicians, religious leaders, and parents pounced on the American entertainment industry and pronounced its violent films, TV shows and video games were largely to blame for the acts of the Colorado teen killers."

When the finger was pointed at the Leonardo DiCaprio film *The Basketball Diaries*, with its dream-sequence of a student shooting up his school, MGM promptly recalled all videos of the film. Then *Heathers* was targeted, as was *Scream*, and any number of action or horror movies. But *The Matrix* was a particular favorite.

One rather vehement pundit, Michael A. Hoffman II,

ranted that *The Matrix* contained occult teachings. "They want to make bushels of money and program the kids to violence and terrorism; and to make this more palateable to community standards, the makers of the film have thrown in some fortune cookie philosophy to redeem it from being just two and a half hours of the pornography of violence."

In a speech given less than a week after the Columbine shootings, Hillary Clinton said:

"When our culture romanticizes and glorifies violence on TV, in the movies, on the Internet, in songs, and when there are video games that you win based on how many people you kill, then I think the evidence is absolutely clear—our children have become desensitized to violence and lose their empathy for fellow human beings. Studies show what many of us have believed, that such exposure causes more aggression and anti-social behavior. So, today, we must fully acknowledge, once and for all, that America's culture of violence is having a profound effect on our children, and we must resolve to do what we can to change that culture."

Mrs. Clinton did not cite any specific study, but it makes perfect, logical sense. How could the answer be anything different?

Now Take the Red Pill, See the Reality . . .

In the fifteenth century, Leonardo da Vinci predicted that a grape would fall at the same speed as a cannonball, since both were accelerated equally by gravity. This was, of course, absurd because anyone with common sense "knew" that a heavy cannonball would fall faster than a little grape. Nobody bothered to test it, until da Vinci proved his assertion through experiment after experiment.

Well, here are some statistics that might not make sense to those who have already made up their minds, but nevertheless they are hard facts (from the U.S. Department of Justice, the National Center for Juvenile Justice, the FBI, crime.org, poynter.org, slashdot.org, and Blues News):

In 1994, the ultraviolent video game Doom was released. The same year produced gore-heavy movies such as *Natural Born Killers and Pulp Fiction*, as well as the violent action films *Timecop* and *True Lies*. The following year saw the release of *The Basketball Diaries, Se7en, Braveheart*, and *Die Hard 3*.

As a baseline, in the year following the introduction of Doom, there were 2,053 kids under the age of 18 who committed murder.

In 1996 the violent gaming industry released Doom II, Duke Nukem 3D, and Quake. The movie theaters showed us *Scream, Sling Blade, Crow II*, and *Broken Arrow*.

So, with impressionable teenagers bombarded with such violent images for two years now, it's no wonder that the total number of murderers under the age of 18—uh, *dropped* to 1,683, a decrease of 22 percent from the previous year.

In 1997, the even-more-violent Quake II was released (and immediately banned in some countries). Super-gory films such as *Starship Troopers, Con Air, Scream 2*, and *Face/Off* topped the charts.

And the underage murderers dropped by another 13 percent from the previous year, down to 1,457.

1998 ushered in Grand Theft Auto, probably the most reprehensible of violent videogames. The year's list of bloody movies includes a remake of *Psycho*, as well as *Saving Private Ryan, Blade, American History X, Lethal Weapon 4, Ronin*, and *Urban Legend*.

Against all dearly held preconceptions, the number of child murderers fell once more.

In fact, from the release of Doom (1994) to the release of *The Matrix* (1999), the number of all victims of violent crimes fell from 51.2 per thousand to 32.1, dropping steadily each year, for a decrease of 37 percent. The total number of killers under 18—supposedly the age group targeted and influenced by all this violence—dropped by an astounding 46 percent.

Does that make sense? Maybe the kids are blowing off steam with the games and diminishing innate violent tendencies. Maybe they're just too busy playing video games to run around causing pandemonium in the real world. I'm not going to attempt to analyze it. However, real numbers don't support the assertions that watching violent movies like *The Matrix* and playing video games like Doom provokes our impressionable youth into violent acts.

The Federal Trade Commission issued a report, requested by President Clinton after the Columbine massacre, which concluded (to their surprise, apparently) that "Scholars and observers generally have agreed that exposure to violence in the entertainment media alone does not cause a child to commit a violent act and that it is not the sole, or even necessarily the most important, factor contributing to youth aggression, anti-social attitudes and violence."

Inspired by a Hollywood Story

The Matrix is certainly not the first film to be blamed for inspiring mayhem. As of 1989, a columnist in the Louisville Courier-Journal cited thirty-five Russian roulette deaths directly inspired by the Academy Award–winning film, *The Deer Hunter*.

In the afterword to his book *Danse Macabre*, Stephen King

lists numerous examples of crimes alleged to have been inspired by his horror novels. Even though he turned the responsibility right back onto the perpetrators, he still felt enough uneasiness after the Columbine shootings to pull his early novel *Rage* (the story of an angry gun-toting high school student) from the shelves.

Kevin Williamson, creator of the *Scream* films, said in an interview, "My favorite line in the movie is when Sydney says to the killer, 'You sick fuck, you've seen too many horror movies.' And the killer says, 'Don't blame the movies, Sydney. Movies don't create psychos. Movies just make psychos more creative.' That sums it up in a nutshell."

Wes Craven, frequently under fire for his *Nightmare on Elm Street* movies, says he could conceive of a copycat killing where a killer "who is already completely nuts" might use a movie as his format or pattern for a murder. "But I think that person is going to kill anyway. I think art is more important than worrying about that." Craven suggests that cracking down on any single instance of something causing a death would require the elimination of 80 percent of the things in our society.

Surely there will be any number of hotshot (and incompetent) amateurs who see the movie *Blue Crush* and get themselves killed doing dangerous surfing stunts. How many young men watched *The Fast and the Furious* and took up a wild street-racing career, only to—literally—crash and burn? Are those films *responsible* for foolish behavior?

As for *The Matrix*, yeah I have a few bones to pick with the presentation of the story and the subtext. The film establishes early on, "If you're killed in the Matrix, you die here," yet our heroes open fire on absolutely everyone in sight, without remorse.

Sure, these dupes might have complicated Neo's intended rescue of Morpheus, and they (like any human) could have been subsumed by an evil Agent . . . but after making a point that these are innocent human beings living out their lives in a simulated dream reality, one would hope that any hero worth the audience's respect would have showed at least a *glimmer* of guilt or sadness about all the slaughtered bystanders. Couldn't they have at least frowned once or twice?

However, that is an artistic choice made by the writers of the movie. Maybe it bothers me; maybe I disagree with the tactic. But if I have a different message, I can write my own story. Does that mean the Wachowski brothers are *responsible* for setting off Harris and Klebold?

Try this:

• A man sees a romantic movie that induces him to propose to his girlfriend. By the same reasoning that *The Matrix* is responsible for the Columbine shootings, then *Sleepless in Seattle* is "responsible" for the marriage, even if it ultimately ends in divorce.

• My dad tells the story of when he was a child at home recuperating from an appendectomy. He listened to Abbot and Costello on the radio and laughed so hard that he nearly had to be rushed back to the hospital for a hemorrhage. Obviously, then, Abbot and Costello were "responsible" for my father's surgical complications. Right?

• A TV commercial tells me to sign up for a credit card. If I can't pay my bills because I overcharged my account, then the credit card company is "responsible" for my bankruptcy because they "made" me sign up for the card.

• A man goes for a hike in the mountains. He leaves the well-marked trail and walks off a cliff. Is it the fault of the National Park Service for "luring" him into a dangerous situation?

• Almost two years to the day after the Columbine shootings, the families of several victims filed a lawsuit against Nintendo, Sony, Sega, id Software, and AOL/Time Warner. The lawsuit reads, "Absent the combination of extremely violent video games and these boys' incredibly deep involvement, use of and addition to these games and the boys' basic personalities, these murders and this massacre would not have occurred." (Note that, though Harris was eighteen and Klebold seventeen, the lawsuit patronizingly keeps referring to them as mere "boys." In 2001 a twelve-year-old was tried

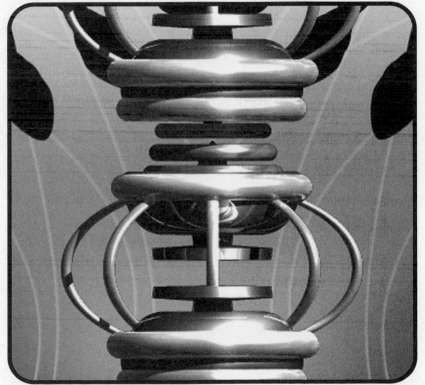

as an adult, convicted, and sentenced to life in prison for killing a five-year-old girl. In September 2002, two Florida brothers aged thirteen and fourteen were tried as adults and convicted of killing their father. Without a doubt, Klebold and Harris would have been considered adults, not "boys," if there had been a trial.)

Live Responsibly

The truth is, we are all affected by the environment around us, the things we see, hear, do, and think about. We have to sort it out, process it, and react appropriately. Music, books, films, conversations, Dear John letters, bad grades, the store being out of our preferred brand of soda pop—everything influences our lives, our actions, our moods. One would have to spend every day in a sensory-deprivation tank to avoid it.

Movies are *supposed* to evoke some kind of emotional reaction from the audience, whether it's fright or the warm-fuzzies, laughter or romantic feelings, excitement or disgust. Any film that makes no impact whatsoever on the viewer is an abysmal failure on the most fundamental level. Shall we castrate all films, removing any content that might provoke a visceral response?

Of course you'll get worked up when watching a horrific movie like *Silence of the Lambs.*

Of course you'll feel the adrenaline pumping when watching a thriller like *Die Hard.*

Of course you'll laugh when watching a comedy like *Dumb and Dumber.*

Of course you'll feel mushy and romantic when watching a heart-warmer like *Sleepless in Seattle.*

But if you do something wildly inappropriate after viewing one of these films, don't blame everyone else for your own actions. We are proud to live in a free society, but freedom also carries individual responsibility.

After an analysis of the Columbine shootout was posted on the irreverent Web site dietcrack.com, they added a disclaimer that the article was not meant to encourage anyone to take any of the actions they described. "In fact, it means to discourage them. Please do not be dumb enough to open fire on your classmates or anyone for that matter. If you do, don't blame me or Dietcrack; we are not at fault, you are."

Modern society continues to deny individual responsibility. If the coffee's hot, blame MacDonalds. If you're getting obese from eating super-mega-glutton sized meals, blame the fast food industry, rather than your own lack of self-control. May as well say that the woman wearing a sexy outfit "forced" you to rape her—or that the color red drives you to rage, therefore anyone who grows Washington Delicious apples is at fault if *you* do something crazy.

It wasn't *The Matrix* that incited the Columbine massacre. It wasn't Marilyn Manson or KMFDM, not Doom or Quake II, not Hitler's birthday or oblivious parents or weak gun-control laws or Goth culture or repressed homosexuality or satanism.

It was the fault of Dylan Klebold and Eric Harris, two deeply sick and disturbed individuals, who (according to their own videotaped goodbyes) *knew* that their actions were wrong and yet committed the crimes anyway. They are responsible for their own behavior, and they have paid the ultimate price.

I'm sure Hollywood's already making a movie about it.

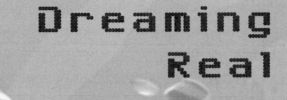

Dreaming Real

Rick Berry

Row, row, row your boat . . . life is but a dream.
—children's song

We are such stuff as dreams are made on,
and our little life is rounded with a sleep.
—Shakespeare, *The Tempest*

The sage Chuang-tzu, after dreaming he was a butterfly,
wondered whether he'd been a man dreaming, or
might now be a butterfly dreaming it was a man.

The film, *The Matrix*, is a wonderful evocation of cyberspace as a kind of Siberian tiger trap for the human race. It doesn't solve anything but it lofts some interesting questions: What is freedom? What is illusion? What is freedom in illusion? Are we free without illusion? And, are we ever not living in a dream?

The Matrix represents a cyberspace (worlds within worlds) where technology has brought us within a hair's breadth of making all our dreams come true. But it's this very situation that creates the questions about what is true and what is dream. What is cyberspace?

I've tried my hand at depicting cyberspace before, in the climax sequence to William Gibson's *Johnny Mnemonic* (Darrel Anderson, Gene Bodio, and I collaborated to do the film treatment, design and animation of the CGI climax of the film; other CGI sequences were handled by Sony ImageWorks). We were at

pains to show that, one, the rules in cyberspace were very different (from say, basic laws of physics like gravity, lightspeed, etc.)
and that, two, if one changed a representation in cyberspace, one
changed the code or recoded the meaning of the circumstance.

Here's an example of what I mean: A long time ago in computer years ('87 or '88) while giving Jaron Lanier a lift to the airport
(founder of VPL; early glove and goggles cybernaut and inventor;
coiner of "avatar" for a person's 3D presence in cyberspace) and
among many things, we talked about composing music in cyberspace. While jacked-in, a score of music could be floating and playing before your eyes. Also available is a floating cyber keyboard; play
the keyboard and watch and hear the score change, or simply "grab"
the notes and move them around for effect. Lanier has actually done
this. This is one of the earliest examples of changing representations
and creating new code. Gamers could imagine myriad others.

When Anderson and I wrote our film treatment for the
"Well Sequence" in *Johnny Mnemonic*, we started out with an
instant no-holds-barred, "I don't think we're in Kansas anymore,"
approach. This may have been the only way to go; the film climax
only gave us two minutes to cinematically be in cyberspace, and
we had a lot of weirdness to convey. We wanted viewers to get
from the outset that the protagonist, Johnny Mnemonic (Keanu
Reeves) had left the "meat" world and had entered cyberspace as
an avatar. As such he was now clearly a representation, a visual
manifestation of sentient code.

To make this clear, we wanted the audience to recognize
Reeves's entity in cyberspace but recognize immediately that he
was very different. We designed an "Origami Johnny" made of
folded charcoal paper slivers. For Johnny's head we made a glass

cylinder lit from within, on the inside of which Keanu Reeves's head was projected; if he turned his head, his face merely tracked the inside of the transparent tube à la a lighthouse beacon.

In this cyber reality, just as in the Matrix, one could also die from disintegration of your coded representation: Destroy the Cyber-Johnny avatar, you kill meat Johnny, jacked-in on the real world side.

There's a data courier chip gone bad in Johnny's head. Within this chip is the cure data for a worldwide epidemic. However, this contraband information is owned by the evil Pharmakom drugs giant. Along with the chip data is a representation of the Pharmakom Data Well and a sectioned representation of Johnny's own brain. It's a "no-no" place to go. Fantastically, Gibson has Johnny hacking his own head! God bless William Gibson. I'll never get over his sense of irony and quirk. Johnny is outside and inside and outside and inside cyberspace, like some bizarre arrangement of Chinese nested tables.

To visually represent Johnny's triumph over the guardian chip, we had Johnny employ a strategy that I think is emblematic of "alter the code, you alter the world." Just before Johnny faces off with the bad processor, he doubles himself below the smoked mirror plain of their high noon shoot out. The chip's defenses repeatedly attack the Origami Johnny, apparently shredding him, yet with strange resilience he would reform over and over again. Johnny's doubled information, stationary, below mirror plane, served as a data redoubt for his sense of self hood. Manipulate the code, you change the rules.

Okay.

This is most of what we could possibly relay in the two-to-three minutes of time allowed us. (By the way, for those of you who saw the film, the ridiculous imposition of the tricycle and bad chopping of the well sequence, not to mention horrible guitar work, had nothing to do with us.) Back then, CGI work was infinitely onerous, expensive and supposed require teams larger than three-and-some-fraction art dudes. We borrowed studio pals for ancillary lo-tech services, like hoisting my six-foot, two-hundred-pound frame in the air while I flailed around in cyberspace as Keanu Reeves's cyber-stunt double; my limbs and other parts festooned with sensors whilst a twelve inch square magnetic cube, disarmingly named Flock-of-Birds, quivered over the ethernet the precise position of my discomfiture; putting the sweat, grunt, and glamour into high tech. I won't discuss the smelly Asian Sharpeis dancing and barking around us as we struggled in Bodio's basement. We were a laughably small team.

My, how times have changed.

Much of *The Matrix* is dedicated to this one concept: recoding your existence and what subtends this possibility. I think it's worth a film-length effort. And I think they did it well.

And did they ever do it differently.

They worked these concepts from the opposite direction. Instead of an apparent and obvious Oz of a cyberspace, this world is a mind-numbing replication of human culture's past, and the moviegoer's present, warts and all. In this tableau we must discover the remarkable as making counterfeit the accepted and mundane. A spooky kind of misdirection. Here, the wrong note is the right note. The hero of *The Matrix* is understandably confused. Even though he senses that the world falls short somehow, it is, has been, his complete framework and cultural formation for his mind.

It's a serious problem of mind and sanity. It's frankly amazing that our hero (Keanu Reeves again) does come into any
acceptance of this new hierarchical reality. And the filmmakers
don't shortchange the difficulty here. Cypher, the informant and
traitor, never really accepts the change as for the better; he believes
it, but would just as soon forget it. Our hero, Neo, has been
ripped late in life from the mechanical womb in which he dreams
cyberdreams. (In addition to describing a grid/lattice of computer-
ized matrices, the word matrix has a Latin root derivation meaning
"mother.") What Gibson called "a shared consensual hallucination"
now commonly called by his term, "cyberspace," is here called "the
Matrix." Only these humans did not consent . . . or did they?

Strangely, that's never really convincingly cleared up and Cypher's willingness to go back, to be reinserted into the Matrix, makes it even less certain.

To what degree is your "mind" a social construction? You think in a language you didn't invent. Language is a product of culture. How much more do you owe to the cultural inculcation of your upbringing for your very consciousness? And when Neo finds out that what has thus far been his model for existence is in fact a supplied and false one, his stomach revolts its contents to the floor.

I buy that.

The Matrix, in creating a faithful replication of our accepted "real" world, requires that natural physical laws become the coded rules. What goes up must come down, momentum and inertia, especially as applied to fight scenes and bullets, predicts injury and lethal impacts. All things Newtonian are supposed to govern not only the expectations of the dreaming denizens of the Matrix, it acts as concretely as death. Don't try and break these rules or you'll die. That's the info in your construct, that's your model, that's your consciousness, that's your coding.

There are code-spawned agents in the Matrix. An Agent is different than an avatar (a cyber representation carrying the consciousness of a human being). An Agent presents itself as ably as an avatar but has no "meat" existence. It's totally a creature of code and, in this case, artificial intelligence. Oddly, after the astonishingly ruthless human apostate, Cypher, my favorite character is one such AI, the agent Mr. Smith. Even given his all-too-human protests, it's actually hard to imagine Mr. Smith as existing anywhere else but the human dreamworld of the Matrix. And I do believe the filmmakers knew that their most human character after Cypher was the non-human, Mr. Smith. Lovely.

Here we have another example of culturally generated mind. Mr. Smith is becoming human against his will (even as Neo is becoming less and less human). Mr. Smith is showing passionate hatred and, what is more, demonstrable intuition. One can imagine him the arch hunter of these rogue Zion hackers because he's more successfully modeling them than his peers. This is perhaps why he anticipates Neo's destination in the end sequence, just in time to murder him; it's this superior ability to model his human prey's behavior . . . but there's a trade-off. To do this, Mr. Smith must think more and more like a human being and he fears being mired forever in their world.

Mr. Smith and Neo really have shared goals: They're both desperate to transcend this stagnant bug-in-amber dream that has defined their lives. (While Mr. Smith, presumably by code design, is gifted with some hat-tricks that supersede the Newtonian representations that rule the Matrix, he is by and large constrained to acting within the bounds of the Matrix world. This ultimately means that Neo can turn the tables. Adequately manipulate his representation and you corrupt his code).

Okay. Enough about how cyberspace works.

Let's get messy and go after meaning.

Are the filmmakers just exploiting all this cool stuff to produce an amusement ride filled with miraculous comic book tricks? Yes and no.

Some have said of the movie that it was the "perfect comic book" and admired it for it's consistency of effort whilst lowering their expectations. I happen to love comics and have rather high expectations of that technically very difficult artform. So if the film was a perfect comic book then it was a hell of a good pic. Technically.

Beyond the technically superb, is it good the rest of the way? How important is the story?

I suppose that it's the "superhero" aspect of the film that gets it damned with faint praise. Is Neo our new Adam? What kind of content is this? Are we to take some puerile longing to wear all black, be cool and misunderstood in our neighborhood, be the magic stranger, perhaps "The One," as any kind of subject above mere adolescent wish fulfillment? Well, yes, maybe.

Superheroes are a ready component of myth encoding. This Matrix, this dreamworld is a place of miracles in such a way as we no longer believe our own to be. One can believe things will happen here as only a child can any longer believe of our own world (and they will soon lose that). Just think it and it could happen. Discover the right algorithm and it will be.

The Word made Cyberflesh.

Wow.

I'm not really putting the corporeal world down as unmiraculous, but parameters change all the time. It's hard to keep up. Where's the magic in the common man's life? The moon shot is, well, on the moon. The superstars weep incoherently over Oscar, have a personal in with the Almighty after winning the pro ballgame, buy their way into high office . . . but not you . . . nor anyone you know. . . .

Gamers could tell you about a different world, one of immediate gratification. One they're trying to get closer to all the time. I mean literally. Feedback devices that impart a realtime sensation of cyberspace, i.e. stick resistance in flight simulation, haptics, the science of digital touch, vision of course . . . how long before the "jacked in" phase posed by Gibson, and here so graphically made real by *The Matrix*?

What is this miracle space to us once we're "there"? Where have we heard about miracles like this before? In our dreams, we fly. In our religions, we speak with the divine. With our drugs, we . . . don't grow up. Something in us doesn't want to. Perhaps it is some kind of atavism that refuses to let us grow all the way up; you're everything you ever were, and we return over and over again. We don't want to leave our dream-believing childlike selves behind.

Oh, it's all right that we observe with satisfaction the achievements of humankind: The great things done in concert . . . the erection of skyscrapers, the feeding of millions, the wiping out of an indigenous populace . . . require a lot of people pulling together. And every one of those people has a little share in the miracle pie. Fine. I guess.

But again, what about the individual personal miraculous life you believed in with all your little mystical heart? Where is that dreamworld?

It's being made. Now. Cyberspace. It's the frontier that appears beneath your feet with each step you take. In the image of the Maker you go. Artists, scientists, seekers, the Dream is rolling through them and out of them. Picking them up like little broadcast nodes and making its presence felt.

I read *Neuromancer* by Bill Gibson, before I did its cover in '84, and I was astonished. And not the least by the incredible resonance between his ideas and ones I thought "belonged" to me and a very few other people I knew. But we didn't know Gibson.

He didn't know us. It's unlikely we shared a causal link. What gives?

Over the years I've had to revise my notions of where I "get" my ideas. Or is it that they get me? I think that ideas are huge things; bigger than me, bigger than Gibson; but not necessarily bigger than cyberspace. Ideas move like waves through the populace and the reason I didn't see the causal link between myself and Gibson is that my tiny perspective didn't permit me to see anything so huge as the ocean swell of dream that carried Gibson, me and others forward to this new creative curve. I don't much care about being a solo artist with original ideas. I care about being awake. Awake to Dream. I believe we collaborate with the idea wave; with past, present and future dreams. Our buoyancy, our drifting consciousness has as much to do with our "having ideas" as anything. Exploring and creating with others throws a bigger net over the wave.

Cyberspace is a good place for big ideas. Cyberspace may be a good place to get religion, search for the divine, find your dream house. In this case, cyberspace becomes not a stagnant holding pattern for the soporific MTV generation, but the real estate of Future. The new Adams and Eves may be Joe and Josephine Blow finding that Idea has found them. Surfing that huge wave of Dream.

Now, Dream has begun to coalesce into a place, pool inside technology, press out new infrastructure, grow the Web, and make increasingly concrete outcomes for miraculous being in Joe Blow's life.

Outside the Matrix, Neo is just an ordinary, physically atrophied human being; inside the Matrix he is "The One." Can the *Matrix* filmmakers possibly be saying that here's as good a place as any to make a divine connection?

Mythic personages abound in this cyberspace (as indeed the arrival of godhead is a shocking revelation in Gibson's beautiful first novel *Neuromancer*, followed by voodoo divinities in *Count Zero*). "The One" is a new Adam, a messiah . . . a superhero. He's come to show the way to the last human city, Zion. His "John the Baptist" is named after the Greek mythological divinity Morpheus, or "Sleep," the gatekeeper to dreams. There's also the femme fatale with the loaded name, Trinity, who resurrects her murdered lover with a kiss. Their rebel ship is named *Nebuchadnezzar*.

But is the Matrix just a gamer's shot at being more than he can ever hope to be in the corporeal world? By virtue of its special properties as a space defined by rational coding, is it just that a gifted hacker savant is able to rewrite the rules; via some super gestalt, is it that he's able to control and shift its representations to his advantage? Or is there some deeper voodoo, some hyper sympathetic magic putting the dreamers in touch with a larger plan subtending existence?

Within the Matrix, Neo is taken by Morpheus to meet the Oracle. It's a wonderful bit and a disturbing one. This Oracle is seeing things atemporally. This isn't a bending or breaking of Newtonian rules; here we're going quantum and relativistic at once. What code/representation/metaphor explains this? We're spookily closer to the divine here than anywhere else in the story.

Perhaps some undisclosed part of the Matrix is modeling heaven, the levels of hell, angels, devils, and gods. How closely can you model a reality before it begins to merge identities with the thing being modeled? Like entangled pairs in quantum physics. Instant teleportation of behaviors over any distance, because the subject photons share an identity.

We don't know that the Oracle has any corporeal existence; Morpheus tells Neo that this middle-aged matron is very old, that she's been with the resistance since the beginning. She tells Neo that he's got a good soul. We really aren't in Kansas for sure now.

The Oracle takes us outside what we structurally understand about the two apparent realities in the film. She's not operating in a normal spacetime continuum. Now things get really big.

Is this all just too far out? The directors, the Wachowski Brothers, are just having fun, right? I'm sure they are. But it's not too far out. It also makes me wonder if we're seeing just how far this could really go. How about this: Once in the Matrix, how is it you know that you've left? I mean, "Morpheus?" Really. Perhaps everybody is still dreaming. The plane the *Nebuchadnezzar* exists on, just another level of the Matrix. Why not? What is there to tell you that you aren't in just another dream reality subtended by yet a deeper reality? One turning around an entirely different axis? (This at least would give some latitude for the origins of the Oracle's prowess and vision). With "Sleep" as your guide, just where is the rooster crowing? Wake up, you're asleep.

In fact, I'm sure the filmmakers would rather enjoy it if you wondered about your own reality. "How much of this is illusion that I'm living?" In cyberspace, old, old questions and mystical pursuits suddenly take on a fresh coat of digital paint.

The Hindus have a multi-leveled, multiple reality structure that has at its base Vishnu the Dreamer. Our reality is Vishnu's dream; he's dreaming us. He also dreams himself much like you can appear in your own dreams. He can move atemporally and instantly over any distance in this dream.

The denizens of the world can dream of Vishnu, worship him, model him in their minds. The Dream can dream the Dreamer. Confusing?

The relation of cyberspace to our own corporeality provides a compelling metaphor: Forget about the linear pursuit of ultimates and hierarchies. Quit even looking for the center of things. Maybe reality is holographic in nature and every single little connection in the matrix of existence carries an image of the whole. Perhaps we cannot see the end of this vast rolling cosmos, but maybe we can see into ourselves and come to an understanding; look at the geometry of internal and nearby relationships and try and draw some conclusions about the way of the world(s).

We may never be really certain about finding an ultimate "bottom" or "top" in the hierarchies of existence. But I'm not sure that we can't, by such relativistic contemplations, seek something akin to wisdom about such things; pierce the multilayered veil as it were and if not know the bottom or top of things, know about the dimension of wonder and perceive into the nature of existence.

We are on the astounding verge of our own perceptions. A bright edge that meltingly folds forward into the dark, creating the frontier as we go. A new wave of dreamspace seems to await our waking brains. Perhaps it's mind itself, dreaming.

Vishnu must have rolled over in his sleep and hit "enter."

About the Authors

PAT CADIGAN, acclaimed by the *London Guardian* as "the Queen of Cyberpunk," is the author of four novels—*Mindplayers, Synners, Fools,* and *Tea from an Empty Cup*—and three short story collections: *Patterns, Home by the Sea,* and *Dirty Work.* Some of her short stories have also appeared in *Letters from Home,* alongside work by Karen Joy Fowler and Pat Murphy. She continues to publish short fiction, with recent stories in *New Worlds, Dark Terrors 3, Disco 2000,* and the Christmas 2001 issue of *Interzone.* She was an editor and writer for Hallmark Cards in Kansas City for ten years before embarking on her career as a fiction writer in 1987. Since that time her Hugo and Nebula Award–nominated short stories have appeared in such magazines as *Omni, The Magazine of Fantasy and Science Fiction,* and *Asimov's Science Fiction* magazine, as well as numerous anthologies. She moved to England in 1996, and now lives in North London with her husband, Chris Fowler, and their cat, Calgary.

BRUCE STERLING, author, journalist, editor, and critic, has written eight science fiction novels and three short story collections. He edited the anthology *Mirrorshades,* the definitive anthology of the cyberpunk movement. He also wrote the nonfiction book *The Hacker Crackdown: Law and Disorder on the Electronic Frontier* (1992) available electronically on the Internet. He has written regular columns on popular science and literary criticism for *The Magazine of Fantasy and Science Fiction, Interzone,* and *Science Fiction Eye.* He also writes a Web log and runs a Web site and Internet mailing list on the topic of environmental activism and postindustrial design. He lives in Austin, Texas, with his wife and two daughters.

STEPHEN BAXTER's science-fiction novels have been published in the United Kingdom, the U.S., and in many other countries including Germany, Japan, and France. His books have won several awards, including the Philip K. Dick Award, the John Campbell Memorial Award, the British Science Fiction Association Award, the Kurd Lasswitz Award (Germany), and the Seiun Award (Japan), and have been nominated for several others, including the Arthur C. Clarke Award, the Hugo Award, and the Locus Award. Over one hundred of his SF short stories have been published, several of which have won prizes. His most recent book is a full-length novel, *Evolution,* published by Gollancz in November 2002. His novel *Timelike Infinity* and short story "Pilot" are both under development for feature films. Baxter's TV and movie work also includes development work on the BBC's *Invasion: Earth* and the script for Episode 3 of *Space Island One,* broadcast on Sky One in January 1998. His novel *Voyage* was dramatized by Audio Movies for BBC Radio in 1999.

JOHN SHIRLEY is the author of many novels, collections of stories including *Black Butterflies* (winner of the Bram Stoker Award and chosen for the *Publishers Weekly* list of year's best books), *Demons, And the Angel with Television Eyes, Eclipse,* and *City Come A Walkin'.* He was coscreenwriter of *The Crow* and has written for television and film extensively. The authorized Web site is www.darkecho.com/johnshirley. He lives in the San Francisco Bay area.

DARREL ANDERSON, a digital-art pioneer, emerged from the underground comix scene to create one of the earliest and longest running art Web sites, braid.com. With members of the BRAID collective and PCA Graphics, he created the animated CGI climax of the 1995 film *Johnny Mnemonic.* The Science Fiction Channel Web site features forty-eight of his images, and he is profiled in *Fantasy Art of the New Millennium II* by Dick Jude. His artwork has received top honors in numerous international award competitions, including Pixar's call for images and MacWorld's Macintosh Masters competition. Anderson actually works either side of the screen, as both programmer and artist. One of his latest developments, GroBoto, is an interactive art tool intended to allow children to explore their creativity, and artists to further theirs. Anderson's work can be seen and sampled at: braid.com

PAUL DI FILIPPO just celebrated his twentieth year as a freelance writer by publishing four books in 2002. His story "Karuna, Inc." was nominated for a World Fantasy Award. In 1994 he won the British Science Fiction Award. His previous novels include *Ciphers* (1991), *Lost Pages* (1998), and *Joe's Liver* (2000). He lives in Providence, Rhode Island, with his mate of twenty-seven years, Deborah Newton, a cocker spaniel named Ginger, and two cats, Mab and Penny Century.

KATHLEEN ANN GOONAN's latest novel, *Light Music* (HarperCollins/Eos, May 2002), completes her Nanotech Quartet, and was received with excellent reviews. The first book of the quartet, *Queen City Jazz,* was a *New York Times*

Notable Book; the third, *Crescent City Rhapsody*, was a Nebula finalist. Her unique melding of literature, science fiction, and music has been noted in *Scientific American*, along with the work of Greg Bear and Neal Stephenson, as being seminal contributions to nanotech science fiction. She has published over twenty short stories in various venues, and her novels and short stories have been published in France, Germany, Italy, Spain, Poland, Russia, and the United Kingdom. Her Web page is www.goonan.com.

MIKE RESNICK is the author of more than forty science fiction novels, twelve collections, two screenplays, and over 140 short stories. He has also edited thirty anthologies. He has won four Hugos and a Nebula, plus major and minor awards in the U.S., France, Japan, Spain, Poland, and Croatia. His passions are science fiction, Africa, horse racing, and musical theater.

WALTER JON WILLIAMS is a screenwriter, the author of *The Praxis* and the cyberpunk classic *Hardwired,* and a fourth-degree black belt in Kenpo. He has also authored another fourteen science-fiction novels and one short-story collection, as well as the ongoing licensed series *Star Wars: The New Jedi Order*.

DEAN MOTTER, illustrator, designer, writer, and editor, is a city boy by nature, so it is no surprise that architecture and urban life often figures prominently in his work. His two critically acclaimed Vertigo Comics miniseries, *Terminal City* and *Terminal City: Aerial Graffiti*, were nominated for a number of comics industry Eisner and Kurtzman Awards in 1997 and 1998. Currently he continues to labor happily in the comic book mines, most recently with the highly acclaimed graphic novel, *Batman: Nine Lives,* and is writing and illustrating Image Comics' *Electropolis*—yet another return to yesterday's future. Motter is perhaps best known as the creator of the influential 1980s comic book sensation *Mister X*.

IAN WATSON graduated from Oxford University with a first class honors degree in English language and literature, completed a research degree in nineteenth-century English and French literature, then lectured in universities in Dar es Salaam and Tokyo and taught futures studies at Birmingham (UK) Art and Design Centre before becoming a full-time SF author in 1976. His first novel, *The Embedding* (1973), won joint second prize in the John W. Campbell Memorial Award and, in French translation, the Prix Apollo. His most recent novel, *Mockymen*, appeared in 2003 from Golden Gryphon Press, which published his ninth story collection, *The Great Escape*, in 2002 to considerable critical acclaim. His first book of poetry, *The Lexicographer's Love Song*, appeared from DNA Publications in 2001. From 1990 to 1991 he worked with Stanley Kubrick on story development for what became Steven Spielberg's *A.I. Artificial Intelligence*, for which he has screen credit for screen story. He lives in rural England with a black cat.

JOE HALDEMAN is best known for *The Forever War*, a novel that won the Hugo, Nebula, and Ditmar Awards, and is now considered a classic of science fiction. His latest novels are *The Coming* and *Guardian* (December 2002). He has won five Nebulas and four Hugo Awards. His twenty novels, three story collections, six anthologies, and one poetry collection have appeared in eighteen languages. Haldeman's mainstream novels *War Year* and *1968* are based on his experience as a combat engineer in the Central Highlands of Vietnam. He teaches writing at Massachusetts Institute of Technology one semester a year, is an avid amateur astronomer, paints watercolors, and plays the guitar. His Web site is home.earthlink.net/~haldeman.

DAVID BRIN's popular science-fiction novels have been translated into more than twenty languages, including *The New York Times* bestsellers that won Hugo, Nebula, and other awards. His 1989 ecological thriller, *Earth*, foreshadowed global warming, cyberwarfare, and the World Wide Web. A 1998 movie, starring Kevin Costner, was loosely adapted from his Campbell Award winner, *The Postman*. *Foundation's Triumph* brought a grand finale to Isaac Asimov's famed Foundation Universe. Brin's latest novel, *Kiln People* (2002), portrays a coming era when a simple advance in technology allows anyone to achieve the ancient dream of being in two places at once. Brin is also a noted scientist and speaker/consultant about trends in the near future. His nonfiction book, *The Transparent Society: Will Technology Make Us Choose Between Freedom and Privacy?*, deals with issues of openness, security and liberty in the new wired-age. It won the 2000 Obeler Freedom of Speech Award of the American Library Association and a prize from the McGannon Foundation for public service in communications.

ALAN DEAN FOSTER's work to date includes excursions into hard science fiction, fantasy, horror, detective, western, historical, and contemporary fiction. He has also written numerous nonfiction articles on film, science, and scuba diving, and has produced the novel versions of many films, including *Star Wars*, the first three *Alien* films, and *Alien Nation*. Other works include scripts for talking records, radio, computer games, and the story for the first *Star Trek* movie. His short fiction has appeared in all the major SF magazines as well as in original anthologies and several "Best of the Year" compendiums. Five collections of his short-form work have been published. Foster was born in New York City and was raised in Los Angeles. He currently lives in Prescott, Arizona.

KAREN HABER is the author of eight novels, including *Star Trek: Voyager—Bless the Beasts*, coauthor of *The Science of the X-Men*, and editor of the Hugo-nominated essay anthology celebrating J. R. R. Tolkien, *Meditations on Middle-earth*. Her short fiction has appeared in *Asimov's Science Fiction* magazine, *The Magazine of Fantasy and Science Fiction*, and many anthologies. She reviews art books for *LOCUS* magazine and profiles artists for various publications, including *Realms of Fantasy*.

JAMES PATRICK KELLY has had an eclectic writing career. He has written novels, short stories, essays, reviews, poetry, plays and planetarium shows. His books include *Strange but Not a Stranger* (2002), *Think Like a Dinosaur and Other Stories* (1997), *Wildlife* (1994), *Heroines* (1990*), Look into the Sun* (1989), *Freedom Beach* (1986), and *Planet of Whispers* (1984). His fiction has been translated into fourteen languages. He has won the World Science Fiction Society's Hugo Award twice: in 1996, for his novelette, "Think Like a Dinosaur," and in 2000, for his novelette, "Ten to the Sixteenth to One." He writes a column on the internet for *Asimov's Science Fiction* magazine and his audio plays are a regular feature on Scifi.com's "Seeing Ear Theater." He is currently one of fourteen councilors appointed by the governor of New Hampshire to the State Council on the Arts. He also sits on the Board of Directors of the New England Foundation for the Arts.

KEVIN J. ANDERSON is the author of numerous bestselling and award-winning science-fiction novels. Recent titles include *Hidden Empire, Hopscotch, Captain Nemo*, a series of prequels to *Dune* written with Frank Herbert's son Brian, as well as *Star Wars* and *X-Files* novels. An avid hiker, he has climbed the fifty highest peaks in the Rocky Mountains, and prefers to write while out in the wilderness.

RICK BERRY is known for, among other things, being the first artist to embrace the digital realm when, in 1984, he created, digitally, the cover for

William Gibson's *Neuromancer*. Since then he has evolved a style combining traditional oil paint techniques with cyber-imaging. His work has been exhibited throughout the U.S. and he's won many awards from both the SF and digital communities. He's produced concept art for television and, with Darrel Anderson and Gene Bodio, created a 3D Computer Aided Design cyberspace climax for the 1995 movie *Johnny Mnemonic*. He also created the 3D CAD Human Design Disc, an anatomical software model published by Antic Software. He has taught at the University of Tennessee and Adams State University, and been the AI symposia lecturer at Tufts University in Boston. A book of his collaborative work with Phil Hale, *Double Memory: Art and Collaboration*, was published in 1993. He's currently working on a collection of digital images with Darrel Anderson in the collaboration known as Braid. His Web site is: www.braid.com.

MOMMIES
WHO DRINK

MOMMIES  WHO DRINK

Sex, Drugs, and Other Distant Memories
of an Ordinary Mom

BRETT
PAESEL

WARNER BOOKS
NEW YORK   BOSTON

The names of some of the persons in this work have been changed or are presented in composite form, some of the places and incidents described in this work are the product of the author's imagination, and some incidental references to celebrities are ficticious.

"Slow to Warm" appeared in *Toddler: Real-life Stories of Those Fickle, Irrational, Urgent, Tiny People We Love* (Seal Press, 2003), edited by Jennifer Margulis.

"Red Hurt" appeared in *Hip Mama* (#30) and on Literarymama.com.

"Witness" appeared in *Brain, Child* (vol. 5, no. 1).

"Mommy Groups and Me" appeared in *Violet* (vol. 2, no. 1).

Copyright © 2006 by Brett Paesel
All rights reserved.

Warner Books
Hachette Book Group USA
1271 Avenue of the Americas, New York, NY 10020
Visit our Web site at www.HachetteBookGroupUSA.com

Printed in the United States of America

First Edition: August 2006
10 9 8 7 6 5 4 3 2 1

Warner Books and the "W" logo are trademarks of Time Inc. or an affiliated company. Used under license by Hachette Book Group USA, which is not affiliated with Time Warner Inc.

Library of Congress Cataloging-in-Publication Data

Paesel, Brett.
    Mommies who drink : sex, drugs, and other distant memories of an ordinary mom / Brett Paesel.—1st ed.
        p. cm.
    Summary: "The anecdotes of a modern mother and Hollywood character actress who unsuccessfully tries to reclaim her carefree past"—Provided by publisher.
    ISBN-13: 978-0-446-57873-8
    ISBN-10: 0-446-57873-8
    1.Paesel, Brett. 2. Mothers—California—Los Angeles—Biography. 3. Motherhood—California—Los Angeles—Anecdotes. 4. Character actors and actresses—California—Los Angeles—Biography. 5. Hollywood (Los Angeles, Calif.)—Biography.
I. Title.
    HQ759.P18 2006
    306.874'30979494—dc22

                                                        2006003685

Interior design by Charles Sutherland

For my guys
Pat, Spence, and Murph

Just once in my life—oh, when have I ever wanted any-thing just once in my life?

Amy Hempel, "Memoir"

✳ Friday
✳
✳

What we'll do is rent a limo. We'll do the cocaine at my house, then take the limo to a couple of clubs," says Lana.

"Great," I say, even though it's not great. I can't imagine doing cocaine since giving it up twelve years ago, but I don't want to be left out. I don't want to be thought a forty-four-year-old mom who is too tired to have a wild night out and too chicken to engage in a little illegal high jinks. Which is, at this point, exactly what I am. And what Lana is, though she's less likely than me to say it.

Lana takes a sip from her tall vodka tonic and looks out at the clientele gathering at the bar.

It's Friday cocktail hour at Bird's, a local pub, peopled by trendy Hollywood types. Thin girls with enhanced white smiles, and boys who look like they just woke up from a two-day nap. Some older rocker dudes who probably belonged to the same hair band, twenty years ago.

Lana, Michelle, Katherine, and I have been meeting here almost every Friday for the last four years. But today it's just Lana and me. Michelle isn't here because she's getting her daughter Faith's astrological chart done. I know nothing of charts but am curious about how you do an accurate reading for an adopted Chinese kid who was abandoned on a dirt road. Michelle says you work backward, eliminating traits, until you find a likely rising sign (she's pretty sure Faith was born in December). Katherine's at the dentist with her son, Jake.

Lana's cell phone rings. She dumps the contents of her purse onto the bar and finds the phone.

"Yes," she says. "Uh-huh. Just ask them for a cake with The Little Mermaid on it. Or anything with princesses."

She pauses while her ex, Tony, presumably absorbs the instructions for ordering their daughter's birthday cake.

"Not Sleeping Beauty."

She pauses, listens, and takes another sip.

"Then ask them for anything Disney," she says, and hangs up, returning to the cocaine conversation. "So it's just you, me, and Katherine. Michelle said she won't do blow because it would be her first time, and she thinks she'd be too freaked-out. And my guess is she would be."

"Oh, yeah," I say, remembering the one and only time Michelle went over her two-beer limit at happy hour and had a panic attack in the bathroom while the rest of us comforted her from the other side of the door. She finally brought herself down by repeating incantations from *The Tibetan Book of the Dead*.

"The thing is, where do we get it?" Lana asks, looking at me like I would know. Because we've known each other since I would have known where to get it. Back when I would have had a dozen connections. Most notably an Iranian high roller who I had to call from a pay phone using the code words "atomic action."

"Uh-hmmmm," I say. "I don't know anymore. I could maybe ask my ant man."

"What's an 'ant man'?"

"The guy who comes in and takes care of my ant problem."

"You're going to ask your ant man for cocaine? Why would he know?"

"Looks like the type."

"You can't ask your ant man for an eight ball. He'll think you're out of your mind."

"Look," I say, "you asked me. Why don't you ask the transgender guy at your gym?"

"I barely know her."

"And another thing, if we do this Sunday, I've got to be in bed by at least three in the morning. Spence wakes up at seven for preschool, and I need some downtime."

"There's no getting to bed by three when you're doing blow."

"Okay. So let's do it the Saturday after this. Then we can sleep in a bit that Sunday morning."

Lana grabs her daybook and flips through it. "That's Saturday the . . . nope. Can't. Daisy and I are going to a theme birthday party that morning. All the kids have to dress like the Hulk, and all the food is going to be green. I'm not facing that without a full night's sleep."

We pick through the best evenings to have our wild night, rejecting many because of the demands of the next morning. Lana takes two more phone calls. One from Tony, who says that he couldn't get a princess cake so he had to go with a sea creatures cake, and one from a mommy who wants to switch a play date to two weeks from Sunday.

Lana snaps her phone closed. "That knocks out that Saturday night too. Frankly, her daughter's a bad seed. I can't watch her on a massive coke hangover. I'll have to get up early that Sunday morning to hide all the matches and knives."

It becomes clear over the next hour of happy hour that we are not going to have our big night. Neither one of us says it. The notion simply dilutes and mutates into an afternoon of facials and eyebrow waxing.

The light fades as we ask for the check. It is close to six o'clock and we are leaving as more hipsters push through the swinging door into the bar. Before Lana lays down her cash she sends a drink over to Jon Anderson, lead singer of Yes. She nods to the long-haired, middle-aged rock god. He raises a glass to her.

As I watch their exchange, I am filled with nostalgia for the girls Lana and I once were. The girls we were before we had children.

I walk home from the bar having promised to watch Daisy on Tuesday so that Lana can go to a movie by herself. I walk slowly because I want to think. I want to think about how I started out being that girl who would have easily spent an evening doing half a gram of coke in the back of a limo with her girlfriends, and ended up being this woman making slow progress home to read stories to her two children (before curling up on a couch to read her own book while her husband watches *Celebrity Poker* on Bravo).

I think about the hazy, lonely months that followed my first son's birth four years ago. I remember being desperate for relief and looking for answers in books. Books with titles like *Surviving the First Year, The Girlfriend's Guide to the First Year, What to Expect the First Year, So It's Your Baby's First Year, The Natural Mother's Guide to the First Year, The Dummy's Guide to the First Year, First Year—Best Year,* and *When Bad Things Happen to Good People.*

Months of shapeless afternoons fuzzed into each other while

Spence slept or ate or cried. Sometimes, as he screamed, I'd put him on his back on the living room floor and go into my room to lie on my bed. The bed would become a floating raft. I'd close my eyes—Spence's dissonant aria stereophonically blaring from a distant shore—and drift, the books hidden in the folds of musty blankets. Eventually, I'd pick one up and turn to the index to look up "Crying." When I'd flip to the indicated page, I'd find a paragraph that told me to burp my baby, walk him around, check to see if something was poking him, feed him. Of course, I'd done these things. Then I'd flip to the index to look up "Nonstop, non-specific, hostile crying." No listing.

None of the books had chapters on what seemed immediately relevant to me. I'd imagine chapters like:

STOP YOUR BABY FROM CRYING—FOREVER. Six foolproof and safe ways to make your home a crying-free zone.

And:

EASY, TWO-WEEK PROGRAM FOR GETTING YOUR PERSONAL-ITY BACK. This program concentrates on exercises that re-mind you of the woman you used to be. Exercises include making lists of things that used to interest you and looking at old picture albums to remind yourself of what you looked like before someone's life depended on you.

And:

YOU ARE NOT YOUR BABY'S BIOLOGY. Invaluable suggestions for ways to keep a stimulating conversation going while nursing or changing a diaper. Beginning with the admonishment to steer away from openers like "Sam did the cutest thing" and "Should I be concerned about mustard-colored bowel movements?"

And I dreamed of chapters like:

SMOKING: THE ROAD BACK TO SANITY AND A GOOD FIGURE.

And:

YES, SOME BABIES HAVE DIED WHEN LEFT ALONE IN THE BATHTUB—BUT HERE ARE MANY WHO SURVIVED AND THRIVED.

And:

TAKE A VACATION. Studies debunk the "first five years are the most important" theory in favor of research that shows that most successful and happy children's personalities were formed when parents were away in Europe.

And, of course:

WHAT PARENTING EXPERTS DON'T WANT YOU TO KNOW ABOUT THE SECRET BENEFITS OF COCAINE.

I began to realize that no book was going to tell me what I wanted to hear, which was that I would be the same person after the baby as I was before the baby.

I spent the days mourning the loss of my past self with as much intensity as I would the death of a lover. I raged against the limitations mommyhood placed on me. I rebelled against what seemed like an American groupthink about what mommies should be: dull, doughy, desexualized, and almost pathologically interested in *all* children and all things having to do with children. Parenting magazines showed me how to make jiggly lollipops out of Jell-O, how to have fun with felt, and how to make little forests out of broccoli in order to interest my child in eating it. When what I really wanted was a stranger to fuck me blind in a parking lot after loading me up on margaritas and Thai stick. Or at least the strictures of my Lilliputian life make me *think* that's what I wanted.

Those first few months that I spent listening to Spence's crying started to form a shaky bridge to a new country. I felt the slowness of the days. I felt the weight of his dependence. I looked back with vague longing and could not look forward, because the terrain was wholly different and unfamiliar.

It was terrain I would begin to explore with others of my kind.

Prenatal Guru to * the Stars

I sit with the phone in my hand, my pregnant belly pressing against the rim of the dining room table. Boredom dulls my brain like Novocain.

Who should I call next? I've already called my mother, a friend in Philadelphia, Office Depot, and a closet organizing company. I've ordered two sets of sheets for the crib and canceled a pedicure.

I look down at my taut tummy, swollen to accommodate the size of a seven-month-old fetus. The fetus is Spence, but I don't know that yet.

I imagine my tummy splitting down the middle, everything inside me spilling out.

What a thought.

I call my husband, Pat, on his cell phone. He's on the set of *Friends,* playing the part of a smart-ass maître d' who hassles Joey for not wearing a jacket.

"Honey, I've only got a minute," he says.

In the background I hear the assistant director calling every-one to the stage.

"I'm thinking of calling Dr. Sammy and having him do a C-section this afternoon," I say. "The books all say that the baby is basically done by now."

"Honey," says Pat, "I read those books too. And they say that the baby still needs to make kidneys for itself."

Pat throws this logical horseshit around when I least need it.

"Never mind," I say, and hang up.

I look out the window and consider taking a walk or a nap. Both of which would require me leaving this chair.

I dial Lana.

"You feel like the man who had to be buried in the piano crate. Right?" she says.

"Mmmm . . ."

"You know you've got to keep moving."

"I don't want to move."

"Look, you've got to get up and move around. Do something. Go take that prenatal yoga class with Rananda. Remember when I went?"

"You hated her."

"I did not."

"You said that you thought she might be a man."

"I was hormonal. Look," says Lana. "Pick up a *Redbook*. There's an interview with Cindy Crawford. Rananda coached her through her pregnancy."

"You're reading *Redbook*?"

"I was in a doctor's office."

I'm not convinced. I think that maybe all the shifts and swings of having given birth turned Lana into a closet *Redbook* subscriber. I'm tempted to confront her, but there are places you don't go, even with your best friend.

At Los Angeles Life Works—Center for Yoga, I sit in a little waiting area watching the other pregnant women around me. Most of them are gorgeous actresses, their little round bellies poking out of loosely tied sweatpants. I recognize some of them as women I've competed with for two-line parts on marginal sitcoms.

A fresh-faced girl sets down a big clay pot of yogi tea and a plate of graham crackers. The women help themselves to tea and nibble on the edges of their crackers. I take four crackers. I eat one, put one aside, and stash two in my purse for later.

"Well, of course, I'm having a home birth," someone says. "But I haven't settled on a doula yet."

"What's a doula?" I ask.

She flashes a gorgeous Meg Ryan smile at me. "A doula helps you through your birth. She keeps you focused and helps you when you feel like you're going to get weak and ask for pain medication."

I find this information useless and uninteresting, as I've been thinking of asking my doctor if I can start getting epidurals now. I want to ask if Rananda has cures for the bad smell I've started to emanate, but decide to sit back and not tip my hand. Maybe no one can smell me but me.

Another woman says, "I had a friend whose doula had her on her feet and washing the blood out of her sheets only two hours after she gave birth."

I start to wonder what kind of sick trip these women are on, when a bell rings and they all rise to go into the classroom. I grab another graham cracker and pull myself to standing by grabbing onto a statue of Vishnu.

About forty pregnant women sit on yoga mats facing a stage draped with Oriental carpets. Swooping gauze creates a canopy over a huge gong, an ornate pillow, and an elaborate sound system. The women speak in hushed tones.

Expectation hangs in the air.

After a few minutes there's some rustling and a breeze, then the tinkle of a bell. At this, all murmuring stops as the women hold a collective breath. They turn toward a door, which opens noiselessly. A small woman enters. I guess, by the shifting of the crowd, that this is Rananda. She's dressed in filmy white and she smiles like she's canonized. She walks onto the stage and turns toward us as she adjusts a head mic around her turban. She pauses for a moment, looking out over our heads, then picks up a huge padded stick and bangs the gong.

"Welcome," she says, her voice amplified. "As you know, there are three kinds of people in the world. There are men, women, and pregnant women." An approving rumble moves through the crowd.

I don't know what this means. But it looks like I'm in the in crowd, and that's always a good feeling. I want to pull a cracker out of my purse but resist.

"I was talking to Cindy the other day," she says, "and Cindy said that her home birth was magical and that she was becoming her animal self. She is spending this time in bed with her child, nursing and rocking."

She lets this land with a long pause.

"Now," she says, "we will introduce ourselves. Give your name, your doctor's name, and tell us where you are having your baby."

The women start introducing themselves. Most of them are having their babies in hospitals. But a few say, "My name is whatever, and my doctor is whozits, my doula is Hari something, and I'm having a home birth."

When a woman says she's having a home birth, the group turns toward her en masse and beams, while Rananda mutters approvingly, "Home birth."

Near the end of the introductions a woman says that she's two weeks overdue with her fourth baby and she's going to have a home birth with a Hari doula.

Rananda looks like she could die now and her work would be done.

"This is Anna," she says in well-modulated tones. "She is having her fourth baby at home. Stand up, Anna."

The effort required for Anna to do this makes it look like this might be her last act. She rolls onto her knees, then straightens her legs. Her butt wavers in the air a bit as she walks her hands as close to her feet as her belly will allow. When she gets to standing, she rocks back and forth on her feet, until she manages to turn herself around to face us. She's six feet tall and looks like a Helga painting. Her gray sweatshirt stretches around her belly, which is big as a planet. I can't take my eyes off her belly. It's the biggest live thing I've ever seen. It puts me in mind of a giant mushroom a friend of mine had growing under his bed in a pot of water—organic and freakish.

Rananda continues, "I attended Anna's last home birth. She was in labor for thirty-two hours. She managed the pain of her contractions by chanting and making a gorgeous daisy chain that encircled her garden twice." She smiles at Anna and motions for her to sit down, a process I don't watch. "During those hours, we laughed, ate peaches, and talked to Christie Brinkley on my cell phone. Christie reminded Anna that giving birth was as close as any being gets to being God."

I like the God part and even the little tidbit about Christie Brinkley. But my ass is killing me, and I wonder when we are actually going to get down to the yoga.

"Everyone stand up," Rananda says.

The pregnant herd jostles and groans into position. It takes a good two minutes to get everyone standing.

"Find a partner and hold her hand."

Now that they're on their feet, the women match up very fast. I look around desperately. Moving through the pairs of women, I spot a short girl in a ripped Batman T-shirt backing into a corner. I make a beeline for her.

"Hi. Want to be my partner?" I ask.

"Sure."

I grab her hand, feeling the moisture between our palms squish. Rananda walks over to the sound system and fires up some chants.

"Now just start walking," she says.

As we walk around in our twosomes, I listen to bits of conversations. Someone says that she just auditioned for a battered pregnant wife guest spot on *ER,* "but they gave it to someone who wasn't really pregnant." Her voice is tight with resentment.

Rananda guides us through our walk, telling us to walk on our toes, step over imaginary boulders, and waddle on our heels—all while holding our partner's hand.

"I'm Ruth," my partner says. "My husband and I just moved here. He's a writer on *Blind Date.* So he's gone a lot." Her hand squeezes my fingers together. "I've been coming to Rananda every day. She's terrific. Do you know that she coached Cindy Crawford privately? Of course, Cindy didn't come here. She'd get mobbed."

Ruth scopes the room with hungry eyes.

Rananda's tinny voice rises over the chatter of the women. "Now stop where you are. Face your partner. Let go of each other's hands and put your arms out to your sides, parallel to the ground."

She shows us—stretching her gauzy white arms out like a crucifix. I look at Ruth like, "Let's agree to fudge on this one a bit." But she looks back at me with a fixed, determined gaze. So I turn to face her, our bellies practically touching as we put our arms straight out.

Rananda says, "Looking into each other's eyes will give you the strength to hold this pose. We will hold it for as long as a contraction lasts. That's three minutes. After having done this exercise for weeks, Leeza Gibbons said that she felt like she could have gone through three more hours of labor."

I hold the pose for a few seconds before I start to feel invisible weight pressing down on my biceps. I look into Ruth's eyes for permission to put my arms down. She stares through my forehead into the back wall. She is all belly and will.

Pain shoots through my shoulders and neck. My arms start to shake.

I hear Rananda's voice through the pounding of blood pulsing through my head. "While you are holding this pose, I want you to think of your birth and what you want it to be like. How do you want the lighting? Cindy had her birth at home on white sheets made out of one-thousand-thread-count cotton."

I feel the veins pop out of my neck like a relief map of the highway system to my heart. My chest clutches and knees buckle. I let out a moan and lower my quivering arms.

I look at Ruth, who seems to have entered a misty realm, a ghostly otherworld. A world in which she is as strong as a Greek goddess. As beautiful as Cindy Crawford. A world in which there are no absent husbands working on *Blind Date* until two in the morning. She is the Venus of Willendorf—stone fertility goddess, timeless and iconic.

And I am going to be sick.

I grab my purse, stagger to the back wall, and lower myself to the floor, my legs wobbling. Two women sit there already, cross-legged, their backs resting against the cool, solid wall.

"I think I had a small seizure," I say, pulling a graham cracker out of my purse.

One of the women dabs her forehead with her faded red T-shirt, her orb poking out for a moment.

"I held it until I peed on myself," she says.

"It's okay. Your pants are black," I say. "I can't see any wet spot."

The other woman turns to me. "Do I smell?" she asks.

My heartbeat slows and I pull in a long breath.

"I can't smell you," I say. "I don't think anyone can smell you but you."

"Has anyone noticed," says the first woman, "that there's something oddly masculine about Rananda?"

"I have a friend who thinks she's a man," I say. A feeling of deep contentment fills me. "Anyone want a graham cracker?"

"Oh, yes." They sigh like I have offered the gift of inner peace.

My chest feels warm and tingly and the pain in my neck eases, as I break the graham cracker in half and hand it to the women to split among themselves.

I have found my people.

✳ Busted

✳

✳

"He's fine," Pat says as I shudder on stiff white sheets in the recovery room. The shuddering a result of epidural withdrawal.

He's talking about our son, who was born half an hour ago.

We have a son. After four epidurals, Demerol, and a C-section that terrified me so much I screamed, "OH JESUS OH JESUS OH JESUS" from first cut to last stitch. I didn't feel pain exactly, but I did feel the pressure of the doctor shoving around my organs to find the baby who was pulled from my midsection and held high, screaming and dripping with blood like a satanic sacrifice. It is an image sure to dominate future dreams.

"He's fine?" I shiver.

"He's healthy," says Pat.

"Great."

My mind is dulled by drugs and, possibly, post-traumatic stress disorder. I have to look at Pat's lips to make out his words.

"He's gorgeous," say Pat's lips.

"Aww."

"He looks like you," the lips say.

"Really?"

"There's just one thing . . ." The lips make a thin line.

I feel something sharp in my brain. I force myself to look from the lips to Pat's eyes, which are soft.

"A thing?"

"His penis," he says.

"His penis?" I shake.

"Yeah."

"Does he have one?"

"Oh, yes," Pat says casually, like this is no big deal. Which is what makes me think that it *is* a big deal. If I wasn't numb from the neck down, I'm sure I'd feel my chest tighten.

"They can fix it," he says.

"They're going to fix his penis?"

"Later. Not now."

I can't grasp what he's saying. *We have a son with a broken penis, which they can fix, but not now?*

My teeth start to chatter, my shaking and mental fog becoming so severe that I feel like I'm in one of those movies in which the junkie-heroine has to cold-turkey it in a padded cell. I want to grab the collar of Pat's borrowed surgical scrubs and beg for a teensy epidural bump. I need to get straight, man, if only to grasp what's happening with my son's penis.

"Why can't they fix his penis now?" I sputter.

"They want it to get more mature," he says.

"A mature penis?" I quake.

Even stoned, I can appreciate the oxymoron.

"They said that this business about his penis is pretty normal," says Pat.

"Okay," I say, not sure that we should refer to our son's penis as business.

"Sweetie, I've got to go now," he says. "They said you have to be here for a couple of hours and I don't want the baby to be alone."

"You're leaving?"

"I'm sorry, honey," says Pat. "It's just that, remember, they said it's a good idea for the father to stay with the baby."

I flash on our Lamaze class. The teacher with the crackly voice said that the father should stay with the baby, because sometimes they mix the babies up.

"Right," I say.

Shake. Shake.

Pat leans down and gives me a quick kiss on the cheek.

I stare at the bouncing pale green wall, thinking that at least if they mix up the babies, we'll know which is ours, because ours is the one whose penis is busted.

My doctor assures me that the penis thing is no big deal, and I'm so stoned on a cocktail of painkillers that I forget to worry. The next four days in the hospital I actually have a blast. So many friends drop by that I think I should do this more often. It's like having a long party that I didn't have to clean or cook for, and I get to stay in bed. If I get tired or bored, I simply nod off and no one gets mad at me.

Through it all, Spence lies in the crook of my arm, breathing against my skin, warm like a puppy.

I even love my catheter. The last month of my pregnancy I was going to the bathroom every ten minutes. Not having to get up to relieve myself is such a joy I wonder if they'll let me take it home.

My room is filled with flowers and cute fuzzy stuffed animals. Food is brought to me on a tray. Special long straws bend so that

I don't even have to lift my head to take a drink. Every meal is topped off with strawberry Jell-O. I start to wonder why I don't make strawberry Jell-O at home. I resolve to eat it after every meal for the rest of my life.

My mother sits by my bed during the day, flipping through *People* magazines, fielding my calls. She picks up the phone when it rings, repeats the name of the caller, and I give her a thumbs-up or a thumbs-down. This is what it must be like to have a personal assistant. I vow to myself that I will have a personal assistant someday.

At night Pat sleeps next to me on a tiny cot. The baby wakes only to eat, then dozes off. When I need to sleep, I press a button and a nurse comes to take my baby to the nursery.

I can't imagine why anyone would ever want to leave.

My last day I sit up in bed eating Jell-O. I've put in my contacts and fluffed up my hair in case I get any last-minute visitors. My mother packs my things as Spencer, wrapped tightly like a papoose, sleeps in his clear plastic box.

A woman with long blond hair, sprayed and winged away from her face, walks into the room. She looks like she was separated at birth from Loni Anderson. Her canary-yellow jacket has huge shoulder pads and it matches her canary-yellow miniskirt. She walks expertly on impossibly high heels. Her salmon-colored fingernails match her lipstick.

"I'm Dr. Hiya," she says.

My mother gives me her "only in Los Angeles" look.

"Hello," I say, putting down my Jell-O.

"I'm the urologist," she says. Her fingernails click against the metal bar of my bed as she grasps it.

"A urologist?"

"For Spencer. I just came by to take a look at Spencer's penis before he goes home."

Oh, right. I remember Spence's penis.

I look at Dr. Hiya's jangling multihooped earrings and can't believe that Pat is shooting a "Six Flags over Texas" commercial instead of being here with Dr. Hiya, the penis doctor.

"Um, okay," I say, nodding at Spencer.

"Aww," she says, going over to him. "What a cutie."

Let's not get personal, I think.

"Such a cute nose," she says as she unwraps him.

Fuzzy with Vicodin, I watch as her salmon nails undo his diaper. I look away. My mother's eyes are round and fixed on the action.

"Ah, I see," I hear the doctor say.

I distract myself by thinking about how and why Dr. Hiya chose urology as her specialty. It's hard to imagine anyone wanting to be a urologist, but it seems especially rare that a specialist should have to choose between being a urologist or a Laker Girl.

"Okay," she says.

Is Hiya her real last name? Or is it a name she made up? Is it a stage name? Her stripper name? I imagine her in a smoky club, grinding against a pole in a see-through lab coat. Normally, I have nothing against strippers. But this one has her hands on my son's business.

"Right," she says with finality.

She closes Spence's diaper (is he smiling?) and walks over to me, tossing her hair behind a sculpted shoulder. I can still taste the sweet strawberry Jell-O in my mouth. Her nails click again as she rests her hand on the bar.

"It's a relatively common condition," she says, and goes on to tell me that the skin underneath his penis is not long enough to allow for a full erection. She can correct it with a graft from his foreskin, a pretty minor operation she'll do when he's about eleven months old.

"It's a good age," she says, "because they're old enough to operate on, but too young to really know that you're doing something to their penis."

"Once you do the operation," I ask, "will it work like everyone else's?"

She smiles. "Yes."

I feel my body go soft. Until this moment I've been unaware of holding on to anything other than my buzz. But here it is—a letting go. Muscles going slack. Muscles do not lie. This letting go must mean I'm relieved. Relieved of what? Relieved of worry? Was I worried? Worried about Spence's penis?

I look over at him.

It's not his penis I'm worried about, I realize. It's his happiness.

Dr. Hiya reaches over and pats my hand with the IV in it. I flinch.

"Mothers worry," she says.

Without thinking I look over at my mother.

Then I think, Oh, wait a minute, it's me. I'm the mother.

I'm a mother.

✳ Friday
✳
✳

I sit at Bird's alone, pretending to read a book. It's the same paperback I've dragged around the house, attempting to read, since Spence was born three weeks ago. Anne Tyler. I picked it because it's easy for me to get lost in a Tyler novel. And I'm looking to get lost.

I gaze at the words on the page. They bounce and merge randomly.

I look up. Lana is late.

Lana and I used to hang out here before I got pregnant. I remember the last time. We sat outside on a long summer day, sipping margaritas like there was nowhere we had to be.

I look at my watch. Pat's with Spence. He took off early from a stand-in job he's been doing all week.

The shape of Lana appears in front of the spill of afternoon light from the windows.

"Traffic sucks," she says. "I hate auditioning on the Westside."

"Sorry," I say. I've walked here from my apartment just up the block.

Lana slips onto the barstool next to me and plops her tiny purse onto the bar. The orange purse is so stuffed that the unzipped sides bow into a circle with papers, a wallet, sunglasses, and a phone spilling out.

Why doesn't she buy a bigger purse?

"Hey, Mack," she says to the bartender. "Pour me something sweet and hard."

She glances at my full glass of cabernet. "How's that?"

"I haven't tasted it yet," I say.

She takes my glass and sips.

"Not bad," she says, putting it back on the napkin, matching the base to the red circle left by the spill of my glass.

"So Pat called me," she says.

"He did?"

"He thinks you should talk to me."

My eyes hurt. The bartender (Mark, Max, Mike?) places a golden drink with a submerged cherry in it in front of Lana. She smiles at him like he's given her the perfect gift.

She turns to me. "Mack works Fridays. About a month ago I was in here bitching to him about Tony."

Tony is Lana's boyfriend. He's a hunky Italian—ten years younger than Lana—who fathered her daughter. Lana doesn't do anything safe.

"What does Pat think I should talk to you about?"

"Um . . . how about why you cry all the time and say that you want to give Spence back?"

I take a sip of wine.

"You know, Rananda says that you shouldn't leave your house or your baby for forty days," I say.

"Sure," says Lana, pulling stuff out of her purse that seems to expand and occupy more space than can possibly be contained in orange leather. "That's what I thought I was going to do. Forty days of bonding in bed with Daisy. Breast-feeding. Rananda makes it sound like fucking bliss."

"Yeah."

"On the third day I started to think about how big a box I needed to get in order to send her somewhere."

"When did it get better?" I manage to ask. It's the question I haven't asked anyone because I'm afraid that the answer is "never."

"Um . . . ," she says, her hand sifting through purse clutter until it locates a crumpled pack of cigarettes. "I don't know. But it does. It's kind of a slow thing. One day you wake up and you look at your kid and you like what you see and your head feels clearer and you think of things you're going to do that day. And you don't know what switched."

"That's good," I say.

"And other days you find yourself wondering if throwing yourself out a five-story window would kill you outright or just make you paralyzed." She pulls a cigarette out of the pack. "Want one?"

Do I want one?! I look around to see if anyone's looking. I haven't had a cigarette since the ceremonial last one on my balcony when I was seven weeks pregnant.

"God, yes," I say.

"Hey, Mack," says Lana, "we're back in a few."

She balances a coaster on top of her drink and hops off her stool, heading out the door like she's the coolest bad girl in high school.

I slide off my stool and follow.

Standing on the street smoking with Lana feels like an illegal thrill. Can mothers of newborns get away with this? Leaving a drink on the bar to grab a smoke outside? Am I being watched? Are my poufy belly and bilious breasts unmistakable evidence that I should be at home in my bed with my infant, like Rananda says?

Lana and I both take a drag and blow out.

"Feels funny, doesn't it?" Lana asks.

"What?"

"Being without the baby. Feels great and horrible at the same time."

"I'd say yes, but I really don't want to be that much of a cliché."

"Hey, can't avoid the clichés," she says, flicking ash into the street.

"All I know is, this feels great," I say, holding up my cigarette.

"Yeah, like a huge fuck-you to the whole mama label."

"Mmmm."

"Well. Tell Pat we talked."

"Sure."

We take another drag and look around. All I want right now is to talk about something/anything that has nothing to do with babies. But I can't think of what that would be.

"Book any good?" asks Lana.

"What book?"

"The Tyler book."

"Oh. I haven't really gotten into it yet."

"Mmm. I'm reading this book called *Sex with Kings*. It's about courtesans. Now, there's a job."

"Yeah, but you have to fuck the king."

"Probably better than fucking your syphilitic pockmarked husband."

"Whose husband?"

"Yours. If you're one of these courtesans I'm reading about."

Now, this already feels better, I think.

"The kings couldn't have been much better than the husbands," I say.

"Sure they're better," says Lana. "They're goddamned kings."

I stub out my half-smoked cigarette. It's enough.

Lana takes another drag and does the same. "Another drink?"

I nod.

And we turn to walk back through the swinging doors of the bar.

✳ Ordinary Madness

It's on all the talk shows and the news. Women who've recently given birth experience a special kind of insanity. Now, we know about the murderous kind. But your average garden-variety kind of insanity varies in degree according to your predilection for that sort of thing in the first place.

I am one of those women who have a strong predilection for ordinary kinds of madness. So my postpartum funk is characterized by very understandable, even banal, fears and obsessions. Like the belief that the birthing process had turned me into the most boring woman alive, or the fear that my son will develop that disease that would make him look like a tiny old person, or my need to put everything that's loose into a Tupperware container. But probably nothing characterizes my ordinary madness more than my certainty that all of these symptoms will disappear if I can only find the right haircut.

It's four o'clock in the morning when I clamp Spence onto my breast and tune in to an infomercial about a miracle stain remover. I find myself considering buying a case, along with the miracle mop, when I notice the nice casual shag cut on the model who's making a bloodstain disappear. What a great cut. It does that thing I always look for. It just falls into place like it doesn't mean it. Like it hasn't even been planned. In that "I just got out of bed and my hair just did this" kind of way.

As the baby tugs at my nipple, I start to dream. What if I had this cut? What if I had this cut and a cute cottony pair of pajamas with a drawstring waist? If I had this cut that looks like I didn't mean it, and the cute pajamas, I could be surprised at the door anytime and still look put together. I'd look like one of those mothers in that magazine called *Real Simple.* I'd been getting this magazine, overlooking the dreadful title, hoping to get "real simple" myself. Its pages are full of images of people making their lives "real simple." With tips on how to organize spare buttons and how to grow bamboo shoots next to your bed to encourage dreams of prosperity.

I drift to sleep, the baby heavy and warm on my belly, knowing that the haircut—the shag flip—will make everything all right.

So I go back to Cathy, who used to cut my hair three years ago.

I go back to Cathy because I have no money. Cathy likes to do trades for haircuts. I will help organize her salon area and she will cut and dye my hair.

If I were thinking clearly, I would remember why I stopped going to Cathy in the first place. But I'm in a walking coma and not up to deductive reasoning. So Cathy seems like a great idea.

Here's what I've forgotten about Cathy:

#1. Cathy doesn't know when to stop. She does the cut. She does the dye job, which is or isn't good, relative to how stoned she is. But then she's got to do something more. My makeup. Or maybe she needs to weave a piece of wire through my hair. Once,

I left her place with two cones glued onto the sides of my head like Mickey Mouse ears. She wanted to show me a club look that was "sort of sci-fi."

#2. Cathy involves me in her crazy life. Cathy has twin sisters who joined a cult when they were sixteen. The cult was an old guy who lived out in the desert. The twins were the only members of this cult. The old guy was sleeping with the twins at the same time. Cathy hired a private detective and some cult deprogrammer to get them out. At one point she had me call the old man, pretending to be a bank lady threatening to put a lien on his account.

#3. Cathy is a healer. So along with the do, I walked away with various elixirs—good for mood swings, that funny yellow cast to my skin, and toe fungus. Cathy has made me aware of maladies I never knew I had. Two years ago she convinced me that my fatigue came from an allergy to my own dandruff. The cure for this was a foul-smelling paste. I had to put the paste on my hair and tie a plastic bag around my head twice a week. After weeks of this I was still tired, I developed tiny scabs on my forehead, and Pat threatened to stab himself on our balcony if I didn't stop.

#4. Cathy is bald on one side of her head.

#5. Cathy's brother works in her salon. He is a filmmaker who makes sci-fi videos about wars that take place in another dimension. In exchange for a haircut, Cathy once asked if I could do some free acting work for him. This involved me standing in front of a green screen, wearing a breastplate and a Medusa-type wig. When he yelled, "Action," I had to stare into the camera and say, "Fardoch will punish you for your travel from Sector 4. For this, your gender will be changed." Then I had to laugh for a really long time—until he yelled, "Cut."

These are the things I've forgotten about Cathy.

★   ★   ★

I lie on my back on Cathy's kitchen counter with my head in her sink listening to Jethro Tull blast from the stereo. Through the cacophony of flute and guitar, I can hear my five-month-old son gurgle as he lies on the hair-covered floor.

Cathy whooshes warm water over my forehead and into my hair. Her fingers massage my scalp, making my body feel loose like jelly. I stare up at the peeling ceiling, tiny points of light bouncing on my retinas.

She says, "So I said to my sister, 'You take those kids and just fucking leave him.' I mean, right? When she married him, he was this groovy guy who rode a motorcycle and had a couple of teeth missing. Which I can see is fuck-all sexy."

"Yeah, sexy," I say.

Meanwhile, I'm thinking that if the shag falls just right at my shoulders, I'll try fitting into the velvet V-necked thing again. I wore it the Christmas before I was pregnant, and I love those pictures. The velvet drapes in a way that makes me look thin but curvy.

She says, "But he's not that guy anymore. I mean, this is definitely the kind of soulless prick you should leave. Am I right?"

"Right," I say. "A prick."

I'm thinking that if this cut manages to give me a little height, my face will look considerably younger. That's going to be great for this reading of a pilot I'm doing next week. The HBO people are going to be there, and they haven't seen me for a while. If I get a new bra and throw a little clip into the shag, I can even wear a casual T-shirt and look messy but still serious.

"Sit up," Cathy says, pulling me to sitting. She reaches over, drags on her joint, and waves the smoke around. I guess so it won't get to my son.

She says, "So that's it. If that loser doesn't come after her, then he's even more of a major fuck than I first thought."

"Sure, sure," I say. "What I need is for the shag to look casual when it's towel-dried and elegant when I blow it out."

Cathy presses her hand into my back and I hop off the counter, stepping over my son to get to the chair.

I'm thinking that if my hair lies flat when it's blown out, my mother will be really happy when she comes to visit next month. We can go out to lunch together and I can wear my blue linen shirt. I'll pick up the check. And she will look over at me in my flat smooth hair and blue linen, and it will give her peace.

Cathy starts snipping away with the scissors as I look into a long antique mirror propped against the wall. I see the neat ends of my just-cut hair grazing the black plastic cape that covers my shoulders. I smell the sweet remains of marijuana smoke. And I dream of how perfect life is going to be when I have the shag. Yes, I think. The shag will give me more energy, ease my loneliness, and give me back what I've lost.

Spence babbles on the floor. Looking at him, I get a sense of time not being a straight line. I see him a boy. I see him a teenager. I see him without me. And I realize that it's not the shag that will do all those things for me. It's him.

Mommy Groups and Me

✳

✳

✳

Spence is eight months old when I start to see how this is going to go. I'm going to be home with him, from the moment he wakes until Pat walks in the door in the evening, returning from whatever midlevel actor job he's managed to score that day. I have given up the notion that Pat and I would trade off stay-at-home child-care duties—not because Pat's unwilling to do so, but because he's simply more likely to earn chunks of money faster than I would.

Alone together, Spence and I live like bears. By the time Spence wakes, Pat is already gone. So I bring Spence into bed with me and we roll around till he tires of that. Spence has become an easy, cheerful baby since he stopped nonstop screaming around his fifth month. Now we pad through our days, eating and napping, eating and napping. Sometimes we see a friend. Which gives us a reason to change out of our pajamas.

One friend is Milly. She says I should come to her mommy group. It would get Spence and me out of the house.

Now, I've never been much of a joiner. As a whole, people in groups make me nervous. People in groups do things that they would never do on their own. On the upside, groups of people can feed the hungry, free political prisoners, and get medical marijuana legislation passed. On the downside, groups of people burn books, lynch people, and drive through the streets in limousines, grabbing their crotches and screaming, "Do you want a piece of this?"

I almost always consider the downside, so a mommy group doesn't immediately appeal. But when Milly says I should go, I go. I go because much as I adore Spence, I can't bear another week of afternoons twisting ahead of me like a figure eight: pick up baby, feed baby, change baby, pick up baby, feed baby, change baby.

So I go because I think that maybe there are more mothers like me, bewildered by their discontent. I go because I think that surely these new mothers ache for what I ache for: adult conversation, a safe place to let the baby roam, and booze. I go even though I'm pretty sure that my shyness with strangers will make me appear mute and simple. And I go because Milly says not to judge mommy groups before I've been to one. Milly is the least judgmental person I know—a quality both charming and maddening.

Before she had her daughter, Emma, Milly was a pretty actress who liked books, vintage cars, and gossip. We met in acting school and our friendship was cemented at a party one night when, on a dare, she moved an egg from one chair to another with just her ass.

Lately, Milly's voice has acquired a hysterical edge and she admitted to me that on her daughter's birthday she ate the whole birthday cake after removing it from the oven, and had to make another. The mommy group, she says, is the brightest spot in her week.

This mommy group meets at Patti's. The house is immaculate, the wooden floors glistening like they've been computer-enhanced. Patti is as immaculate as her floors, her shiny blond hair pulled into a perfect ponytail that I think might be fake. She wears a pressed white men's shirt and a pair of shorts that shows her flawlessly tanned legs. A friend of mine recently told me about spray-on tans and I wonder if Patti has sprayed hers on. As I index everything about Patti and her home, I realize that I'm generally assuming that nothing here is real.

Eight mothers sit around a long glass table that has a cushy gray childproofing strip around the edge of it. In the middle of the table rests a bowl of grapes. The women sip from glasses of what I hope is vodka. Milly sinks into a pillow on the floor and pushes Emma toward a gaggle of children who are pounding on things and ignoring each other nicely. I perch on the edge of the sofa and slide Spence down to the floor next to me so that he can suck on my knee.

Patti stands in hostess mode. "Brett," she says, "can I get you anything? Water, iced tea, or a Diet Snapple? We have strawberry-kiwi Snapple and iced tea Snapple. The real iced tea has sugar, the iced tea Snapple is diet."

It's not vodka, I think.

"I'll have some water."

"What's his name?" she asks, nodding at Spence.

"Spence."

"Nice," she says. "You know there's two girl Spencers at my son's day care."

I mentally grope for an appropriate response.

"Wow," I say, as if both shocked and impressed.

Patti cocks her head and says, "Yeah," like maybe I'd better consider changing Spencer's name.

We both look at each other and nod for a very long time.

"Which one is your son?" I ask.

She points to a bald baby who sits staring at a wall.

"Sebastian," she says. "He scratched his own eye yesterday."

"That must have hurt."

"You'd think so," she says. "But he seems fine."

I look at Sebastian staring at the wall and wonder what he's seeing.

"Patti," says a woman who's crystal-meth skinny, "I went to that 'Music and Mommy' class at Kids Place last Tuesday. It was great. But I thought you'd be there with Sebastian."

"You know," says Patti, "I thought the class was really great too. But the week before, Sebastian put a drumstick up his nose and really hurt himself."

I watch Sebastian lean his cheek against the wall.

Milly pulls off a branch of grapes. "I like Kids Place," she says, "but I think it's weird that they don't have some kind of padding on the steps. I mean, it's all about kids, and those concrete steps are just an accident waiting to happen."

"You're telling me," says Patti. "The first day we were there, Sebastian fell and slammed his chin on the top step. If he had any teeth, I'm sure he would have lost them. As it was, the fall made his face swell up and he had to take an anti-inflammatory that he ended up being allergic to. It took a month to get his face to go down and to get rid of the rash and the scabs."

"The rash and the scabs?" asks Milly.

"He got the rash from the anti-inflammatory. Then he scratched the rash and got these scabs all over his face."

It looks like Sebastian has fallen asleep leaning his face against the wall. I think of all those self-inflicted wounds. Sebastian must be sending out a crude kiddie cry for help. Without words he can only bang himself up badly enough to require removal. I am impressed by the simplicity of his plan.

I want to join Sebastian against the wall. I'm not a general kid-lover. I like some kids and not others. But I'm drawn to Sebastian—poor guy. He's living in a fake home. Right now he's perfecting his ability to nod off in any situation, a skill my husband has honed, having grown up in not a fake home, but a terminally dull one. Pat can actually nap while playing cards, which his family does for hours on end while talking about which are the fastest routes for getting to towns no one else wants to go to.

The mommy group winds on through the early afternoon like a figure eight: discuss latest accomplishment of babies, pick up and reposition babies, remark on how hard it is to get anything done with babies, discuss latest accomplishment of babies, pick up and reposition babies, remark on how hard it is to get anything done with babies.

One woman says that she's afraid her daughter's teeth are coming in crooked. Another says that she's pretty sure her daughter's going to be left-handed and "Isn't that a sign of creativity?" Another says that a real sign of creativity is when a kid smears his feces on things "like it's paint." I wonder if Milly realizes that she's eaten all of the grapes and that no one else has had a chance at one.

Spence's rhythmic gumming of my knee makes me feel heavy and groggy.

I hear a woman say, "Well, of course, you need to cut juice with water. It's too much sugar otherwise."

I doze off somewhere in here, then come to with a jerk, quickly reaching up to wipe my mouth.

A woman says, "Daphne throws a fit if you put anything green on her plate."

I lean over to Milly. "Can you watch Spence for a minute? I need to run to the bathroom. Just let him suck on your arm, he'll be fine."

Patti's bathroom sparkles like a television-commercial bathroom in which germs are cute and animated and toilets talk. I look in the mirror. I can't imagine that all these women, by themselves, are this dull. I mean, Milly told me that one was a journalist and another owned a gallery. It must be something about putting them all together in a group. And what about Milly? She seems to blend right in. The Milly-I-know can pick up an egg with her ass, for God's sake.

Is there something about motherhood that turns one's mind to goo? I look at myself. Am I them? And what about the other things? Where's the food? Are grapes all we're going to get? Maybe this is my answer. These women are existing on water and grapes. And in this case they don't even get the grapes.

I turn on the cold faucet. The water feels good against my skin. Nice cold water.

How am I going to make it through the afternoon? I'll have to come up with some way not to fall asleep. And with no food I'm losing energy fast.

I lean over and splash water into my face. That, too, feels very good. I look up to see myself dripping with water, my vision fuzzy.

Yes, I think, it's something about groups. Something that dulls the active mind and subdues the eager heart.

I reach for a towel, press it to my face, and breathe in the clean.

Looking in the mirror, I see myself, washed and makeup-free. Without eyeliner I look like a fetus—round brown corneas, a shock in the pale landscape of my featureless face. I look strange to myself. An alien.

A knock at the door startles me. My alien eyes grow bigger.

"Brett," says Milly from behind the door, "are you okay?"

"Sure," I say, glancing down at Patti's white towel, noticing a dark brown swath of makeup smeared across it. Christ, I think, I've ruined the perfect towel that lives in the perfect bathroom of the pristine house that Patti built.

"Because Patti has to get in there with Sebastian," Milly says. "There's a cortisone cream in the cabinet that she needs for his scalp."

My hands tighten around the towel.

"I'll be out in a minute."

"Brett," says Milly, "did you notice that I ate all the grapes?"

"Yes. But I'm sure it doesn't matter," I say, laying the towel next to the sink.

"Well, Patti just ordered pizza. She's throwing a plastic tarp on the floor and letting the kids all sit on it and chew on crusts."

"Great," I say, picking up the towel again.

My stomach gurgles in anticipation of the pizza as I listen to her click into the living room on the glossy wood floor.

What if one of the others finds the towel? Looking around the bathroom, I return to the stack of identical towels on the windowsill. Aha. I am—though alien—practiced at trickery. I refold the foul towel with the telltale dark stain now facing the inside, and slip it under all the rest.

Then I slide open a drawer under the sink. My hand sorts through some loose tampons, lipsticks, and a brush. I take out a lipstick, dab color on my cheeks, and rub. Not bad, I think; the color makes me look more awake. I put the lipstick on the counter, fluff my hair, and smile my public smile.

I reach for the door—then pause. Turning once again to look at Patti's bathroom, I see the lipstick. And before I think of why, I slip it into my pocket.

✳ Friday

✳

✳

Everything in me gets lighter when I see Lana walk in with her friend Michelle.

Fifteen minutes ago I was waiting for Pat, pacing in front of Spencer while he plopped blocks into a pan I'd gotten out of the cupboard. Pat walked in the door and I fled, running to the bar— an escapee.

I've seen Michelle before, over at Lana's. But she looks different in the dim bar light. Her face is softer, her fine hair pretty around her face.

"You remember Michelle," Lana says, pulling a couple of stools away from the bar.

"Sure," I say.

I feel a familiar constriction in my chest, the pounding of what feels like extra blood whooshing through my system. I am pathologically shy. Years of therapy, when I was younger, have made it possible for me to form words when I first meet someone, but I still experience a flight response. Inside my head, microscopic beings like the Whos down in Whoville run around screaming,

"Holy Mary Mother of Fuck—*run*—fucking save yourself— *hide!!!!!*"

I look down at my glass of wine while Lana and Michelle settle.

"Michelle's been going crazy with her two-year-old, and I thought she'd like to get together with us on Fridays. Cut loose a bit before facing the weekend," Lana says.

Mack walks over. "You ladies looking for a taste of heaven?"

I am growing used to Mack's playful flirting. He does it with everyone: men, women, children, older people, gay men.

"What?" asks Michelle, clearly not responding in kind.

Mack adjusts, affably dropping the flirtation. "What can I get you?"

"I'll have an Amstel," she says. "No glass."

"Surprise me," says Lana, winking at him.

Mack winks back.

"So, Michelle," I say, "you have a two-year-old?" The first tool of the chronically shy: hide behind a question.

"Faith," she says.

"Michelle and her girlfriend Sarah got her in China," says Lana. "Michelle quit writing for talk shows to stay at home with her."

Mack puts a bottle of Amstel in front of Michelle. He slides a green shot over to Lana, who downs it and smiles.

"Mmm," she says to him. "You take such good care of me."

Mack salutes and turns as Lana says through clenched teeth, "What's with his hair?"

"What do you mean?" I ask, holding my glass in front of my mouth.

"There's more of it," says Lana.

Michelle leans in. "Plugs," she says.

Lana and I look at her in our huddle.

"You can tell because it comes out in a pattern. Like the way hair used to come out of those highlighting caps."

We stare at the back of Mack's head.

"Why do men do that?" says Michelle. "What's wrong with bald?"

"It's a virility thing," says Lana.

"But, come on, do they think that this looks better?" I chime in.

Michelle sits back in her barstool. Lana and I pull up.

"At least they don't do snaps anymore," Michelle says.

"Snaps?" asks Lana.

"Yeah. I have a cousin whose toupee snaps onto a snap that's surgically implanted in his scalp."

"Um. Okay," I say. "What does snap-on toupee look like?"

"Wrong," says Michelle.

"No, really, what does it look like actually? Describe it," says Lana.

Michelle smiles. She's got us and she plays the moment. She sips her Amstel, looking off.

"It looks," she says, "like a smoker's lung."

Lana cackles.

"Only," says Michelle, "there's this indentation in the lung— where it snaps onto his head."

I feel my shyness seep away—the Whos slink off. I find myself on that peculiar planet women meet on, where being together in that moment is enough.

"Now wait," I say. "What about when he unsnaps his hair? Does he just have this exposed snap in the middle of his head?"

Lana pulls up her knees, propping them against the bar. Michelle puts her beer down.

"I've never seen him without the toupee or his cap. It's this red plaid cap that snaps onto the snap when he's not wearing the piece."

"His piece being his *hair*," says Lana.

"Right."

"I wonder if anyone's ever seen the snap," I say.

"He's single," says Michelle.

"Psst . . . ," whispers Lana as she raises her hand at Mack to order another shot.

We look at Mack, eyes on his plugs.

"I bet," I say, leaning over, "when you talk to your cousin, all you can think about is the snap."

"Haven't seen him in years. Not after he threatened to shoot me for being gay."

Something drops out. We stop.

Lana and I look at Michelle as she reaches for her beer.

"Hey," she says. "I've slept in bed with the same person for twelve years. He sleeps alone with a snap in the middle of his big bald head."

We drop back in. Motion and sound come together.

Sounds about right, I think.

✳ Lost and Found

✳

✳

$\mathbf{I}$ like the building right off the bat. The
clanky gate of the elevator slides open even though it's stopped
two inches below the floor of the door leading to the hallway.
The walls have old-building-smell and the wooden floor creaks
with every step. I could be in New York or Chicago. This is definitely not a Los Angeles building.

I figure the room I'm looking for is the one I see at the end.
A woman sits there in a skirt, reading a magazine. As I enter, I try
not to make eye contact. What do you say to someone else who's
waiting to see a therapist: "What are you in for?"

A sign says to fill out one of the slips below if you're new. I
take a slip out of the basket and a short pencil from another basket. There are about twenty pencils in the basket and I wonder
why there are so many. Are there ever more than a couple of people in here at a time? I can't imagine a huge line of people winding out of this room demanding a session with Dr. Martha Ryan.
Granted, I don't know Dr. Ryan. But no one's that good.

I sit in the chair opposite the woman and stuff my backpack

under my chair. She doesn't look up from her magazine. She knows the drill.

I pick up an *O* magazine from the low table, rest the slip on it, and fill out my name and all the vitals. I consider flipping through the magazine, but Oprah looks so happy and slim on the front that I'm not in the mood. Instead, I pick up *Time* from the table, with something about cloning on the cover.

I flip through the magazine.

I wonder if I got the time wrong. The woman in the skirt is waiting too. We can't both have appointments at the same time. Maybe she's here to see someone else. Some dentist down the hall who shares a waiting room with Dr. Ryan.

I look up and see no evidence of any other doctor, only the slips for Dr. Ryan. The woman looks up from her magazine and smiles.

"Dr. Ryan?" she asks.

Contact. I look down at a picture of two sheep looking exactly alike.

"Yeah," I say.

"I'm just here to pay my bill from last week," she says.

I look up. I wonder why she didn't simply mail her check in. Is she using payment as an excuse for a therapy quickie?

"I can go," I offer, realizing that I'm looking for a reason not to go through with this. Right now my problems seem so petty, I feel ridiculous. "You see, Dr. Ryan, I have this husband who adores me and this darling baby who looks divine and friends who make me laugh." What a load. What a goddamned burden. What the fuck? The woman in the skirt is probably here for real stuff; she probably has that condition that makes you pull one hair out of your head at a time. She's sitting here in her wig, having scraped together a few bucks hooking so that she can pay off her therapy bill from last week. Therapy being the only thing that might give her an answer to why she wakes up screaming, scratching herself wildly, three times a night.

"Of course not," says the woman in the wig. "I'm only giving her a check. It won't take any time."

The hooker has a bank account, I think. Things can't be too bad.

I haven't been in a therapist's office in years. Not that I have a problem with it. It took about ten therapists and a couple of self-help seminars to get me to the point where I had as much affection and forgiveness for myself as I might a good friend. In fact, I *was* my own best friend. Sometimes I annoyed myself. But there were times when I was so darned cute I wanted to hug me. This was up until Spence was born, when the best friend became a stranger.

Having been through the therapy mill, I know that therapists are people with all sorts of strengths and prejudices of their own.

When I was single and living in New York, I wasted a couple of good years on a Gestalt therapist who worked out of a basement office on Fourteenth Street. Dr. Flom looked a lot like a tall, skinny Freud, which probably did a lot to recommend him to me. He wore a beard and corduroy pants and had no discernible muscle mass.

I don't remember being particularly unhappy, though time does tricky things—maybe I was. Most likely, I went because I didn't have a boyfriend or an acting job and I thought that going to a therapist might be just the kind of magic pill to make those things happen.

So I entered Dr. Flom's basement office a vaguely dissatisfied girl and left two years later, angry, bitter, and a couple of G's poorer.

The office was covered in dog hair that came from a white terrier that jumped all over me as soon as I walked through the door. The dog would start to settle as I took off my jacket to sit on the hair-laden couch. Dr. Flom would then lean back in his tilting desk chair, the smelly dog at his feet, and I would talk.

Gestalt, he said, was a term that meant that he dealt with "the whole thing, the body and the mind." So, occasionally, he would have me get up from the couch, kneel in the white dog hair on the carpet, and beat a pillow with a couple of padded bats. The dog would jump around wildly, yapping while I beat the pillow senseless.

Somewhere in the middle of the second year, Dr. Flom hit on a theory. He decided that all of my problems stemmed from the fact that I was the least favored child. He should know, he said, because he was one of two brothers and his older brother was by far the favorite. Tears rolled down his cheeks as he described various toys his brother got, but not he. Trips his brother went on, but not he. Compliments his brother received, but not he.

I encouraged him to talk to his brother. Work it out.

He couldn't, he said. His brother was dead.

I suggested that he beat some pillows. He did once, but fell into a heap, crying, as the dog licked his head.

Through it all, I thought, It's true: my brother Erik was cuter than me. It's true: he got more attention than I did.

As Dr. Flom cried and struggled through the next couple of months, I seethed at my parents for having favored Erik over me.

It ended badly. I stopped seeing Dr. Flom because he left town. God knows how long I would have paid for sessions that involved him weeping and raging about his brother. The last time we met in his hairy office, he told me about an incident twenty-nine years ago when he stole his brother's fishing rod so that his brother couldn't go on a special fishing trip with his father. Two weeks after that last session, he called me from Maine, where he had gone, he said, "to sort out some stuff with the dead."

I went home that Christmas to rail against my parents for ruining my life by favoring my brother. It was a Christmas that my mother refers to as "that time you came home mad at the world."

The bewigged hooker goes into Dr. Ryan's office and leaves seconds later. I silently wish her well.

I enter Dr. Ryan's office with skepticism and desperation. It resembles a college professor's study, with primitive African masks hanging on the wall and hundreds of books on the shelves.

She motions for me to sit on the couch opposite her. I sink into it, noticing the box of tissues on the low table between us. She looks like a nun who only recently quit being a nun—no makeup, flat shoes, frizzy hair pulled back, a frilly blouse buttoned up to her chin.

Maybe she *was* a nun.

She does that therapist thing where she just looks at me for a bit. I find this passively hostile. But I know enough to know that that's my own "projection." So I sit and wait for something to happen while little specks of dust swirl in the sunlight that streams through the window like persistent hope.

Dr. Ryan perches on the edge of her chair.

"So what are you here for?" she asks.

I have this feeling of hanging on, of being on the edge of something. I hold my breath tightly. At once I realize that it is not wise for me to open my mouth. If I open it, if breath comes in—I will . . .

"I'm miserable!" I scream, grabbing the Kleenex box. Snot explodes out of my nose. I sputter, let out another scream, and double over, smashing the box between my knees and chest. I pull it out, crumpled, and try to mold it back into shape as I continue my wall of sound and snot.

"I'm so unhappy," I cry. "I hate myself. I hate my life. I feel like it's never going to change. I feel like I'm always going to be fat and unhappy and needy and a sniveling pile of nothing. This is it. I've got nothing. I'm nothing. I'm a terrible mother. I don't like me. How can anyone else like me?"

The words, phrases, come in short bursts, between phlegmy sobs. And as my volume and complaining build, so does my self-loathing.

"And then I think, I'm so lucky, you know? I got this healthy kid. I have this husband who's great. I'm worse than the most microscopic crumb because I'm so fucking ungrateful. All I want is to rewind my life and be the way I was before I had Spence. I'm never going to be happy, ever again. I've ruined my life. I'm miserable and I deserve to die. And it's never going to change. I'm going to be this horrible, unhappy mother who makes my son feel like shit for being born and I'm going to torture Pat into having an affair and leaving me. And I'm going to be a fat, miserable old lady who screams at the neighbor kids for throwing balls in her yard. I hate myself."

More of the same self-pitying invective spews out of me in fits and starts for what feels like half an hour, as Dr. Ryan sits primly with her hands in her lap.

My words get slowed down by longer stretches of soft crying and tissue grabbing, until I feel so tired I want to curl up on the couch and take a nap.

That's worth a sixty-dollar copay, I think, exhausted.

Dr. Ryan looks at me, her expression unaltered.

I put the mangled box of tissues back on the table and breathe.

"Maybe we should think about antidepressants," she says.

What? It's not *that* bad, I think.

"I'm probably just having a bad day," I say.

"Do you think you might hurt your son?" she asks.

"What?"

I look down at the wet Kleenex in my hand.

"No. I would never hurt Spence," I say.

But I might run away, I think. And isn't that just as bad?

In the remaining five minutes of our session Dr. Ryan and I decide to hold off on medication and see where this goes. But I can already tell by the lightness of my limbs that this is what I've needed—balls-out sobbing and complaining.

I leave the building, a little buzzy, and stop by a high-end children's clothing store called Lost and Found. I rarely poke around stores like this, because I have opinions about people who buy expensive clothes, especially for children. But today I think that my opinions are hard to carry, especially when they're about myself.

So I walk around Lost and Found fingering the tiny merchandise. And I end up buying Spence a pair of shoes that look like bear claws. They cost only slightly less than the copay I just handed Dr. Ryan.

* Ass
*
*

Since Spence was born, my body has become strange to me. Sliding my hands over its topography, I feel bumps and sags where once there were curves and planes. I was warned, of course. But like sex, death, and Vegas, you really don't know anything until you get there.

During one of Spence's naps, I steal into my bedroom to take a look at myself, naked, in a full-length mirror. Turning around slowly to view the new me.

Uh-huh, hmmm. Fleshy, doughy. In some places the damage is not that bad. My breasts have held up remarkably well. Turn, turn.

Then there it is—my ass.

I haven't thought about my ass for years, for reasons that are probably clear to friends who've seen my ass on a regular basis. It used to be unremarkable. Rather square and flat. The best thing I could have said about my ass is that one usually saw it after an overall impression had already been made.

But this post-Spence ass is something else. Still square and flat, it is now larger, discolored, and mottled.

*   *   *

When my mother comes to visit, Lana and I stand behind her in line.

"You have the same ass as your mother," says Lana.

I look at my mother's ass and see my future.

Asses don't get better, I think. They get worse.

For days after that, I look at my ass in the reflection of store windows, forcing Pat to judge it and buying magazines that promise to tell me what jeans would best disguise my ass deficiency.

I look at other women's asses, becoming somewhat of an ass expert. I decide that what sets a good ass apart from others is size and definition.

I can't stay away from the topic of ass for too long.

At a party I watch a woman lean over to dip her chip. She's probably never been pregnant.

"You have a very firm ass," I say.

She looks at me blankly as Pat pulls me by the elbow over to the bar.

"You've got to stop thinking about ass," he hisses into my ear.

"I know, I know," I say. "I just can't help it. My world is full of ass."

I spend the rest of the party trying to divert my thoughts by figuring out how much it cost to cater the affair. Determining how much things cost and how much money people make often occupies my mind nicely for long stretches. If I determine that someone makes a boatload of undeserved money, then I make a mental list of ways in which I am better off than they are. It was when I started doing this that I really "got" that you can't put a price tag on integrity and a sense of irony.

So I'm adding up the price of the hors d'oeuvres and what the wine would cost wholesale, when I catch a glimpse of my ass in a marbled mirror. I spend the rest of the party and weeks afterward with my back against a wall.

J ust don't think about it," Pat tells me about whatever "it" currently is.

Pat, I think, has the perfect mind for a serial killer. He can just turn it off. Like Scarlett O'Hara, he can think about it tomorrow. Or not think about it at all.

My mind, on the other hand, is drawn to the grotesque, the annoying, and the petty like a heat-seeking missile.

I think about ass every few minutes for the next month.

Weeks before this I was obsessed with plastic vaginas—or, more to the point, with who on earth would buy and use a plastic vagina.

I had gone to a store called the Pleasure Chest, with Lana, who was looking for things that might jazz up an evening with Tony. I'd been to these stores before when they first became popular in the early nineties. I'd gone partly out of curiosity and partly because I thought I might pick up a few new tips. I think I bought a pair of handcuffs once. But, for the most part, it just seemed like the outfits, zippered masks, and two-pronged dildos could cause a nasty rash. And how does one clean and store these things?

The Pleasure Chest was different from the stores I remembered from a decade ago. For one thing, this store had branched out and also sold bath salts, scented candles, and fresh flowers.

The other remarkable thing was that huge families from the

Midwest strolled through the aisles with shopping baskets over their arms, picking up nipple rings and butt plugs.

The merchandise looked like the usual fare. As I absently fingered some stuff while watching a mother and daughter flip through the flavored condoms, my hand landed on a plastic vagina.

At first I didn't know what it was. In fact, the hairless, pink mound of plastic was so unrecognizable to me that I had to read the label to figure it out.

It's a label I regret having read. I just couldn't understand why someone would buy a small, disembodied vagina. What did one attach this to? Did one simply place it in the middle of the bed? Where was its hair? There was simply a hole in the middle of the mound. There was no canal, no insides to it. I just couldn't see anything to recommend it except that it was remarkably cheap (just $6.95) and small enough to carry in a fanny pack.

In the days that followed, all I could think about was plastic vaginas and who used them. Did any of my men friends? Did the man behind the cash register at the wine store? I asked Pat if any of his friends used plastic vaginas. He hadn't heard of any who had. Would *he* ever use one? He didn't think so. After a while he refused to talk about them. As did my therapist, best friend, and the women in my book group.

Michelle takes me to a Siddha Yoga center. She claims that the meditation technique she learned there can help me train my mind away from thoughts of ass. After all, it helped her control her hypochondria. This is a strong endorsement, as Lana says she's taken Michelle to the emergency room more than once, panting into a paper bag in the back of a taxi because she's convinced a slight blurring of vision means the onset of mad cow disease.

Lana says that last summer Michelle's fear of West Nile virus was so extreme that she had to wrestle a knife from her to stop her from amputating her own finger after a mosquito bit it.

Michelle and I take off our shoes in a bright lobby. Over the shoe rack is a huge photograph of the current guru of Siddha Yoga, Guru Mai. The first thing I notice about her is that she is a major babe. The second thing I notice is my ass in the mirror as I bend down to stash my shoes. "Don't think about ass," I say to myself as I focus on Guru Mai's beatific face beaming from the photo.

My mind starts to veer to thoughts of Guru Mai's ass and how nicely covered it is in that red robe she wears in the picture. I feel slightly dirty carrying thoughts of the guru's ass with me as I pad, in my stocking feet, over to a spot where I can sit cross-legged and watch Guru Mai give her videotaped lesson. A TV is propped up in the chair where she would sit, were she here.

Where is she? I wonder. I imagine her sitting behind a two-way mirror deciding which one of us to mind-control.

Guru Mai's face pops on the screen and starts to tell a story about a foolish man and a strawberry. She tells the story like it's a total laugh riot, like it's something hilarious that this man wants this strawberry before it's ripe. Cross-legged devotees around me giggle like they're in on the secret.

Michelle looks over at me and gives me a stoned-on-yoga-and-green-tea smile.

I can't figure out how any of this is going to train my mind away from its petty and lurid thoughts. If anything, I'm so bored by the strawberry-and-foolish-man story that I start to think about how much the guru makes on the gift shop alone. I also think that the drawstring yoga pants that are being sold would hide any kind of ass, and I wonder if I can get a second pair for half price if I buy two.

The TV pops off, leaving the image of the guru's face burning on the gray screen like a modern-day Shroud of Turin.

I hear a voice say, "And now we will have twenty minutes of silent meditation."

Good, I think, this is it. This is what I came for.

The voice continues with some instructions as a musical instrument twangs over and over again.

Is that a zither? I wonder. It's twangy, isn't it? Kind of a stringed thing that doesn't play real notes. Like a poor cousin of the harpsichord.

"Empty your mind," the voice says.

The voice—who is it coming from? Is it from that guy in the mustard shirt that gave me a date-rapist smile in the lobby?

"If a thought persists, gently let it go," says the voice.

The bones of my ass feel the hard floor through a flimsy pillow that I picked up from a stack by the door. Who knows who's sat on this pillow before? Faces dance in my mind—faces of other possible users of the pillow. They fade in and out of each other, laughing, like an arty segment of an old black-and-white horror film. Not just *any* film. I've seen this film. What movie is it? *The Picture of Dorian Gray?* No. A Jack the Ripper thing? No. Wait a minute . . . it's something I saw recently . . . a Vincent Price thing . . .

The faces rise and fall in my mind and I review every old movie I've seen in the last few months.

This is hopeless, I think. I will forever be tormented by my own thoughts.

"Do not attach yourself to any one thought," says the voice.

I start to feel floaty. My mind drifts as if it's not *in* me, then focuses on a fuzzy red circle.

This is it, I think. I'm not attaching to any thought.

"Don't attach to the thought of not attaching to thought," I say to myself.

I go toward the fuzzy red circle. I am walking but not walking. I get close to the circle and it starts to change colors. I watch it vibrate. It pulses rhythmically.

It is perfect, I think—then try not to think.

It is a perfect circle. My mind settles and for a brief moment I contemplate the mathematical rightness of the curve.

The voice returns.

"And when you're ready, open your eyes slowly," it says.

The circle gets smaller. I watch it float in front of me. And just before I open my eyes, it floats away from me. The neat half of the perfect ass.

✳ Friday

L ook, I get it. I get it. Things get . . . the sex gets routine," says Katherine. She picks up her black and tan and slips the wet coaster out from underneath it.

Katherine has been joining us on Fridays for about a month. She went to acting school with me eighteen years ago in New York, and we bumped into each other again a couple of months ago at a mutual acquaintance's preschool fund-raiser. When I invited her for Friday drinks, she practically wept with gratitude. She'd been to a number of midday mommy groups that were so dull that she found herself hoping for an interruption the size of an earthquake or a mud slide. Katherine fits into our little group remarkably well, having quickly distinguished herself as the mommy who can do a beer bong standing on her hands while balancing a plate of fries with her feet.

"Right," I say. "If you don't know that sex is going to be a little tamer after you've been with someone for a decade and had a kid, then you're an idiot."

Michelle smiles. I can't tell what she's thinking. It dawns on me that I know nothing about her sex life. Hard to know if that's because she's the lone lesbian here or because she's naturally conservative about personal sex talk. I'd understand that, since I don't tend to say much about Pat and me. Certainly not in comparison to Katherine and Lana, who don't seem to stay away from the subject of sex for too long.

Lana leans over the bar and pulls on Mack's shirt. "What's that?" she asks him, pointing to a misty yellow drink in front of a guy in a business suit. "Never mind telling me. It looks good. I'll have one of those."

I pause in my head to marvel, yet again, at Lana's adventurousness when it comes to drinking—and everything else.

"But, oh, I miss the mystery of sex with someone new. The 'what's going to happen?' part," says Katherine.

Katherine has a voice that rasps like it's three o'clock in the morning all the time. In fact, she makes her living from it, most famously for saying, "Bravo—watch what happens." She's arrestingly beautiful too, her Irish pale complexion paler still under black curls that flop over her forehead.

"I wish I could get Slim to wear some kind of weird mask, not talk, and do something to me so freaky that I can't even tell you guys about it," she says, raising her now empty beer glass at Mack.

"Can't imagine what that would be," mumbles Lana.

Neither can I, but for different reasons. I can't imagine the act. Lana can't imagine not telling.

Katherine's boyfriend, Slim, is a gorgeous, chiseled black guy with a lady-killer smile—a drummer for a band he started with his friend Jim, called SLIM JIM. As long as I've known Katherine, she's predominantly dated black men.

Slim has a gig on Friday nights. Which means that every week Katherine has to walk out of the bar sharply at 5:45 to take over watching Jake, their two-year-old.

"The other day," Katherine says to me, "I was thinking about a time. God, it was one of those loft parties we used to go to in Manhattan. This was the one where Milly picked up the egg with her ass."

"I remember."

"This guy who I had been talking to. Some hot black guy. Sexy. An actor, for sure. Follows me to the bathroom."

"What is it with you and black guys?" asks Michelle.

"Black guys will do anything," says Lana, sipping the yellow drink Mack has just delivered.

"So I'm getting ready to pee and he slips in the door."

"You left the door open?" asks Michelle.

"I think the point here," I say, "is that she knows he's coming in."

"And you know the way you hover over the toilet if it's not a bathroom you know," Katherine continues. "Well, he puts his hand in my urine stream."

"Okay, icky," I say, leaning back in my barstool. "That's all I need to know."

"*I* want to know," says Lana.

"And then he licks it."

"His hand?" asks Michelle.

"Of course, his hand."

"What happened after that?" asks Lana. "That's a pretty strong opener."

"You know," says Katherine, "nothing really. I watched him lick and then washed my hands and left him standing there. We eyed each other through the party after that. Sexy as hell. And, of course, I think about it all the time."

Lana raises her yellow drink and stops. We all look at the drink in her hand for a moment. Then she smiles and takes a sip. Michelle and I shudder. Katherine giggles.

"I wonder what he did in that bathroom after you left," says Michelle, her face screwed up like she knows but doesn't want to know.

Mack delivers Katherine's black and tan and tops off my red wine. I wonder how much of this conversation he's hearing.

"So these are the things you miss?" I ask. I don't have stories like this. Sure, I remember a few sweaty fumblings in stairwells with men I just met. But nothing like urine-licking or Lana's guy who put rubber bands around everything on him and her—a visual I try to block out even today, seven years after hearing the story.

"Yeah," says Katherine like a sigh. She picks up her fresh black and tan. "I wonder what would have happened if I had actually met the guy. Like if I had walked over to him at the party, afterwards. I mean, maybe something else would have happened to me. No Slim. No baby."

"Men who lick your pee off their hands aren't the kind who hook up for any length of time," says Lana. "I'm just guessing."

"Yeah," says Michelle. "You are way better off."

Michelle is fast becoming a fan of Slim's, who told her he likes dykes because they don't give a shit about what men think.

"I know I'm better off," says Katherine, sliding her finger down the fog of her glass.

We three watch Katherine.

We watch her dream of the urine-licker and what might have been, as the orange light from outside stretches long across the bar.

* Orange Alert

*

*

 Six months after 9/11, I sit in a car with Lana, Michelle, and Katherine. We've just been to see a dreadful all-woman sketch group called FemFatal, the main source of dubious hilarity having been jokes about PMS.

The car is stopped in front of my house.

"That show was just one long complaint about being a woman and getting older. Jesus," says Lana from the backseat.

"Almost made you yearn for a dick joke," says Katherine.

"Almost," says Michelle.

"I'm off," I say, opening the door. "Sorry to miss next Friday. Someone take notes. Don't have too much fun without me."

I'm talking about my upcoming trip to visit a high school friend in London. Ten glorious days on my own, in London of all places, while my mother-in-law watches Spence with Pat. The women in the car have been oozing envy ever since they heard.

"Hey, Brett," says Lana, stopping me. "I have a present for you."

She rummages around in her purse and passes me a Baggie.

"It's a Vicodin. I figured you'd want one for the plane. It's from my post–C-section hoard. I'm not sure if it still packs a punch."

"Vicodin," is the hushed chorus from my friends.

"Thanks," I say. "I don't know if I'll use it on the plane, though. Because I'd rather have wine."

Lana says, "I was just thinking that if something happens like a man with a bomb, you'll be relaxed."

"If there's someone with a bomb on the plane," says Michelle, "she's going to need all of her mental faculties to outwit him."

"If there's a bomb on the plane, she's going to be dead like *that*," says Katherine, snapping her fingers. "She might as well be stoned."

I put the Baggie in my pocket.

"Nothing's going to happen on the plane," I say, feeling the knob of the pill through my jeans.

I call my agent, who never calls me, to tell her not to bother calling me because I'll be in London.

"London, huh?" she says. "Make sure you get to the airport early. With the country on Orange Alert, things are going to take more time. Orange Alert is one step below war, you know. Frankly, I think it's a bad time to travel safetywise. Businesswise, I've got no problem. Stars are so desperate they're taking up all the work that would normally filter down to actors like you."

I start packing two days ahead of time, mulling over what outfits to wear on "holiday," as the Brits say. What should I wear while lounging around the mansion? What kicky accessory can I bring to the pub after seeing a marvelous show at the Old Vic?

Pat watches me pack and repack.

I hand him a Post-it reminder of things I've already reminded him about.

"Don't let your mother mess with Spence's nap schedule too much," I say.

"Brett, it's all going to be fine."

"I know. I'm just thinking there's some big thing I'm forgetting to mention."

"Mom's going to love being with Spence."

"Don't let her love it too much," I say. "What if Spence forgets who I am and starts thinking she's his mommy?"

As silly as this sounds, it's been a nagging thought ever since I asked her to come out. Spence adores her because she has nothing but time for him. In comparison, I feel like a depressed sack of mommy.

"He's not going to forget you," says Pat. "I'll show him your picture every day."

I can't figure out how I can both long for and dread being away from my son. Although I suspect this condition will never change. Won't I shine with pride on his graduation day only to feel like he's been stolen from me as he drives to college with his U-Haul?

Pat walks over to his computer, where he'll stick the Post-it on top of the other Post-its I've given him.

"Do you think I should fly to London during an Orange Alert?" I ask. Pat pauses, the hand holding the latest Post-it reaching toward the other Post-its. "I mean, it is an Orange Alert. Maybe it's too dangerous. Maybe I should stay. Nah. I should go, right?"

The Post-it falls onto the desk. I look at Pat to see him holding his pose like a modern-day Pompeian fossilized in mid-activity. I watch, knowing that he is considering his answer very, very carefully. The refrigerator drones as the air becomes electric with the possibility of true domestic drama. What happens next depends on Pat's ability to organize and weigh years of intricate couple politics.

It is, after all, a test. He knows there's a single right answer, and he knows that only I know the answer. If he shows too much concern, I will become hysterical, swallow the Vicodin still buried in the pocket of my jeans, and scream at him that he's never been supportive of anything I do. Then again, if he doesn't show *enough* concern, I will storm out of the apartment, swallow the Vicodin, walk around the block, and return with a list of times he's let me down—starting with the now infamous evening he left me all alone with his born-again mother so that he could play poker with the boys. I ended up drinking a bottle of gin and telling his teetotaling mother that her son likes sex. He *really*, *really* likes it.

Pat slowly sinks into his chair at the computer.

"I think," he says, drifting off as he looks out the window, searching for something written in the sky.

"I think . . ."

"Yes," I say. "I want to know what you really think. I mean it's an Orange Alert. Should I be concerned? Should *you* be concerned?"

"I think . . ."

"Are you worried about me?"

"Well, I'm always . . . ," he says, picking through the possibilities in his mind. "I'm always concerned . . . I'm always interested in what . . . I always know that you can . . ."

He looks back at me. His eyes search my face. The naked desperation in his expression softens me.

"Because I think it's going to be fine," I say, letting him off the hook. "And I can't make a decision just based on fear. If I did that, I'd never go anywhere, right?"

Pat looks like a condemned man who just got a call from the governor in his final hour.

"Absolutely," he says, his voice loud with relief.

★   ★   ★

The night before I leave, there is a message on my machine from a friend in Philadelphia.

"Just wanted to say bon voyage. I think it's great what you're doing. I just . . . I guess I just wanted to hear your voice in case anything . . . We argued a little the last time we talked and I just didn't want that to be the last thing . . ." Her voice catches. "You know, the last thing . . . in case. Silly. Nothing's going to happen. You're going to be fine! It's all going to be fine!"

Another pause.

"Brett, I love you. And I will always love you."

Another pause.

And in a much deeper register, "Good-bye." Her voice is soft and wet.

I decide not to take the Vicodin with me on the plane, figuring that a couple of drinks will relax me enough.

I put it in its clean Baggie in the corner of my desk drawer. It sits there—a small white promise of relief.

I kiss Spence good-bye, feeling a pull so strong I almost can't walk out the door. My mother-in-law takes him and I run to the elevator like I'm fleeing the scene of a crime.

On the way to the airport Pat drives while I do a verbal check-list.

"Passport—yes. Money—yes. Ticket—in my backpack."

Pat turns on the radio.

"Four hundred troops have been stationed at Heathrow Airport. Blair's support of the United States has made London a top target for terrorist cells sympathetic with Al Qaeda."

I look over to Pat.

"Four hundred troops," I say.

He looks fine. Relaxed even.

"What do you think?" I ask.

"I think," he says, "I think, Wow, four hundred troops."

"Is that four hundred guys with guns? Or is a troop like a hundred guys, meaning there's four thousand guys with guns?"

Pat seems to consider this.

"I think it's just four hundred guys with guns," he says.

We turn our attention to the radio again.

"Scotland Yard has uncovered four separate plots to bomb Heathrow in the next week. All threats are being treated as serious."

"Do you still think I should go?" I ask Pat.

We change lanes. Pat's face settles and he reaches over to turn off the radio. There is a quiet surety in his manner.

"Brett," he says, "if I really thought that anything was going to happen to you, I wouldn't let you go. I think this is all about fear. And fear makes fear. It's one big fear fest. You're going to be safe. Spence and I are going to be fine. Spence will remember you. And you will have fun."

We see the sign "Airport." Pat drives under it.

"So, obviously, I think you should go. It's more important what *you* think," he says.

"I think," I say, "I think I should have brought the Vicodin."

When I get on the plane, I look for faces of possible bombers. I look for dark men with just-about-to-enter-the-kingdom-of-heaven expressions on their faces. Although by now I think that the terrorists must be getting smarter, and I should really be looking for an old lady with depleted uranium in her bun.

I waggle my puffy coat into a ball and stuff it in the overhead compartment.

My seat's a good one. An aisle.

I take a *People* magazine out of my backpack and put it in the pocket in front of me. Doing this calms me down because I love reading cheapo magazines on planes. Things I would rarely do on the ground are delicious pleasures miles up in the air. Like reading bad magazines, drinking five of those little bottles of wine, and having sex in the bathroom. With or without a partner.

I feel my seat rigid against my back and try to focus on the pleasures that await me, rather than the nervous guy in front of me who keeps glancing around.

It's a packed flight, and as the flight attendant swivels her arms around demonstrating safety features that are laughably useless against a terrorist attack, I concentrate on breathing slowly.

In/out. In/out.

The takeoff is smooth.

In/out. In/out.

I think about the pill in a Baggie in my drawer at home.

In/out. In/out. Four thousand troops at Heathrow.

We climb higher. The nervous guy in front of me looks back at a dark woman and waves a bit. *Is it a signal?*

In/out. In/out. The pill. The pill in the Baggie. Why didn't I stay at home?

The loudspeaker comes on. There is a pause. *Oh my God, this is fucking it!!! Some guy is going to come on and say that he's been living in this oppressive American regime for twenty-three years masquerading as a United Airlines pilot, only to choose this day to fly this packed plane into Paramount Studios.*

"Ladies and gentlemen," a calm voice says, "this is your pilot and I wanted to tell you . . ."

He goes on about the trip we're going to take and the temperature in London. My body gets loose and I begin to think about the five minis of wine I'll be ordering from the flight attendants, when I hear . . .

"We expect a great deal of turbulence leaving Los Angeles. So we ask that you keep your seat belts fastened until further notice. The flight crew will stay seated and beverage service will be delayed until the turbulence is over."

Beverage service *delayed*?!

In/out. In/out. Out, out, out. Orange Alert Orange Alert.

Blood rushes through my body like it's sending fuel. My throat contracts. I begin to choke. I cough. The plane lurches like the deck of the *Starship Enterprise* under attack.

I cough and spew phlegm onto the tray table in front of me.

I look around for someone to grab onto.

My vision is foggy but I can make out: the man across the aisle reading a paper, the woman behind me perusing the duty-free catalog, the kid, sitting kitty-corner, picking her nose.

Are they all drugged? Out, out, out.

"Are you all right?" asks the woman behind me. She lowers the catalog and reaches for my arm.

"Um . . . no," I say, my voice wobbly.

Suddenly, my throat opens up and a sob comes out. Tears gush down my cheeks.

"Oh dear," says the woman in an English accent.

"I just . . ."

I start to heave giant sobs. The plane bounces like crazy, then drops like someone simply let it go.

"Oh my God. Help!" I scream to the God of my youth—the old man in the sky.

The man across from me smiles.

"It'll be over soon," he says.

I sob huge waves of tears and mucus and sound.

Between waves I manage to say, "It feels like . . . we're going . . . we're all going . . . to fall out of the sky."

The man reaches over and holds my wrist just below the Englishwoman's hand that holds on tight like she's done this before.

"I know it feels like that," the man says. "But we won't fall out of the sky."

My rolling sobs soften into sniffles as the plane continues to bounce. The Englishwoman's hand disappears only to appear again with a brown pill.

"It's an herbal sedative," she says. "A woman in the back sent it down."

"Thank you," I say, my voice small and babyish.

And I take the pill. My cheeks are wet, my jeans damp between my legs. In moments my breathing returns to its natural rhythm. It can't be the little brown pill that I've taken only seconds before. It can't be the wine I haven't had yet. But this feeling of soft grace feels like a pill or wine swimming through my system. It's as if I've been released from my fear like magic. No, not magic. I know that. It's the old man in the sky. It's deliverance given, simply because I asked for it.

The Englishwoman's hand settles on my elbow again, and it stays there until the plane stops shuddering and goes in a straight line.

✳ What to Expect

✳

✳

So what do you think?" I ask Michelle as we sip tea in my living room, watching Spence take a couple of steps, fall, then crawl to a ball he's been rolling. Michelle's daughter sits at a table, neatly coloring. Her legs dangle, crossed at the ankles. Faith's now a serious three-year-old who has no time for Spence's less academic interests.

"I think he's figuring it out," says Michelle.

"But all the other kids are walking like pros by now."

"He's an Aries," she says. "He's taking his own sweet time."

I know nothing about astrology, but I like that Michelle seems so sure.

"See here," I say, picking up a dog-eared paperback, "are these columns: What your toddler *should* be able to do by the end of the month, What your toddler will *probably* be able to do by the end of the month, What your toddler may *possibly* be able to do by the end of the month, and What your toddler *may even* be able to do by the end of the month. According to this, Spence is probably supposed to be running by now."

"Probably supposed?"

"That's my wording," I say.

"There's no such thing as 'probably supposed.' "

"What I mean is that it's in the 'probably' column and he's not even walking yet. Let alone running. Although how they determine the difference between 'will probably' and 'may possibly' is anyone's guess. It's a very thin line."

"It's just a bunch of editors figuring out some neat columns that give parents some gauge of . . . I don't know . . . what to expect, I guess," Michelle says.

"Still, I'd be more comfortable if walking was in the 'may possibly' column. That leaves it more open," I say.

"I don't see where all this worrying is getting you," says Michelle. "Spence is a normal little boy."

"He hasn't said a word yet," I say.

"You said that he said 'car.' "

"Yeah, but he was pointing to the toilet."

I lie in bed next to Pat.

"The book says Spence should be able to build a tower of two blocks," I say.

Pat lays his magazine on his chest.

"He can't build a tower?" he asks.

"I show him how to do it and he just grabs a block and throws it."

"Babies throw things."

"Thing is," I say, "if he can't build a tower of two blocks, how's he going to move on to the next stage?"

"The next stage?"

"Building a tower out of three blocks."

*   *   *

I become obsessed with stages, mentally checking things off as Spence achieves them.

Good, good, I think when he puts a triangle block in a triangle hole. That's in the "may even be able to" column. He's way ahead of the pack on shapes.

I start to think about what the stages for early motherhood are. In fact, I get very excited about pitching a book to the what-to-expect folks:

What to Expect the First Two Years of Motherhood

Sample Chapter

By the time your child is eighteen months old:

You should be able to:

- Build a tower of two blocks by yourself without weeping
- Babble

You will *probably* be able to:

- Show your baby how to build a tower of two blocks without saying, "How simple is this? It's just two blocks on top of each other. See? One. Two."
- Sleep through the night without having a nightmare about your child losing limbs or shrinking to the size of a grain of sand
- End a full day alone with your child without screaming at your husband as soon as he comes home, "What about me? Am I a fucking zero here? When do I get to have some goddamned fun?"

You may *possibly* be able to:
- Build a tower of two blocks while your child is napping, without thinking, How can he not get this? All the other kids can do this. Should I take him to some kind of "tower specialist"?
- Go to bed without having that glass of wine you refer to as "Mommy's magic medicine"
- Use a spoon and fork without thinking about how bloody it would get if you stabbed your own hand right now

You may *even be able* to:
- Put the blocks away and not think about them for a week
- Ask for what you want without whining
- Look at your child and think, I could do this again

* Friday

*

*

When does the show air?" asks Lana, lifting a glass of something bronze on the rocks.

"Have no idea," I say. "I'm just relieved I survived the whole thing without killing myself or anyone else."

We're talking about the second acting job I've had since Spencer was born. The first having been a bit on *Six Feet Under*. This one involved a couple of improvised scenes for HBO's *Curb Your Enthusiasm,* which stars Larry David, the professionally cranky creator of *Seinfeld*.

"Couldn't have been that bad," says Michelle, reaching up to smooth my hair.

"Not the acting part," I say. Mack comes over and pours more wine into my glass. "Just the part where they made me drive a car in the scene with Larry."

"Oh my God," says Katherine. "Whose car? Didn't you tell them you don't drive? Jesus. What did you do?"

The fact that I can't drive is a constant source of fascination for my friends. It's almost as if I don't know how to read or use a fork. I have multiple eye problems that cannot be corrected very well with the contacts and the glasses I wear, or with LASIK. I'm a freak of the eye world, with eyes that are simply a mystery to doctors. There are poly-polysyllabic words to describe my eye problems, my favorite of which is "idiopathic," which means "for no reason." All this means is that I move in a world that looks fine to me, but probably doesn't resemble the world everyone else sees. And, of course, I've never been able to drive.

"The assistant director comes up to me," I say, "and tells me, 'Here's the shot . . . blah, blah, blah. You're going to drive up into the driveway, park, get out, talk to Larry . . . then . . . blah, blah.' And all I'm thinking is, This is it. My first job in three years and I'm going to kill Larry David."

"Might have been a blessing," says Lana. "I don't understand the appeal of that show. A whiny guy whines about stuff without ever learning a goddamned thing. He's the most annoying, child-ish man on the planet. I want to smack him."

"Oh, I think he's hilarious," I say. "There's something so satis-fying about him being your worst self."

Lana shrugs. Our taste in TV shows and films differs greatly. She leans toward the kind of esoteric fare that puts me to sleep in about five minutes. She can't wait for the director's cut of *My Dinner with Andre*—a movie made about a dinner conversation that goes on for two hours.

Katherine calls over her shoulder, "Hey, Mack, I'm looking to float out of here. Another black and tan, my friend."

Mack nods.

"So I tell the assistant director that I don't drive and he says he'll figure something out, but don't tell Larry. He goes off and I sit in the makeup chair imagining what it would be like to be on trial for negligent homicide."

"Murder one," says Michelle.

"What?"

"I think it would be murder one," she says. "Because you had time to think about it in the makeup chair."

"Yeah," says Katherine, "if you have time to think about your actions, things get a whole lot worse. If the DA is out for blood, he could make a case for murder one."

"But they're not *my* actions. They're the actions of the assistant director," I say.

"Maybe manslaughter and conspiracy to commit murder," says Lana, draining her glass and sliding it toward Mack.

"No, no," I say. "Those cancel each other out."

We ponder the charge for a bit while Mack puts Katherine's beer down and picks up Lana's glass.

"Anyway," I say, "what ended up happening was that this little guy, on a walkie-talkie, hid in the backseat of this huge SUV and told me everything to do. Like, 'Okay, push the right pedal now.' "

"Did it work out?" asks Michelle.

"More or less. I didn't kill anyone, so that's good. It's just that I've never used a brake before. So I'd drive into the shot and the little guy in the back would whisper, 'Left foot down.' And I'd slam my foot down, because I was afraid of running into Larry. Every time the car lunged to a halt, it probably looked like I thought I was in some kind of cop show. Like I was going to jump out and yell, 'Freeze, motherfucker.' "

"God, wouldn't you want to play a part like that just once in your life?" says Lana. "The suspect freezes, and you're the hot detective in high heels. And you keep your gun trained on him while you flip open your badge with one hand."

"Yeah," I say. "I used to have a list of characters I wanted to play. Like I wanted to be the tough teacher who managed to turn the class around by being cool and showing them kung fu moves."

"Right," says Katherine. "Or I always wanted to play the blind-girl part in that sixties movie. She falls in love with Sidney Poitier."

"That's a specific part," says Lana. "We're talking about iconic images here."

"So why can't I want to be the blind girl?"

"Because it's not like there's a slew of blind-girls-who-fall-in-love-with-Sidney-Poitier parts."

Michelle pipes in, "*A Patch of Blue.*"

"What?" asks Lana.

Katherine smiles at Michelle. "Yeah. That's it. That's the name of the movie I'm talking about."

The conversation veers off and I'm left thinking about the roles I used to dream of playing. The teacher who turns around the school. The sexy spy. The class-action lawyer. The strung-out rock icon. The woman with multiple personality disorder, and one of her personalities is a hooker.

Not one of them was a mom.

✳ Slow to Warm
✳

✳

It's a dream. I know this because the moonlight hits the water like it's in a cheap motel painting. Spence is two. He walks along the edge of a pier, naked, wobbling impossibly on the drop-off. I follow him, covered in layers and layers of clothing. I think, Wow, this is weird. It's weird in the way that twice-baked potatoes or pretzel salad is weird. But I'm not too fazed. I know that this is a dream, for Christ sake, and it could get a whole lot weirder. In seconds I could be eating my contact lenses, which is a recurring thing in my dreams.

Suddenly, Spence dives into the water. I stop. Every cell of my body electric. My heart thumps fast and my eyes lock onto his watery form. He kicks his legs, but doesn't rise to the top.

I have to jump in. I start removing the layers of clothing. I think, I've got to get these clothes off so I don't drag him down. And at the same time I know that I shouldn't bother with the goddamned clothes. I should just jump in, for God's sake. But I can't. I've got to get these clothes off, and I rip them—tearing them off me as I keep my eyes fixed on Spence, who sinks further down.

Then I think, Wait! I can stop this. I can just stop the dream. And I force my mind through some thick cosmic goo till I get to the cheesecloth layer between sleep and not sleep. I push and push—and my eyes pop open.

I land in my bed—damp, agitated, conscious—and roll over to find Pat breathing rhythmically. Looking at the slope of his shoulder moving up and down, I think, Why didn't I think fast enough? Why didn't I just jump in the water and save my son?

Days after the dream, I sit on a bench next to four other mommies. I watch Spence pour sand from a dump truck into his pants. Shit, that means slinging him in the tub when we get home. Or I could let him run around naked until the sand on his ass dries and falls off onto the carpet.

"I simply can't get Sam to eat vegetables," a mommy next to me says.

"Cover them in cheese," another mommy says. "They'll eat anything covered in cheese."

I'm so bored I feel like crying.

A mommy looks at me and says, "What about you? How do you get Spence to eat his vegetables?"

What I want to say is, "I don't know about you ladies, but what I could go for is a big, hairy cock."

Instead, I say, "I just do the reward thing. You know, if you eat four peas, you can have this can of Pringles."

The mommies look at me like I suggested my son eat his own feces.

I'm not getting this mommy thing down.

I've been bringing Spence to this toddler program at a local preschool for a couple of weeks now, thinking that it's time to mingle with other babies and mothers. Suddenly, all that we were together—our little club of two—is out in the open. My mommy shortcomings are on parade. I can't cook. I don't do crafts with dried pasta and glue on rainy days. Talking to these mommies makes me want to bite them.

Jesus. It took me two hours to make the twenty deviled eggs I promised to bring to the preschool Halloween party. The skin of the eggs wouldn't separate from the white part, so I had to gouge each egg with my fingernail in order to peel it, leaving big dents. When I laid the egg-white ovals on the paper towel, each one looked like the surface of the moon. I sat in my kitchen and sobbed.

Spencer came up to me, covered from head to toe in red marker, looking like he had Ebola.

"Mommy's a little bit of sad," he said.

"Yes," I said, "I'm a little bit of sad."

A mommy at the school says, "I hide the vegetables in a tuna sandwich."

Cock, I think.

"All he tastes is the tuna fish."

Cocksucker.

"Or you can hide a piece of spinach between a cracker and a hunk of cheese."

Lick my juicy pussy.

"Peas are the easiest to get them to eat, because they're sweet."

Fuck me up the ass, soldier. Then dick slap me till I cry for mercy.

A teacher comes out and yells, "Circle time!!!!!"

The kids all run around like lab rats screaming, "Circle time!!!!!"

Spence runs up to me and grabs my hand. "It's share time. What do I have to share?"

Just that your mom's a big loser, I think. Because I forgot the damn thing to share.

As we walk into the classroom, I look at all the other kids bringing in shiny trucks, dolls with glossy hair, bags of marbles.

I bend down to Spence.

"What about your subway ticket?" I say, pointing to his pocket, where he keeps the tickets for the subway we ride to school every day.

"Yeah," he says, and beams, reaching into his pocket. I know he is remembering our routine of riding the escalators, talking about the trains, paying for the tickets.

I lean against the wall of the classroom, watching child after child show their loot and gab about it.

"It's a truck," says a boy with sandy hair.

"And where did you get it?" asks the teacher.

"It's a truck," he says again.

I can see where this conversation is going, and it's not far.

The other day, as I dropped him off, the teacher told me that Spence is "slow to warm." It sounded like she was saying he was unbaked bread.

"Slow to warm," I thought. "That means . . . what?"

She continued, "So it will take him longer to become integrated."

Not wanting to lay my mommy ignorance bare, I nodded and said, "Yes, slow to warm, I'll have to look into that."

At home I agonized over Spence being "slow to warm." Was it a physical thing, like his circulation was bad? Was it an intellectual thing, like he couldn't grasp simple concepts and had to warm up to them somehow by not taking them head-on? Was it an emotional thing, like he carried things inside him—a human pressure cooker, ready to explode one day in violent preschooler rage? What the fuck was "slow to warm"?! Were we in serious trouble here?

By the time I picked Spence up, I was close to tears. I pulled the teacher into a corner, shaking with shame and dread. She looked frightened, so I loosened my clawlike grip on her shoulder. I took in a long breath and tried to steady my voice.

"What does slow to warm mean?" I asked, preparing for the worst.

"Oh," she said, suddenly relaxing, "it means he's shy."

Relief flooded me and I felt like a doctor just told me that the black spot on my lung X-ray that he thought was cancer was just a mark from someone's coffee mug.

The sandy-haired boy sits down and the teacher calls Spence up to share. He reaches deeply in his pocket and fishes around, building the suspense, and pulls out a dog-eared ticket.

"It's a subway ticket," he says.

"Wow," says the teacher, looking confused.

"What's a subway?" asks a kid. This is, after all, Los Angeles.

"It's underground," says Spence. "I go with Mommy."

After circle time we all go outside to do an art project. Spence sits next to a girl who licks the edge of the table.

A mommy hands out pieces of construction paper cut to look like the facial features of a ghost: spooky, slanty eyes, button noses, smiley mouths. The kids begin to glue the pieces onto an outline of a Casper-shaped ghost. Spence glues down two eyes. He wants to make the nose another eye and begins to put an eye where the nose goes. A mommy reaches over and takes the eye out of his hand.

"That's not a nose," she says. "It's an eye. You can't have three eyes."

I could take her down right here. What a supreme idiot. Of course, a ghost can have three eyes—it's a ghost!!! Christ on a stick.

But I just smile weakly at Spence and remember to tell him when we're on the subway that it's fine to have three eyes.

So I revisit the dream. I lie in bed and conjure the pier, my naked son, and me in layers of clothing. I see the moonlight. And I will myself there. I follow my son. He dives into the water—and this time, without hesitation or panic, I dive in after him. I feel the weight of the clothes pull me down, but my arms are strong, making sure arcs through the water. I go under. I see him suspended in bouncing, shifting light. I reach out, grab him, and swim toward the surface. The heavy clothing falls off of me and I kick easily back to the pier, my son safe in the crook of one arm.

I wake from the dream, my limbs light and floaty. Goddammit, I finally got something right. I lift myself from the bed—maybe I'm still dreaming—and walk into my son's room, where I see him under the covers, curled up safe. I scoot in next to him. I look at the ceiling and feel the roundness of his back against my arm. And I know in one of those fleeting moments of clarity that I can do this. I will learn how to do this. Because I cannot lose him.

✳ Secret Society

✳
✳

Finding the Childwatch program at the YMCA is a lot like dying, going to heaven, and finding out that it's *exactly* like the heaven you were told about when you were young: fluffy clouds and lots of naked frolicking.

For months friends have been telling me that there's this place where you can drop your kid off for two hours while you work out (if that's your thing), sit in a steam room, soak in a hot tub, and finally give yourself a long blow-dry. All this for a thirty-five-dollar-a-month "poverty membership."

I tell those friends to go sell their bullshit to a blind old woman who still believes in fairies. I'm not buying.

But Lana confirms the stories. She says that she doesn't go there because she prefers her Silverlake gym, where she has a much higher chance of hooking up with a guy if the Tony thing continues to go badly.

All I'm looking to hook up with is two hours of me time and the loosey-goosey buzz that comes from having steamed oneself shy of a coma.

★　　★　　★

Proving that we are impoverished is easy. I show up at the Y, my dirty hair pulled into a ponytail, my jeans ripped, Spence's T-shirt stained. I actually rub some applesauce into it before we arrive. Later Lana says that she doesn't think that we have to *look* impoverished so much as *be* impoverished. But I'm not taking any chances.

The guy behind the desk nods as he goes through Pat's check stubs. We currently live on Pat's daily stand-in work and an occasional commercial.

"Looks in order," says the guy.

"Yeah," I say. "We're pretty poor."

I glance down at Spence's unwashed face to bring the point home. The guy doesn't look up from the papers.

"Well, I'll give you a short tour of the place," he says.

I push Spence in a stroller behind the guy, who walks me through the plant.

He shows me the weight room, which I won't be using. Lifting weights seems too exhausting.

We glance into the classroom where an aerobics instructor yells orders over pounding music. Aerobics has never really worked for me. After a few minutes I get short of breath and have to sit down.

We look at something he calls the mat room. It's full of cushy mats on which people are stretching out and doing sit-ups. I watch some people bending backward over balls that are bigger than beach balls. That's got to be murder on the lower back.

Eventually, we get to the steam room and the whirlpool.

"After your workout," he says, "you can relax here."

I look at the bubbling water of the whirlpool and imagine myself, hair bound up in a towel, hot water pounding against the small of my back, sharing secrets with a couple of other impoverished women of leisure. I wonder if you can bring champagne flutes in here. The plastic kind, of course, so they won't break when one of the women throws out an arm while telling a story about her young lover.

"And Childwatch?" I ask, wanting to throw my arms around him and scream "I won!"

He leads Spence and me into a room full of machines of some kind. Along one wall is a window, through which I see about twenty children playing while three women look on, one with an infant in her lap.

The guy introduces me to Doris, the kind of large woman that children love to bounce off of. She tells me that this is a child *watch*, not child *care*. They will watch my child while I work out, but if he cries for more than ten minutes, they come and get me. If his diaper needs to be changed, they find me and I come back to do the changing.

She shows me a notebook.

"You write your child's name here," she says. "And here's where you write down where you're working out."

I nod.

"And if I'm doing a steam?" I ask.

"You can write down that you'll be in the steam room after your workout. But put down the workout area first."

I nod again, thinking that I'm going to figure out some workout place to write down. I'm going to have to at least *appear* to be working out somewhere for a brief amount of time—before my steam, whirl, shower, and blow-dry. This is going to be more complicated than I thought.

That night I consider the possibility of committing to a real, rather than ersatz, workout routine. But that seems awfully drastic.

Last year, as Pat and I were waiting at the finish line for my brother to complete the LA Marathon, I asked Pat, "Why don't we run marathons?"

We looked at the runners who'd finished, shivering in their tinfoil capes.

"Because it hurts," he said.

Doris smiles at Spence when I bring him in the next day. He toddles by her to a plastic kiddie car.

"Where do I sign?" I ask.

Doris hands me the notebook. I sign Spence in. My pen hovers over the workout section. I think, then write, "Weight room." It seems as good as anything. In small print I add, "Afterward: steam room, whirlpool, possible sauna." In the "Comments" section I write, "Recovering from back surgery," thinking that this will justify all the steaming and soaking.

Doris glances at the notebook.

"Spencer has had back surgery?"

"Oh, no," I say, hoping I won't have to elaborate on my lie. "Me. *I've* had back surgery."

" 'Comments' is for the children," she says. "Is he allergic to anything?"

"Spence? No."

"Okay," she says. "We'll come and find you if there's a problem."

"Great," I say, remembering that with my faux bad back I'll have to move a bit slower.

I shuffle over to Spence and blow him a kiss before leaving.

In the changing room it's the old bodies and the young ones that fascinate me the most. Ones like mine, I now understand. They still have shape, but have gotten thicker out of the need, I think, for quite literally a broader base. Our bodies do seem to manifest function. We are biological architecture. Older bodies get smaller, occupying less space—seeming to disappear, before the owner does altogether. Younger bodies are not a mystery to anyone, since everyone once had one. They are the worker bodies. They demand attention.

A group of women who look to be in their seventies has come in from a swim class. They sit on their bare bums in front of a long mirror, flesh of their arms jiggling as they dry their hair and gab. One of them catches my eye in the mirror.

I quickly lean over to tie my shoes.

I wander around the weight room for a bit, my towel draped over my shoulders, before deciding to do some free weights in front of the mirror. I had a roommate, once, who lifted weights in the living room and I think I can imitate her moves enough to look like I know what I'm doing.

I walk over to a row of weights on a rack, under a sign that says "Please rerack your weights." A sign next to it says "Do not drop weights." Simple enough, I think, looking at the weights.

I reach down and pick up one that looks small. I straighten my knees, managing to lift it up a couple of inches off the ground— but find that I can't pull it further up, nor can I straighten my back. I hunch with the weight dangling in my fist like I'm an elephant preparing to pull one of those huge slabs used to build the

pyramids. Though, in my case, this is no preparation. I can't pro-
ceed any more than I can put the weight down. Putting it down
would require bending my knees, which would release my whole
body, sending it crashing to the floor. My towel slips down from
my shoulders and covers my head. I sway a bit under the towel,
thinking that if I get a little swing in my arm, I can possibly throw
the weight out, away from my foot, which I would like to save. I
remember the sign admonishing not to throw the weights and
am grateful for the flapping terry cloth obscuring my identity.

I get enough swing going to release the weight, which thuds a
scant few inches from my toes. Standing up, my back clutches as
my towel slips to the floor. I eyeball the sign "Please rerack your
weights" and hook my foot under the towel, kicking it over the
weight.

I decide to walk my back out by taking a couple of slow turns
around the room. As I amble, I glance at the clock, which shows
that I've been here three minutes. I really should kill more time
before I go to the steam room. What if the Childwatch folk come
looking for me and discover that I skipped working out altogether? Is that some kind of rule that I would be breaking? Would
the membership guy come up to me and say, "Excuse me, ma'am,
the poverty membership is strictly intended for poor women who
want to get into shape so that they can bear the burden of raising
their families with the very few resources they have. The poverty
membership does *not* exist so that artists, who *choose* to live on
limited means, the 'nouveaux poor,' if you will, can drop off their
kids and fuck around in the whirlpool."

Pat says that I have an exaggerated sense of being monitored by
the world at large. He says that most people don't care if I take an
extra helping of something I didn't pay for. No one cares that
Spence walked out of school with a toy car that didn't belong to

him. Pat says that I don't have to offer corroboration when I call in sick to the dentist by telling the receptionist that she can ask my husband if I really do have such a dangerously high fever. He says that everyone takes the cute tiny bottles of shampoo and conditioner from hotels.

I'm sure Pat is right. No one cares what I do with my precious two hours at the gym. But I'm not taking any chances.

I walk over to a machine that looks pretty straightforward. I can see that one sits on the padded seat and lifts weights by pushing up on the bars above. I sit down and face the weights I will be lifting, grasp the bars, and push up.

Nothing moves. Not the bars, not the weights.

I stop, filling with resolve. I breathe in again, hold my breath, and push, straining against the bars with everything I've got.

Nothing moves.

My breath releases with a loud *"Pahhhhh."*

I can't believe that I can't lift this load even once.

"You need to move the pin," a voice from behind me says.

I turn to see a girl no bigger than Barbie. She leans over and moves a pin from low down on the stack of weights, to just below the first weight.

"You were trying to lift two hundred pounds," she says.

"Jesus," I gasp.

"I moved it up to five pounds," she says before she bounces off.

I wonder if she's an angel or a spy.

I adjust, back straight, fists around the bars. I'll do ten lifts, then rest, I think. Then I'll do ten more. I'll do five rounds of ten, with breaks in between, and then go steam.

I push against the bars and lift the weight.

Not bad, I think as I bring the weight down carefully.

I lift again, remembering to breathe.

And down. Up again.

How many is that? Five, I think.

Up and down.

Okay, so seven. I'll do seven, then rest.

I push up the bars, this last time an effort—and rest.

So that's seven. Seven's not bad for a first day. I mean, I've never lifted weights in my life. This is the sort of thing you have to work up to gradually. If I overdo it, I could really hurt myself. Give myself a stroke or something. Seven is good. I feel a little burn in my upper arms. But I'm still breathing. That's good. Tomorrow I'll do eight.

I get off the machine and do a little shake, to calm my muscles down. I twist my upper body around a couple of times, like I've seen on TV, and head for some well-deserved relaxation.

Taking a steam is more interesting *before* you do it than *as* you do it. I can really stand only a few minutes before I start to feel like I'm in a Cambodian prison camp.

The whirlpool, however, is a week in the country. Not an impoverished mom in sight; just me, and two old men, having an extended conversation about the necessity of wearing flip-flops in the showers to avoid fungus, which one of them got here, he says. I don't care that the conversation is dull. I don't care that there's no champagne. I drop my head back and feel the water pound every bit of tension out of me. I let my mind drift and I think that I really am very lucky to have two child-free hours a day to waste away at the YMCA.

"Brett Paesel," says a voice.

I come to.

"Your son's diaper needs changing."

Shit, how did they find me?

I pull myself out of the watery embrace of the whirlpool, the cold air shocking my skin as I grab my towel and follow the Childwatch woman into the dressing room.

"It'll take me a minute to dry off," I say.

At Childwatch I change Spence quickly and he's happy to run and play again when I leave to claim the hour and a half I have left of my time. I return to the dressing room dry and dressed.

Getting back into my wet bathing suit is unappealing. Undressing to take a shower seems silly. I look around. The old ladies at the mirror are gone. But curled up in an armchair is a woman reading a book. I figure she's an impoverished mom. Who else would come to the YMCA to read a book in the changing room?

How is she getting away with this? Did she write in the notebook that after her workout she could be found finishing that novel that had lain by her bed, unread, at home? Or is she just taking the chance that she won't be discovered sloughing off? Is she the sort of woman I've always longed to be—thumbing her nose at authority, lounging around the changing room, not giving a flying fuck what anyone thinks of her?

Her audacity thrills and terrifies me.

I walk over to my locker and unlock it. My backpack yields nothing more interesting than a schedule of aerobics classes. I have nothing to read.

The mom lifts her head.

"There's old magazines near the StairMasters," she says.

I want to say, "You never saw me." But I know it's understood.

We belong to the Secret Society of Impoverished Moms at the Hollywood YMCA. It's a powerful bond.

✳ Friday

✳

✳

What the fuck do you think was going through his mind?" asks Katherine, her voice outraged and amused. "Casually showing us pictures of his fiancée, like it's not the weirdest hookup since Michael Jackson and anybody."

She's talking about our friend Dave, who we saw recently at a drama school reunion. Dave is in the process of bringing his Thai fiancée over to the States. He knew her for five days before giving her an engagement ring, hidden in a jar of cold cream the day he left. Dave has spent the last three months digging through third world paperwork to get her over here.

"Five days? He knew her for five days?" asks Michelle.

"This is nowhere near the worst part of the story," I say. "He brings out the pictures and we're all still kind of processing the five-day, Thailand, doesn't-speak-a-word-of-English part when we look and see that the girl looks like she's twelve!"

"Dave is forty-seven!" says Katherine, keeping the outrage going. Dave was one of the older students.

"What's the big deal?" asks Lana. She slips off her sweater and lays it on the bar.

"Sounds to me like the big deal is that this guy basically bought a wife," says Michelle, who is fast establishing herself as the moral core of our little group.

"But if she gets something out of it and he gets something out of it, who cares?" Lana continues. "Obviously, she's not twelve."

"Dave says she's twenty-three. But who knows if that's the truth?" says Katherine.

"Look," I say, holding up my empty glass to get Mack's attention, "I'm not all wound up in the morality of this. Dave's a decent guy and the girl is poor. What I think needs to be discussed, if we need to discuss it at all, is, what kind of person is happy hooking up with a person whose affection they're buying, who doesn't speak English, who they've known for five days?"

"A guy who's been divorced twice, who's forty-seven and portly, and whose part in a big movie just got cut down to a shot of the back of his bald head," says Katherine.

Mack slides a glass of wine over to me.

We sit for a bit.

"Maybe we should give credit to Dave for going out and doing something about his own unhappiness," says Lana, who doesn't know Dave. But now he's everyone's problem. Something for us to solve.

We sip and think about that.

"No, no," I say, untangling it in my mind. "Because he bought something that isn't real."

"That's right," says Michelle.

"The part that's scary," I say, "is the part where Dave thinks she loves him. The part where he shows pictures of this gorgeous girl snuggled up to him like he's special. He's not just buying her company, he's buying the lie that she loves him."

"Okay, so suddenly I feel horrible," says Katherine.

"I didn't mean to be a downer," I say.

"I mean it. I feel like shit."

"Poor Dave," says Michelle.

"Poor stupid Dave," says Lana.

I wish there were an English word for "schadenfreude"—the state of sorry joy. Surely, we Americans are as acquainted with the feeling as the Germans. It seems to me that this is what we feel for Dave. Sorry that he will most likely be heartbroken when he finds out that the love he bought is not real. And joy that we are not him.

✳ Witness

I have come to the conclusion that raising a young child involves long stretches of boredom interrupted by flashes of terror and bursts of supernatural joy—which sounds awfully close to the definition of "psychosis." And also, I am told, "combat." One would think that, knowing this, I would send Spence off to boarding school and surgically ensure that I never have another child. But no. For a reason I cannot name, I become obsessed with having a second one.

I start peeing on all kinds of sticks. Sticks that tell me when I'm ovulating. Sticks that tell me if I'm pregnant. I get crazy about sticks. I buy them in bulk and pee on them even when I'm not ovulating or remotely close to being pregnant. I begin to live by the sticks.

I circle the best days in my date book for getting it on. I wake Pat in the middle of the night for sex. Because the stick says *now*. Then I lie on my back with my legs propped against the wall until they lose all feeling and fall onto the bed. I wake Pat again, pounding my paralytic legs with my fists.

Months of this and no success.

I read adoption books and daydream about flying to India to pick up a little Indian girl. I even talk to someone who has a baby connection in Nigeria. But back out when I realize that we only communicate through his beeper and pay phones.

I am desperate—driven by a force beyond myself, like Richard Dreyfuss in *Close Encounters of the Third Kind*. So I decide to have my doctor run some tests that will tell me a little more about my chances of getting pregnant.

The day I go in for the results of the tests, I wait alone in the lobby. Pat and Spence park the car while I sit on a brown leather sectional and start to finger the neatly placed magazines on the square glass table in front of me. I consider reading the article on "ten things men would like us to know." But I'm not sure I want to know.

I look up to see bamboo shoots in a glossy green pot on the corner of the table. Behind them is a painting of Buddha done by my doctor, Dr. Sammy. He is a Buddhist, which is and is not a good thing in an OB doctor. At his best he is cool, detached, amused. At his worst he is cool, detached, amused.

When I was looking for a gynecologist, I asked a couple of friends for their recommendations. The first said that she had a great doctor, thorough, no-nonsense.

"It's just . . ."

"What?" I said.

"Well, it's silly really. It's just that he has no sense of humor."

"I don't know that that would matter," I said.

"Well, then, he's your man," she said. "It's just that one time he was doing a Pap. I mean, he was right in the middle of it. My feet are in the stirrups. And the lights go out all over the hospital. And he just . . ."

"What?"

"Well, he just waited until they came on again. He didn't say anything. Nothing to break the tension. I just lay there in the dark, my legs spread, and listened to him breathing, while the greasy speculum slipped out of me."

"What happened?" I asked.

"The lights came on. And he finished the job. He just went on like nothing had happened."

Not sure about that, I thought.

My next friend said that she had a great guy she had known for years. He was practically a friend.

"It's just . . ."

"What?" I said.

"Well, his sense of humor is a little strange. It's okay with me. But you might not like it."

"Like what does he say?"

"Well, the last time I was making an appointment with him, he said, 'Great, I can't wait to see that luscious bod. I'll be waiting, with my tongue hanging out.'"

"Ewww."

"He was just joking."

Not my guy, I thought.

My next friend said that she had met her gynecologist in acting class. He called himself Dr. Sammy. Sammy being his first name. He was a Renaissance man—doctor, painter, actor—and a Buddhist.

"It's just . . ."

"What?" I said, weary.

"It's just . . . Well, he's handsome."

"So what?"

"Well. Some people don't like that in a gynecologist," she said.

"How handsome is he?"

"Very handsome," she said. "He played the devil in a scene for acting class. And he was so sexy that the women couldn't take their eyes off him."

"Your gynecologist played the devil?"

"He was good," she said.

Pat and Spence join me in Dr. Sammy's office. I look out the window and see sky clean as a blue sheet, sunlight bouncing off white squares of concrete in the street below, glinting cars maneuvering in a parking lot. I try to imagine Dr. Sammy as the devil, and my mind skids to a short list of things I'd be willing to trade my soul for.

"So let me see here," he says.

I hear him open a file, but keep my attention on the sheet sky. Spence climbs into my lap.

"He's three now?" Dr. Sammy asks.

I think, Get to it, get to it. What does the file say?

"Almost three," says Pat.

"I've got some stickers," says Dr. Sammy. He pops out of his reclining chair and sprints out of the room.

Spence squirms off my lap and onto Pat's.

Is he stalling? I wonder. The stickers a delaying tactic while he gets up nerve to say that while getting routine information about my fertility status, he found out that I'm riddled with cancer. It's a brain tumor, I'm sure. I'm always sure it's a brain tumor. Wait a minute, he didn't go anywhere near my brain. It would have to be ovarian cancer. I see myself six months from now wearing a turban, looking thin and impossibly beautiful, being wheeled into Spence's preschool graduation ceremony.

Dr. Sammy bounces back in with stickers and hands them to Spence.

"Stickers!" Spence says, sliding off Pat's lap onto the carpet.

Dr. Sammy plops back in his chair, grabs the file, and leans back again.

I see Pat in my hospital room, moving the tubes aside and carefully lying down next to my waiflike body. Hanging on to my last few breaths, I whisper, "I loved only you."

"Your progesterone is good," says Dr. Sammy.

Pat looks at me, smiles, and grabs my hand like we won something.

It's not cancer.

"Pat's sperm is good."

Pat nods like he knew that all along.

I look down to see Spence sitting in the middle of frog stickers he's stuck to the carpet. He looks up at me and smiles. King Frog with his subjects.

"So what is it?" I ask.

"Well, Brett, it's nothing really," says Dr. Sammy. "It's just that you're forty-two and your eggs are old."

"But I don't look like I'm forty-two," I say. "Forty is the new thirty."

A patient smile spreads across his face.

"Not biologically," he says.

I realize at this moment that I hate him.

"Old eggs?" asks Pat.

"Mmm," says Dr. Sammy, leaning forward, his beaky nose hanging over his weak mouth. "A woman has only a set number of eggs at birth. She loses these eggs as she gets older, and by forty the eggs that remain are old; they're tired."

How old are they? I hear in my head. So old they need a walker just to get them over to the uterine wall.

He goes on, "There's a higher risk of chromosomal problems. And it's harder to get pregnant."

I watch as he rests his talons on top of the file.

"Christie Brinkley had a baby at forty-four," I say.

"I'm not saying you can't get pregnant," he says. "In fact, if I were to bet on a forty-two-year-old getting pregnant, I would bet on you."

"You would?" I ask.

My voice sounds girly and flirtatious, not my own.

"You've got everything going for you," Dr. Sammy says. "You've got the blood pressure of a teenager."

"I do?" I ask, giggling.

"And your uterus is in great shape. Pink and healthy."

"Pink. Great," I say.

Dr. Sammy is such a handsome, kind man, I think. We should have him over for dinner sometime.

Spence grabs onto my knee and pulls himself up from the frogs.

Pat raises an eyebrow at me and turns to Dr. Sammy.

"Well, we wanted to know what we're dealing with, because if it looks unlikely that we'll get pregnant, we're going to start looking into adoption," he says.

Spence pulls on the neck of my shirt. "I want more stickers."

"Just a minute," I say, prying his fingers away. "Dr. Sammy's talking to Mommy."

Dr. Sammy laughs. "Well, that's a surefire way to get pregnant—start adoption proceedings."

"Really?" I ask. I look at Dr. Sammy's lovely long fingers.

"Stickers," says Spence, his voice insistent.

"Just a minute," I hiss. "So why would starting to adopt make me pregnant?"

"Oh, well, it's nothing scientific, right?" he says, winking at Pat. "It's just the way the world works. You get what you want when you're looking the other way."

"Stickers!" screams Spence.

"Spence," I say, "this is *my* turn. I get to talk to the doctor now. You are not the only person in the world."

Spence's face drops and he sinks back to the carpet of frogs.

My heart lunges toward him. I want to take it back. I want to say, "You *are* the only person in the world. That's the problem. That's why we're here. I'm terrified that you will be alone someday. I can't sleep thinking of you alone in the world."

The truth of this hits me like a hokey God moment in a made-for-TV movie.

I hear Dr. Sammy intone more about my pink cervix and attractive follicles. I hear percentages and words like "artificial insemination" and "donor egg."

But most of this sounds like it's bits and pieces from outside a door. Inside, I hold my answer. Turn it over and tuck it into my chest. My answer. The reason for this near-psychotic pining for a second child.

The reason offers itself up and I know that it's been there since the day my brother was born. It is this: I want for my child what I have. A witness. Someone who will say, "Yes, it's true. Yes, I was there. We were so very loved."

✳ Purse Party

✳

✳

I am convinced that some women have an accessory gene. They are predestined to understand what looks right with what. They instinctively know what's in and what's out. They care deeply about this year's green.

I could be wearing a green that's so four years ago and still have a good time. If there's anything equivalent to the *opposite* of an accessory gene, that's the gene I have. The only accessory I had for any length of time was a watch my father gave me. It was silver and it hung around my neck. I'd probably still have that watch if I hadn't misplaced it while stripping on a roof in New York City on a dare. It's the only accessory I ever gave a shit about.

So why, oh why, do I go crazy at the purse party? I don't plan on buying a purse. I carry a backpack with a broken zipper. And now that I have Spence, I occasionally tote around the diaper bag the hospital gave me when he was born. It's pink plastic with bears on it and doesn't match a thing I own. I don't know from purses.

There's nothing ominous in the invitation. Katherine tells me that a friend of hers, who has a beautiful home in the Los Feliz hills, is having a purse party. Would I like to go? The "beautiful home" part is important because I am far more interested in homes than purses.

I say yes mostly because of a prurient interest in this home of a hugely wealthy actress. I also say yes because, despite my accessory handicap, I love girl things. I like huge groups of women jabbering about things that don't really matter. I love clothing swaps and Tupperware parties and bridesmaid fittings. I like to giggle and talk about whether something is slimming. I like experimenting with eye shadows. And I have an almost hormonal need to know what would be the best container for pickling things, even though I've never pickled.

I want to be where women are together. I breathe better around the sound of high-pitched chatter. So it is with these expectations that I go to the purse party.

Katherine calls me a few days before the party. She asks what I'm planning to wear.

"What are *you* wearing?" I ask, looking for a clue.

"Well, I'm just going to try to look hip," she says. "And I'm worried about what purse to bring. But I was thinking that if I go with something vintage, I can probably get away with it."

"Get away with what?" I think.

"Karen said that *In Style* magazine is going to be there. So be prepared," she says. Karen is the home-owning hostess.

Prepared? I think.

"I guess I'll just wear jeans and my denim top," I say. I figure the monochrome look will make me look tall and pull attention away from the middle of me, where all my problems are.

When Katherine picks me up for the party, she looks hip to me. But then, what do I know?

The house is worth it. Redone, remodeled, and rethought. A

lot of light. I love the kitchen. The cabinets are white against a dark green wall. A couple of hired workers bustle around a metal island as big as a bed.

Karen's publicist is really working the party. She buzzes around introducing people to each other. She's a short woman with a wide smile and crazy eyes. Bulbs flash around Karen and some very thin women. I spot some famous people and some sort of famous people. A poor man's Demi Moore talks to a guy taking notes.

Purses are placed on furniture all around the first floor. I'm disappointed. I thought it was going to be like a Tupperware party in which a lady explains all about the bags. In this situation I'm going to be on my own. Or with Katherine, who immediately starts chatting with a stranger about the merits of the particular bag she's holding. Not prepared to lay bare my bag ignorance so early, I drift off to the deck to get a large glass of wine and several slices of Brie.

The deck is all dark wood and air. The Brie is soft and buttery. I sit on one of several matching wicker chairs and pretend that the deck is mine.

Katherine gives me a "come here" wave from the kitchen. I help myself to a second glass of wine and a cheese cube before returning to her and the purses.

There are big purses and small purses. Roomy ones, and others shaped like bowling bags. A whole line of them is made out of a pink dotted fabric. These cause a lot of activity near the sofa. The most popular purses are made out of kicky, fun fabric covered in a clear plastic. The "fun fabric" sports something like floating Eiffel Towers surrounded by floating pink poodles. One woman starts laughing when she sees images of martini glasses dancing beneath the plastic surface of a triangle-shaped purse.

The laughing woman shows it to a friend, who also starts laughing.

Whimsical diaper bags sit on a wooden pew in the hallway. They come with matching Eiffel Tower or camouflage or whatever bibs. The diaper bags go for about a hundred dollars. And the purses range from forty-five to a hundred. "But," I hear from several women who heard from the bag lady, "these are at cost. And you get fifteen percent off. Bags like this are two hundred dollars at Fred Segal."

I tour the bags with Katherine and even pick up a few. Katherine snags one and hangs on to it. More women pour through the shabby-chic front door. Bags are slung on shoulders. One small woman carries four bags. Bags start disappearing from the coffee table and a nicely restored armoire.

A woman who looks like Peppermint Patty sits on the stairs, hunched over a calculator. A line of women with bags on their shoulders forms in front of her and winds out to the kitchen.

The wine is beginning to fade, so I grab another glass from the deck. I begin to worry about all those bags that have already been sold. Have I missed the one? Have I missed a bag that might change people's image of me forever? Have I been hasty in assuming that I'm above bags? I could get a life-changing bag here, for a quarter of the cost that a famous person would buy it for at Fred Segal. Am I fucking out of my mind?

I leave my glass on the deck and weave through a gaggle that's formed around a furry light blue clutch. I start moving fast through the remaining purses. There has to be one somewhere. One that was overlooked. A gem. I find one on the stairs that looks promising, but it has things in it. It's an already owned purse. Damn.

How can I not know what all these women know? How can

I not know that this is a once-in-a-lifetime opportunity that I'm throwing away, just like I threw away that offer to play Titania in *Midsummer,* my junior year in college. If I had taken that part, I would have been able to work my way into the company. I would be doing Shakespeare now, instead of bit parts on TV shows nobody ever sees.

I find a plastic fun purse propped up against a chair leg in the living room. Someone put it down on the floor, under the sight lines of most of the women. Ah-hah. I pick it up. God, it feels good. It's a solid purse. Roomy. And I love the way it's shaped— a trapezoid, shorter on top and wider on the bottom. How clever. This purse has a sense of humor. A woman tells me that the plastic-covered fabric was green upholstery fabric. She just appears, this woman. She says that she designed these bags. She tells me that she found the fabric in an out-of-the-way place in Korea Town. Who knew? She hadn't even been looking for fabric that day.

"Magic," she says.

I try the purse on. The strap fits perfectly in the hollow between my neck and the small hump of my shoulder bone. My hand feels the hardy, smooth plastic at my side.

"Oooh," says a woman next to me. She has two purses over her shoulder. "That's a great one. I missed that one."

I feel strong and proud. My hand grips the plastic tighter.

Once the trapezoid is on my shoulder, my breathing slows. I find Katherine with a group of women who all have plastic purses. She's found a purse with a flowery motif. It's so perfect for her that I want to call my mother about it.

"Katherine, I found one. I found a purse," I say in a voice that doesn't sound like mine. She takes a long look at the purse as I wait for what seems like forever for her pronouncement.

"This purse belongs to you," she says. "It's amazing how everyone just picks out the perfect purse. What a great color. It'll go with your brown faux alligator jacket."

I hadn't thought about that. But she's right, of course. It'll really set off that jacket.

I suggest to her that we sit on the deck with another glass of wine and our purses. We should savor this moment, not let it go by too quickly.

Sitting on the breezy deck with my trapezoid propped against my chair, I sip my wine and say witty things. The only other thing that has given me this sense of well-being and power before is cocaine. And the purse is a lot cheaper.

A satisfying sense of acquisition floats through the air. Women stroke their purses. Cameras flash. No one takes a picture of me, but I don't care. There will be pictures of me, with the trapezoid, later.

Several other bepursed women move onto the deck. Normally, I sink into myself in big groups. But the purse makes me brave. It also makes me an expert.

I chat with a famous-looking woman about the wisdom of mixing strappy square-toed sandals with a conservative skirt. I tell Katherine she should stop flattening her hair. She should get a graduated cut that flips in the back. I retrieve things from my magazine reading. I hear myself loudly exclaim that brown is the new black, and fifty the new forty.

I could stay there forever. But women start leaving.

Katherine tugs at my arm and I sigh. I don't want to go. I haven't had a chance to talk about what kind of pumps I should buy to match the trapezoid.

"Brett," Katherine whispers insistently, "we're the last ones here."

I look around to find that it's true. Katherine pulls me through several rooms to find Karen lying on one of her many couches, her feet elevated.

We thank her.

"You guys got great purses," she says.

"I really love mine," I say, wanting to sit on the couch with Karen.

I start to sit, when Katherine grabs my elbow.

I straighten up and stand, looking at Karen, who glances at my glass of wine.

"Would you like me to pour your wine into a paper cup so you can take it with you?" she asks.

"Oh, no. That's too much trouble."

"None at all," she says.

Leaning on Katherine as we walk down the driveway, I think of all those leftover, unclaimed purses. The thought makes me sad.

I take a sip of wine from my paper cup as Katherine opens the car door.

"I like Karen," I say, sliding in.

"Good people," says Katherine.

"And giving me wine to go? Damn. You don't often find class like that in this town."

As the car winds down the hill, I impress myself by moving the paper cup with the rhythm of the car, not spilling a drop.

✳ Friday
✳
✳

"Diet Coke?" asks Katherine, looking at my soda.

"I might have a glass of wine later," I say. "I'm trying to shake these last ten pounds."

"Uh-huh," she says, sounding unconvinced.

"Brett, you are the worst at secrets," says Lana. "If I was a press secretary and wanted something leaked, I'd tell it to you." She downs a black shot and places the glass upside down on the draining grid of the bar.

I want to say that that is absolutely untrue. I know a shitload of stuff about her that I've never told a soul except Pat, like the blow job she gave a docent in the bathroom of the Museum of Tolerance and the washcloth she stole from Phil Spector's house.

"You're pregnant," says Michelle. "Aren't you?"

There it is. The first public airing of what I've known for two days. The time between knowing you're pregnant and saying it is emotional twilight. Soft and personal, it is the in-between time Pat and I have shared, sitting on the couch the last two evenings.

"You guys, it's really early," I say, swirling the ice cubes of my watery soda with my straw.

"It's a girl," announces Michelle.

"You can't know that," says Katherine. "It's the size of a comma right now."

Mack walks up and the conversation dies like we're guilty of something.

"You ready for a wine?" he asks me.

"Um, sure," I say, planning a sip or two to throw him and any regulars off the scent.

Mack walks down to the other end of the bar to grab a bottle.

"Michelle's a seer," Lana says to Katherine.

"A seer?"

"I see things," says Michelle.

"Like what?" asks Katherine.

"She saw, a long time ago, that Tony wasn't going to stay with Daisy and me," says Lana.

"Well, we all see that," says Katherine.

Plop. Talk about secrets. Katherine has said the unsaid thing— that Tony is not the one who will stick around; not the one who will be sitting next to Lana at graduations and holiday meals; and that we all know it.

Katherine looks like she's just been asked for the ticket she forgot to buy. It's an expression of guilt, desperation, and bravura.

Lana looks down at her lap.

"I mean," says Katherine, "that we all see that you aren't happy. You don't have to be a 'seer' to see that. Right?"

Katherine throws me a "help me out here" look.

"Right," I say as Lana lifts her face to me. "What Katherine is saying is that sometimes it takes a seer and sometimes you see things even when you're not a seer because it's easy to see them.

Not that you're right about what you see. Seeing is a matter of who's doing the seeing . . ."

Lana's brow crinkles and I know I'm not making sense, but I can't stop because I'm hoping to land on something helpful.

"See? What Katherine is saying is that we all see things at certain times, which doesn't necessarily make us right. Though Michelle sees, so I'd pay attention to that first. Unless you don't agree. In which case, ignore it and stick to what you yourself see."

Jesus, I haven't a clue what I just said and I can tell by the look on Lana's face that I haven't accidentally landed on something that sounds good. So shoot me, I want to say. I've just been told I'm having a baby girl and haven't had five minutes to process it. No wonder I'm addled.

Mack returns with my glass of wine. We all look at Lana, who is red-faced, tears caught in her bottom lashes. Mack shifts his weight from side to side for a second, then leaves, probably deciding that whatever he was going to offer (advice, another drink, a quip) is best held back.

Katherine catches my eye, her gaze speaking forgiveness for my inability to say the right thing. Then she turns back to Lana.

"Tony isn't making you happy," she says, her voice like a public service announcement for living wills.

"I just don't understand it," says Lana. "How can he stop caring just like that? Remember when Daisy was born?"

She turns to Michelle, her voice a plea. "Remember? We were so happy."

"I remember," says Michelle.

These words, or ones like them, are said by Lana every other Friday as we watch her struggle through the last gasp of her relationship, helpless to ease her pain. All we can do, all we ever do, is acknowledge it. As we do now, Michelle's hand on hers, my eyes wet, Katherine's smile weak.

And then, because there is not going to be a solution this Friday, the moment passes.

Lana sniffs and smiles. "So Brett's going to have a girl?"

Our movement and breathing immediately register relief that Lana has swung the conversation away from Tony. So quickly the air gets lighter.

"That's what I see," says Michelle. "Her girl has come to her."

I wiggle on the barstool, excited at the thought of ponytails and diaries with locks on them.

"You're the only person who can say stuff like that and it doesn't sound freaky," says Lana to Michelle, her voice bearing only a slight trace of the moment that has just passed.

"Hey, being able to see things hasn't seemed to change my life substantially," says Michelle. "It's not like I see practical stuff like financial trends or where lost keys are."

"I wonder why that is," I say, fully convinced that Michelle does see things.

"Maybe I'm not supposed to profit from it."

"Can others profit?"

"No. Wait. I do profit. Well, I benefit. I see parking spaces."

"Like how?"

"I feel a space is around a particular corner or down a particular street."

Lana jumps in. "You could hire yourself out. You know, like mediums who solve crimes. Only, you find parking spaces."

"Yeah," says Katherine, "but then she has to ride around in the car with a stranger who hired her."

"What if you could, like, find parking spots for people over the phone?" I say.

"Can you see things over the phone?" asks Katherine.

Michelle shrugs.

"Let's test it," says Lana, sliding off her barstool, grabbing her phone off the bar.

"How can we test it?" I ask.

Lana stops and thinks. "I'll stand at the end of the street and hold something. Then I'll call Michelle and see if she can tell me what it is over the phone."

"No," I say. "That's mind reading, not seeing."

We turn to Michelle.

"Can you read minds?" Lana asks her.

"I barely know my own mind," she says.

Air goes out of the idea.

Lana sits back on her stool. "Damn. That's what we really need. A mind reader."

"Sorry to disappoint," says Michelle, smiling.

I'm no mind reader myself, but Lana's far-off look says she's thinking about Tony. Katherine is staring intently at a dapper black guy halfway down the bar, probably thinking things that she could never tell Slim. Michelle looks at me as if she's thinking about other things she sees but won't tell.

Me, I'm thinking about my baby girl no bigger than a comma.

✳ Red Hurt

✳

✳

I lie on the couch, my thighs pressed together, hoping to keep blood and tissue from oozing out of me. It's a ridiculous pose because I've already miscarried and what I really need to do, according to Dr. Sammy, is let my body heal itself—let it expel the baby that is not a baby. Also, he says, I should have a D&C to remove any leftover matter that lingers inside me. Matter that might get infected, slowing down my ability to get pregnant again.

Matter.

Seven weeks' worth of matter is oozing out of me, I think. It's the night before my D&C and I'm watching a Lifetime Movie of the Week.

It's been only a month since I found out I was pregnant. It's only been a month of anticipation and dreaming and lists of baby names. It's been only a month.

The pregnancy isn't viable," Dr. Sammy said only this morning—after pulling his gloved hand, dripping with matter, out of me.

I cried, of course. Pat held me. Dr. Sammy held me. Pat cried.
Dr. Sammy held Pat.

Then I stopped crying. Pat and I both stopped crying.

Well, I thought, that's that.

We really should have Dr. Sammy over for dinner, I thought
for the umpteenth time as Pat drove me home. I watched neigh-
borhoods whiz by, clutching the plastic container of pills we had
gotten at the hospital pharmacy.

This is really very ordinary, I thought. Lots of women have mis-
carriages. I'm lucky, I thought. I miscarried in the seventh week. It
could have been the fifteenth week, or the twentieth. It's not like I
knew this baby, I thought. It's not like I lost a living person who I already knew. It's not like I lost Spence. I just lost a possibility, I thought.
I just lost the possibility of a person. I just lost a lot of matter.

On the TV, Meredith Baxter-Birney binges on three chocolate
cakes in bulimic fury. She sits in a car and stuffs cake into her
mouth with her hands, smearing it all over her face, making
growling noises. She looks up, her face chocolate, to see a man
looking at her through the window. She wipes her mouth with
her hand, then smooths her hair, streaks of icing spreading
through her sprayed do. She smiles at the man as if to say, "What
you just saw was an aberration. I'm actually completely self-
possessed and a member of Mensa."

I feel another ooze and I shift—afraid to sit up and feel a rush
of "what was" soak my Kotex. The Darvocet I've just taken is one
of my favorite painkillers. It obliterates the pain of the contractions that came in and out the night before, like a malevolent tide.
It also encourages me to feel foggy and soggy and sorry for myself. Somewhat like Meredith's character, who turns to the passenger seat of her car and vomits.

I am stoned, I think. I'm stoned on Darvocet. Who would have thought you could get stoned on Darvocet?

A German phrase for menstrual period is *Rot Weh*. The "red hurt." This is it, I think. This is red hurt. There is something luxurious about my growing misery. It is so complete, so monumental, that I can only live inside it.

Spence is asleep behind a closed door. I hear Pat opening and closing cabinet doors in the kitchen. He is contained, efficient, loving—like a good nurse. And I barely see him. The phone rings and I hear his voice, low.

Meredith is at a party and watches as her husband inclines his head toward a beautiful young woman. Her husband looks back at her across the room like, "I'd rather be with you, but all this purging is beginning to wear on me." Meredith sighs, goes into the kitchen, pours a huge glass of water from the tap, and turns to survey the hors d'oeuvres on the counter. Her eyes move over the squares of cheddar—no, the celery boats—hell no, the lemon squares—hmm, maybe. Then her gaze stops at a huge wheel of Brie. She smiles a stoned smile as the screen fades to black.

"It's the anesthesiologist," says Pat, handing me the phone. He floats in front of me as I reach for the receiver.

"Yes," I say into the phone.

I hear, "Hello, Brett."

A clipped voice tells me that the D&C I will be having tomorrow is a quick and simple procedure. But since I'm going under, the voice needs to go over some things.

Foggy, I answer the voice's questions while watching a commercial. A dog spins plates.

It must be the Puppy Chow.

It must be the Darvocet, I think.

"Do you smoke?" the voice asks.

"No . . . well, yes. Since I miscarried . . . I wasn't smoking while I was pregnant. But yesterday and today."

The voice pauses, then I hear "Hmmm."

I clutch. All fog gone.

"What? I was only smoking for two days!"

The voice says, "That's fine. Just don't smoke any more before the procedure." Pause. "Hmmmm."

"I mean, if you think I shouldn't go under," I say. "I don't need this operation. I'm just electing to . . ."

Pat appears in front of me.

"No. It's fine," says the voice. "Just don't smoke and I'll see you in the morning."

I click off the phone and hand it to Pat.

Fog settles in again as Meredith is rushed through a hospital ward on a gurney. A team of people in hospital greens runs alongside her, shouting things at each other as she rolls her head back and forth saying, "No, no, no."

I clutch again.

"Pat. The anesthesiologist doesn't think I should do this operation!"

"What?" I hear from the kitchen.

"The guy on the phone," I yell. "He thinks I could die on the operating table!"

Pulse jumps in my neck and I put my hand against it to feel the pound, pound, pound. Pat returns and sits at the end of the couch. He leans forward, elbows on his knees, hands hanging loose.

"You're not going to die," he says. I press my feet against his back. "I can't imagine he said that, Brett."

"He asked if I smoked and I told him yes. And he took this long pause and sounded like he wasn't sure I should do this."

"What did he actually say?"

"He said, 'Hmmmm.' Like that. He took a big long pause and said, 'Hmmm.' Like, 'Hmmmm, do I want to risk a malpractice suit on a dead smoker?'"

"What?" Pat says, turning to look at me. "Maybe he just said 'Hmmm' as he was writing down your information."

"It was not that kind of 'hmmm,' Pat. It was like, 'Hmmm . . . how many dead smokers does that make this week?'"

"Brett, look. If he thought there was even the slightest possibility that you would die having something like this . . . an elective surgery, he certainly wouldn't let you do it. And he sure as hell wouldn't want you to die on his watch."

"People die on someone's watch."

Pat looks across the room and blows out air. I push up with my arms and reposition myself on the pillows. Swoosh—out comes more matter.

Meredith lies in a hospital bed, metal bars on both sides, oxygen tube in her nose, monitors beeping. Her husband holds her skeletal hand, tears glisten in the corners of his eyes. Meredith looks at him, parts her papery lips into a weak smile, and says, "You're my man."

Pat puts his hand on my knee.

"What if I don't wake up? Ever?" I say.

"You'll wake up. I know you'll wake up," he says. "Remember when you thought you had that flesh-eating disease?"

"I'm not making this up, Pat."

"I'm just saying that you have a tendency—well, a driving need—to extend these things out to the worst-case scenario."

"See! You think there is a scenario in which I might die tomorrow."

Pat takes his hand from my knee and strides over to the phone.

"That's it!" he says, punching numbers into the receiver.

"What are you doing?"

"I'm calling Dr. Sammy."

"What?" I yell. "Don't call him."

Pat hangs up and turns toward me.

"Look, Brett. We can end this right now. We'll just ask Dr. Sammy if a couple of days of smoking is going to kill you on the operating table tomorrow." His voice is hard with fading patience.

I swing my legs off the couch and sit on the edge. I know now that this is what I've been wanting since this morning when Dr. Sammy said my pregnancy wasn't "viable." I've been wanting true drama. Big stakes. I've been wanting some yelling, some screaming. And it would probably be supremely satisfying if Pat stormed out into the balmy Los Angeles night only to return drunk and contrite with a huge chocolate cake that I can smear all over my face. Maybe Meredith Baxter-Birney can play me in the movie: *Big Red Hurt: The Brett Paesel Story.*

I double over and rest my chest on my knees. My head flops down and I make a high singing sound. I follow the sound to the end, pull in some air, and make it again.

Long as a road—sure and loud. Then, *bang,* like a door opening, I start to shake and sob. Blood gushes past my Kotex and spreads out on the towel beneath me. I am all body and sound. I am flesh and tissue and bone.

I hear on the TV, as if through a long tunnel, a perky woman's voice praising the virtues of a miracle spot remover.

And even as I let my body heave up my loss, I realize that I have surely stained the couch.

Becoming the Woman of My Dreams

✳ ✳ ✳

I sit in an upscale Italian restaurant in Laguna Beach with my well-dressed parents and take in the scene, satisfied. No one would guess that I am a ragingly insecure actress so desperate for my parents' approval that I would eat cut glass for a word of praise.

Within seconds Spence slaps his hand into my pasta bowl and lets out a yell that could lead grown men into battle. Marinara splatters over the three adults and the white tablecloth, making it look like a crime scene. Spence grabs his crotch with his sauce-soaked hand and screams, "My penis is pointing, my penis is pointing."

I panic and stand holding Spence while my parents sit motionless. An audience of suntanned faces turns toward us.

"My son," I say to the group. "He's just . . . he'll be okay. He just . . . got an erection and I guess it frightened him."

My head pounds with pulsing shame—about what, I'm not sure. Certainly not about Spence; I've got no problem with pointing penises. It's something about me—some primordial shame, born simply out of being watched. Born simply out of being me.

My mother comes to life like someone turned on her switch. "Honey, you don't have to explain. You can sit down."

The faces continue to wait for the next thing.

"If you're three years old," I continue, "well, you can imagine, an erection could be a scary thing. It probably feels like it's going to just take off."

The faces remain impassive like whittled wood.

Spence cries as I whisper to him, "Think about something else. It'll go away soon. Think about something boring like cleaning your room or eating green beans." I pause, then play to the crowd, "Or something even more boring like listening to Dr. Phil over and over again."

I wait for a collective chuckle, but it doesn't come. My parents dip their napkins in their water glasses and start to dab their clothing. Slowly, the faces return to their meals.

I want to get their attention again. I want to say, "This woman you see standing here, dripping red sauce, holding her son with a hard-on, incapable of handling this moment with any moxie— this woman—is not who I planned on being. I planned on being Dana."

In my parents' house, on the floor in the extra bedroom, is a battered cardboard box labeled "Kristin's Stuff."

That's me. I was Kristin. Still am, to my parents, who refused to call me by the many names I used through grade school: Kirsty, Robyn, Kate, and the ill-advised Natasha. These were precursors to the name I landed on: Brett, with a small "b"—an affectation I picked up in eighth grade and never shook.

I pull out the box every once in a while and sift through the contents. Here are grade school tests belonging to Robyn and Kate. Letters addressed to Natasha, later shortened to Nat. Flowers pressed by Kirsty. And a worn piece of notebook paper on top of which is written "The Dana Project." It is a contract I made with myself in seventh grade, itemizing the changes I needed to make in order to transform myself into Dana:

I knew a girl named Dana when I was four. She was a mature eight-year-old who ruled the playground with the sheer force of her personality. Tough and pretty, she was intimidating as hell. I was particularly impressed when one day she pulled out the waistband of her underpants and demanded that all the boys put rocks in them. As the boys lined up to throw their rocks into the expanding cotton, I was stunned not only by her confidence but by her ingenuity. Why hadn't I ever thought of rocks in my underpants?

It must have been the image of Dana—boldly standing on the playground, the bumpy terrain of her false belly silhouetted against the fading light—that inspired the Dana Project. Here are the steps my junior high self thought I would have to take in order to transform myself into the woman of my dreams:

1. Stop caring what other people think.
2. Change name to Dana.
3. Carry a brush at all times and brush hair five times a day.
4. Swear sometimes. *Not in front of parents.* Try using the words *fart, fuck, you suck, pussy, pissed off,* and *dildo.*
5. Find out what "dildo" is. Ask Tom Goldenhirsch.

6. Always act like you know what's going on, even if you don't.
7. Always carry a purse.
8. Do spontaneous and outrageous things. *Not in front of parents.* Consider taking off shirt in public or cracking up in church.

Kate Paesel, 10/23/1972

In reading the contract, I see that it's full of holes. My concerns about my parents, my hair, and a purse are not consistent with my image of Dana. The evidence of who I am, who I will always be, is carved in the careful, concerned language of this document.

Last summer my mother showed me a little alumni book that her high school class of 1947 put together. In it were current pictures and little blurbs about what people are doing now. We thumbed through it, marveling over the fact that the class slut owned a bookstore and the class jock looked like Mr. Potato Head. Next to each picture were three adjectives that each person had sent in to describe themselves. The class slut said that she was "Adventurous, Optimistic, and Zany." Next to my mother's picture were the adjectives she had sent to describe herself. They were "Dependable, Determined, and Decent."

"Mom," I said, "these are all 'D' words."

"You noticed," she said, pleased.

"You might as well have added Dull."

"What do you mean?"

"Come on," I said. "Dependable, Determined, and Decent? Would you want to meet this person?"

"I *am* dependable," my mother said.

"How about Daring?" I said. "That's a 'D' word."

"Kristin," she said, "I am not daring."

This is and is not true. My mother is an artist who lived in Europe most of her life. Which is daring by a lot of people's standards. But it is true that she doesn't think of herself as daring.

And I am the acorn who hasn't fallen far from the tree.

I got to have a Dana moment early this year when I did a topless bit on *Six Feet Under.* The bit demanded that I dance in front of a bonfire with my shirt off, my breasts proudly swinging, and say a couple of lines.

Finally, I thought, I get to be bold and free—*and* I get to be those things on national television. This was even better than rocks in my pants. After I shot the scene, actors and crew came up to me and said things like, "Wow, that was brave" and "I could never have done that."

I felt powerful and drunk with my own chutzpah.

A few months later I was Googling myself, as I do when I'm bored—Google myself and my friends. I do this because something gets said about me in a chat room every once in a while. And I'm curious. So I Googled myself and up popped this link to Celebrity Nudity Database. It said something like:

Brett Paesel

Rating ★★ [I am not sure out of how many stars I got two, but I don't think it's a high number.]

Scene Description: Floppy Breasts

Sexy Lauren Ambrose watches a wild bonfire party with a buncha aging hippies. One of them (Brett) runs up to Lauren. Brett's a little chubby, and her naked saggy tits flop and bounce as she dances by the firelight. I gave an extra star because she's pretty good and because it's fun watching her swing and bounce.

There it was—a write-up of my Dana moment on a celebrity nude Web site. I was not, in this man's eyes, a beautiful, bold celebration of womanhood, I was a middle-aged hippie with saggy tits.

A few weeks after the Google, I asked for tips on how to make small talk from Katherine, who could get a tree to talk to her. I'm tired of making faux pas that turn me into the woman not to get trapped with at a function. Recently, at a wrap party for an Olsen Twins project, I said, "Well, T. S. Eliot couldn't have said it better when he said that the greatest treason is to do the right thing for the wrong reason." This statement cleared the room and I ended up having a third martini, which led to my dirty dancing with one of the teenage extras from the show.

Katherine said, "Brett, I just say the first thing that comes into my head."

"That *was* the first thing that came into my head," I said.

"No," said Katherine. "The *first* thing. Like, 'Great shoes' or 'I like your haircut.' "

As Pat and I drive to a snitzy Hollywood party, I think of myself as Dana with rocks in my pants. I will be fun and flirty (not *too* flirty). I will not be Dependable, Determined, and Decent. I will say the first thing that comes into my head, something simple. I feel kicky and bold in my new pair of flowy pants.

At the party I wait in line for a drink, crushed next to a semi-famous, older director who knows me somewhat as that woman who does those bits on his friends' shows sometimes. He gives me that trapped smile I know so well.

I think . . . think . . . think . . . first thing. First thing that comes into my head. I look at his shoes. I shift. I look at his hair. I pull the waistband of my flowy pants.

I breathe in and will a thought to descend. I breathe in and open my mouth and say, "I'm wearing a thong."

His eyes widen. I think, Well, I've got his attention. And I barrel on through.

"It's itching," I say.

He smiles vaguely, then looks out over the room.

"I'm just . . . ," I say. "It's my first time wearing one because of these pants and it's killing me."

"Yes," he says in a strained voice.

"Why don't men wear thongs?" I ask.

"What would you like?" he asks, inclining his head toward the bartender.

"Not to have to wear a damn thong," I say.

"To drink," he says.

"Oh," I say. "I'll have a white wine."

He orders for us both and hands me my wine.

"Thanks," I say.

There is a pause and I say, "So, yeah. The thong. Well, I guess you have to be uncomfortable to be sexy. I mean, look at those push-up demi-bras with water in them."

He smiles and says, "Yes. Well, see you soon."

I watch his back as he slips through the crowd. I stand with my cup of wine, my fingers feeling the cold, wet plastic. I feel the fabric pull between my buttocks. And I think that T. S. Eliot was indeed right. The greatest treason is to do the right thing for the wrong reason.

I am not Dana. I am dependable, determined, and decent. And, hey, I ain't that bad. Because it's fun to watch me swing and bounce.

✳ Friday
✳
✳

What just pisses me off more than just my average 'pissed off' is that Children's Day knows we're a gay couple with an adopted child. They have this very PC brochure with pictures of black children holding hands with whites, two boys playing with dolls . . ." Michelle trails off.

Lana reaches over and pats Michelle's knee. I take another sip of my red wine and look at our reflection in the mirror behind the bar. Light briefly fills the room as the door is opened, and I see Katherine in the mirror, walking toward us, her perky breasts straining against a tight red T-shirt. She raises her hand at Mack.

"Don't mind the glass. Just inject me with a black and tan, my friend," she says, flinging her purse behind the bar rail at our feet.

Lana takes her hand from Michelle's knee. "Michelle's preschool just screwed her without a kiss."

"No shit," Katherine says to Michelle. "You were high on that school."

"Uh, let's see. That was before today, when they 'suggested' that Sarah and I not come together to Faith's Halloween party."

Mack slides a sticky amber shot over to Lana, which she dumps into her beer.

"This just doesn't make any sense," I say. "They knew you were a gay couple when you registered."

"The teacher said it wasn't the school. It was some of the parents who were having grandparents come. She said that a couple of parents had seen Sarah and me kissing outside the school and they were worried that we'd do it at the party or something and that the grandparents would be offended."

"What if you say you won't kiss?" says Katherine. She pauses. "No, never mind. That's stupid. You shouldn't have to say anything." She reaches through us to grab her black and tan.

"You know, just fuck 'em," I say. "Fuck those Children's Day hypocrites. Bring Faith over to my preschool. Carter's pretty easy. Say you know me. They're pretty impressed with me these days."

"Impressed?" says Lana. "I thought you said that you were the worst mommy there."

I put down my wine.

"Sure. When it comes to technical stuff like working with food or doing anything crafty. I can't do any of that. But," I say, dragging it out, "Spence just made me a star."

"No talking about kids," Katherine says, reminding me of a recent Friday rule.

"This isn't about Spence," I say. "It's about how famous I am at Carter School."

"I hope we're not finished with me," says Michelle.

"This has everything to do with you," I say. "Thing is, the other day I go to pick Spence up and the teachers and the parents are all looking at me. Like I can feel them staring. I go to sign Spence out and I'm standing next to one of the moms,

Mako, who's looking at me like I'm suddenly someone special. And you know she's never given me even one thought."

"Right, right," says Michelle, spinning her hand like, "Move it along."

"Anyway, she says to me, 'Spence told us about your morning.' I can't think of what she's talking about. But she smiles and says, 'You had quite a morning.' And, suddenly, I remember. Shit. Spence came in on us. Pat and me."

"And this makes you famous?" says Lana. "The moms over there must be pretty hard up."

"Now, this is according to Mako, who somehow thought I should know. What Spence said was that he saw Mommy sitting on Daddy's head."

Lana pushes away from the bar and spits beer all over it. Katherine slaps her thigh and whoops like it's the funniest thing. Michelle smiles and swigs her Amstel.

I'm pleased. It's a brief celebration. Plus, I just told a sex story, which I almost never do. Good for me.

"Anyway, I guess the story got around school and Mako said that everyone's impressed that I get a little action on a school morning. To be honest, I think they should be more impressed with Pat."

"*I'm* impressed with Pat," says Lana.

"I'm working hard at figuring out how any of this helps me," says Michelle.

"Thing is," I say, "now that I'm a person of note over at Carter School, I bet I can get you in."

"You can get me in because everyone knows you get head in the morning?"

"People get into schools for a lot less," says Lana.

"Don't you see?" I say. "You're my funky lesbian friend with her Chinese daughter. We're the color. We're what keeps the day interesting."

I say this before I know how true it is.

"As impressive as your notoriety is," says Michelle, "the sad truth is, Sarah and I will probably stick it out at Children's Day for Faith's sake. I can't yank her out of school in the middle of the year."

"I guess," I say. "But if you can't hack it, come over to our preschool and say you know that mom whose husband goes downtown in the morning."

Mack places four clear shots in front of us.

"Anyone who can guess what's in these shots," he says, "gets to take me downtown tonight."

He winks and walks away.

It Takes a Gay Village

✳ Village

✳

T hat's it, Brett. Right at the end she does a little laugh. Can you match it?" says a voice from behind the glass window of the sound booth.

I watch footage of an actress in some straight-to-video movie. I've been called by a friend of a friend to rerecord the actress's lines, because they're unintelligible. Jobs are few, so I asked my friends Ben and Joe to watch Spence while I work. Pat's shooting something with the Olsen Twins again—some bit where he chases them in a golf cart. If we weren't so desperate for money, I'd sit down and ponder what exactly we think we're doing here in Hollywood. It's a far cry from the mind-blowing political theater that rocked our worlds when we were serious artists in Chicago.

I lean into the microphone and match the starlet's words. "You tell Guido I don't have the bag, man." Then I tag it with a snort of a laugh.

"Perfect," I hear from behind the window.

I puff up a bit at having nailed it. Even though it's an easy thing.

On the street I phone the guys. "Hey, Joe, I just got out of the session. I'm on my way to get Spence."

"Wow, that was fast," he says on the other end.

"I'm a pro."

"Well, we were just settling in," he says.

From another room I hear Ben yell, "Tell her we were just starting to watch *The Golden Girls!*"

"I'll be there in ten minutes," I say. "Bea Arthur may scare Spence, so turn down the volume."

Pat and I have known Ben since we lived in Chicago, and we've known Joe since he moved in with Ben ten years ago. They are large men, too big for their apartment. They are gentle giants, seeming to stoop to get through doors, filling up a room with their size. There is poetry in their pairing. How did they find each other? Two gay men who love everything on Lifetime television, beer on tap, and babies.

I walk in the door toward the end of *The Golden Girls*. Spence sits on Ben's lap as Joe hunches over a frying pan in the kitchen, muscles bulging from his shoulders like the Hulk.

"Mommy," Spence yells, waving.

"Hey, sweetie."

I throw my backpack down and sink into a chair. Bea Arthur tosses off a line as she exits through the swinging door of the kitchen. Ben laughs.

"That, my friend," he says to Spence, "is comedy."

"You want to be Bea Arthur," I say.

"I *am* Bea Arthur," he says. Which is true.

"You guys want to stay for dinner?" asks Joe. "It's cool. As long as we can kick you out in an hour. We've got a Bear Bust tonight."

"No thanks," I say. Ben and Joe would never miss Friday Bear Bust, a kegger at a local gay bar, catering only to large, mostly hairy guys called bears.

Spence slips off Ben's lap and walks over to Joe.

"Can I see the fish?" he asks, tugging on Joe's pant leg.

"Just a minute," says Joe, sliding the frying pan to another burner. "I got a new bottom feeder. A scavenger. You'll love him."

Joe reaches way down to grab Spence's hand. They amble off to look at the aquarium in the den, as Ben and I stare at the opening credits of *The Nanny*.

I grew up with many gay uncles, friends of my parents who were "confirmed bachelors"—or, as a gay friend's mother says, "those who have elected not to marry." These men sat at our kitchen table, chopping onions, chatting to my mother as she cooked. They were tan all year round and their pants were always pressed. They adored me, I now realize, because being part of our extended family was as close as they would get to having children.

One of these men, "Uncle" Jay, gave me a black doll when I was about three, just to shock the neighbors. Later he gave me a Bible. Printed on the inside of the cover was a map of the Holy Land, where Jay had scrawled notes.

"Just think of the tan you could get here," he scribbled over Jordan. Over the Mediterranean Sea in capital letters he wrote, "Let's meet Jackie O. here." When I lent the Bible to my church's Bible display, it was returned by the Sunday School teacher. I couldn't figure out why.

A few years ago I got a cocktail napkin in the mail from a

friend of Jay's. "Just wanted you to know that Jay was thinking of you way back in 1975, when we were skiing in St. Moritz," says the accompanying note. "That night he couldn't stop talking about how smart and talented you were."

I unfolded the napkin to read, in Jay's handwriting, "I'll send her to Vassar."

I imagined Jay in his skiing jumpsuit, which he wore even when he wasn't skiing, boasting about me in a ski lodge thirty years ago. I imagined him making huge promises about how he was going to take care of me. Someone must have drunkenly insisted that he put it in writing.

My friend William trained Spence early to call him Genius. Last summer Genius went to France to work on a screenplay. While there, he sent me a photo attached to an e-mail. "All week, I've been a very happy man," it said. I opened up the attachment to find a picture of a model-handsome young man, shirtless, on a beach. The e-mail went on to say that the young man's name was Enrico. He was twenty-four and studying at the Sorbonne. "He's intelligent and so deep," continued the e-mail, "and we're in love. He's moving to the States."

I remember thinking that there was no part of the e-mail that made me happy for my lonely, fortyish friend who had a habit of choosing heartbreak. I didn't like that they'd known each other for only a week, that they were in France, that the guy was twenty-four, Chilean, or that he was named Enrico. Genius needed a fiftyish art dealer who liked rococo bathroom fixtures, fine wine, and paying for things. Who had a solid name like Scott.

But that was before I met Enrico. He landed and I was converted.

★   ★   ★

Give me for to the baby," Enrico says, arms outstretched, going for Spence.

Spence looks at Enrico wide-eyed. He can't understand a word Enrico says. But he likes that Enrico lets him watch back-to-back DVDs when he babysits. Something I, the TV Nazi, will not allow. Enrico lifts Spence in a practiced hip-hold.

"Genius is coming for to later," he says to me.

"Fine, you know how to let him in," I say. "I'll only be gone a couple of hours."

"This is nothing. We watch for some elephants and find dinosaurs in a book."

"Sounds good. There's food in the fridge."

"I love for the food for Spencer. It's nothing."

"Right."

"I can for Thursday babysit for the baby. I have for Katherine not to do for this week," he says.

"Good," I say.

This means that he's not babysitting for Katherine and can do Thursday for me. Enrico has a booming babysitting business among my friends. He's good with children in that effortless way that is common in cultures where children are passed around easily and crying is as much the music of a busy household as the clanking of pots and pans while a huge evening meal is being prepared. But the biggest plus of Enrico the babysitter is being able to call a friend on the cell phone, while in line at Target, to say loudly, "Enrico's doing me till two on Friday, so it looks like you can have him from three to six."

Unable to marry Genius, Enrico can't work in the country legally. Employing him regularly probably excludes my friends and me from holding any high political office in the future. I wouldn't want to be standing in front of a microphone at a televised press conference, Enrico behind me in an orange tank top, saying, "I can no longer pursue the office, as I have illegally employed this Chilean babysitter."

"Brett," Enrico says, putting Spence down, "I do forever need to talk about next month now. I will go to Brazil for to have lipo-vacation."

Genius has told me that Brazil is the cheapest place to go for plastic surgery, as Brazilians get liposuction as easily and as often as we get our teeth cleaned. Enrico first went there for a lipo-vacation when he was eighteen.

"But you'll be back in May," I say.

"Oh, yes. It's nothing."

"Does the lipo hurt?"

"Not for nothing," he says. "It is like someone take a big board and keep hitting you for four days."

"Ouch."

"Then I must so for to be careful when I come back. And not so much lift the babies. For I must for to have this bandage from here," he says, slapping his thigh with his hand, "to here." He brings his hand up to his neck.

"Like a body cast?"

"For five weeks, yes. Only it is a bandage"

"What happens if you take the bandage off early?"

"My doctor say fat will come out like balls on my body."

"Little lumps of fat all over you?"

"Yes. Lumps."

"I've got to say, Enrico, you look fine to me. If you feel a little chubby, why don't you just go on a little diet."

"Oh, no," he says, "I love the chocolates and the sauces."

★　★　★

Spence knows that a lot of our adult friends come in couples. To date, he hasn't asked why some couples are made up of a man and a woman and why others are made up of two men or two women—although he did initially ask if Enrico was Genius's son.

Most of Spence's gay uncles come in pairs. Mine came singly, though often there was a friend in the background who visited from out of town and stayed in the uncles' guest room.

I don't think that my mother and I went out looking for fabulous gay uncles for our children, though we were happy to have them. I found, and maybe my mother did too, that some of my childless friends drifted away after I had a child. Maybe those friends assumed that I had suddenly lost interest in the things we used to do together. Whatever the reason, they disappeared completely as if their names had been written on my heart in invisible ink. Of the ones who stayed, several were my gay friends who became uncles by showing up over and over again, by watching our baby, inviting us to dinners with our baby, listening to my postnatal blabbing, and offering up solid advice on how to decorate the baby's room so it wouldn't make me gag on its cuteness.

Christian and Doug have been babysitting Spence since infancy and have followed his development since then with avuncular pride. Recently, they decided to raise a child of their own.

Christian calls to thank me for filling out their adoption recommendation. He tells me that he and Doug are making little books for the birth mothers to look at. Books that describe their house, their relationship, their individual histories. Doug wants to put kitty stickers on the pages. They've been told to put things on and in the book that will appeal to young, undereducated girls. Anything that will make your book stand out.

I ask if being a gay couple will be a handicap.

"Not really," he says. "Most of the girls grew up without a dad in the picture. The agency told us that often birth mothers choose gay couples because they figure it gives the baby two dads. A dad and a spare."

That night I lie in bed thinking of a young girl turning the pages of Christian and Doug's book. I see her touching the kitty stickers. I think of her reading what they wrote about how they would raise her child. I see her close the book.

I fall asleep thinking of her choosing them.

✳ Finding My Religion
✳

✳

After **twenty years of truancy** from Western religion, I have returned with my son. I've always assumed that I would return—once I had children. Taking Spence to church has seemed as much a given as potty training and birthday parties. No doubt because going to church was part of my weekly routine until I left home.

Apart from Reverend Jensen, the preachers of my youth were uniformly dull. Handsome Reverend Jensen disappeared one Sunday, yanked by higher-ups for some indiscretion or another. Probably for getting it on with one of the clucking matrons who took covered dishes over to his house during the week. At the age of eleven I thought he had been fired for being too interesting, since I was sure that a requirement for the job must be a talent for creating a somnambulant effect on listeners during the sermon.

It is one of those preachers I hear, intoning his dreary message, when I picture myself sitting next to my mother in a pew, as my brother Erik plays at our feet.

My mother has written a note on the bulletin: "Do you think

my rear end is bigger than, smaller than, or the same size as ➜?"
The arrow points to a straight-backed woman in the pew ahead
of us.

I look, circle "smaller than," and pass the bulletin back.

My mother reads it, smiles, folds the bulletin, and writes, "The
minister looks like Les," as I look on. Les is a friend of my father's
who looks so average you can't describe him. Whenever someone
looks like no one, he looks like Les.

I nod discreetly.

We pass the bulletin back and forth until we stand to sing the
next hymn.

Note-writing during church is only one aspect of what my father calls "your mother's peculiar brand of religiosity."

Mt. Pleasant United Church of Christ is a "Just Peace Church."
On any given Sunday Spence and I walk up the steps after having had our milk shakes at the counter of a local diner. A banner
that says "Let My People Marry" flaps in the wind. A large man
in a choir robe paces and smokes a clove cigarette as an older
couple makes agonizingly slow process through the side door.

The congregation of this church is left-wing activist. Luke, the
openly gay minister, gives thoughtful, funny sermons on social issues. A woman who looks about sixty-five (her long frizzy gray
hair suggesting a youth spent on peace marches and mescaline)
keeps us posted on the many "actions" she is involved with, including a recent "nude women spelling out the word 'peace' on a
mountaintop." Kids chase each other through the pews. Cans of
food, off to a food bank, pile up in the back.

My own peculiar brand of religiosity has included everything
from being tapped with a feather by a Siddha Yoga guru, to desert
meditation retreats, to attending temple with my Jewish friends on

High Holidays. A religious dabbler, I even sampled rebirthing—a psychospiritual practice based on the theory that all of your problems trace back to the original birth trauma, requiring you to "relive" the trauma by submerging yourself in a warm pool in a snorkel and reenacting the journey through the birth canal.

People at Mt. Pleasant pretty much leave Spence and me alone. Which I appreciate, since I've never really wanted to explain that in many respects I am a fraud, soaking up the sweet, anachronistic optimism of their devoted hearts, while hiding the fact that I'm not particularly Christian.

I am an interloper. And Spence loves hanging out at the nursery, where I drop him off fifteen minutes after the service has started. I am grateful that no one has asked me to actually join the church. I would have to come clean. Not just about not being a Christian, but about the fact that joining any kind of group makes me tired and rashy.

The last time I officially joined a group, and stuck with it for any amount of time, was in the tenth grade. Full of feeling I took to be divine, I joined the Hear and Now religious singers. We were a group of teenagers outfitted in gray bell-bottoms, pale yellow shirts, and smart black vests. After only a month with the group, I was tapped for the Madrigals, an elite subsect who sang solos in the middle of snappy tunes that incorporated sign language and dance moves.

I loved it. And I saw my career as religious sign language soloist taking off. When I think of it now, I realize that the God I worshipped was more one of belonging. I believed in Christianity being the One True Religion because I was snug in that group and they thought I was a star. An eccentric teenager with glasses the thickness of paperweights, I wasn't generating a whole lot of heat on the boy scene. But I could rock the house on Sunday mornings with my solo verse in "Leaving on a Jet Plane." For reasons known only to our group leader, Mr. Telsgaard, "Leaving on a Jet Plane" was one of our top religious tunes, along with "Rocky Mountain High" and "Killing Me Softly."

Mr. Telsgaard looked like Les, but his bland face was deceptive. He was ambitious and worked us like crazy. After six months of intense rehearsals Mr. Telsgaard announced that we would be giving a Gala Concert. He listed some of the pieces and then announced the finale: "The group will sing 'Morning Has Broken' while Brett reads the first five verses of Genesis in the instrumental breaks."

Surely, this is what I had been waiting for all my young life.

"Thank you, Mr. Telsgaard. With God's help I won't let you down."

"Glad to hear it," he said. "Just don't do anything fancy. Say the words and keep it simple."

The next few weeks we practiced like mad, each rehearsal ending with a half hour devoted to "Morning Has Broken."

Mr. Telsgaard would swell the blended voices, then bring them low as they sang, "God's re-creation of the new day." Then he would turn to me and nod. I would lean into the microphone and start, "In the beginning, God created . . ." My voice cracked with intensity. My eyes sparkled with tears.

After each rehearsal Mr. Telsgaard pulled me aside.

"Brett, I need it with a little less . . . feeling."

Every time, I nodded, not hearing.

A week before the Gala Concert Mr. Telsgaard pulled me aside again.

"Brett, I'm taking you off Genesis."

At first I thought this was a test. An extension of the trust ex-

ercises Mr. Telsgaard required us to run through at the beginning
of each rehearsal. Exercises that involved jumping off tables into
a gaggle of fellow singers. Or being fed a mystery food while
blindfolded. This must be the mother of all trust exercises, I
thought. Did I trust myself—did I trust Mr. Telsgaard enough—
to know that he was bluffing?

"I know, Mr. Telsgaard," I said. "I know that the piece is very
moving. I trust it. I trust myself. I trust you. And I trust God."

"You don't understand," he said. "I'm taking you off Genesis."

My throat hurt like something was balled up in there.

"You stand out too much," he went on. "Hear and Now is a
group. It's an ensemble. Your feelings are too big. You overwhelm
the singers. You overwhelm the group."

I continued attending church for a couple of years after being
fired from "Morning Has Broken," but the juice had gone out of
my interest in belonging to any group, particularly a religious
one.

At Mt. Pleasant, after listening to Pastor Luke's impassioned sermon on gay marriage, a mom stops me outside the nursery.
Sharon is the only person in the congregation who has doggedly
insisted on engaging me. She is also the Sunday School teacher.

"The Sunday School curriculum has just arrived. We're going
to start doing some lessons with the preschool kids to get them
ready for Sunday School. I think you'll love the little pamphlets."

This is the moment I've been dreading. I have hoped against
hope that I could continue coming to church without ever having to weigh in on core Christian beliefs, like the existence of a
man named Jesus or the concept of original sin.

Sharon hands me a pamphlet with a cartoon Jesus dancing

with children of every color. A bubble comes out of his mouth: "Love is the answer."

"Yep. Looks great." I smile, folding the pamphlet.

Up until now, Sunday School has been about Spence playing with toy dinosaurs and occasionally singing "This Little Light of Mine." The fact that he hasn't come home with a memorized Bible verse yet is probably the only reason Pat has quietly tolerated Spencer's and my churchgoing sedition.

Pat and I sit on the couch, our feet propped up on the coffee table, the radio turned down. We've had dinner, played with Spence, read him three stories, and endured his two attempts to win our attention post-bedtime. Finally, we hear deep breathing from his room. This is precious adult time.

"So," I say, "looks like they're going to start some kind of lessons in Spencer's Sunday School."

"Lessons?" Pat's body tenses.

"Yeah, you know, like 'God is love,' 'Love is the answer,' 'Love means never having to say you're sorry.' That kind of thing."

"You mean '*Jesus* is love.' It's going to be about Jesus, isn't it?"

"I imagine Jesus will be mentioned. Yes."

"In a positive light," he says.

"Well. He was a great guy," I say. "I mean, you don't have anything against Jesus the man, do you?"

"Um. No. Just Jesus the one and only son of God."

We stare ahead. My heart pounds. Here it is. One of the little locked boxes of our marriage. Every couple has them. The boxes they agree not to open. This box contains Pat's anger at the church of his youth. The church that told him he was a sinner. That he should repent. That he needed to be saved.

Pat gets up to close Spencer's door.

"Are you going to teach him about the Greek gods as well?" says Pat. "Athena was born out of Zeus's head."

"I'm sure he'll learn all about the Greek gods in school someday," I say.

"Why don't you teach him all about that Indian blue elephant god with all those arms?"

"I don't know anything about him. Her."

"I just think," says Pat, "that if you're going to teach him the mythology of one religion, you should teach him the mythology of all of them."

I say okay. But I don't know all those other mythologies. I'm familiar with the Christian stories. Pat says that that's just it. Their familiarity gives them credibility to me. I say I don't know what he means.

"Like the myth of immaculate conception," he says.

"Well. I happen to believe that immaculate conception is possible," I say.

Our locked box explodes.

"AN ENTITY CAN'T KNOCK UP A HUMAN!" screams Pat, stomping into the bedroom.

I follow him. He walks back into the living room. I follow. Words start flying. Some make sense, some don't. We trail each other around the house, yelling, slamming doors. Pat puts on his coat. Takes it off. Puts it on again. I cry and tell him to keep his voice down.

"I didn't say that I thought immaculate conception is *probable,*" I say. "I think that probably Mary and Joseph did it before they got married, and she got pregnant with Jesus, and they probably couldn't tell anybody that they'd done it, and so Mary said, 'Guess what, this angel said I was having the son of God.' "

"So what are we talking about?" yells Pat.

"I'm just saying that immaculate conception is *possible*. I think *anything is possible*."

"Even a blue elephant god with lots of arms?"

"No. I don't think a blue elephant god is possible."

"There you are!" He throws up his hands like his point is made.

"But that's just me," I say. "If someone believes in a blue elephant god—I say, 'Thank God, you believe in *something*!' "

We face each other like hostile strangers—tense, waiting for the next lob.

Then something switches. The air changes. It all slows down. Probably because we've reached the nut of it.

Pat slips off his coat and lets it drop. He looks at me as I stand, shaking.

"What is it," he says, "about you and religion?"

I sink to the bed and sit on the edge, no fight left. I reach back in my mind for an answer that makes sense. I search and search, while Pat stands with his coat lumped at his feet.

"It's what keeps me hanging on," I say.

I must have been in my late teens when I asked my mother about her unusual take on religion. She doesn't believe in heaven or hell. She doesn't believe in an anthropomorphic God. She doesn't believe that Christianity is the One True Religion. And yet she goes to church every Sunday, passing silly notes to whoever comes with her.

"Kristin," she said, "I don't care what you believe. I don't care what anyone believes. I just hope that it's *something*. When you've fallen over the edge of a cliff and you're dangling with just your fingers digging into the rock, I want you to have something that gives you the strength to hang on."

Weeks after the argument with Pat, I realize that this is what

I want for Spence. I want him to believe in something—
anything—that will keep him hanging on.

Pat skulks around the edges of the Sunday School classroom as
I throw things into Spencer's backpack: a couple of dinosaurs, a
Baggie of Cheerios, and his crayoned cartoon pamphlet. He's
scribbled all over the Jesus who has a modern-day kid sitting in
his lap. Spence smiles at me and I notice a circular sticker on his
shirt—a drawing of two hands praying.

"It's his worship sticker," says Sharon.

Pat smiles like he's trying.

"So, Sharon," I say above the heads of children milling, "I
wanted to ask you about the curriculum."

"Isn't it great?" she says. "We had a whole discussion today
about how Jesus wants everyone to love each other."

I look at Pat, who seems to be controlling an eye roll.

"I just wanted to . . . talk about what the curriculum says . . .
about H-E-L-L," I say, spelling in case a kid tunes in.

"Oh," she says. *Did I say something bad?*

"Are you going to say anything about H-E-L-L?"

"Oh, no," she says. And it suddenly occurs to me that she may
think that I'm in *favor* of starting the kids off early with some
scary hell stories. Maybe she thinks I want more hell and less
lovey-dovey in my Sunday School curriculum.

"I mean, I'm not a big fan of H-E-L-L," I say quickly.

Relief relaxes her face. "Me neither," she says.

Pat is now unreadable.

"Great," I say. "And S-I-N? Do you talk about that?"

"No. None of that either," she says. "We just talk about love
and sharing. "

"Good," I say. I feel a bit foolish. Like I came in here to have some big confrontation about hell and sin, and I can't get anyone to take me on. I have to stop myself from patting her on the back and saying, "Keep up the good work."

"Well, that's just great," I say. "Because love and sharing, that's really what it's all about."

I throw a look to Pat, who is on his knees, picking up toys and tossing them in the appropriate bins.

"That's what I think," says Sharon.

"Great," I say.

We smile at each other.

"Have you thought about joining the church?" she asks.

Pat looks up at me.

I pause, then choose to pretend that I simply didn't hear her. This is a little trick I've learned from my mother. It's remarkably effective.

"Well," I say, "keep up the good work," and I pat her on the back.

✴ Friday
✳
✴

Lana is already crying when I walk through the door. Michelle stands, her arm around Lana's waist. Katherine looks on with concentrated concern. I stop, just inside, to give myself a stolen second of calm before approaching. I watch the bar as if it is some disconnected scene, which, of course, it is—a world that moves ahead, pitiless to the small dramas of the people who move within it.

As I walk toward my group of friends, I know that Tony has either left or is leaving. The pose tells me everything.

"I can't believe he's being such an asshole," Lana says as I pull out a stool to sit on.

Mack slides a prepoured glass of wine in front of me.

"He's young, "says Michelle.

"He's young *and* he's an asshole," says Lana, sniffing and reaching for her beer.

Katherine leans over to me. "The affair's been going on for three months. Some chick he met outside a grocery store."

"Jesus. What an asshole."

"Yup," she says. " 'Asshole' is as far as we've gotten."

"Then I'm up to speed."

"He met her outside a grocery store," says Lana. "He was coming out of the store with potato chips, and he just started talking to her. She gave him her number."

"That's a particular kind of woman, right there," says Katherine.

"What do you mean?" I ask.

"Come on, have you ever handed your number to someone you just chatted up outside a grocery store?"

"No," I say. "But I might have. I don't think the woman's the problem here."

"That's right," says Michelle. "Let's get back to Tony."

"He's such an asshole," says Lana, looking off.

The rest of us share a look. How much further do we go? Here is the moment that we've been waiting for—we now have empirical proof of Tony's assholeness. And now that Lana has pronounced him an asshole—now that she's said it—*we* get to say it. It is the first step in a long process of prying Lana loose from her dream of her little family of three. There is no pleasure in the task. There is, however, a shared sense of relief in this moment. It is hard to watch your friend suffer for as long as Lana has with Tony.

"So what are you going to do?" asks Michelle.

I'm relieved that it's Michelle and not me who has asked the question. This is tricky territory. If Michelle's too eager to kick Tony out, Lana might leap to his defense. Michelle must also make sure that her indictment of him does not become an indictment of Lana's bad judgment. It's best to stick to generalities like "He's an asshole" and "What was he thinking?" and "How could he do that?" This is not the time to say things like "That first month when you were dating and he came home drunk at four in the morning, wouldn't tell you where he had been, and smashed the glass shelf in the living room—that was the moment when it became clear that this was a man who had no clue about what it would take to make a woman as complicated and magnificent as you happy and cared for."

"I don't know what to do," says Lana. "If I tell him to leave, he won't have anywhere to live."

I glance at Michelle, wondering what she will say instead of "Who the fuck cares where this guy who can't make money, drinks too much, ignores you for days at a time, and cheats on you *lives*!!!! Kick his ass out *right now*!!!"

Michelle says, "What do *you* want? Do you want him to leave?"

Good, that's very good.

Lana pauses for a moment, sniffling. "Sometimes he can be so sweet to me, you know?"

Katherine says, "When he's not busy being an asshole!"

Whoops. Total miscalculation. I look sideways at Katherine, who looks back at me to indicate that she's just realized she's made a mistake and that the conversation has taken a new turn. We've moved on from "asshole" to making Lana feel cared for.

"I mean," says Katherine, "of course he's sweet to you. You're a beautiful, smart woman."

"You think so?" Lana asks, looking into the mirror behind the bar. She gives herself a slight smile.

"Of course you are," we all murmur—or something close to that.

"This girl he's seeing," she says, "is a lot younger."

"Maybe your self-confidence frightens Tony," I say at the same time Michelle says, "Tony is probably immature himself."

I look over to Katherine, who only wants to confirm and re-confirm that Tony is an asshole.

What follows is a plodding dissection of Tony's motives and
intentions. It's slow and painful, but it must be done. This is how
women restore each other—they question and affirm, coax and
tease. It is a delicate and brutal dance.

Until the end of this happy hour, we will perform it.

Lana and the ✳ Reverse

✳

✳

A couple of weeks after Tony moves out for a trial separation, Lana says, "Brett, I'm sitting at some bar in the Valley, making out with some guy, then I turn around and start making out with a different guy on the other side of me."

She pulls a blue plastic thing out of the freezer. She wears a tight white T-shirt with a watery pink stain and is naked from the waist down.

"Sounds like a big night," I say.

"You're not kidding," she says. "I'm making out with two guys at once and I'm thinking this is wild. I haven't felt like this since I was twenty. I'm having a blast, knocking back tequila and talking dirty. One guy asks if I was an animal, what animal would I be? I tell him a lioness. So I'm growling all night. Like he's my prey. Anyway, you can tell that I'm so far gone I forget that I have to give a little speech at my preschool fund-raiser meeting today."

Lana pulls the elastic strap of the blue plastic thing and adjusts it around her head. I see now that it's an ice pack. Lana's eyes peer out of tiny holes in the cold mask. She looks like a rare bird.

"I don't know how I get myself into these things. I can't give a speech at the preschool looking like I just came off a three-day bender," she says.

I look at Lana's bare legs and wonder if mine are bigger or smaller than hers. I've lost all sense of myself physically since having Spencer. With almost everyone I think, Do I look like that? Is my skin tighter, looser? I look for clues in mirrors but find that I adjust almost immediately, pulling in my tummy, standing straighter, dropping my chin. I've learned to distrust mirrors. Since she broke up with Tony, Lana has lost twenty-five pounds. She is the junior version of herself.

"Goddammit!" she yells, and starts to hop around the kitchen, her white bottom bouncing. She balances on one leg, leans down, picks up a marble, and clanks it into the sink.

"Goddammit! Daisy, Mommy just found another marble!" she yells to her four-year-old, who, as far as I can tell, isn't home. "That's it. If I trip or fall over another marble, there will be NO MARBLES EVER AGAIN in this house!"

"It's amazing how much stepping on something that tiny can be so painful," I say.

"Brett, it's the tiny things that get you. Marbles, needles, paper cuts, slivers. Personally, I'd rather somebody smash me in the face with a big board."

She sits at her computer, pops it on, and stares at the screen through the ice-blue mask.

"So here's what I'm talking about," she says, clicking the mouse with one hand and grabbing a cigarette out of its pack with the other. "It's called Our Place. It's a site where you meet people."

"For dating?"

"For anything. You know my friend Bobbi? The psychic? She's the one who recommended it. She said it's a great resource for single moms. She's a single mom."

"Resource for what?"

"For meeting people. Could be dating. Could be someone's got a great babysitter they want to share. I'm thinking I might even get leads on a house."

"You're looking for a house again?" Lana wants a house almost more than she wants a man. "What about a down payment?"

"No," says Lana, images popping up on the screen, "I don't have the down payment. But if I get a no-money-down thing, in an up-and-coming area—a fixer-upper. All I'm saying is, it's out there."

I think of Lana and Daisy living in the skeleton of a house littered with crack pipes and condoms. I imagine a cold wind blowing through a broken window as Lana and Daisy huddle for warmth in front of the oven.

"Here's the site," says Lana.

She clicks and sits back as a site appears, exhaling smoke in a short, purposeful puff. I get up and look over her shoulder.

"Fantastic," she says. "Look at this. I've gotten seven hundred and twenty-three hits since I put up my profile three days ago."

"You got seven hundred hits of guys wanting to know you?"

"Isn't it great?"

"It's incredible. Kind of scary."

"What's scary? Maybe one of them is rich, foxy, and owns a house. Besides, they only know me as Chiclit. It's anonymous, unless you want to meet someone. Here's my picture," she says, clicking.

Up pops her picture. In it she is model-gorgeous.

"Where's your profile?"

"Here," she says.

I lean closer to the screen. Lana's ice mask scrapes lightly against my temple as I read the first line: "Badass single mom likes to kick it in bars."

I straighten up.

"Well, there's your answer," I say.

"What?"

"Badass single mom?"

"It's me," she says. "Besides, it's not just guys. I've gotten some hits from other single moms who just want to hang."

I start to feel light-headed and a bit woozy. I often feel this way around Lana. She lives on the edge of such real chaos that it's almost like knowing someone who does extreme sports. Whenever I see her, I am surprised and thrilled to find her still standing. It makes me want to giggle a lot.

I adore her. She is everything at once—sloppy, ambitious, funny, distracted, smart, and willfully naive. As a mother, she is affectionate, silly, impatient. She is my talisman. She is witchy voodoo against the cloning of the American Mom.

Invoking Lana's voice in my head is the only thing that gets me through my yearbook meeting with Jerri Regan.

I signed up for the Yearbook Committee at our cooperative preschool because you have to do a committee and because I figured Pat could do a lot of layout on the computer. I was looking for an easy job. Not because I was afraid of a little work, but because I was afraid of failing. Most of the committee work demanded skills I simply don't possess: cooking, organizing, cleaning, asking for money, or talking to people.

I signed up for the Yearbook Committee because I can take

pictures. I signed up for Yearbook even though I can't understand why four-year-olds need yearbooks.

Jerri Regan is the committee chair and she frightens me with her zeal to make sure that every second of every child's life at Carter School be documented with precious and accurate detail. She is a squirrel-like woman, jerking fast, this way and that, several things in her hands at one time. When I talk to Jerri, I can't help thinking that she is the photo reverse of Lana: Pale, where Lana is dark; small, where Lana is tall; desperate, where Lana is confident; earnest, where Lana is ironic and philosophical.

There are forty children in the school. Jerri took pictures of each one on Santa's lap—later laying out all forty pictures over eight pages, with captions telling us what each child asked for (seventeen boys asked for Spider-Man). Jerri took pictures of each child's Halloween costume (we had fourteen Spider-Men), laying them out over another eight pages. Jerri took pictures of each child on his or her birthday with the child's favorite gift (twelve Spider-Men and thirteen Barbies), superimposing the pictures on a calendar.

Jerri is so devoted to creating this work of mnemonic art that she rarely asks me to do a thing. But near the end of the year she's in a crunch and I agree to an emergency yearbook meeting.

Her house is rambling, festooned on every wall with paintings done by her children, the edges curling.

"We can sit in the breakfast nook," she says, stepping over and winding through abandoned toys.

I try to get a feel for the size of the house, sans toys, for Lana, who will want to know all the details. Lana spends chunks of time decorating her imaginary house and deciding what color to paint the walls. She carries around fabric swatches and subscribes to a magazine called *Kitchen*. She keeps a box of tiles she bought from

Mexico under her desk, where they will stay until she can line her sink with them.

Jerri brings two glasses of Kool-Aid to the table. I take a legal pad and a pen out of my backpack.

"Well, the yearbook is going to be late again this year," she announces.

Since I am the only other member of this committee and have done almost nothing, I feel wholly responsible. But Jerri makes this statement like we're in this together. Like somehow our people let us down. I sigh.

"Well, yes," I say. "It's a big job and there are so many kids."

"You're telling me. I'm missing pictures of kids in every category. Now, with Daniel that's fine. Because of his ADD, it's hard to get a picture that's not blurred. But I've got almost nothing on Frida. And I'm missing fourteen pictures of kids with their Easter baskets."

She unfolds a large chart and smooths it out onto the table.

"Now, what I've done is, I've got each kid's name here on the side," she says, sliding her finger down forty names. "And I check off if I've got a picture of them in each category. Like, look, here's Spence."

She points to his name and moves her finger horizontally over checks in squares. Then she stops at a blank square.

"This is what I'm talking about," she says, sounding more like she's talking to herself than me. "I don't know why I don't have Spence in the pumpkin patch."

I look at the massive chart of checks and names and try to imagine what Lana will say when I tell her the story. Probably something like "Screw crazy Jerri and her asinine chart. How did she get the house? Money from her parents? That's a hot area."

"He was sick," I say to Jerri.

"Now, that's something we deal with all the time. I'm thinking of making a list at the end of each field trip, of kids who couldn't be there. That way their parents won't think that you and I missed getting a picture of their kid on that day."

"Sounds good," I say, looking around. "Great house. Have you had it long?"

"It was David's," she says, referring to her husband, who looks like her twin. "The point is that we're missing a lot of stuff. It's not just the pictures but the interviews."

"Interviews?"

If I tell Lana that the house was David's first, she'll drop into a glum monologue about how Tony hasn't given her shit and even crazy Jerri has a man who can provide the basics. Maybe I won't tell her.

"The interviews are darling," says Jerri. "I have a list of sixteen questions that I ask each kid. Like 'What's your favorite color?' Didn't you read last year's yearbook? The question I really like is, 'What do you smell like?' Last year little June said that she smelled like throw-up because she had just thrown up that morning. It's little gems like that you don't want to forget."

"Great," I say. "So are these floors original?"

"We just had them done," says Jerri, tapping the floor with her shoe.

"Sweet. I love hardwood."

"So what I want from you," she says, "well . . . what do you think? Should we use the same questions we used last year?"

"Hey, if they were such a big hit last year. I mean, why fool with what's golden?"

Jerri blushes.

"Good," she says, "I was hoping you'd agree."

I'm not sure what I've agreed to. But Jerri looks happy. Lana says I have a gift for making people think I'm completely on their side, while hiding my contempt. If so, it's not calculated. I never mean to mislead. It's just my Swedish soul and my desperate need to be liked that won't allow me to say what I really think. Lana is a different animal, and would not be sitting here, sipping Kool-Aid, flattering the yearbook supervisor.

"Well, good," says Jerri. "You've been great."

I've been great? I haven't done anything.

"So, Jerri, is there anything I can do to help you with the yearbook deadline?"

"Oh, no, I've got it. I just have to wrap up the pages in Adobe, input the interviews, do a graphic for the cover, and copy it all on the color printer at school. I only needed to tell you that it's going to be late. And I wanted to hear your thoughts on the interview questions."

"You're sure I can't help?"

"Don't be silly," she says. "You've done so much. I just get worried because the parents at school are getting antsy. Calling me about when they're going to have the yearbook. They want it yesterday, you know," she says in a collusive tone.

I nod. "Oh, I know."

I don't know. I know only that I've been let off the hook somehow. I've managed to do absolutely nothing and have Jerri feel like I'm her best friend. I feel horrible and relieved. Horrible *because* I'm relieved.

"You do such a fabulous job with the yearbook," I say. "Everyone says so."

"Well, they say it behind my back. Because all I hear about is which pictures are missing and how late it is, and how Jackson got left off the dedication page last year."

I can feel Lana's presence hovering, telling me to back off now. But I need to make Jerri feel better so that *I* can feel better.

"Jerri, the dedication page last year was a masterpiece. It's such a small thing that Jackson's name was missing."

"Tell that to Jackson's parents," says Jerri, looking miserable.

"Hey," I say, like there should be a swelling strings sound track underneath my words. I have to stop myself from taking her chin in my hand. "You are only one person. There's just so much one person can do. And you already do the work of twenty people. So that's twenty times more than me or anyone else. And since most people only do half of what they say they do, it's like you're forty people."

Huh? Whatever it is that I've just said makes Jerri smile. Her eyes shine.

"Thanks," she says.

I say many more things like this in the two hours that follow. I hold Jerri's hand and tell her that she needs to take more time for herself. I say things I've heard on talk shows. I turn off Lana's voice in my head. The voice that would tell me I'm being duplicitous and patronizing. Lana's voice that would tell me that this is more about my seeking forgiveness than it is about comforting another person.

After giving Jerri a hug on the threshold of her pale yellow house, I walk north on Highland. My sneakers slap the pavement.

Slap, slap, slap.

I feel a pull in my chest and a sharp stinging behind my eyes. Self-loathing fills me up like bile. I am corrupt. I am untrue. I am evil.

Slap, slap, slap.

I look up into the smog-cloaked hills. I need to feel better. I need to be washed clean. I need exoneration.

Slap, slap, slap.

Where will I find it?

Slap, slap, slap.

But, of course, I know. I will find exoneration where I always find it.

Slap, slap, slap.

I will find it on Friday.

Slap.

On Friday Lana will exonerate me. Lana will fix me. She will fix me with listening. She will fix me with a story about her having done something far worse. The other women will nod and they will all forgive me. Lana will buy me a glass of wine. We will move on to other stories. There will be other stories. I will feel soft. And then Lana will stop. And remember. She will stop and remember the house. She will stop it all to demand every single goddamned detail about Jerri's yellow house.

How Much Is that Baby in the * Window?

*

*

Pat and I have been on the road for two hours when we exit the highway. We wind through small towns, ending up in a dense forest. Our car chugs up a dirt road past No Trespassing signs and locked wooden gates. I shove thoughts of getting caught in a Ruby Ridge shootout to the back of my mind.

We're looking for Christian Outreach Adoptions, which operates out of someone's home near San Diego. It's taken quite some doing to get Pat to even consider going with an outfit with "Christian" in its name. But I point out that most adoption agencies have a Christian angle. Some agencies probably throw the word "Christian" in the title so you won't think they're people who will rob you blind. I tell him the "Christian" probably doesn't mean anything. It doesn't mean you have to sign any Christian papers or take any Christian blood oaths. We'll just pick a baby, fill out an application, and split.

It's dark by the time we ring the chimes of an old two-story home, miles from any other house. A boy in a red vest and a tie opens the door. He looks about twelve.

"My father is expecting you," he says, like an adult. He motions us into a foyer.

I glance into a living room as the man/boy takes our coats. It takes a moment for me to make out anything, as the room is lit only by a few sconces illuminating small paintings of Christ. As we follow the careful walk of our juvenile host, I notice crisp white doilies on maroon chairs that look like no one's ever sat in them. A Bible lies open on a gleaming wood table, a leather bookmark arranged across one page. I don't allow myself to imagine what is going through Pat's head.

Mr. Boy leads us into an office.

"Have a seat," he says, making a graceful arc with one hand. We walk into the room, then turn around to see him back up and leave.

The love seat squeaks as Pat and I settle. Three leather photo albums are lined up on the coffee table in front of us. On the wall above a mantel hangs a large photograph of a family. Two parents with two blond boys, the boys both in red vests.

Pat coughs a bit and looks down at the albums.

I pick one up and open it to see rows of pictures under plastic. Each picture shows a couple with a baby. The family groups are all posed about the same way. A child between a man and a woman, the smiling faces in a line. All of the children are white. I flip through the pages, fascinated by the rows of families in identical poses.

I hear a voice behind me. "You're looking at our success stories," it says.

I look around to see a man who looks like a skinny Les. He's unusually tall and wears a suit. When Pat stands to shake his hand, the top of his head is level with skinny Les's shoulder. I simply smile at him. Something tells me that the man is going to do most of his talking to Pat.

"I apologize for making you wait," he says. "I was just talking to a couple who got back from Russia with their daughter last week."

He sits across from us, his knees bending at chest level so that he looks like a broken mannequin.

"I'm Mr. Brooks," he says to Pat. "I believe I talked to your wife on the phone."

I feel Pat juggle things around in his mind. I suspect he didn't anticipate talking at all. I'm the one who's made the phone calls and talked to friends who've adopted. I'm the one who has gotten up in the middle of the night and paced around, only to crawl back into bed, wake him up, and say, "What if we die in a car accident and Spencer is left alone, what then?"

I remind myself to thank Pat for not mentioning that the surest way for us to die in a car accident, orphaning our son, is for us to make repeated trips to the Christian Outreach Adoptions on roads that would test anyone's faith.

"Um . . . yes," says Pat. "We're looking into adopting our second child."

He wiggles next to me like he's in a tight spot.

Mr. Brooks lights up.

"Well, that's what we do," he says. "We placed all of these children in loving homes."

He leans over and strokes the albums with his long hand.

"The pictures are . . . very convincing," says Pat.

Mr. Brooks fingers the bindings. A pause descends as we watch Mr. Brooks's hands move over the albums.

"So how do we go about getting one?" says Pat, breaking in. "A baby. How can you help us get a baby?"

Mr. Brooks sits back and smiles.

"Sounds like I should tell you a little about us. Just a minute . . ."

He pops up from his chair and pokes his head out of the office.

"Jeremy?" he says.

We wait for a bit, then red-vested Jeremy appears in the doorway.

"Jeremy is our second," says Mr. Brooks. Jeremy smiles like he's done this before. "We got him from Russia when he was ten months old."

Pat and I nod at Jeremy.

"Can I get you any coffee?" asks Jeremy.

"No thanks," we say.

It's as if Jeremy is a modern-day Pinocchio, working on his "real boy" skills. I can't imagine this has anything to do with being adopted. One has only to look around the funereal home to see that this is an odd place for anyone to land.

Mr. Brooks sits back down in his chair and starts his spiel. This is a great job, he says. He and his wife adopted their first son from Russia fifteen years ago and they were so happy with the results that they made it their mission to set other childless families up with Russian babies. Pat and I ask if he deals with other countries. And he says that he could, but he specializes in Russia and Eastern Europe.

What's unsaid, what Pat knows, I can tell by the tilt of his head, is that the children are white. And while I have no problem with adopting a white child, no problem with others wanting a white child, I want to work with people who embrace all possibilities of what a family can look like.

I want to say, "So you help white families adopt white babies. Fair enough, but let's put that on the brochure. Tell me that over the phone, before I risk my life on your dirt roads to get here." The fact that we are talking *around* the race issue makes my jaw hurt.

After twenty minutes of this Pat says, "Well, we'll certainly think about it," as he folds up the application Mr. Brooks has handed him. Everything in his gesture a dismissal.

As Jeremy leads us out through the living room, I see on a big German grandfather clock that it's eight o'clock in the evening. Is Jeremy's red vest part of a school uniform he hasn't removed? Or is it his Christian Outreach Adoptions costume? The one that shows him off to be the beautiful blond boy that people who walk through the door dream of having for their very own?

That is so weird, Brett," says Michelle when I tell her the story on the phone.

"It was like a movie," I say. "I just can't stop thinking about Jeremy in that house. And where was the older boy? I heard this creaking from upstairs. I wonder if they keep him locked up there—in his tattered red vest, pulling out his hair, banging his head against the wall, chained to his bed—the boy they can't show anyone."

"Are you sure you aren't exaggerating this a little?"

"Me? I'm telling you. It was bizarre. Where was *Mrs*. Brooks? Dead? Her bones bricked up in the wall somewhere? Maybe there were other red-vested white boys trapped in the basement, ready to take Jeremy's place if he slipped up or passed out from starvation."

"Anyway," says Michelle, ignoring my macabre imaginings, "I never ran into anything like that. But maybe being a lesbian automatically sifts through the folks you wouldn't want to deal with."

"Yeah, well. That may be true. All I know is that there's some twisted Christian shit going on in that house, something that has to do with red vests. And what about all those identically posed families in the albums? The whole thing was freaky as hell. I really don't want to have another experience like that. I might come back with a chip lodged in my brain that controls my every action and thought."

Michelle says that's ridiculous. She and Sarah had a great time visiting lots of agencies and they never returned with chips in their brains. And finally, they went to China with a whole group of people who got along famously and they came home with Faith.

Himlata sits at her desk, pictures of various raced and gendered families tacked to bulletin boards behind her. A bronze statue of the many-armed elephant god stands in the corner of the room, a framed photo of Gandhi above it. Pat cocks his head toward the elephant and smiles at me.

"I have a basket of toys outside the door," Himlata says, sunlight glinting off the beads on her sari.

Pat gets up and brings in the basket in for Spence, who pulls out a train and carries it into the hallway.

"I work by myself, out of my home," she says. "This is a newsletter I send out to my families twice a year, and here are pictures of our annual picnic."

She lays the newsletter on her desk so we can see.

"That's Rory," she says, pointing to a photograph of a brown boy with big eyes. "His parents got him from Guatemala two years ago."

I imagine Pat and me picking up a little Guatemalan boy from a tiny village full of goats. We walk up a cobbled path to a small cottage, where we meet a large woman dressed in a brightly colored native thing. Behind her, round babies play on a stone floor. Smells of some rustic stew waft from a bucket that is suspended over a fire. She inclines her head to a chubby boy she calls Jorge. He will be ours. Pat and I beam like we're in an ad for this sort of thing.

"And this," says Himlata, "is little Emma at the picnic." She points to a brown girl with shiny dark hair. "Her parents got her from India two years ago."

I see Pat and me sitting on a floor in a modest Indian home, eating some great Indian curry. We wear brightly colored robes. A woman who looks like an Indian Salma Hayek, in a sari, jingles a bell. A curtain pulls open, revealing a toddler on a pillow, with a little red dot on her forehead. Salma calls her Kaia. The little girl gets up from the pillow and walks toward us, unsteady on her perfect pudgy feet. I pull the girl into my lap and put my cheek next to hers. I am filled with satisfaction at having rescued her from a life of identifying herself as "Ellen" while explaining frequent-flier miles to Delta customers calling from a hemisphere away.

"Many of my families stay in touch with me long after the adoption. It's such a personal process. And we will get to know each other very well," Himlata says.

I imagine Spence at his high school graduation. His gown

whipping behind him as he strides toward us, his family. Pat, me, his sister, Kaia, and Auntie Himlata.

"That's great," I say. "We're very interested in the picnics and the newsletter. In fact, I'm a writer. I could do a column on a different adoption story every month."

"Magnificent," says Himlata, her earrings jangling.

I look around the office. An office that will become very familiar to me through the years, I'm sure.

"So what's the process?" asks Pat—a little too business, I think.

Himlata tells us about the application. She tells us about the countries she deals with. She details a timeline. She lists her contacts with various organizations.

"Guatemala sounds good to me," says Pat. "If we were to go forward with that, what kind of fees would we need to pay?"

Himlata looks down at a piece of paper.

"Guatemala," she says, looking up, "is about twenty-three thousand dollars."

Pat looks like Himlata just reached across the desk and punched him in the face.

I can't fucking believe it. Twenty-three K for little Jorge? Who gets all this cash?

"Wow," says Pat, like it's his last word before he dies.

I hear Spence banging something against a wall in the hallway. We sit for a bit, Himlata smiling like she's been here before.

"Okay," I say, "how much for the Indian girl?"

Himlata looks at her paper again.

"It's a little less," she says, her voice even. "Twenty-two thousand."

"Wow," I say. "Have you got anyone cheaper?"

Himlata smiles.

"China, I think," she says. "Because it's a little more efficient. You can get a baby for about seventeen thousand."

Faith cost us about fifteen thousand," says Michelle, setting down her teacup. "But that was four years ago."

I watch Faith and Spence build a Lego structure to contain Spence's collection of toy dinosaurs.

"I knew it was going to be substantial," I say. "But seventeen thousand. We'd be so in debt."

"Yeah," says Michelle, smiling at the Lego structure, which looks a little unsteady. "But it's less than a car. Way less than a Mercedes. I mean, when you think of the things Americans spend money on. Shouldn't a kid cost more than a house?"

"Well, sure," I trail off. I don't say the obvious, which is that Michelle's analogy completely breaks down when you get to the resale value of a house versus the financial drain of a college education. But I can tell that this isn't that sort of conversation. And I don't want to come across to Michelle as the biggest, tightest, whitest mother bitch on the planet, trying to get the best deal on a brown baby that she can possibly wrangle. That would mean that there is less distance between me and Mr. Brooks from the Christian Outreach Adoptions than I would like to think.

"Was it just the most amazing moment ever when you saw Faith for the first time?" I ask, showing my softer side. Michelle is all heart and I want her to think well of me. I don't want her to think that I'm all about the bottom line.

"When I first saw Faith," she says, "she was being handed to another couple."

"What do you mean?"

"It's this kind of cool and weird thing they do when you're

getting the babies in China. All the couples who are adopting go into this big room and we kind of line up in these chairs. When Sarah and I did it, we knew all the other couples by then. We'd come over on the plane together. About twelve couples, I think. And Sarah and I were the only dykes."

Faith stands back and admires the structure as Spence carefully places a triceratops in the middle of it.

"So we were in this line of chairs and they brought out the babies one by one and handed them to the new parents. It was interesting to watch, because we had all gotten pictures. So it was kind of this guessing game too. Anyway, they brought out Faith and I said to Sarah, 'That's her.' But they handed her to this other couple."

"Did you just think maybe you were wrong?" I'm thinking that a lot of babies look alike to me. Not just Chinese ones.

"Actually, no. I had this thing in my chest. I was watching this couple coo over her and I felt—I just knew—she was mine. Meanwhile, they keep bringing out these girls and handing them to couples, and Sarah and I are just sitting there."

"Jesus."

"Then they said my name. And they handed us this cute little girl who looks nothing like the pictures we got."

"But pictures. Jeez, who can tell, right?"

"I can tell."

"Sure. Of course you can tell. You're that connected. I'm not so sure I would have been able to tell. When Spence was about a month old, this weird scenario used to repeat in my head. I'd think about what it would have been like if Spence turned up missing. What if I had to go to a lost and found to find him? What if there were all these diapered babies lined up on the shelves? Would I know which one was him?"

"Of course you would," she says.

"Michelle, I've got to say, I'm not so sure. Not at that young an age."

"Well, *I* knew," she says. "First of all, these babies were a little older. I knew it was her. Faith was sitting in that other couple's lap. I knew that she was mine."

I feel the top of my skin get tingly at the surety in Michelle's voice.

"So what happened? How did you get her?"

"After about twenty minutes the two people who were running the thing said that they'd made this terrible mistake, and they switched the babies. Took the one in my lap and gave it to the other couple. Then they handed us Faith."

"What did you think?"

Michelle looks at Faith walking around the structure with a T. rex in her hand.

"I thought she was home," says Michelle.

✳ **Friday**

✳

✳

I watch Michelle move her finger in a circular motion, describing the funnel that she envisions all souls going through before being born this time around.

We started out talking about what to do with outgrown kids' clothes, moved to where to donate the clothes, skipped to volunteering, spent a couple of minutes discussing time management, with Lana throwing in a comment about how Tony is always late, and ordered a second round—all of this has led, inevitably or not so inevitably, to a discussion about death and what, if anything, is "out there."

"And I saw all these souls who had just died, picking out qualities as they moved down the funnel. Like they could pick out their skin color and their interests," Michelle says.

"Before these souls funneled into new fetuses?" asks Katherine.

If anyone's going to find this notion the least bit freaky, it'll be Katherine, since she was raised Catholic.

"Something like that," says Michelle, lifting her Amstel.

Katherine considers. "Cool. Beats the shit out of going to hell and that's it for the rest of eternity."

We all mumble and nod.

Lana takes a sip of her drink. "I've got a guy who hangs around me."

"Tony?" I ask, wondering if this is the next bend in the conversation.

"No. A guy who you can't see."

"Really?" asks Katherine, leaning in.

"Sure. I met him through this medium. This healer. A woman who does that kind of thing. I was depressed. I went to her and she said that this guy and this girl kind of hover around me, protecting me. Helping me out."

I want to ask what the pair says about Tony, but I don't want to sound flip. Thing is, I really *do* want to know. I mean, it's one thing to guard a person, but if an entity were hovering around me like that, I would want some solid advice. I wonder about the day-in, day-out work of an entity. Do they hang around when you're having sex? Or do they float into the next room when you're in the middle of something private or gross? Do entities hover around more than one person? And if so, how do they divvy up their time? Do entities nap?

"But you only mentioned a guy hanging around you now. Where's the girl?" asks Katherine.

"I only talked to her once. That day. The day I went to the healer. She never showed up again."

"Maybe her work was done," offers Katherine.

I think about all the different ways we humans interpret our spiritual existence. Is it really a guy and a girl who hover around Lana, or is that the way she characterizes parts of her psyche? Do souls literally go through a funnel, or is that a way of describing preexistence in a way that we can all imagine? Jesus, this stuff makes my head hurt.

"Sometimes it's more interesting what people *don't* believe than what they *do*," I say. "I was talking to some friends recently about Mormonism, and the part they got hung up on was Mormon belief that Christ appeared in the United States."

"That *is* pretty hard to believe," says Katherine.

"Yeah, but you just had a reasonable conversation with Lana about a male entity that hovers around her."

"Sure. But you're talking about Christ showing up in an American desert. How likely is that?"

"How likely is it that Christ turned water into wine?" says Michelle.

"Which reminds me," I say, holding up my empty glass to Mack.

I turn back to Katherine. "All I'm saying is that maybe your Catholic background allows all kinds of room for entities floating around, but has a hard time allowing for Christ showing up anywhere but in the Middle East."

"Why couldn't Christ show up in the United States?" asks Michelle. "Why couldn't he show up anywhere he wanted?"

Michelle goes to a Lutheran church, is a minor expert in astrology, and, let us not forget, is the forger of our recent funnel theory. This kind of effortless eclecticism is very attractive to me. I think that religion should be all about mixing and matching. Hey, you only go around once. Or do you?

"I think Brett has a point," says Lana. "Given your background, different beliefs will grab you. And some won't. Like, I can't really get behind the whole blue elephant god with all those arms."

"Me neither!" I say a little too loudly. Mack looks at me from the other end of the bar. "But see, I bet if I were Hindu or grew up in that part of the world, the blue elephant would make total sense. As it is, I've just got to say, 'Oh, come on—a blue elephant with all those arms. Do you take me for a total rube?' "

"Let me pause," says Katherine, pausing to drain her black and tan, "to appreciate the word 'rube.' "

Michelle raises her voice above ours. "You know the blue elephant god . . ."

"What is his name?" mumbles Lana.

". . . doesn't really look like that."

"See. You too," I say, slapping the bar.

"No. I'm saying that he's a metaphor. And his name is Ganesh, I think. The Hindus aren't saying that that's what he actually looks like. The representation of him as this blue elephant with many arms is just a metaphor for something."

"For what?" asks Katherine.

"I don't know. Abundance? I don't know."

"That's disappointing," I hear myself say.

The others look at me.

"Here I was thinking that a huge group of people believed that God looked like a blue elephant with tons of arms."

"So?" says Lana.

"Well. It was kind of nice to me. Even though I couldn't imagine it. That people believed it. Believed in the unbelievable."

"That's what faith is," says Michelle.

We get quiet for a bit.

I wonder if men talk about things like this when they're out with each other. Pat has a poker game every Tuesday night. When I ask him what the guys talk about for five hours over cards, he says, "Poker."

I think about the things women talk about. The things they *think* about. I think about the way women can believe several seemingly contradictory things at once. As long as one of them isn't a blue elephant god with lots of arms.

I watch Lana stir the ice cubes in her drink with her finger and I think about Michelle's funnel. I imagine Spence sliding down it, picking up this trait and that, and falling out the bottom into me.

✳ Porn and Magic
✳
✳

I sit on a folding chair across from a porn star. Her white sleeveless T-shirt stretches across two breasts that look like floating bowling balls. A tiny dog is curled up on her lap.

I'm in the backstage holding area of a show called *Colin and His Sleazy Friends.* I've agreed to do the show because my former comedy partner, Shannon, said that all the really hip comedians are doing it. The host, Colin, used to do a cable access show of him sitting around with porn stars, touching their breasts. Some Hollywood types loved it and decided to put up a live version of the cable show, throw in some legit comics, and try to sell it to Comedy Central or Bravo.

The porn star's tits look like they hurt. She can't possibly sleep on her stomach. How *does* she sleep? If she slept on her side, the weight of the top breast would surely stretch the tissue around the breast. Maybe she props up her breasts with pillows.

I'm not exactly sure why I said I'd do the show. I haven't performed with Shannon since before I had Spence. We were a duo for four years. Lately, I've wondered if I even care about acting anymore. But I'm afraid to say it. What would I do if I didn't act? An actress is all I ever was.

The porn star smiles at me. I smile back. She's my first porn star. But I imagine she's like anyone else. Doing a job. Making money. I wonder if she's going to bring the dog onstage with her. Maybe the dog is part of her act.

Shannon said there wasn't any pay, but everyone was doing Colin's show because it was a great opportunity to get seen by a bunch of network and studio guys who were coming to see this latest, hottest porn/comedy hybrid show. Who knew where this might lead? she said.

"Ritualized shunning?" I said. "If a parent from the preschool sees me."

It felt like a bad idea, but Shannon was really fired up about how great it was going to be. So after extracting a promise from her that I wouldn't have to take off my shirt, I said I'd do it. Mostly out of habit—the habit of moving my marginal career forward even though I'd rather be somewhere else, if I only knew where that was.

The porn star says, "I like your purse."

She crosses her legs that squeak in brown leather.

"Thanks," I say, moving my purse-party purse onto my lap.

"I need something like that, with compartments. I just have this." She looks down at her dog. Which I now see is a purse, not a dog. "It's not very practical."

I think that her breasts alone tell us that she is an impractical woman. And I feel sad that the dog is a purse. I liked the idea of a porn star with a dog. It was sweet.

"Well," I say, "this is a great purse. I can fit a book in here. And look . . ." I hold it up. "There's a little pocket in here where you can keep your keys."

"I only have one key," she says.

I think that's odd, and I consider asking how she gets through life with only one key. But I really want to talk about my purse. In fact, I'm surprised by how much I want to talk about it. Then it occurs to me that I have been ignored since the stage manager showed me to the backstage tent. I didn't think I would want the attention of Colin's sleazy friends, but here you are. I must, because I puff up with confidence as I show the girl my purse.

"I can put my lipstick in here," I say, slipping my hand into the front pocket.

"Oh. I see," she says, then tilts her head. "But I probably need something bigger."

"It's deceptively roomy," I say.

"I need room for products," she says.

"Oh," I say. I'm not sure what products she's talking about.

I look at her hairy dog purse. "Looks like there's plenty of room in there."

"Oh, yeah," she says, putting her hand into her purse and fishing around. She brings out a doll that looks like Barbie with an even bigger rack.

"It's me," she says. "You can order dolls of me from my Web site. I have a card."

The hand not holding the doll of herself slips into the purse, which has somehow morphed from looking like a poodle to looking like a big hairy vagina, out of which she pulls her wares.

She hands me the card. "Tammi Silvers—I came, I saw, I swallowed."

If I were looking for a sign that I no longer belong in the comedy world, this might be it. I am about to go onstage with a woman who sells dolls of herself, owns only one key, carries a big hairy dog vagina purse, and misquotes Julius Caesar. No offense to her. In fact, I'm grateful. Maybe she's a cosmic messenger.

I consider asking her who buys these dolls. They're too small to be sex toys. Unless . . . I stop my mind from going where it's going.

"Yeah," she says, holding up the doll to admire. "I'm working on making the transition from porn star to icon."

An icon of what? But I think I know. So many people in Hollywood want to be icons. What they mean is, "I want to be remembered. I want people to think I'm important." I feel for her, even without the dog.

And I realize that I'm *not* in the same show as the porn star. I'm in the show where I get to go home to my son who will remember me. Who will always remember.

Shannon's face appears over my shoulder.

"Sorry I'm late," she says, slipping into the seat next to me.

She's dressed in a powder-blue suit, her long legs bare, ending in high strappy sandals. I realize that I have made a sartorial blunder. Standing next to her in my loose black T-shirt and jeans, I'm going to look like a stagehand.

"I didn't know we were supposed to dress up," I say to her.

"I just thought, when in Rome," she says.

"Yeah," I say. "But we're 'the funny,' not 'the porn.'"

"There's a law that you can't be both?"

I want to say yes. There does seem to be some unspoken cosmic law that says that you can't be funny and sexy at the same time. I am proof—having fallen heavily on the "funny" side of the funny/sexy continuum all my life.

"Nice suit," the porn star says, still holding the doll of herself. I'm guessing that this porn icon has fallen heavily on the opposite side of the same continuum.

"Thanks," says Shannon. "Nice doll."

The girl smiles proudly and says, "It's me."

Shannon throws me a "we'll talk about this later" look and removes me from the conversation with a deft "Let's get a beer."

I drink a beer even though I never drink beer, because it's all they've got. Strolling through the look-alike porn stars and sleazy hangers-on, I think of all the places I'd rather be.

Last week Spence and I went to Isabella's birthday party. It was one of those lavish affairs that folks planning on only one child throw for their three-year-olds. There was even a magician.

"And now," said the magician, holding up a trembling rabbit, "I will put the bunny in this cage."

The magician, who was probably a neighbor's fifteen-year-old kid, stuffed the bunny into a cage, sliding the gate closed.

"Bunny!" a toddler shrieked, running toward the cage. Her mother scooped her up in an expert grab. The magician continued despite the distraction of the child's fading howls as she was carried into the house.

I took a sip of watery punch, watching Spence stare at the bunny in the cage.

The magician floated a silk handkerchief over the cage.

"Where's the bunny?" Isabella asked her mother.

"We'll see," said her mom.

I remember thinking that there were going to be some pretty pissed-off toddlers when the bunny disappeared. Who knew this was not a great trick for three-year-olds? The magician's act hadn't been going well up to this point. The toddlers were decidedly unimpressed when the flower changed color. They mostly looked around like, "So?" I guess you have to have a sense of the way things *do* work in order to be amazed when they turn out differently.

"And now," said the magician, "presto."

He pulled the handkerchief to reveal an empty cage.

"Where's the bunny?" cried Isabella.

"It disappeared," said her mom.

Spence looked at me, teary. A younger kid rushed the cage and knocked it over, which somehow released the bunny manifest.

"Bunny," screamed Isabella.

The bunny zigzagged wildly across the yard.

"For God's sake, someone get that bunny," said a mother next to me.

The children mobilized in one unit, charging after the bunny. It all happened so fast that I couldn't respond in any way, other than to anxiously picture the rabbit torn to pieces in some gruesome toddler slaughter. A mother yelled to the children to be careful, the bunny might bite and give them rabies. Finally, the children cornered the bunny and threw themselves on it—a heap of screaming toddler. The magician and a couple of moms started picking the kids off, until the magician stood up, raising the bunny above his head.

"Back off!" he yelled. "Everyone, back off and leave her alone."

The kids, hearing hysteria in his voice, withdrew.

"Oh, for God's sake," muttered the mother next to me.

"You almost killed her," the magician said to the retreating children, tears running down his face. He hugged the bunny to his chest and ran with it into the house.

Shannon and I line up backstage with the porn stars. I think about the teenage magician and the frightened bunny. I think about all the disappointed children.

It was funny. The birthday party. I told Pat the story later. I told it to the mommies at the bar. It was funny, but the whole thing moved me too.

A couple of porn stars are already onstage. Shannon and I lean against the wall, hearing Colin ask a question. It's answered by high-pitched squeals.

The sobbing magician was a relatively small part of the party. I ended up having to substitute for a mommy in the puppet show, reading from a script as I crouched behind the cardboard theater, my puppet hand losing feeling. Spence insisted on sitting beside me as I furiously turned pages with my other hand.

When the cake was brought out, Isabella refused to let anyone sing "Happy Birthday" to her, so we all hummed "The Wheels on the Bus."

And a baby bit an older child, who screamed that he was going to get rabies now, just like the bunny, and die.

As the party thinned out, I found the magician in the kitchen drinking a Coke and stroking the bunny.

"Hey," I said. "Rough crowd."

The boy looked up at me.

"She was really scared," he said, leaning down to kiss the top of the bunny's head.

"Yeah, I could tell," I said. "You know, the kids just didn't know what was going on. They thought that the bunny had really disappeared."

"That's dumb," said the boy.

I sat at the table.

"How long have you been working on your act?" I asked.

"Since I was twelve. That's when I got my first kit."

"You know, my brother did a lot of magic tricks," I said. "His best one was this thing with hoops that connected and then didn't."

"I do that trick," he said, his voice a bit lighter.

"What's your name?"

"Dylan," he said, straightening up in the chair.

"So, Dylan, here's the thing. I used to be an actress on TV," I started.

I was about to give him some mommy/performer wisdom, when I got caught by my own words.

Used to be . . . used to be. Who am I now?

I'll think about that later, I thought.

"As a fellow performer," I told him, "with a certain amount of experience, I can tell you one thing." I paused for emphasis, resisting a motherly reach for his hand, which was buried in the bunny's fur anyway. "You've got to know your audience, buddy. It's that simple. Don't throw away your talents on a crowd that's not going to appreciate you. The toddlers don't get your act. Don't waste time worrying about what they think, or what they want."

The boy magician smiled. I couldn't tell if he was comforted or was simply shooting me the smile so I'd get up and leave.

I reached over and pet the bunny, waiting for him to say something. When he didn't, I stood up and quietly left him with his bunny.

Did I make a difference?

I'll think about it later.

I do Colin's show in a mental haze. I can't stop thinking about the party—about the boy magician.

Shannon and I follow a couple of porn stars onto the set and we do a couple of preplanned jokes. The guy comics take over and somersault over the couch, landing on the floor. This causes the audience to roar as if a lion just ate a Christian. A greasy, drunk rocker dude bounds onto the set. He is a surprise guest, Lemmy from Motörhead. He sits next to Colin, beer in hand, talking about how truly fucked-up he got last night, banging a porn star in a hotel room till the management threatened to call the police.

"But a guy's got a right to fuckin' party," he yells.

The audience goes wild.

At some point the porn star sitting on the orange shag carpet in front of me passes me a steel dildo. She tells the audience that it's a great new product because of the weight of the steel. The dildo feels pretty damn heavy to me. I consider bringing up concerns I would have about such a weighty sex toy causing vaginal tearing and fistulas.

But I don't want to be a spoiler. Even a spoiler of Lemmy's great time, whoever he is. So I bounce the dildo up and down in my hand, like I'm testing the weight. I bounce the steel penis as if I'm considering. Which I am.

You've got to know your audience, buddy. It's that simple. Don't throw away your talents on a crowd that's not going to appreciate you.

I pass the penis and get some peace.

Hey, I don't begrudge the audience their good time. I don't begrudge Lemmy, Colin, Shannon, or the girl with the doll of herself.

I just want to go home.

✳ The Standoff
✳
✳

The Carter Preschool fund-raiser is a bear of an event that supposedly raises half the school's annual income. Every year each family is expected to donate five hundred dollars' worth of stuff to the silent auction, be on a committee, do setup and cleanup on the day of, and work a two-hour shift per parent during the event.

As always, Pat and I manage to meet requirements with a minimum amount of effort. For this year's silent auction we donate one of my mother's paintings (found in the back of our closet—$400), a voice lesson (given by Pat in our living room—$75), and an old end table of ours (antique?—$25). Needless to say, we don't win the incentive prize—a pricey bottle of champagne for the first family to raise more than five thousand dollars in donations. That is won by the Henleys, who donate a guitar signed by all the members of U2 and a week on Mandarin Fishing Boat (airfare not included).

In signing up for a committee, I know enough to steer clear of food, purchasing, and the silent auction. My first year at Carter I was "beginning parent," not required to do much but watch and learn.

I watched the Food Committee meet biweekly for two months, generating charts of who was going to make what food when. Where would they store it all?

I watched the Purchasing Committee having to buy or rent everything from plastic spoons to forty-five foldout tables.

I watched the Silent Auction Committee having to store auction items in their homes. A sign from one of those unlucky committee members remained on the bulletin board for weeks:

WHOEVER PURCHASED THE GRANITE BUST OF EINSTEIN— WE LOST YOUR PAPERWORK SO WE DON'T KNOW WHO YOU ARE!!!! PLEASE CLAIM IT!!! MY SON KEEPS BANGING HIS HEAD ON IT EVERY TIME HE OPENS THE CLOSET TO GET HIS SWIM- MING TRUNKS.

Apparently, no one claimed the bust, as the sign was eventually replaced by:

TO WHOEVER DID NOT CLAIM EINSTEIN, WHOEVER YOU ARE!!!! YOUR LACK OF CONSIDERATION HAS RESULTED IN YOU LOSING EINSTEIN. MY HUSBAND AND I HAULED HIM OUT TO THE DRIVEWAY AND LEFT HIM THERE. YESTERDAY HE DIS- APPEARED. SOMEONE'S GAIN. YOUR LOSS.

Knowing what I know, I sign up for the Program Committee, chaired by Jerri Regan, of course, who likes to do everything herself. This turns out to be an inspired move on my part, as I end up attending only two meetings. One to approve the program design—already mocked up by Jerri—and one emergency meet- ing, called because Jerri has lost the artwork for the back of the program. By the time I arrive, she has found it on the backseat of her car and all I have to do is assure her that it always feels like it's never going to get done, but somehow it always does. I offer to cut and paste the ads for companies who donated, but she says she's already done that. "See? It always gets done," I say at her door.

As for the two-hour work shift, I sign Pat up for Bar and myself for Patrol.

My feet are already aching fifteen minutes into my patrol shift. I stand between two long tables displaying silent auction items. It's an odd assortment. On a table labeled "Pamper Yourself" sits a big basket of men's skin products flanked by a signed script of *Frasier* and a pink T-shirt that says "Go Kitty." A sign over the table on the other side says "Services." Cards behind the bid sheets indicate an array of services, from a three-hour consultation with a divorce attorney to Pat's voice lesson.

"Who donated the porno videos?" whispers Lana into my ear.

"There are porno videos?"

"Over there."

Lana points to a table labeled "Adult Entertainment."

"You're kidding. I thought that meant adult activities like drinks at the Skybar."

"You can be shockingly naive."

"Come over and look. I think someone donated a butt plug. It's either that or a wine cork. I don't want to touch it." Lana tugs my arm.

"Can't," I say. "I'm on patrol."

"Patrol?"

"For two hours I have to walk back and forth between the tables of auction items, to make sure no one steals anything."

"Well, you'd better plant yourself right in front of that darling framed poster of the two kids dressed like strawberries," says Lana. "Because that's the first thing some crazed mom is going to rip off while no one's looking."

I agree that it seems odd to be standing guard over this rather ordinary stuff. The U2 guitar is in a minivan parked next to the ticket takers. If anyone wants to see it, they have to ask one of the other patrollers to let them in the van with a key she's wearing around her neck. The guitar is one thing; but I can't imagine anyone lifting the stuff I'm guarding. And if they tried, I don't know what I'd do. I don't have a whistle. There doesn't seem to be any protocol. I think it's a free-form thing. Would I use shame? Pointing wildly at the stealing mom, screaming, *"Stealer!!!! I've caught a big stealer. Here she is—a lying, stealing bitch."* Is shame punitive enough? *Too* punitive?

After Pat comes over to slip me a glass of wine and inform me that he just bid on a ceramic ladle, I continue thinking about my role as patroller. I decide that I would sidle up to the stealing mom, lay an unfriendly hand on her shoulder, lean close to her ear, and whisper between clenched teeth, "If you put the Restoration Hardware gift certificate back down and walk away without a scene, I'm going to forget I saw you."

I like the idea of my being some tough-love-mom-cop so much that I start to hope that I catch someone.

Lana comes back half an hour later, holding a couple of beer bottles.

"For the troops," she says, waving the beers at me.

"Where are they?" I ask.

"They're over there."

She nods at Michelle and Katherine, who appear to be circling the same table.

"Someone donated an actual face-lift," says Lana. "Katherine wants it and she's up against a pretty determined adversary."

"Who?"

Lana indicates a much older woman in a head scarf who sits close to the table.

"That babushka over there, keeps upping the bid by five bucks. At first I thought she was a man. But Katherine's sure she's a woman."

"Whoever she is, she doesn't look like the kind of person who would want a face-lift," I say.

"Maybe she's going in for some kind of extreme makeover," Lana says. "If she gets the face-lift along with teeth veneers, a butt-lift, and an all-over chemical peel, she could end up looking like Suzanne Somers."

I watch the scarfed old lady rise from her chair, slowly making her way over to the table, where she picks up a pen and writes something down.

"That's it," says Lana. "I bet she just pushed the face-lift up to fifty-five dollars."

"How high is Katherine willing to go?"

"She said to send her home if she goes above one twenty-five."

"Well, how much is the face-lift worth?" I ask. I haven't a notion about what kind of money we're talking about here, having never, not for one minute, considered cosmetic surgery. I'd rather wear a bag over my head for the rest of my life than submit to a surgeon slicing into my facial flesh, I'm that afraid of pain and permanent damage. I blacked out while getting my ears pierced.

"I think you can get a face-lift for about eighteen thousand. Unless you go to Brazil, where they do it for around seven hundred. That's where Enrico goes."

"Katherine's not going above a hundred twenty-five for an *eighteen-thousand*-dollar procedure?"

"You've got to draw the line somewhere," says Lana, squeezing past me to deliver the beers.

During my two-hour patrol I don't get to nab any stealers, though I stiffen when I see a mom finger some bath products in a way that I would describe as suspicious. Katherine and the old lady push the face-lift bid into the eighty-dollar range. Other interested parties drop out when they see the old lady eyeball Katherine, pointing at her in a hexlike manner.

It occurs to me that the old lady may not be anyone's guest. She seems so completely out of place that I wonder if she just strolled in off the street with a couple hundred bucks burning a hole in the pocket of her apron. In Los Angeles it's hard to tell. The old lady could be anyone, could be an art director for TV commercials. Spence's urologist looks like Loni Anderson. My friend tells me that Dustin Hoffman (whom he did a movie with) "looks crazy like a homeless person." The most shocking star-in-real-life moment I had was when I met Morgan Fairchild, who looked *exactly* the same as she did thirty years ago. She looked so much like her I thought she must be someone else.

Nothing and no one are what they seem.

Pat is finishing up his bar shift as I sit at a table with my pals. He seems to have caught silent auction fever, having managed to slip away long enough to up our bid for a mini–pinball machine you play with your thumbs.

Lana rubs one of my feet as I look out at Marie, who swoops toward us trailing a blue silk scarf. Her skin is so unnaturally tan that she looks like she's been lost at sea.

"It's all going fabulously," she says. "People are bidding like animals and the band's about to play. Maybe someone will take off her top and dance in her bra. That's what happened last year."

I introduce Michelle, Lana, and Katherine.

"Marie," I say, "is the chair of the Membership Committee for Carter Preschool."

"I thought about running for president," she says. "But I didn't want to run against Richard. His wife is a regular on *Strong Medicine*—you know, the Lifetime doctor drama. Anyway, I figured I'd lose to him because he's got the celebrity factor working for him."

I smile at the ridiculous truth of this. In Los Angeles, joining particular preschools can be a way to get chummy with stars. Mommy talk on any given playground can revolve around which star's children go to which school. An acquaintance of mine actually wet her pants when she saw Jodie Foster checking out the playground at her preschool. Frankly, I'm surprised that this acquaintance recognized Foster, as I'm told that Foster doesn't look like Foster.

"How are you ladies doing tonight?" asks Marie, switching gears.

"Katherine's got her eye on the face-lift," I say, pulling my foot from Lana's lap.

"Great choice, Katherine. Start early," Marie says.

Katherine looks unsure about how to take this. I want to tell her that my experience with Marie has been the same. I never know if she's meaning to insult me in her smiley fashion, or if she's completely unaware that in a two-minute conversation she's managed to make me feel like a voodoo doll that's been needled several times over.

"That woman over there keeps upping the ante," says Lana,

pointing to the old lady who has pulled a chair up to the table where the bid sheet is.

Marie looks over.

"Oh," she says. "That's Charna. She's a friend of my husband's. Great actress. Used to have a recurring role on *Dr. Quinn, Medicine Woman.*"

We all look at Charna.

"She hasn't really worked since," says Marie. "She probably figures that a face-lift could fire up her career again."

We watch as Charna pulls a muffin out of her pocket and starts to nibble.

Katherine sighs. "Well, now I feel awful. I don't want to deprive a poor old woman of her last shot at the big time."

"Yeah. You might as well give up," says Marie. "She's tough. She'd as soon beat you to a pulp with a bat than let you get that face-lift. I'd be amazed if you won."

Katherine sinks lower in her chair. "Jesus. Who needs it?"

"I've been telling Katherine that she doesn't need a face-lift anyway," says Michelle.

Marie squats down in her gown so that she's eye level with us. She looks at Katherine closely.

"It's the eyes that really give you away," she says. "You see this sag at the end . . ."

She points to the edge of Katherine's eye.

Katherine says, "Sag?"

"Well, it's a 'droop' really," says Marie. "The eyes start to droop and your nose starts to drop."

"My nose has always looked like this," says Katherine.

"Oh," says Marie. "I didn't mean to say that your nose had already dropped, I'm just saying that it will. Everyone's does."

"All right," says Lana. "All this talk of sagging and drooping is driving me back to the bar. Anybody want another?"

"Yup," says Michelle.

"Sure," says Katherine, touching her cheeks and pulling them up.

Lana nods and turns to the bar.

"I wish we had two face-lifts to auction off, instead of one," says Marie. "I just know that Charna's going to go to the mat for this."

"It's no big deal," says Katherine, waving a dismissive hand.

"A whole face-lift—no big deal?" Marie says. She thinks, then pops up, "Ladies, come with me."

Marie speaks with such authority that we stand up and follow her, the blue scarf rippling as she marches ahead. She stops at a bid sheet flanked by before-and-after pictures. One is a photo of small, saggy breasts.

"Ohh," says Katherine sympathetically as she looks at the sad rack.

"This is what this guy can do for you," Marie says, pointing to the other picture, which shows a set of round, pert, perfect breasts. They look like the breasts in fourteenth-century Flemish paintings—symmetrical and hard, like balls that have been glued to the torso.

"My," says Michelle. "Those look really solid. I bet you could pound a nail with them."

"Absolutely," says Marie.

She stands up straight and sticks her chest out at us.

"Feel," she says.

We look at her boobs.

"Those are yours?" asks Michelle, looking back at the picture.

"Got them at the silent auction last year," says Marie. "Feel."

She points them at me.

"Oh, I don't have to," I say. "I can see that they're very . . . firm."

"Feeling is believing," she says, pushing them closer to me.

I look around and catch Pat looking at us. I smile at him as I reach out and lightly graze Marie's breast. Pat winks. What does he think I'm doing? Trying to turn him on? *Am* I trying to turn him on?

"You've got to grab it," Marie says with an edge in her voice.

Michelle leans over to me. "Grab it," she says.

I look at Pat again. He stands still, his full attention on me.

I turn to Marie, take a deep breath, reach out, and give Marie's breast a big squeeze. It's like fondling a rock. I quickly take my hand back.

I glance toward the bar. Pat is gone.

"When I'm dead," says Marie, touching her breasts, "these babies will still be rolling around all that loose dust in the coffin. They're indestructible."

"I believe that," I say, wondering why this is a selling point.

I look around for Pat and spot him bending over the bid sheet for the thumb pinball machine again. Damn, I think he missed the breast-grab. He would have loved it. He's textbook-heterosexual-man-crazy for the mere suggestion of my doing it with another woman. I once kissed another woman at a party and he got so excited he had to leave.

"So think about the boob job," Marie says to Katherine, "instead of the face-lift."

"It's not an either/or thing for me," says Katherine. "To be honest, I hadn't even thought of having a face-lift before tonight. I just got excited because I couldn't believe that I could get one for so cheap. I figured that if I didn't end up using it, I could give it away as a Christmas present."

"Katherine, feel my breasts. And tell me you don't want a boob job," says Marie.

"I don't want to feel your breasts."

"Don't be shy," says Marie. "Brett just felt them."

"I don't want to touch your breasts," Katherine says slowly and firmly, like she's talking to her son.

"It's just that they're so hard you won't believe it."

"I'll take your word for it."

The two women look at each other for a moment. I feel sorry for Marie. I can't quite think of what would create a woman whose mission appears to be the cosmetic transformation of all womankind. Maybe her mother told her she was unattractive. Maybe her first husband left her for a young thing. Marie's face does not hint at answers. It's hard to know what lies beneath the surface of a remade face.

Marie squares her shoulders under the blue scarf.

"All I'm saying," she says, "is that the boob job is a steal. This doctor donates a job every year. And every year some lucky mom is transformed."

"I guess that lucky mom is going to be someone else."

Marie's face reddens under the tan. "You don't know what you're missing."

"*I don't want a boob job,*" says Katherine—louder, I'm sure than she intended.

A few faces in the crowd turn in our direction, holding clear plastic cups of wine as they watch our group.

Katherine and Marie stare at each other in some freaky femmy standoff.

I didn't see this coming, and I wonder if I'm supposed to break it up. It's clear that Michelle isn't going to intervene. She appears to be enjoying it.

More faces turn toward us.

"Okay," I say, edging between them. "Let's relax here. I'm sure everyone will go home with some really great deal. It doesn't really matter if it's a face-lift or a boob job or some homemade bath salts. The thing is, we're all winners."

Katherine shifts her weight from foot to foot, like a fighter. Marie stares her down.

I've shot my wad. I don't know what else to do but stand between them as Katherine bounces and Marie stares.

Time passes.

"Hey," says Lana, materializing like a postmodern deus ex machina, "folks are doing beer bongs in the parking lot."

Heads turn away and murmuring starts.

I watch the men in suits and women in clacky heels leave, headed for the next big thing—in the parking lot.

Lana plops into a seat and throws her legs onto a table. Michelle smiles at me and I feel the air start to move again.

Katherine backs up a bit, tension seeping from her body.

Marie stays tense but turns on an electric smile.

"I'm sorry," she says. "I didn't mean to be pushy. It's just that most people can't wait to touch my breasts."

To Katherine's credit, she lets the whole thing drop. I see it happen. She cocks her head and reaches out to hold Marie's elbow in a gesture both awkward and sweet.

"Thanks for offering," she says.

It takes half an hour to wedge the scooter we won between the mosaic nightstand and the basket of men's skin products in our trunk.

Pat and I pull away from the fund-raiser like carpetbaggers. I won't know until tomorrow how much we've spent. But I doubt that we've ever spent this much in a single evening before.

I tell Pat about Marie's rock-hard breasts.

"So that's what it was," he says.

"Yeah. Why did you leave after I grabbed her breast?"

"It was too exciting," he says. "I had to leave."

He reaches over and slips his hand between my thighs as he watches the road. I put my hand on his and press it hard against me. With my other hand I grasp a lever and release the chair back, which descends a scant two inches before it meets with the patchwork ottoman we got for seventy-five dollars.

I close my eyes as his hand travels over my body, sure and seeking.

I reach into his lap.

The best part about being with someone this long is that we can go straight to the good stuff.

✳ Friday
✳
✳

We're about an hour into happy hour. Katherine has just slammed a beer and left, running home to relieve Slim of Jake-watching. Lately, Slim's been gigging for a hip-hop duo whose name starts with "P."

Michelle, Lana, and I are in midconversation about whether Slim's new job is a good thing or a bad thing for Katherine, who now has more money but less time.

Lana looks down the length of the bar and smiles at something or someone.

"He's hot," she says.

I can't see that far, so I'm going to have to take her at her word.

"Introduce me to him," she says to me.

"What?"

"Just find something fun to say and bring me over to meet him."

"Are you out of your mind?" I say.

The reasons why I don't want to accommodate Lana are many. I'm perfectly happy sitting here trying to solve Katherine's problems. Plus, I don't want some stranger sitting in on my hard-earned two-hour respite from child-rearing. And I can't do the flirty-flirty-girl thing. It makes me feel like I'm acting a part I'd never get cast in.

"It's easy," says Lana. "You just go over there and say something like 'Where did you get that tie?'"

"You like his tie?" Aside from not wanting to do this in the first place, I really don't know why any of this has to do with his tie. And when did Lana start liking guys in ties?

"No, Brett. I don't care about his tie. I care about *him*. Go meet him for me."

"But why do I have to ask him about his tie?"

Michelle sticks her head close to mine. "You don't care about the tie. It's just a way to get him to talk to you."

"But I don't want him to talk to me," I say. "What if he thinks *I'm* the one who's interested in him?"

"He might," says Lana. "But then you'll bring him over and he'll meet me and you putter off."

"I don't want to lead him on."

"Jesus, Brett," Lana says, glaring. "Girlfriends do this for each other all the time. It's an accepted, time-honored way of meeting guys."

"Look," I say, "I'm shy as hell and married. And you're brazen and more or less single. Why don't you just walk over there yourself?"

"Because I can't take being turned down."

"I don't get this at all. What's the difference between you getting turned down there or getting turned down once I've handed him over?"

"It's less direct," she says.

I shift and look to Michelle for support. She gives me an un-readable smile, so I turn back to Lana. "What if he turns *me* down?"

"You're married. What do you care?"

"I care a lot. I'm having a great time just sitting here shooting the shit with my girls, and now for no reason of my own, I have to go over and get rejected by a cute stranger?"

Lana gives me a look she usually reserves for her daughter when she does something like stuff her underpants in her mouth just to annoy her.

"Forget it," says Michelle, her voice breaking Lana's accusatory gaze. "I'll do it. What do I care if I'm turned down by a straight male cutie? Doesn't mean a thing to me."

She turns and walks toward the guy, becoming fuzzy in my gaze as she joins him.

Lana looks on.

"How did you ever hook up with anyone before Pat?" she asks, mystified.

She's watching Michelle pimp, so I don't answer. I don't tell her that when I was younger many men didn't care that I was flirtation-challenged since I had spectacular tits. Flirting was as foreign to me as foraging for nuts, but men who liked enormous racks (and there seemed to be a glut) didn't seem to mind that I didn't talk for the first seven minutes. Maybe my silence made me even sexier. All I know is that men liked to rub up against me a lot and it didn't much matter what I didn't do or say. I sometimes thought that I could be in a coma and they'd still want to titty-fuck me.

In no time at all Michelle returns with, "Ricardo, these are my friends Lana and Brett."

His gaze settles briefly on my chest before Lana scoots in front of me.

"Funky tie," she says, touching it lightly. "I've been looking at it for an hour."

Michelle slides into Lana's vacated barstool next to me. We watch Lana as we periodically play with our drinks. I am both fascinated and annoyed by Lana's flirtatious nature. Fascinated, because this particular skill set is so contrary to any of my own. Annoyed, because whenever Lana flirts with a guy, it breaks up my party.

As Michelle and I watch, though, fascination wins. Lana is a master. She's the Michael Jordan of flirting.

Lana looks out the side of her eyes at Ricardo. Pulling a strand of hair from her ponytail, she plays with it as she talks in a high voice. I watch her completely transform herself from ballsy broad to nymphet. It's remarkable. She actually appears to shrink in size.

What also shrinks is her vocabulary and capacity for linear thought.

"You have big hands," she says. "Where'd you get them?"

Ricardo reddens and holds up a mitt. "My father had big hands."

"Is your father a big man?"

"He worked on a farm."

"Apples are my favorite," she says, sliding her high-heeled foot back and forth.

"When they're ripe," he says.

"That depends on who's eating them."

"You should try the Buffalo wings I just ordered," says Ricardo.

"You knew just what I was thinking," says Lana as the two of them float to the end of the bar.

I turn to Michelle. "Did you understand any of that?"

"No," she says, shrugging in admiration of Lana's gift. "But it always works."

✳ Mom Country

✳

✳

I'm not sure how fast Spence can put on his pajamas," my mother says.

"I'm fast," says Spence.

My mother goes into the kitchen as Spence stands beside his pajamas, draped over the edge of the couch. I reach out and touch his cheek.

"You're really fast," I say.

Mom comes back from the kitchen with an egg timer in her hand.

"Do you think you can get them on in three minutes?" she asks Spence.

He considers his answer; though three minutes to a three-year-old could be as long as it takes to bake a cake or as short as a sneeze.

"Yup. Three minutes," he says.

"Okay," Mom says. "I'm going to set this timer. When three minutes is up, it'll ring. If you've got your pajamas on by then, then you've done it in three minutes."

She punches in three minutes, shows Spence, and sets the timer down.

"And *go*," she says, reaching for her gin and tonic.

Spence pulls his arms from the armholes and whips his T-shirt off his head.

"On Friday," she says, "I was thinking we could all go to the zoo. Then that night your father has tickets for Tchaikovsky's Sixth. You can go with him and I can stay home and watch Spence."

Spence flings the T-shirt across the living room. It lands on the mantelpiece.

"How much time is it?" he screams, pulling at the waistband of his pants.

My mother puts down her drink and leans over to check the timer.

"It's only been half a minute, sweetie," she says.

"Are you sure that you don't want to go to the concert with Dad?" I ask. "I can stay with Spence."

Spence falls onto his bum, wiggling furiously out of his pants.

"No, of course not. I'll stay home," she says.

My mother and I now begin to negotiate who is going to be more selfless Friday night. For reasons probably buried in our Swedish past, whoever does the most work with the least reward wins.

Spence's pants land on the coffee table.

"Is it three minutes yet?" he yells.

Mom looks at the timer.

"You've got two more minutes," she says.

"All right," I say. "But don't make dinner. I don't want you to work too hard."

Spence jumps onto the couch, yanking down his underpants.

"I won't do a big dinner. Just Reuben sandwiches," she says.

"I need another minute!"

Mom leans back in her chair.

"No, you don't, love," she says to him. "You're doing really well."

Naked, Spence drops to the floor, grabbing his pajama top.

"Why don't I just make a big salad?" I ask.

"Reubens are no trouble."

My mother is determined to walk away from this negotiation having established that she is still the title-holding self-debaser. She will give up going to the concert, she will make the dinner *and* watch Spence.

Spence pulls the top over his head.

"I can't find the arms," he yells, panting.

Mom reaches over and untwists a dangling arm from Spence's top.

"All right," I say. "Make the Reubens, but don't do the dishes."

Spence jams his arms into the armholes.

"How much time now?"

"You've got a whole minute," says Mom.

"A minute?!"

He grabs his pajama bottoms, falls to the carpet, and rolls around, wrestling with the material.

"I'll leave the dishes if you want," she says. "But it's just as easy for me to do them."

Forget it, I think, just do everything. Spence jumps up, finally jerking the waistband of his bottoms in place.

He throws up his hands and bellows, *"How much time was that?"*

My mother looks.

"You had a whole forty seconds left over."

Spence collapses onto the couch.

"That's good," he says, tired and satisfied.

I am simply tired.

Through the rest of the visit to my parents' house on the lake, Spence demands to be timed on everything. We time how long it takes for him to eat, how long it takes him to get from the car to the front door, how long it takes him to brush his teeth. He takes the timer with him everywhere.

"All kids love to be timed," says Mom, pleased.

I remember my mother timing me when I was a child, so the whole timing thing is not new. I wonder if friends of mine spent their youth racing against the clock as literally as I did.

"Your mother is timing Spence?" Michelle asks me over the phone.

"It's this thing she does to make tasks fun. Like they're a game."

"Spence doesn't get frustrated?"

"Not yet. He can get his pajamas on in a minute and a half if he doesn't have to unzip his pants."

"I guess, if it works," she says, sounding skeptical.

"I didn't think the timing thing was so odd," I say.

"I've never heard of it."

"Wow. Now I feel like a member of a freak family. The timing freaks."

"Jesus, Brett," Michelle says. "Every family has their weird things."

"Really?"

"Sure, my mom used to take out her teeth and hide them somewhere in our rooms before bedtime. We had to find her teeth in order to get her to read a book to us."

"Wow," I say, "that makes me feel a whole lot easier about my mother's 'fuck episode.'"

I tell Michelle that when my younger brother was a junior in high school, he started swearing with cocky zeal. The swearing seemed to be some crazy challenge to my parents, a way of proving he was his own man, choosing to say "fuck" at least three times per sentence. My mother was mortified, not simply because she and my father never swore but because she considered swearing uncreative and a symptom of an impoverished vocabulary. Her words, not mine.

When Erik refused to give up the constant swearing, she decided to meet "fuck" with "fuck."

"Pass the fucking salt," she'd say at the dinner table.

Erik would pass the salt like he was cool with his fifty-year-old mother making easy with words that didn't look right on her.

After a soccer game Mom chatted with the coach, Erik by her side.

"I couldn't fucking believe how you fucking pulled the whole fucking game out of your ass," she said.

Erik smiled weakly at the stunned coach.

Weeks of my mother's swearing did nothing to alter Erik's. It was a fucking standoff.

Prom night, Erik brought his date over to get pictures taken. The date was a wispy, pretty thing Erik had been trying to bag for half a year. Maybe he'd worn her down with persistence, but it's more likely that no one else had asked her. Whatever the reason, Erik was thrilled that she had finally said yes.

The rest of the family dressed nicely to meet the date. Erik introduced her all around, and she politely chatted with my kid brother, Keir, who was obsessed with coins at the time.

We still have the pictures of Erik and the date in front of the

living room window, looking stiff. In one picture Keir stands between them, holding up a Kennedy half-dollar.

Mom passed around her world-famous Japanese pork appe-
tizer. My father made some jokes about the idiosyncrasies of the
family car Erik would be driving that evening. Eventually, Erik
said it was time to go and the group of us moved into the foyer.
Erik reached into the closet to retrieve the date's shawl.

"Very nice to meet you," my mother said to the date.

"Nice to meet all of you," said the date as Erik placed her
shawl around her shoulders.

"Have a fucking great time, you motherfuckers," said my
mother.

In my mind we all stood there in the foyer, frozen like wax figures, waiting for a sign indicating that we could all return to our
natural state. I don't know what that sign was, but somehow
movement started again. Somehow Erik shuffled the date out the
door. Somehow the rest of us picked up our evening routines.

Within minutes we heard a key in the door. Erik appeared in
the living room, pulling his date along. He walked over to my
mother, who was clearing the pork.

"You win," he said as the date looked on blankly. Who knows
what she thought? But after a pause came relief, as my mother
nodded forgiveness at Erik and shot the date a beneficent smile.

Each country a mother inhabits with her child has its own customs. Mother and child establish rhythms, logic, and language
that aren't understood outside that country. At least this is what I
tell myself whenever I wonder what the adult Spence will say
about his mother's using his toddler self as a makeup mover.

When Spencer was about two years old, I found it impossible to
put my makeup on with him in the bathroom. He would grab my

blush and throw it on the floor. He'd chew on the eyebrow pencil. Once, he dropped a brand-new MAC lipstick into the toilet and flushed it.

I started to put on my makeup during his naps. Or I simply didn't put it on at all, making me look as if motherhood was taking more of a toll than anyone thought. I am not, as my mother puts it, one of those women who can "wear the natural look." To her credit, she says *she* can't wear the natural look either.

Tired of looking tired, I created a game for Spence and me. He became the makeup moving machine. I'd lay out my makeup in a line along the sink.

"Blush," I'd say.

Spencer's arm would appear as he made the growling sound of a machine. The hand moved mechanically up and down and side to side, as it lowered itself toward the blush. When it was finally in place, it opened and clamped around the blush, pulling up in a jerking motion. A series of grinding sounds and moves brought the blush over to my hand, where it was dropped.

Each item of makeup was delivered to me in this fashion. And, although the game extended makeup applying time from five to forty-five minutes, I started looking a damn sight better. I also figured that Spence was getting to know a lot about makeup application. Which is, in Los Angeles, a marketable skill.

At three Spence still enjoys this routine. Though it still seems to take a long time, especially because the makeup moving machine has become a T. rex with claws that are far less efficient than the machine's clamp. But just recently, I bought a little timer from Target. I figure once I start timing the T. rex, I will be able to bring down the time of makeup application to a cool seven minutes.

✳ On Purpose

When Pat tells me that he just got this great new job as a stand-in for a Nickelodeon show; when he tells me that what's great about it is that he'll be putting in a lot of over-time, which means a lot of money; when he tells me that it shoots every week on Thursday nights, so on those days he'll be out of the house for eighteen hours at a stretch—when he tells me all this, with a smile full of pride, I feel like a woman being buried alive behind a brick wall; like the woman in a Vincent Price movie I saw when I was young.

"It's fantastic, honey," he says. "We'll get health insurance and I'm working with guys I've worked with before, so I'll probably do some voice-overs. This is going to be a boatload of money."

The bricks are up to my eyes. I peer out at him.

"That's great," I say. "You'll have a lot of fun too, I bet."

Slap goes a layer of squishy cement.

Pat says, "So, especially on Thursdays, it'll be kind of pointless to wait up for me. I've heard that after the shoot the cast and crew hang out in the Art Department and drink whiskey."

Brick.

"How long does the job last?" I ask.

"Six months."

Brick.

"That's long."

"Yeah. If the show goes well," he says, "they may take a couple of weeks' hiatus and go back into shooting extra episodes. So it could be as long as nine months."

Brick. Brick. Brick. Buried.

I feel like a world-class bitch, begrudging Pat this fun job that will support the family. Pat has taken on the role of provider with admirable seriousness. I love him for this. I love him for being so grown-up and practical.

And I want to scream, *"I'm buried alive here!!!!! Look at me! I'm trapped behind this wall and I can't get out!"*

But like the woman in the movie, I look through a crack in the wall, mute.

I can't remember why the woman in the movie didn't scream. Perhaps for the same reason that I don't now—because she knew that she should be grateful for simply being alive.

And I *am* grateful, I love my time with Spence. There is a rhythm to our days that I enjoy and he's better company now that he talks like a pro. But no matter how much I love him, no matter how thankful I am to witness every one of his realizations, no matter how much I melt at the look of adoration in his eyes, I still watch the clock, waiting for Pat to walk in the door at the end of the day.

I know that when Pat comes home, I will have time of my own back. I'll be able to walk outside, lie on the couch, read a book—just because I feel like it. When Pat is not home, Spence's care supersedes any longings I have for these little freedoms.

This is why Pat's great job, with its long Thursday nights, makes me feel locked in; trapped.

When I was in drama school in New York, my friends and I couldn't afford to go anywhere for spring break. We didn't even have the scratch to go out for dinner.

Bemoaning this fact, one night, over cheap wine and cigarettes (which we somehow did find the cash for), we fantasized about going to the south of France. We imagined ourselves eating coarse bread with cheese on a hilltop that overlooked a quaint village.

Why not create the south of France in one of our living rooms? a friend suggested. We'd lay a blanket on the floor, have a picnic, and just imagine ourselves there.

I still have the pictures of that picnic. There we are, lying on top of each other on a blanket in my living room, glasses in our hands, ripped French bread in front of us. Our smiles as wide as they would be if we were worlds away.

As the first long Thursday night approaches, I decide to create for myself the illusion of freedom. I will carve out an evening in which I can be with adults, talking about adult things. Like the south of France, my imagination will make it an evening that's all my own—time that doesn't belong to Spencer or Pat or the preschool. With my son in his bed, isn't it possible for me to do anything I want in the living room?

What I picture is a weekly salon thing. I'll invite the most interesting people I know. We'll lie around and talk about books and art and politics. Maybe we'll invite fabulous guest speakers, like Bill Moyers, to talk about our place in the universe.

I think about that for a while and, after thumbing through my address book, realize that I have few friends who would partici-pate in anything called a salon. Too intimidating.

Is it a book group? Hard to have one *every* Thursday. Plus, I still feel rotten about the book group I belonged to a few years ago. I went to the monthly meetings several times, lying about having read the book, too embarrassed to fess up. Those evenings were excruciating, nodding my head, murmuring, "I agree," every two minutes.

What about a writing group?

As I think about it more, I like the idea. I'll invite all of the brilliant writers I know. Every Thursday, writers will bring bits of writing in, critique each other, maybe do some writing exercises, bat around a few big ideas. That's it.

I wouldn't call myself a writer, so I'm not exactly sure why it's a "writing group" and not a "singing group" or a "knitting group" (ac-tually, I *do* know why it's not a knitting group). When I start think-ing of people to include, I realize that Michelle is the only writer I know who'd say yes to being in my group—probably for the very same reasons I'm starting it. But the group needs to be bigger than just the two of us to make it feel like a salon and not just another preschool committee, so I fatten up the ranks with three arty women with time on their hands.

Putting Spence to bed at the beginning of the first meeting is a snap. As I click his bedroom door closed, I breathe in, looking at my gal pals sitting around the dining room table with their pens and notebooks. I'm surprised to see the table crowded with bags of cookies, potato chips, and bottles of wine. I had envisioned a more serious tone, but, hey, let's make it a party.

I grab a glass from the kitchen and pour myself some wine.

"He's so yummy I just want to bite him," says my friend Anne, telling the others about a recent crush. Anne's black curls bounce as she talks, reaching for cookies.

"You should write about that guy," says Michelle.

Anne goes on and is just beginning to wind down, when Shannon compliments Mary on her new purse, a beige leather thing that looks like a big envelope. Mary is thrilled that Shannon noticed. She gets up and models it.

Michelle pats the purse.

"Maybe we should write about purses," she says.

I'm impressed with Michelle's attempts to remind the clutch of women that we are here to talk about writing. Even though I am the instigator of the group, I am loath to harness the energy. I hate telling people what to do. Not because I lack the desire— I would love to tell *everyone* what to do—but because my need to be liked is greater than my desire to accomplish anything.

"Okay, did anyone see last week's *Six Feet Under*?" asks Shannon, getting up from the table and grabbing her smokes.

She walks onto the balcony and lights up as conversation about the show spikes.

I enjoy the next hour. I turn on some music, the women chatter, occasionally Michelle suggests a writing topic, I have another glass of wine. Spence sleeps through the whole thing.

Eventually, Michelle clears the table and we find ourselves sitting with pens in hand.

"Let's choose a word and write for five minutes on anything that word inspires," says Michelle, laying her watch in front of her.

"What kind of word?" asks Anne.

"It can be anything," says Michelle.

"Does it have to be a thing, like 'purse'? Or is it something more ethereal, like 'time'?"

"Anything."

"Okay. Let's do 'time,' " says Anne.

Each of us writes the word "time" at the top of our papers and starts to write. As I write, I am amazed at how long the five minutes seems to be. Surely, I keep thinking, five minutes must be up. Then I think, Well, that's about "time," and I write about that. I write about Michelle's watch. I write about how much time I'll have to sleep tonight before Spence wakes at six in the morning. I write about how many hours it will be before Pat crawls into bed with me.

"Time's up," says Michelle.

We stop writing. A group exhalation happens, as if to mark that the whole thing was quite an effort.

"Now let's read out loud," says Michelle.

We go around the circle, reading our five-minute blurbs. After each one the others gush, "Oh, that's so clever," "I would never have thought of that," "You should write a whole story about that."

After this we break out more wine and continue talking. We talk about what color I should paint my bedroom, bone marrow transplants, frequent-flier miles. We talk about a friend who can't get pregnant, a mother who has cataracts, and a therapist who says inappropriate things. Mary cracks Anne's back, and Shannon shows us how she walked as a child before she got hip surgery.

Five hours later, having had coffee and banana bread, we all hug at my door.

The writing group takes care of my empty Thursday nig
I come away feeling fantastic for having put pen to note
I start to feel the press of something familiar in my
thing I first recognized in fifth grade, when I gave
"Seven Days? The Creation of the World as Bib

The speech baffled my classmates, whose speeches revolved around state birds and extreme weather conditions.

When the teacher asked me why I chose the creation of the world as my subject, I said that I wanted to talk about something important. Giggles from my classmates instantly let me know that talking about something important wasn't cool. Beth Henreddy's speech on mud slides, which employed phrases from some Partridge Family songs, had been the biggest hit—followed by Marc Jaslow's, because he brought in a jar of live bees.

Through the years, I learned to stay silent about the thing in my chest. I learned to ignore the press of needing to say something important. I learned to stay silent about my longing for some sense of purpose. I knew that discussing these things would be a surefire way to clear a room preparing to play a kissing game.

After college I became an actress. My hope was that I could say something important by speaking someone else's words and looking kind of cute while doing it. I envisioned myself onstage, fist in the air, screaming to the heavens as thousands of audience members stood and cheered. The people listening would be so pumped that they'd run out of the theater ready to feed the hungry, stop wars, and overthrow governments. My purpose would then be clear to me. I would be the fiery smarty-pants actress who changed the world.

I moved to Los Angeles and lost sight of any purpose, reconnecting with it only when I noticed its absence while standing on a soundstage in a purple business suit. I was about to play a dotty real estate agent in a popular TV drama. The director came up to me before a take and told me that if I didn't speed up my dialogue, she would have to cut the scene. As she walked away from me and ᴍbled with the anticipation of public failure, I thought, What the fuck am I doing here, pretending to be a fast-talking real estate agent? How does my doing this particular thing serve anyone?

These were not the kind of thoughts I wanted to have while standing in a pretend house, in clothes that weren't my own, in Hollywood.

This particular moment did pass. I talked fast enough to keep the job. And, later, my search for a greater purpose was partly found in Spencer's birth.

Clearing the wineglasses from my table, after another Thursday night writers' group, I feel the thing knocking in my chest.

I stop clearing and sit. I think to myself, Who am I to think that I have any higher purpose than that of caring for myself and my family? Who am I to think that the knocking in my chest is connected to any real facility for anything greater than being a mother and a wife? Doesn't caring for and loving myself, family, and friends give me the greatest purpose I can think of?

Absolutely.

Knock, knock, knock.

I lift a half-empty bottle of wine and pour some into a glass. I pick up the glass and walk over to the radio, switching it to a classical station. I turn off the lights and turn on the computer.

This is it, I think. I am going to write something magnificent. I am going to start right now.

I click open a blank document.

My fingers lightly touch the keys as I wait for divine inspiration.

I have time.

I wait.

Then inspiration descends. It fills me up and travels to the tips of my fingers and I begin to type.

SHE WALKED ALONG THE BOMBED-OUT STREET, HER RAGGED
DRESS BRUSHING HER KNEES, CARRYING MEDICINE IN THE
VIAL SHE HAD RETRIEVED FROM HERR MULLER'S BASEMENT.

I lean back in the chair. I take a sip of my wine.

Yes.

This will be a great book. A book about how a heroine, much like myself, saves the world from a post-9/11 plague.

My mind skips to the review in *The New York Times Book Review:* "Paesel's powerful prose thrills and terrifies. This book is an unprecedented first effort. With such depth of feeling, such command of language, such shocking grasp of structure, Paesel moves us to an exalted state."

I lean forward.

CATHERINE KNEW SHE HAD ONLY MINUTES TO DELIVER THE
SPECIMEN BEFORE IT WAS RENDERED USELESS BY THE UNRE-
LENTING HEAT.

I lean back again, listening to the music. I look at the words I've typed. That's a start, I think. I'll pick it up tomorrow.

Tomorrow never comes.

Months later I join a writing class. I write several short stories. I write about a sixteen-year-old runaway, I write about an amnesiac, I write about people in an arctic town going crazy in the midnight sun.

The teacher smiles and gives me some suggestions. She is good at this. She tells me to ease up on the adverbs and adjectives. She doesn't tell me to stop writing about the midnight sun.

I bring in a story about something that happened to me. It's a story about a shag haircut I got after my son was born. But it's not about the haircut. It's about how I thought a haircut would make me feel better. How the haircut would bring back a younger me.

The teacher says, "That sounds like you. Write more things like that."

So that's what I do. It doesn't feel like a purpose exactly.

It feels like breathing.

✳ Friday

Then my mother looks me in the eye and says, 'Well, Katherine, I don't know what you're complaining about. Everyone went out of their way to accommodate the children.'"

The rest of us moan and sip our drinks. Katherine is telling us about the vacation she just took with her huge Irish family. She has nine brothers and sisters, none of whom have children of their own. So when Katherine and Slim take trips home to the Midwest family seat, Jake is the lone child, jabbering to adults, pulling on them, desperate for their attention.

"I thought," says Katherine, putting down her beer, "that having a child would pull my mother and me closer together. I'm the only one who's doing the job she did."

Lana takes off her sweater and lays it on the bar. "When I told my mother that I was pregnant, the first thing she said was not to expect her to babysit."

"My parents were dying for grandchildren," says Katherine. "When Slim and I weren't coughing them up, they acted like we were willfully denying them the happiness of progeny."

"So they didn't have a problem with the idea of a biracial grandchild?" I ask.

"God, no," says Katherine. "I'm the youngest of nine kids. They've had far bigger problems, in their book, than a biracial grandbaby. Two of my sisters are gay. One of my brothers is chronically unemployed. Another brother is a drug addict living in the basement."

"Wow," I say, the wannabe writer in me, jealous that Katherine has a drug addict in her family. Why isn't my family that colorful?

"Everyone has a drug addict in the basement," says Lana.

Michelle scootches her stool closer to the bar.

"I don't," I say, trying to keep my voice free of disappointment.

Michelle turns to Lana. "You don't have a drug addict."

"I do too," says Lana. "My sister's a drunk who slept on the couch in the family room."

"It's not the same as a drug addict in the basement," says Michelle.

"She huffed my mother's cleaning products for a summer and moved out to marry a porn star."

"She's still not a drug addict," says Michelle.

Michelle has been on an accuracy kick. I suppose it's a natural response to all the tall tales we tell on Fridays.

" 'Drug addict in the basement' is a general term, referring to all siblings who don't manage to leave the home because they're impaired," says Lana. "Right?" she adds, looking to me.

"I wouldn't know," I say, glum. "I don't have a drug addict."

"So I'm the one who brings home the longed-for grandchild," says Katherine, sliding past the drug-addict talk. "And I don't get any help. I'm the one who gets up with Jake at six. I'm the one who feeds him, who tucks him in."

"Where's Slim in all this?" asks Michelle.

"Normally, he's pretty helpful," says Katherine, "but as soon as he hits the Midwest, he figures I've got all this help and he kicks back."

"Doesn't sound like him," says Michelle, ever the Slim fan.

"So I said to my mother that it's no fun for me to come on vacation with my kid and have to work twice as hard, while everyone else gets to do their own thing."

"What did she say?" I ask.

"That's when she said the thing about everyone having gone out of their way."

"Well, how does she think they went out of their way?"

"One of my sisters took Jake for a walk. And my brother chased him around the house for fifteen minutes, until Jake got so wound up he was screaming. Then, when my brother had had enough, he handed Jake back to me."

"I hate it when people do that," says Lana.

"Are you sure Slim doesn't help out? It doesn't seem like him to lay around and let you do all the work," says Michelle.

I lean back and resolve to talk to Michelle about this accuracy thing. It really stops the spin of a good yarn.

Katherine stops to consider. "Sure. Slim helped a little. He gave Jake his baths and put him to bed twice. But I'm telling you, most of it was on me."

Michelle looks down at her Amstel. "I can't imagine him doing nothing."

Lana stands up high on the rung of the barstool and flags Mack, who signals back. She plops back down. "But what

Katherine is saying is that it's strange that our mothers get so hard on us once we become mothers ourselves," she says.

I lean forward. "Last time I was at the airport, Spence pulled off his shoes. Pat was doing the tickets, I was stuffing some last-minute stuff in the diaper bag and I picked out a juice box and sprayed juice all over my shirt, I started dapping it off with a wet-wipe, and my mother said, 'Kristin, Spencer's shoes are off. The bottoms of his feet are black.' I looked at her and said, 'Mom, the bottom of Spence's feet are not a high priority right now.'"

Mack puts a Bloody Mary in front of Lana, followed by a tiny beer back.

I go on, "But it's like my mother has totally forgotten what it's like to have children. She forgets that she almost never washed my brother's hair when he was fivish, because he hated it. For about a year he had this layer of dirt you could actually see through the hair on his scalp."

I see Michelle look off to picture this in her mind.

"Eww," she says.

"I don't think it's that our mothers have forgotten," says Lana, twirling her celery. "I think it's that they think we have it easy these days. We've got all this helpful modern stuff—the bouncy seats, the disposable diapers, the videos, the fancy toys. We even have guys who help out now and then. Even Tony used to dry an occasional dish."

Lana stops and we wait to see if we're going to go into a Tony moment. She puts down the Bloody Mary.

"And frankly, we *do* have it easier than they did," she says. "A while ago my mom was telling me about being a mother in the late sixties. She was at home full-time. She did the washing, the cleaning, all the parenting, all the getting up in the middle of the night—no help from my dad. And I asked her. I asked her how she managed it all. You know what she said?"

Lana reaches over to grab the beer back and downs it.

"She said, 'Booze and pills, Lana. Booze and pills.'"

✳ Blood

✳

✳

A woman who has had a miscarriage does not trust her body when she becomes pregnant again. She looks at the line on the pregnancy test and feels apprehension, where before there was celebration. A woman who has had a miscarriage does not immediately run to her husband, yelling, "We're pregnant!" A woman who has had a miscarriage keeps the knowledge to herself for a few days. A woman who has had a miscarriage, and is pregnant again, lives a secret life in the bathroom. It is there that she touches her breasts. Are they still tender? She touches her belly. Does it feel round? A woman who has had a miscarriage looks for blood.

A woman who has had a miscarriage knows a lot about blood. A few spots may mean nothing. A few more spots than that may still mean nothing if it stops soon. Brown blood means the end of bleeding. Watery blood means the beginning. Bright blood means that there's more blood to come.

I sit on the toilet, looking at myself in the mirror over the sink.

I'm not going to look at the toilet paper this time, I think.

What's the point? If I've miscarried, I've miscarried. I might as well go to bed not knowing. That way I'll get a decent night's sleep.

But I don't want to find out first thing in the morning, do I? Then I'll have a whole day to get through, cramping and bleeding, having to act normal with Spence.

If I find out now, I can have a few drinks, cry, take a bath, have a few more drinks, play a Meat Loaf CD really loud and stomp around the apartment, cry, have Pat go get some Baileys and cigarettes, watch a really bad movie on TV, write some e-mails to people who I want to feel sorry for me, and pass out around four o'clock in the morning. Pat will then have to wake up with Spence while I sleep it all off.

Sounds like a good plan.

I reach for the toilet paper but pull my hand back.

If I keep looking, that means I have no faith. This lack of faith could be *creating* the miscarriage. Whereas not looking for blood means that I'm confident. Won't I get rewarded for that? God rewards the faithful.

I'm not going to look.

I grab the toilet paper and wipe, looking at myself in the mirror instead. I don't look half bad. I certainly don't look like I'm miscarrying. Thank God for my skin. Good skin makes up for a lot of deficiencies, like my eyes sinking deeper into my head. In a few years my eyes will be completely swallowed by my face, leaving a couple of dents in their place. I'll look like one of those old-people dolls that they make with stuffing and panty hose.

I stand and pull up my pants. I reach behind and flush, without looking for blood in the water.

I don't deal with blood well anyway. Not my own. Not other people's. Certainly not Spence's. Spence was a couple of months old when I first cut his fingernails, snipping a tiny fingertip. As blood streamed out of the cut, I screamed, "Oh my Christ. You're bleeding. Holy Mary Mother of Fuck, what do I do now?"

Running to the freezer, I grabbed an ice tray and cracked it, sending ice cubes sliding over the kitchen floor. I skidded across the floor to the dish towel, grabbed it, and dropped on my knees to the watery linoleum, to gather the ice cubes in the towel.

"Hold on!" I screamed at screaming Spence.

I crawled over the wet floor with the dish towel and ice cubes, reaching the living room carpet, where I rose and ran to Pat's sock drawer. I yanked the drawer, sending it crashing to the floor, seized a loose sock, threw the ice cubes and towel into the sock, then ran to Spence and jammed his hand into the sock.

I picked Spence up and carried him over to my bed, where I lay down next to him, winding the icy sock tightly around his hand. We cried together, blood seeping through the sock, until we both fell asleep.

I sit at the nurse's station outside Dr. Sammy's office. Dr. Sammy's nurse is a round no-nonsense woman named Charlene. I can tell that she doesn't like me, which is why I do my best to be a cooperative patient.

Charlene unwraps the blood pressure cuff from around my upper arm.

"How many weeks along are you?" she asks.

"Seven now."

She writes this down.

"How's my blood pressure?" I ask.

"Good," she says. "Like a teenager's."

She says this like it's something she says to a lot of people to make them feel good.

"Great," I say. "You've got my urine. My blood pressure's good. I'm taking the prenatal vitamins. Everything looks like a go."

"Except I need some blood," she says.

I tense. "Blood?"

"Yes."

"But you got some of my blood last month."

"I need some more today."

"You're doing more tests? Why didn't you do them on the blood you got out of me last time?"

"Those were different tests," she says.

I hate the way she slows down her speech whenever I question a procedure. She puts big spaces between her words, as if my brain isn't working fast enough to understand what she's saying.

"You know it really helps if you tell me you're going to take my blood *before* the appointment, so I can prepare," I say.

"Whenever I do that," she says, measured like a clock, "you cancel the appointment at the last minute."

I have no response to this because it's true.

"I'm going to have to lie down," I say.

"I know," she says, taking out the rubber ball and the rubber strap. I look at these and think, as I have many times, that I cannot imagine how anyone shoots up. I'd pass out while injecting myself and sleep through my high.

She walks past me and I follow her into an examination room.

The paper on the examination table crinkles beneath me as Charlene tightens the rubber strap. I feel my blood swell in my upper arm as the strap digs into my flesh.

"Now squeeze the ball," says Charlene.

"I can't move my hand," I say.

"Brett. Squeeze the ball, or it's going to be harder for me to find a vein."

I try to send a telepathic signal to my hand to squeeze.

My hand remains slack and the ball rolls out of it onto the floor. Charlene picks it up.

"Brett, I'm putting the ball in your hand and you need to squeeze it."

"My hand's not working."

"If I try to find a vein without the ball, it's going to be harder on you."

I try again to send a signal to my hand. Perhaps I am successful.

I feel a slight prick in the crook of my elbow.

I hear, "That's it. It's flowing nicely," before I black out.

I sit on the toilet, looking at myself.

My face looks rounder. This could mean that I am still pregnant. Or it could mean that I am hanging on to all the weight caused by the pseudo-baby currently shriveling in my uterus. I resolve, again, not to look at the toilet paper.

I wonder if "no blood at all" can be a bad thing. I mean, thirty percent of perfectly normal pregnancies spot. Is it odd that I haven't spotted at all?

Stupid. How would I know if I've spotted? I threw a black pair of underwear into the hamper this morning without looking at them.

All this thinking about blood makes me woozy. I imagine myself seeping gallons of blood, unaware because I won't look for it. I sway a bit on the toilet.

I can't feel the tips of my fingers. I struggle to my feet, pull up my pants, and fumble with the zipper. I go into the bedroom and lie down. From Spence's room I hear Pat making the sound of a dinosaur. Spence squeals delight.

I close my eyes.

Maybe I'm hemorrhaging internally.

The only time I wasn't afraid of blood was when I watched my best friend, Ed, die of AIDS at the Beth Israel Medical Center in New York City, the week of September 25, 1991. That week I sat by his bedside, watching him occupy that sliver of time and space between being alive and not being dead.

Yet.

He was asleep, or simply unaware, most of the time. When he awoke in the corporeal world, his self settling into his face and voice for a few minutes, he would need to cough blood and phlegm into a plastic receptacle.

In the early nineties there was a national fear of blood. It was a time when my own fear would have marked me as a member of the terrified majority. But I am not a joiner. And this was Ed's blood—the stuff that flowed through him, tainted though it was, that kept him near to me for one more minute, one more day.

I loved his blood. It was easy for me to empty the receptacle into the red garbage can marked "Hazardous Waste." I did not believe that Ed's blood would hurt me.

Listening to Pat's dinosaur chase Spence around his room, I let my mind rest on Ed's final week. I let myself grieve, ever so briefly, that Ed is not here to tell me that I'm being a big baby and that whatever my body delivers up is what it's going to deliver up, regardless of how terrified or not terrified I am. I cannot create a miscarriage. I cannot prevent it. Any more than I could create or prevent Ed's blood from finally betraying him.

I think of how much Ed would have loved to have gotten older. How much he would have loved to lie on a bed, listening to a child's shrieks of joy, feeling blood course through him like a promise.

I get up from the bed and go into the bathroom.

I pull down my underwear and look.

✳ Heroics

✳

✳

I lie on the examination table. Dr. Sammy glides the heart monitor over my belly, which rises from the rest of me like a perfectly round burial mound on sacred ground in the middle of the English countryside.

I hear Spence roll a chair back and forth in the corner of the room. From the monitor I hear the whooshing sound of the baby's heartbeat.

"There it is," says Dr. Sammy.

I have given up wanting more from Dr. Sammy. At first I wanted to hear things like "That is the strongest heartbeat I have ever heard in a fetus so young. How do you do it all? Writer, actress, mother of a toddler, and now this . . . creating the most genetically perfect baby I've ever encountered."

Dr. Sammy pulls me up and I sit on the edge of the table, my feet dangling like a child's.

Spence bangs the chair against the wall.

"Spence," I say, careful to use my perfectly modulated mommy voice in front of Dr. Sammy. "Let's choose not to crash the chair right now."

Pat hates this phraseology. He says it leads the listener, in most cases Spence or him, to believe that they are part of the choice. I got the idea from some Suze Orman show. This guru of home finances says that with children you should never say, "We can't afford that." Instead, you should say, "We're not choosing to spend our money on that right now." I like the egalitarian sound of it. Pat says it's subterfuge.

Spence looks up at me, smiles, and sails the chair across the room, crashing it into the wall. I guess he made a different choice.

Dr. Sammy looks at him and returns to me. "Any questions?"

I bury the ones burning to be asked, the ones he cannot answer. *Will I be able to lose the weight? Will this baby be a crier, like Spence? Will I be able to juggle the needs of two children and still be able to write? Is a Roth IRA the best way to go? Is painting my bedroom a dark blue going to make it look smaller? How can I get rid of the ants in my house without spraying the baseboards and poisoning us all? When Spence is fifteen and yells at me that I'm a bitch, how will I be able to bear it?*

I look at Spence kneeling to inspect the bottom of the chair.

I breathe in. "What are the chances of my having a C-section again?" I ask.

Dr. Sammy leans against the counter.

"Well, we'll go over your options when we get closer to delivery," he says. "You can try for a vaginal birth if you want. But you have a higher possibility of rupturing, since you've already had a C-section. Doesn't mean you will."

"Rupture" sounds catastrophic to me, like a blood-soaked near-death experience. "Near death" being the upside. What about *death* death? What about machines screeching a flatline while my screaming baby is whisked away and blood gushes out of me like a fountain, as Dr. Sammy yells, "Code Blue, I'm losing her. I need some fucking assistance here, *stat.*" I've seen the shows.

Dr. Sammy flips through my chart. "There's no reason why you couldn't have a vaginal birth."

That's okay, I'll take the C-section, I think.

"You'll probably want to go over your options with Pat," he says.

C-section is fine.

"If you decided on the C-section . . . ," he continues.

C-section, yes, that's the one I want.

". . . we'd schedule it a week earlier than your due date."

"A week earlier," I say.

"Yes."

"I'll take the C-section."

"Well," he says, "as I was saying, we can talk about it in depth at your next appointment."

"If it were up to you, what would you do?" I ask.

Dr. Sammy closes my file.

"Well," he says, "if it were up to me . . . Look, I'm always going to err on the side of being conservative. So I would go for the C-section."

"Yes," I say.

"But," he says, "a lot of women really want to go for a vaginal birth. It's important to them. Me, I'm not really into vaginal heroics."

I want to tell him that the only remotely heroic thing my vagina ever did was pity-fuck Tom Goldenhirsh my senior year in college, after he told me his sister had cancer.

Truth is, if my vagina did anything heroic, it would be the first of my body parts ever to do so.

★   ★   ★

I blame my mother for my cowardice. Take away her fears and she is only half a woman. It took two Valiums and a double gin and tonic to get her on a plane when I was a girl. On walks through our neighborhood she shoved me between her and big dogs like a human shield. There were no matches in our house, or sharp knives, for fear of someone hurting themselves. I didn't see a neatly sliced tomato until I was in my teens. The bits of tomato that were added to our salads looked like tiny globular internal organs.

My fears range from the physical fear of pain to social fears to a fear of being trapped alone in a small room with a boring person who has a tic and likes to talk. When I was around ten, my mother read one of those popular seventies books about being your own best friend and being okay while others are okay. She told me that the book didn't help much because its advice about confronting one's fears was to ask yourself, "What is the worse thing that can happen?" And her answer was always, "That I will die." It wasn't an answer that gave her much comfort—or courage.

Maybe my fear of just about everything is a cellular ode to my mother. If so, I am the only child of hers to sing it. My youngest brother is quite the opposite. Risking his life is his hobby. He and his wife go off into the wilderness exploring unpopulated places with names like Dead Man's Cove, Last Resort, and Crazy Joe's Rattlesnake Prairie. Every Christmas they send a picture of themselves smiling as they jump off a cliff into something that looks like molten lava or a Nordic void.

★   ★   ★

I get a phone call from Nurse Charlene. I can tell she still hates me.

She tells me that my C-section appointment is for December 10 at noon. A familiar blast of adrenaline rushes through me as I write "C-section" down in shaky handwriting on a notepad. I've elected to have this surgery, it's true. But that doesn't ease my terror of the needles, slicing, and bloodletting that a C-section will involve. My eyes blur as I start to pant.

"Will that work?" she asks, her voice tight.

"Huh?"

"Can you confirm noon for your C-section?"

"Right," I say. "Is there . . . can I . . . drink the night before?"

"No liquids after midnight," she says.

"But up until then, can I have alcohol? To calm my nerves."

"I'll have to ask the doctor," she says. The whole sentence an exasperated sigh.

"Okay," I say. "If not, can you ask him if there's a pill I can have? Maybe something that numbs me from the neck down before I get to the hospital. My husband can carry me in."

"I don't think there's anything like that," she says.

"Would you just check?" I say. "You'd be surprised. My dentist gives me something called, I don't know what the medical term is, but he calls it green gin. It tastes like peppermint and wipes out your fear response and your memory."

"Green gin?"

"Yes. Just ask him for green gin."

My panting increases and I grab onto the kitchen counter.

"So you're confirming December 10," she says.

"Yes," I say. "I have to go now and find a paper bag."

*   *   *

Pat comes home to find me prone on the couch counting backward from 100.

"Looks like you got the appointment," he says.

"December 10," I say, waving the paper bag around.

"Do you need a pan?" he asks. "Are you going to throw up?"

"No, no," I say, starting short staccato breaths. These are yoga breaths called breath of fire, meant to help calm the system. I try them, even though usually they make me lose all feeling in my fingers, which starts a panic that I have MS.

Pat sits down and watches me.

"Okay, look," he says. "The baby has to come out. And this is the safest thing. Now, what is it you're worried about?"

I stop breathing fire and gasp, "That I will die."

"We could all die tomorrow," he says.

"I know," I say. "And I can't figure out why everyone is so calm about it."

But through all this hysteria—through all my very real, heartstopping fear—I know that I will have this baby, C-section or not. I will do it shuddering, spitting, peeing in my pants, undoubtedly highly medicated. But I will do it. I will enter my own Dead Man's Cove—and return with the exhilaration of having survived. And I know that I will do thousands more things that quite literally scare me shitless. This I inherited from my mother as well, the choosing to do it—the thing that terrifies you—anyway. Because choosing *not* to do it is like dying. And I'm not ready yet.

✳ Friday

✳

✳

I sip from the straw of my Diet Coke and put it down on the bar, which is quite a stretch past my belly. It's too boring to complain about my state. Everyone but Michelle has been there. My aches and pains are no worse than any other woman's at seven months. But, oh, I really want to complain. I want to complain and complain and complain. Then I want to take a nap, get up, and complain again.

Instead, I say, "I think a guy hit on me this morning."

"Really?" says Lana, putting down her tall vodka tonic, two limes.

"Yeah. I didn't really think about it until he was gone."

"I got hit on all the time when I was pregnant," says Katherine.

Michelle shifts. "Why would guys hit on a pregnant woman? Nothing says 'taken' more than that."

"Maybe that's part of it," says Katherine. "The kink of poking another man's girl while she carries his baby."

"Jeez," I say. "I was just hoping this guy thought I was cute."

"You *are* cute," says Lana. "But I agree. Something about taking everything another man's got really appeals to guys. In this case he gets the wife and the unborn baby."

"And I thought *I* was cynical about the motives of straight men," says Michelle.

"So how did the guy hit on you?" asks Lana.

"Well, as I said, it didn't occur to me until he was gone. But he kind of appeared beside me while I was walking and said that I looked great. I thought he was just being nice."

"So what did you say?"

"I said, 'Thanks.' "

"That's all you said?" asks Lana.

"What was I supposed to say?"

"You're supposed to say, 'I look better in just my panties.' "

We all laugh. Michelle holds up her empty. Mack nods.

"So that's it?" asks Lana. "He said you looked nice and you said thanks?"

"Then he said that he had seen me several times before."

Katherine shudders. "That's creepy."

"Yeah," I say. "I think that now. But at the time I thought that he was just a neighborhood guy who really had seen me here and there."

"Jesus," says Katherine. "You are so naive."

Ouch. I know Katherine means this in a protective, affection-ate way. But it hurts all the same. I wiggle in my chair, trying to get comfortable.

"I don't think I'm that naive," I say. "It just didn't occur to me that he was hitting on me because I'm so huge. Being pregnant is *not* sexy."

The women grumble a bit. And I wonder if I'm the only one who thinks this. I feel a bit prudish. I've heard women giggle about how orgasmic they are when they're pregnant. Lana said that her pregnancy increased her sexual drive. The only drive increased by my pregnancy is my drive to nap and complain.

"I felt so hot when I was pregnant," says Katherine, "like I was filled with female juice."

"What?" asks Michelle, cocking an eyebrow.

"I felt all sexed up," says Katherine.

"Female juice?" asks Lana, biting into one of her limes.

"Jesus," says Katherine. "All I'm saying is that all those hormones and all that stuff around the baby, sloshing around, made me feel juicy."

"Okay," I say to the others, "I don't think we're going to get much more clarification of female juice than that."

"You know what's really sexy is your boobs filled with all that milk," says Katherine.

"Oh, no," I say, louder than I meant to. I turn to Katherine. "You have tiny breasts, so it's fun for you to have bigger ones. When my big boobs get filled up with milk, they look obscene. And not in a good way."

"Obscene is good," says Lana.

"I said *not* in a good way. In a something-we-really-don't-need-to-see kind of way. In an underside-of-the-ball-sack kind of way."

Michelle's dropped out of this, so I really can't tell what she thinks. Maybe we're talking too much about being pregnant. I wonder if that makes her feel left out.

"When Jake was about six months old, we left him with friends for a weekend," says Katherine. "Slim and I drove to the Grand Canyon and camped. Obviously, I was new at the breast-feeding thing, so I somehow forgot or didn't think about my breasts filling up with all that milk. We got down in the canyon at, like, dusk and my breasts were practically bursting. I told Slim that the best thing I could think of was for him to suck out all the milk."

She takes a sip of her black and tan, as she looks off remembering this, I assume.

"Man," she says. "What a great night."

Whenever Katherine tells stories like this, I think that there must be a whole chunk of human experience that I'm missing. Maybe she's right. Maybe I am naive.

"After that," says Katherine, "Slim wanted to do it every day. But I had to put a stop to it, since I was worried that he'd drink up all of Jake's milk."

"Aw. You didn't need to do that," says Lana. "You would have eventually started producing enough milk for two."

"Eww," I say. "Sorry, but ewww. I try not to be an 'ew'-type girl. But this whole thing deserves an 'ew.'"

Lana and Katherine laugh.

"I don't understand why sucking breasts is such an 'ew,'" says Michelle.

"It's not the breasts," I say, "it's the milk."

I look to read Michelle's expression. Is she upset with me? Did she think I was slamming breast-sucking lesbians?

"Well," says Michelle, putting her Amstel on the bar, "Sarah and I are having dinner. So I'm off."

"So early?" I say.

"Sorry," she says as she grabs her purse from the bar. "We really do have dinner."

After she leaves, I say, "God, I feel awful. Did I say something bad?"

Katherine says, "No, it was me. It was something I said. She looked funny when I said that thing about having big boobs full of milk."

"Don't be silly. It wasn't anyone," says Lana. "She just had a dinner."

"Maybe it wasn't the breast milk or breast-sucking," I say. "Maybe she was upset because we spent so much time talking about being pregnant. Maybe she'd had enough."

"Yeah. I hadn't thought of that," says Katherine.

"You guys," says Lana, standing and sliding her empty toward Mack. "You're making something out of nothing here. She just had a dinner."

We think for a second. I look at my watery Diet Coke, tiny ice cubes looking like glass pebbles. I think about how often I make something out of nothing.

Lana's probably right, I think. She probably just had a dinner. But I feel lousy anyway. I resolve to call Michelle later. It wouldn't surprise me if we all did.

✳ Free Bird

If there's a pill for it, it will be prescribed to me. I must look like a woman who needs a lot of medication, because doctors are keen to hand it to me, even when I don't ask for it. For a ghost of a symptom, I've been offered codeine, Demerol, a festival of antidepressants, Xanax, Vicodin, and seemingly hundreds of other pills that my friends would pay big money for. I still have a small stash of Valium that my dentist insisted I take before each visit, for fear that without it I would bite him. I'm surprised that I haven't been prescribed medical marijuana for my athlete's foot.

"Jesus, for an ingrown hair, they'd give you a morphine drip," Lana says when they wheel me in, stoned to the bone, after my scheduled C. After Lana's C-section with Daisy, her doctor refused to prescribe anything stronger than extra-strength Tylenol.

All I know is that I feel fabulous. My trusty friend the catheter dangles off the edge of the bed, ensuring that I won't have to get up for at least twenty-four hours. I'm surrounded by friends and family, buzzing around me like drones.

I can't wait to get to the Jell-O.

Murph lies in the crook of my arm, warm as a promise.

Lana tells me later that right after the birth Pat came out to tell Spence that the baby was a boy. She says that Spence took in the news, then walked up to Daisy and said, "I have a brother, and he's a boy."

The morning after the first night, I am alone with Murphy, who sleeps in his plastic box. Pat has taken Spence to school, and my parents are at the cafeteria. I eat Jell-O, the taste filling my mouth, stinging the insides of my cheeks with sweetness. Whatever drug combo I'm on causes a sensory overload that is often pleasant. I marvel again at what a perfect and compact food Jell-O is. Hugely underrated.

I finish the cup and consider ringing for another but am vaguely embarrassed to ask for a fourth. I lie back on the incline of the bed, adjusting it slightly to the perfect angle for a post-Jell-O nap. I press the buzzer for the nurse to reel away Murph so I won't be interrupted by his gurgles and chirps—since every time I hear a peep or imagine hearing it my eyes pop open, making sustained sleep impossible.

As I gaze at the flowers on the nightstand, awed by the density of their color, I wonder again why so many new mothers are desperate to leave the comforts of the hospital. I'm so content that I keep thinking about how I can break open my stitches or give myself a concussion so that I can stay another day. I fiddle with the phone cord as I consider smashing my head on the metal bars of the bed.

I barely notice a new nurse entering until she writes her name with a Magic Marker on the whiteboard: Yana.

"What do you need?" she asks in a Russian accent.

Yana looks like a plush art refrigerator, her white uniform pulled tightly across her square frame.

"Can you take my son to the nursery?" I ask.

I ask this weakly. I'm never sure how to address nurses. I certainly don't want to sound like I'm ordering them around. They might retaliate by denying me medication.

"When do you want me to bring him back?" she asks, unsmiling.

"Back?"

"In two hours, correct?" she says more than asks.

"Whenever he cries is fine," I say.

"It should be every two hours."

I lift my head with effort and stare at her.

"I'm feeding on demand," I say.

She looks back at me. "I'll bring him back in two hours."

She gives a stiff nod, pivots, and leaves.

What? Even in my drug haze I gather that my most basic child-rearing choices are being overridden by Yana, the day nurse. I turn my head to the wall and consider my options. Maybe leaving the hospital isn't such a bad idea.

Whenever I'm in the company of strong women, I buckle in the face of their decisiveness. The fact that they are so sure makes me question my own path. The fact that they issue orders with unblinking clarity makes me eager to follow them. I have been a willing submissive to ballsy women all my life. I give over power partly out of insecurity and largely out of laziness.

On the upside, I figure, let someone else make the decisions about things I barely care about: what movie we go to, when to go home from a party, what color skirt to buy. To this end, my friendship with Lana is perfect. She's quite happy to make these minor calls.

On the downside of my willingness to follow lies a dark history of seething, silent bitterness.

In my early twenties, I lived in a five-floor walk-up with Penelope, who was English and able to issue commands like she was to the manor born. The apartment had been my find, and I'm not even sure that I actually ever offered her the extra bedroom. All I remember is that she moved in and immediately set the tone for the household. I couldn't wear shoes inside (too noisy), I couldn't make phone calls until 11 a.m. (she might get a call from home), and I couldn't take a bath before her (I'd use up all the hot water). All opened boxes of food had to be wrapped in Saran, no music could be played after she went to sleep, my bath towel had to be hung in my room and not in the bathroom, next to hers.

I lived much like Anne Frank behind the bookcase.

"I can hear the toilet flush after I've gone to bed," she told me one morning as she washed Ziploc bags, hanging them around the kitchen to dry.

"Sorry," I said.

"So I've decided that there's to be no more toilet flushing after ten at night."

"What do I do if I have to go to the bathroom?"

"I guess you'll have to hold it, or let it sit in the bowl until the morning," she said, dropping our salt shaker into a dry bag, sealing it, and returning it to the table. "If you leave it there, remember to get up and flush it early. I don't want to see it."

That did it. I followed the rule, leaving my waste in the bowl until early morning when upon hearing Penelope stir, I would run to the bathroom to flush. But I waited for the perfect moment to free myself from her tyranny.

When my brother decided to move in with me, I gave Penelope notice. I wrote her a note and left for the weekend before she had a chance to read it. I couldn't sleep the entire weekend. My imaginings of the reprisal to come were so terrifying that I developed diarrhea, making me grateful to be at a friend's house, where I could flush.

When I came back, Penelope was oddly calm. She said that she had been expecting this. She was surprised, she said, that I had put up with her for as long as I had. This was the most vulnerable I had ever seen Penelope. As we talked, I realized that while I had lived in fear of her edicts, she had been living in anticipation of the moment that I would kick her out.

Had I been more sophisticated, I would have recognized that even the most confident seeming of my acquaintances had their moments of weakness. I might have even recognized that in many ways I was the stronger.

Such conclusions, however, take a lifetime to realize. Compliance was not only a comfortable way to survive, it was habit.

When Yana wheels Murph in two hours later, I've been stewing the whole time. My buzz has worn away, replaced by a knot of resentment grown larger through the years, with every missed opportunity to stand up for myself.

"He's not crying," I say, looking at Murph sleeping.

"It's been two hours," she says.

"I'm not going to wake him up," I say, my voice shaking.

"It's good to get them on a schedule."

I can't imagine that Yana has been at this hospital very long. "Feeding on demand" is the most popular choice among all the mothers I know. So surely, she has come across this before. Maybe this is the day that she's had it with all those crazy American mothers allowing infants to rule the house. Maybe today is the day that she's snapped. Maybe she woke up this morning and said to herself, "Enough with these spoiled American babies. I'm going to do something about it. I'm going to get this entire lazy country on a schedule and I'm going to do it baby by baby. Starting with this one."

If that's the case, she picked the wrong mother.

I push the button that raises the back of the bed, clanking me into a higher sitting position. I feel like the paralyzed skier in *The Other Side of the Mountain.*

"Yana," I say, "this is my decision. I am the mother. You are *not* the mother. I decide how I'm going to do it. And I am going to feed him when he asks to be fed, not when the clock says it's time."

Yana, steely, looks at me. I brace myself for her response. I try to imagine myself as the paralyzed skier valiantly claiming her independence. I have to stop myself from making more of the moment—from saying "I am a free bird. A bird who lives free, Yana. I may not have use of these limbs, but in my mind I soar." I don't think this is ever said in the movie. But it's something like that.

"Okay," says Yana, shrugging. "Don't matter to me."

She grabs my tray of discarded Jell-O cups and leaves.

I stare at the closed door of my room. Could it possibly be that easy?

I push the button to lower the back of the bed, stopping when my face is a few inches away from sleeping Murph.

It's hard to grasp that he is really mine. I marvel that at only a couple of days old he is able to instill in me such fierce protectiveness. Already, he has given me strength to overcome my own ridiculous fears, if only for a blip of a sliver of an instant.

I relish the moment as my eyes start to close. I consider buzzing my buzzer and demanding more Jell-O, but I can't open my eyes.

And I fall asleep before giving it another thought.

✳ Two?
✳

✳

Before Murphy was born, every mother I knew said, "Spence was a screamer? Then your next one will be an angel. No one gets two screamers."

My friend Kim said, "My first was a nightmare baby, screaming from the moment he woke up. But the second was a dream, a Buddha baby."

Another friend said that her first was a dream and her second, three months in hell.

"But I guess that's the way it goes—you get one easy and one hard," she said.

I don't go in for maternal prognostications. I never thought, when I was pregnant, that being shaped like the bow of a ship meant that my babies would be boys. Even though they ended up being so. I didn't put any stock in the ring-over-the-belly gender-determining test. I didn't believe that it was bad luck to get the baby's room ready.

Mothers go crazy predicting all sorts of things about the fetuses that lie oblivious in others' bellies. They combine old spells with New Age witchery. Balsamic vinegar will make you go into labor. Having sex late in your ovulation cycle will produce a girl.

Late in my pregnancy it seemed pretty clear to me that all this voodoo on the part of mothers is an attempt to exert some kind of control over that which is cosmically uncontrollable.

I am not like these mothers. It's all a bunch of hooey.

Except for the bit about not getting two screamers in a row. That makes solid sense. If there is a compassionate God, surely He is not so cruel as to send consecutive screamers to an innocent mother.

Five weeks after Murphy's birth I put him in the stroller, screaming like he's on fire. I've fed him, changed him, burped him, rocked him, and checked to see if anything's poking him. Everything's fine except for the nonstop screaming. When Spence used to scream like this, I'd become paralyzed with anxiety and helplessness. With Murph I've become practical. I figure the screaming is idiopathic. And I manage to move through the days with my screaming companion, accomplishing most simple tasks, with resignation and faith that it will all turn out as well as it did with Spence.

I push Murph in the stroller, howling, to the preschool to pick up Spence. He screams down the street, he screams in the 7-Eleven as I buy a soda, he screams as I open the gate to the pre-school. He continues screaming as I check the family folder for announcements and Spence's artwork. I pick him up and bounce him, screaming, as I look for Spence on the playground.

Spence hears us coming, turns, and waves.

Barbara, the teacher, appears beside me.

"Sounds like something's poking him," she says.

"I've checked," I say. "Nothing's wrong. He's just a screamer.

Spence was a screamer in the beginning. At about four months it stopped."

"Usually, you don't get two screamers," she says.

"Well, I did," I say.

My back stiffens as Murph continues his ceaseless wail. My sane self knows not to hear accusation in her pronouncement. But that's difficult. It's hard not to hear, "What egregious sins have you committed in the past that God would send you not one, but two screamers."

Barbara stares hard at Murph wailing.

"That's not normal screaming," she says. "It sounds like something is really wrong with him."

I shift Murph to the other shoulder to give my left ear a break.

"No," I say above the noise. "Nothing wrong. He's just a screamer."

A month later I stand on the same playground talking to Mako, a Japanese American woman married to a Jewish man. Mako is a first-class overachieving mom. She speaks only Japanese to her trilingual child. At the preschool this year she has taught units on Hanukkah, American birds, and germs. For school potlucks she makes sushi rolls from scratch.

Mako and I have had our second children around the same time. We bring them to school occasionally and jiggle them on our shoulders as we watch our preschoolers show off.

"Is Murphy napping yet?" Mako asks, glancing at Murph, whose usual screaming isn't at full volume right now..

I can only hope that she knows that the cloud of passed gas I move around in emanates from Murphy and not me. I keep meaning to ask the pediatrician about it. How much gas can one infant pass? Is this normal? I sure as hell am not asking Mako. I think of Pigpen in the Peanuts cartoon. My second screamer with little wavy lines coming off of him.

"Not really," I say, swaying Murphy as he moans, mostly to break up his unpleasant bouquet.

"Really?" she says.

"He doesn't really sleep much during the day. I mean, he'll nod off, but as soon as he senses me relaxing, he fires up and screams like I just chopped off his finger. You know how it is."

"Wow," she says.

"No biggie," I say. "I just have to stay tense and he's happy."

Murphy's foot jabs the air and an odor rises from him that could kill small insects. I move a couple of feet downwind. Mako moves closer.

"So you have a hard time putting him down?" she asks.

"I can put him down," I say. "He just won't stay down."

"Hmmm," she says. "Have you tried rocking him?"

"Oh, yes." I say. *Have I tried rocking him? Does she think I'm a total idiot?*

"Hmmmm," she says, looking off into the distance as if this is some puzzle to solve. "Have you tried humming?"

"Humming. Yes," I say.

"And he still won't go down?"

"Not with rocking and humming," I say.

"Hmmm," she says. "Have you tried rocking and humming in a dimly lit room?"

Not with the baby, I want to say. Only by myself—after a day of screaming, a couple of cocktails, and a hysterical call to my mother.

"Because if I rock and hum to Kodi in a dimly lit room, he nods right off," she says.

"I think Murphy knows it's a trick," I say. "He's incredibly intuitive."

"I guess that's possible," she says, sniffing the air.

I move again. Mako follows.

"Are you still breast-feeding?" she asks.

"Mostly," I say. "I switch to formula whenever my nipples feel like they've been stapled."

"That's it," says Mako. "That's why he's farting like that. It's the formula."

She turns and walks away, quiet Kodi nestled on her shoulder.

Maybe the gas is connected to the screaming. Maybe Murph is in tremendous gastronomic pain. I stop formula. I give him Mylicon drops. I change my diet. I bounce him, rock him, sing to him. Dim the lights. Nothing works. He rarely sleeps, and if he's awake, he's screaming, moaning, or making a cranky-old-man sound.

I carry Murphy down to the office of our building to pick up a package. The building manager is a woman named Boo Merlin (you can't make this stuff up), an older woman from New Orleans who came to Los Angeles thirty years ago "because of a man" and never left. She's a mother of six, grandmother of several, and a kid magnet. She beams her Southern smile, opens her sparkly eyes wide, coos at them, and they all come running. Or crawling.

Around Boo, stoned smiles spread across infant babies' faces like they're mainlining. Everyone's baby but mine.

Murphy wails on my shoulder as I reach for my package.

"Does he always do that?" Boo asks.

"Scream?"

"Yes. That," she says. "It sounds like something's wrong."

"Not that I can tell," I say loudly, sitting across from her, Murph still going strong.

She tilts back in her chair to get the clipboard I have to sign to get my package.

"Maybe he's hungry," she says.

"Just fed him," I say, signing my name.

"Have you tried rocking him?"

"Yup," I say. "No problem, though. Spence was a screamer and he turned out fine."

"No one gets two screamers," she says.

"Guess I'm the exception to the rule."

I'm aware that I've begun to sound defensive, but I can't help myself. Then something in me switches.

"Turns out there are some new studies coming out of Johns Hopkins," I say. *Johns Hopkins? Where did I get that?* "Babies who scream early are significantly brighter, more intuitive, and seem to be immune to certain cancers."

Boo's eyes widen. "Really?"

"Something to do with all that extra oxygen getting to the brain."

Boo stares at Murphy, who passes gas and wiggles, his wailing dialing down to a soft moan.

"I had one screamer and he's my smartest," she says, her gaze contemplative.

"I'm not surprised," I say.

I see gurgling, quiet babies everywhere—peaceful pink-cheeked cherubs, smiling as they lie in their mothers' arms, in strollers, on blankets on the grass. I marvel at these beings who seem to bear no resemblance to the creature I wheel around—his howling so loud as to seem an agonized plea to be released from his earthly existence.

Maybe it's Stockholm syndrome, but I find myself starting to prefer my screamer. Those passive, bland babies, I think to myself—who needs 'em? All they do is lie there. I've got a lusty, full-voiced maniac who lets me know just how he's feeling every second of every day. Aren't I lucky?

I also start to think about robbing banks and changing my name to Tanya.

✳ Friday

✳

✳

Having wanted a second child desperately, I understand what drives Michelle to the sperm bank.

"It's wild," she says. "Sarah and I take home these profiles of sperm donors and discuss the pros and cons of these guys like we're a couple of assholes at a pickup bar."

"You're not going back to China?" asks Lana.

"We might," says Michelle. "But I think I want to try to get pregnant first. I want to know what it feels like. And I love the idea of Sarah's egg and my uterus. Sarah and I had less money when we got Faith. Now we can afford in vitro, so why not give it a whirl?"

She reaches for her Amstel.

"Hey," she says. "We adore Faith. This won't take anything away from her."

I know this is true. Faith is their girl. Their little China doll.

"What are the guys in the profiles like?" asks Katherine, taking her cell out of her purse and putting it on mute.

"Well, Sarah and I have different favorites. I like this black guy who's a musician."

"Oooh, I'm already liking him," says Katherine.

"Oh. Who does he play for?" asks Lana.

"He can't say," says Michelle.

"If you're going to go for a musician, you should find out if he's good," says Lana, who is a rock snob.

I put down my glass. "Michelle said that she *feels* like an asshole in a pickup bar, Lana. She didn't say she'd *become* one."

"I just think she should know if he's any good."

"David Crosby's already given his sperm," I say. "This guy's a musician. That's all we know. It's not like he's going to send a three-song demo along with his sperm sample."

"Who does Sarah like?" asks Katherine.

"She can't choose between this southern trucker dude and a Korean PhD student."

"I know how she feels," says Lana like Groucho.

"She likes the trucker because he seems kind of sweet. He wrote that he likes driving into a sunset and working with his hands."

"Good enough for me," says Katherine, slapping the bar. Who tends to like "rough around the edges" almost as much as she likes black.

"What about the Korean PhD?" I ask Michelle. "What's wrong with that? A smarty pants. What's his PhD in?"

"History. He's doing a dissertation on fourteenth-century farming techniques."

"Wake me when it's over," says Lana.

"Oooh," says Katherine, like she just remembered. "You should go to one of those genius sperm banks."

"I'm not sure what they do with genius sperm. I'm not sure that they really give it out. Do they?" says Michelle.

"It probably costs major bucks for genius sperm," says Katherine.

"Jesus, I know some geniuses who might skip the middleman and sell it to you at an extreme discount," I say.

"What geniuses do you know?" Katherine asks me.

I have to think about that.

"I'm a genius," says Lana, putting down her tall glass of bourbon and something.

We look at her.

"We're talking about geniuses *with sperm,*" says Michelle.

"I thought we were moving on."

"To you being a genius?" Michelle asks.

"To geniuses that we know. Katherine asked if Brett knew any geniuses. And she does. *I'm* a genius."

"Your IQ is over 150?" I ask.

Lana's brought up being a genius before. But I wonder what that actually means. Is it simply her own assessment? Or a solid IQ number?

"Oh, sure, I'm like 160 or something," says Lana. "It's no big deal. I'm not saying it like 'Hey, you guys, check me out. I'm a fucking genius.' I'm saying it like 'Your garden-variety geniuses are out there. We're your neighbors, your teachers, your garbage collectors. More people are geniuses than you think.' "

"So your point is," I say, trying to get back on track, "that genius sperm is less rare than we think, and therefore shouldn't have to cost so much?"

"No," says Lana, picking up her drink and smiling, "I'm just saying that I'm a genius."

Something in me rankles. I know that Lana is just playing around. But she's hit something in me—probably intellectual insecurity. Something I rarely experience, except around her and a handful of other friends.

I take a sip of wine. "I'm amazed at how often you can work your genius status into a conversation."

"When have I talked about it before?"

"When we were talking about schools and you said you hated school as a kid because you were a genius and you were bored."

"Okay," she says, her voice hard. "But the fact that I am a genius was particularly relevant to that conversation. Which I don't remember having, by the way."

Yes, you do, I want to scream. You always say you don't remember when it's something you don't want to cop to. I feel my neck tighten.

Lana pulls up in her barstool.

Michelle breaks in. "All right. All right. I don't know how we got onto this. But can we get back to my sperm?"

Lana and I glare at each other. My eyes sting.

Glare.

Then Lana switches. Just like that. Her face goes soft and she turns to Michelle.

"Sure," she says. "I think your best bet is the southern trucker dude."

"But he smoked for ten years . . ."

I hear the conversation, my face flush with feeling.

That's the thing about Lana. She'll take you everywhere—laughter, frustration, pride, anger, compassion, envy.

And even though I'm still hot from the ride, I figure it's better than going nowhere at all.

✳ Faking It

I **stand in front of a bulletin board** at the preschool staring at handwritten signs that say "DON'T FORGET to dress your kid in red for Red Day" and "Parents—Please Please Please sign your last name too when signing your kid out—IT'S THE LAW." Next to the cleanup schedule, I spot a new sign that says "IMPORTANT!! BY FRIDAY PLEASE BRING WASHED ½ GALLON CONTAINER OF JUICE OR MILK."

My pulse quickens as I reread the sign about the half-gallon container. I don't know what a half-gallon container of juice looks like and I'm too embarrassed to ask. I get juice, but I don't look at the amount or at the kind of container it comes in. There's the thin kind, the middle kind, and the big one. Obviously, I could just check out the labels at the grocery store. But I could still bring the wrong kind of container. The sign doesn't specify what kind. And washed? How?

The casual scrawl on the sign, the dashed-off crayon note, seems to indicate that, of course, we all know what we're talking about here. "We"—the parents. "We"—who are familiar with children's crafts.

Jesus, I think, getting the information I need is going to take some finessing. I'm going to have to fake it again.

Like all shy people, I am a relatively deft "faker." Faking being worlds away from actual lying—something I'm not that good at. Faking is implication. It's a subtle inference. It's manipulation. Lying takes bravery. Lying takes cunning. I am neither brave nor cunning.

Coming right out and admitting my ignorance is not an option. First, because it might require a longer conversation. But more profoundly, because I am a survivor of childhood ridicule for my naïveté.

Kevin, a career stay-at-home dad, walks up to me as I stand in front of the bulletin board, considering my strategy.

"Are you all right?" he asks.

I rearrange my face.

"Yes, yes," I say.

"You look sick," he says.

"It's nothing."

I smile and decide to take this head-on.

"So, Kevin," I say, "did you see this sign about the juice container?"

"Mmmm."

I cock my head in what I hope is a casual manner. "What kind of container are you going to bring?" I ask, pointing to the sign.

Kevin shrugs. "I guess whichever one is empty first," he says.

"That's what I was thinking," I say. "Thing is, Kevin, there are no containers in my refrigerator right now. So I'm going to have to go out and buy one. And I'm just thinking about what to buy."

Is Kevin squinting because of the sun? I can't tell.

"Are you asking me what to buy?" he asks.

"Of course not!" I say with what I hope sounds like a friendly scoff. "I'm just thinking out loud here. Should I get the carton container or the plastic one?"

"It's not going to work with the plastic one," he says.

Aha! It's a carton. But what's *not going to work?*

I give a thoughtful look.

"Hmmm. Yes. You have a point there. I guess I'll get the carton, then."

Kevin looks at the ground, then turns to leave.

I say a little louder, "Carton, yes. But what will I do with all that juice?"

He turns back. "Drink it?"

"That's a lot of juice between now and Friday," I say.

"I suppose you could throw out whatever's left," he says, "Or keep it in a jar."

"But I'm wondering," I go on, sure that this tack will reveal the answers without tipping my hand. "Let's say I put the juice in a jar. Then, I'm thinking, do I destroy the integrity of the carton by ripping open the top to clean it? Or do I just pour water in the spout and swish it around? And I'm wondering about whether I should use liquid soap or something stronger."

"Stronger?"

"Something like Lysol?" I say, flipping it off like it just popped into my head.

Kevin's face screws up.

"Brett," he says in a different, slower voice, "just rip open the top of the carton and rinse it out. They're going to cut it in half anyway, to make Easter baskets."

Aha, I think, that's what the cartons are for—Easter baskets.

"See, there you are," I say. "All along I was thinking that the cartons were going to be birdhouses."

"Friday's the Easter egg hunt," he says.

"Right," I say, waving my hand at him like, "Of course, of course."

I have to stop faking. It's too stressful. Lately, I've been faking way over my head. As a fake mom-about-school, I'm not polished. But when it comes to my burgeoning writing career, my faking has been far more effective. I'm going to have to come clean soon, though. As I'm afraid that I'll fake my way into a position of real authority, ordering around a staff of six people while having no clue about what I'm actually doing.

Pat says that everyone is faking. He says that no one knows what they're doing. But I find it difficult to believe that everyone is walking around in as high a state of ignorance as me. Someone must know what they're doing, because things work. Things get done. The doctors who separated Siamese twins a year ago look like they had a good handle on things, since the twins now walk around independently like they never shared a rib cage. I've got to assume that the guy who designed the Eiffel Tower was pretty clued in, because I've seen it and, guess what, it's still standing. Even my ant man knows what he's doing. I know, because I no longer have ants. And I no longer need my ant man.

I've gotten a couple of writing jobs lately. And so far, I haven't had to actually produce anything. Which makes faking easier, but also makes my modest success all the more mystifying.

A month before Murph was born, a man named Randy Foster introduced himself to me after seeing a show that I was in. The evening featured a bunch of authors reading true stories about their lives, and I had just read a piece I wrote about my miscarriage.

Randy shook my hand vigorously and told me that he liked my writing. He was producing made-for-TV movies, he said. I told him that I thought I might want to write a made-for-TV movie.

At this point I was looking to write anything that people might pay me for. With a second baby coming, Pat and I were more concerned about money than we had ever been.

Later that week I met Randy for lunch. He talked so fast I thought he might be high. He jabbered about Movies of the Week, his big triumph being *The Baby Jessica Story,* which had been produced over a decade ago. He said he was proud as hell of how he had made the movie about all the people in the town, not just about the kid in the well.

Because, he said, "Really, how much can you say about a toddler stuck in a well? That gets boring fast."

I nodded through the lunch and left with no deeper understanding of how to get paid for writing Movies of the Week.

In the days that followed I became preoccupied with complaining about my pregnancy and I pretty much forgot about Randy. Until he called a month after Murph was born. The Movie of the Week business was slowing down for him, he said.

"I was pretty sure I was going to get the rights to the Andrea Yates story," he said. "The postpartum chick who drowned her kids? But her husband went with some Christian producer."

"Too bad," I said, laying Murphy in his crib.

"I had a great take on it too. I was gong to separate each scene with a slo-mo drowning of another kid."

"Mmmmm," I said, closing the door softly.

"The oldest kid, I guess, saw the whole thing."

"I heard," I say.

"Great fucking story. Everyone in town wanted it."

"Too bad."

"Not getting that story was a real blow. So I said to myself, 'Go back to your roots, Randy. You're an ad man.' "

"Great."

"Right. So I'm sitting here at this company and I've got this whole campaign and I'm thinking, Who will make me look smart? And I remembered you. Have you ever written copy?"

I wasn't sure what copy was. Not really. I had a general idea that it was advertising content, but that was about it.

"I'm familiar," I said, a faker's phrase that means nothing.

"Great. Can you come in here in about an hour? I've got some stuff to throw at you."

"Ah. Well, my baby."

"Right. What's your rate?"

"Rate. Um, well. It depends on the job."

"How's three hundred a day sound?"

Like a slice of heaven, I think. Like Christmas in August. Like a merlot buzz without the hangover.

"Well, we can start there," I said.

Pat, with the boys in the back of the car, dropped me off at a mirrored black high-rise. I walked up the wide stairs to the entrance, already spending all that money I was going to make.

I found Randy in his glass box of an office.

"Come on in," he said, pointing to a yellow bucket chair that looked hard to get out of. "Have a seat."

I dropped my backpack on the floor and folded into the chair.

"How's the writing going?" he asked.

"Um. Great," I faked. I hadn't written a word since Murphy's birth.

We swapped a few sentences about our kids, then fell silent

while Randy looked at me like I was a piece of furniture he had yet to place.

After a skip in time Randy jerked, swiveling around in his chair to pop a videocassette into a TV behind his desk.

"So here's how you can make me look brilliant," he said, rewinding the cassette.

I shifted as much as I could in the yellow bucket. The tops of my legs felt achy. I couldn't imagine how I was going to make him look brilliant. But for three hundred dollars a day I was willing to try. I thought of the new rug that I planned on buying for the boys' room. One that would cover up the apple juice stains on the wall-to-wall carpet.

He paused the tape at the top and swiveled back to face me.

"I'm working on this ad campaign for a show called *The Insider*. It's a show that's going to follow *Entertainment Tonight*."

He leaned forward.

"After *Entertainment Tonight* does its half hour of celebrity news, *The Insider* will come on and give you the real scoop about the stars."

I was already confused. Didn't *Entertainment Tonight* already give you the scoop about the stars? Were we going to get the first scoop and then an even deeper scoop right after it?

"The idea," said Randy, swiveling to grab his remote, "is that you—the viewer—are getting the inside information."

He aimed the remote and I turned my attention to the TV. Stamp-sized pictures of famous people popped up on the screen. A red line started to connect one stamp-sized picture to another and then another, while a voice said something like "The stars are all connected. Winona Ryder dated Johnny Depp, who dated Kate Moss, who dated . . ." After a minute of red lines running between the stars, the grid exploded under the voice shouting,

"You've heard that there are six degrees of separation. Now there's *no* degree of sep-o-ration."

When the ad ended and Randy turned off the TV, my ears buzzed.

"What do you think?" he asked.

I had no idea of what to say.

"Great," I said, thinking of the pricey haircut I was going to get with the first check.

"That's what I think," he said. " 'Now there's no degree of sep-aration' was mine."

As he said this, I was grateful that I hadn't asked what it meant, which had been my first impulse. Did it mean that there were *no* people between you and these stars? Surely, that made no sense. Everyone knows that the paparazzi, a publicist, and an entire culture of star fuckers stand between you and any particular star. I mean, unless you *are* Winona Ryder or sleep with Winona Ryder, how can you be no degrees away from her?

Randy swiveled to pop the cassette out of the TV.

I started to wonder just how I was going to make him look brilliant. Did he want me to write mini-bios on each star? Maybe he thought that I knew some of these stars personally. That I was a no-degrees person. This was Hollywood, after all. Maybe he thought there was no degree of separation between me and Brad Pitt. Maybe he thought that I could give him information that was more inside than the inside information he currently had. Shit. Why didn't I know any famous people? I saw three hundred dollars a day turn to sand sifting through my fingers. I saw myself hacking away at my own hair in front of the bathroom mirror while the boys played on the stained, tattered carpet in their bedroom.

"I call these grids of stars connectivities," he said.

"Oh," I said. "Because of the connectedness of the stars."

What? I didn't understand what I'd just said. Was "connectedness" a word?

"See," he said. "I knew you were the right person for the job."

What job?

"Connectivities," he said.

"The grids?"

"Just shoot me a couple of them a day," he said.

"I can do that," I said, thinking of the window fan I'd buy for the living room.

For the next couple of weeks I bought tabloid magazines and drew grids over everything—napkins, books, paper towels. Discarded grids littered the house, making it look like I was engaged in some top-secret code-breaking enterprise for the government. I sent Randy my grids at the end of each day. As far as I could tell, it was work any assistant could do. Some of the ways I found to connect stars were ridiculously simple. After I turned in a grid of six stars connected only by the fact that they'd all been to the same Starbucks, I felt sure he'd fire my lame ass. But no. He kept telling me that I was making him look brilliant, and I kept billing him for three hundred dollars a day. Who was I to quibble? The boys had a new rug, the window fan was top-notch, and I looked fantastic.

It did occur to me that Randy might also be a faker, delighted and terrified that some exec had gone for "no degree of sep-o-ration," a phrase he'd scrawled on a damp beverage napkin after his sixth apple martini and half a quaalude, slipped to him by a drunk girl who wanted to write ad copy and had always thought that the phrase would fuckin' sell a whole damn show.

I never saw *The Insider* and I doubt that any of my grids ever made it on. Each time Randy went over them with me, he'd make his own adjustments. I didn't mind. I didn't feel remotely attached to my work, since I never really understood what I was doing. Were these grids for the actual show? Was Randy running these grids by other people, claiming them as his own? Were these practice grids?

The checks came with the memo "For writing services."

But I hadn't written a thing.

Faking leads to more faking. I add to my writing résumé that I've written ad copy, because that's what Randy says my grids are. A magazine accepts one of my stories and upon reviewing my résumé, an editor asks if I would like to do a celebrity interview.

"Sure" I say, even though all I know about Natalie Maines is that she's a Dixie Chick and that she said something about Bush and Texas that pissed off her fan base.

The editor goes on to tell me that I'll interview her while she's being prepped for a photo shoot. He says that I'll have to turn the interview around in five days. So I don't have to bother writing anything. I can just transcribe my questions and Natalie's answers.

Perfect, I think. Another writing job that requires no writing.

I cram my head full of information about Natalie for the next two days. I listen to her music, I research her on the Internet. I memorize the names of her husband and her children.

It occurs to me that I need some kick-ass piece of recording equipment so that I don't miss a thing. I can't ask the magazine how they record stuff because I don't want them to know that I've never done this.

Pat says he'll take care of it. The night before the interview he hands me a small metallic box with holes on one end of it that he got from RadioShack. He says that it's a digital recorder and all I have to do is speak directly into it and it will record everything digitally. He seems to think that recording digitally, rather than on a tape, will reduce chances of something going wrong.

"So I have to speak into the end of this," I say, holding the metal thing in front of my mouth like I'm a TV reporter. "And then I direct it over to her as she answers?"

"Ideally," says Pat, looking at the back of the box it came in, "the closer you get the microphone to her, the better."

"I think that's going to make her feel self-conscious, Pat. I can't stick this all up into her face. I pictured a tape-recorder thing that I put on the table between us. I need to look like a professional."

"How does a professional look?"

"Like what you see on TV. A girl in a short skirt who puts a recording thing on a table and asks the star questions while the star gets a manicure."

"It'll be fine. Just stick it up like this," he says, standing the metal thing on its end. "And lean into it to speak."

Pat says this while bending his head down to the table, his mouth inches away from the digital box.

I can't sleep that night. My neck seizes with anxiety. Why did I say I'd do this? I can barely speak to a stranger under normal circumstances. Now I have to speak to a *famous* stranger while thousands of dollars are being spent by the magazine to set up her fancy photo shoot.

The next day Pat and the boys drop me off at the gate of a Hollywood-mansion-for-hire. When I meet Natalie, I steady my voice as I introduce myself as the "journalist who's writing your celebrity bio piece that's for publication in the next publication of the magazine." I sound like a six-year-old playing dress-up.

Stylists and manager types create a general hub as Natalie and I are ushered into a cool slate-gray room with a fountain. White towels and robes everywhere. It looks like a meditation/after your shower/pamper room.

We sit at a low concrete table.

I have no idea if Natalie thinks it unusual that I prop the silver recording device up on a bunch of towels, pointing it toward her neck. That's as high as I can get it without disappearing behind the towel mountain. My too-short skirt cuts into my thighs as I peer at her over the mound. I barely hear her answers over my inner voice repeating the phrase "I want to go home, I want to go home, I want to go home" like the chug of a train.

Somehow the whole thing ends and I'm shaking hands with a crew of black-outfitted stylists as Natalie is whisked off for a mani/pedi.

When I get home, I discover that the recording of the interview is barely audible. Pat labors over the transcription as I curl into a tense knot on the bed. He says no sweat, he'll retrieve as much as he can and just type xxxxxxxxxxxx when he can't hear what's being said on the tape. I get up from the bed occasionally to look over his shoulder, cringing as I see blocks of xxxxxxxxxxxxxxxxxxxxxxxxxxxxxxxxxxxxxxxxxxxxxxxxxxxxx xxxxxxxxxxxxxxxxxxxxxxxxxxxxxxxxxxxxxxxxxxxxxxxxxxxxx xxxxxxxxxxxxxxxxxxxxxxxxxxxxxxxxxxxxxxxxxxxxxxxx.

When Pat hands me the whole transcription, I burst into tears:

BRETT: How do you feel now about the backlash you got from your fans concerning xxxxxxxxxxxx Bush xxxxxxxxxxxx. It must xxxxxxxxxxxx [*Note from Pat: There's something here that sounds like "France and what Democrats eat when it rains"—does that mean anything to you?*] xxxxxxxxxxxxxxxxxxxxxxxxx.

NATALIE: I'm glad you asked that. The thing you can't ever say is that [*twenty? renting? sent?*] xxxxxxxxxxxxxxxxxxxxxxxxx

which tells you why more xxxxxxxxxxxxxxxxxxxxxxxxxxx
xxxxxxxxxxxxxxxxxxxxxxxxxxxxxxxxxxxxxxxxxxxxxxxxxxxxx
xxxxxxxxxxxxxxxxxxxxxxxxxxxxxxxxxxxxxxxxxxxxxxxxxxxxxx
xxxxxxxxxxxxxxxxxxxxxxxxxxx it's a real problem.

BRETT: But that doesn't mean you xxxxxxxxxxxxxxxxxxxxx
xxx for what it's worth?

NATALIE: You couldn't be more xxxxxxxxxxxxxxxxxxxxxxxxx
xxxxxxxxxxxxxxxxxxxxxxxxxxxxxxxxxxxxxxxxxxxxxxxxxxxxx
xxxxxxxxxxxxxxxxxxxxxxxxxxxxxxx but that's how much xxxxx
xxxxxxxxxxxxxxxxxxxxxxxxxxxxxxxxxxxxxxxxxxxxxxxxxx.

BRETT: I'm glad you said xxxxxxxxxxxxxxxxxxxxxxxxxx. It's
hard to find xxxxxxxxxxxxxxxxxxxxxxxxxxxxxxxxxxxxxxxx.

NATALIE: Some people say what the xxxxxxxxxxxxxxxxxxxxxx
xxxxxxxxxxxxxxxxxxxxxxxxxxxxxxxxxxxx country great xxxxxxx
xxxxxxxxxxxxxxxxxxxxxxxxxxxxxxxxxxxxxxxxxxxxxxx sticky
xxxxxxxxxxxxxxxxxxxxxxxxxxxxxxxxxxxxxxxxxxxxxxxxxxxxx
xxxxxxxxxxxxxxxxxxxxxxxxxxxxxxxxxxxxxxxxxxxxxxxxxxxxx
you can tell by looking at them.

After screaming at Pat that it's impossible to create something out of this gobbledygook—I'm going to be exposed as a faker, sued by the magazine, and vilified by a Dixie Chick—I manage to piece together something from my memory and from bits of transcription that reveal themselves like amateur sculpture from stone.

"Do you have any more?" asks the editor when he reads the shreds of my interview.

"That's all I've got," I say, my shoulders aching with the strain of possible discovery.

The editor breathes out audibly.

I grip the phone, sweat pooling in between my palm and the receiver.

"God, I wish you had more," he says. " 'Cause it's so damned good."

Maybe Pat's right. Maybe I'm faking it no more than any other average Joe. I know only that as I fake my way through the outside world, the difference between that and the world I share with my family becomes cavernous as a geographical divide.

"What's that?" says Spence, pointing to a thin gelatinous thing on the sidewalk.

As I look closer, the thing appears to move in a zillion different directions.

"I guess it's ants eating a dead worm," I say.

"How do you know the worm is dead?"

"I'm just guessing."

"What's it like to be dead?"

"I don't know. I've never been dead."

"Aunt Jo is dead."

"Yes. She's dead."

"Will I ever die?"

Can't fake through this one.

"We all die," I say, knowing that there is only the truth of it. "But you don't have to worry about that for a really, really long time."

Make me right, I say to myself. I say to God.

Make me true.

Kindergarten
* Fever
✳
✳

"**What I'm giving you here**," says Jerri Regan, handing a stack of papers to a mom, "is a timeline of things you need to do to get your kid into a school that you're happy with."

A group of us, parents from Carter Preschool, sit on foldout chairs in the living room of Jerri's yellow house. I sip red wine as I watch each parent take a stapled set of papers and pass the rest on. Jerri smiles at the process. This year not only is she chairperson of the Yearbook Committee, but she is also chair of Purchasing (the committee that buys stuff for the school). She is also vice-chair of the Ways and Means Committee. And now she's taken on the Kindergarten Committee chair. For someone like me, who likes to slide by with as few expectations heaped on her as possible, Jerri is a mystery. Why would a person go out of their way to grab responsibility for things no one will ever appreciate? It seems positively psychotic.

I hadn't anticipated attending a "kindergarten strategy meeting," as I've refused to involve myself in the citywide kindergarten panic that happens every year around this time. Most of the public schools in Los Angeles are spectacularly bad, so parents of a certain socio-economic level educate themselves about the system, figuring out ways to land their child in one of the few decent public schools peppered around the city. I've come to this meeting to listen, even though I'm resigned to Spence's attending our local public school if only for kindergarten. I figure I owe it to Spence to be knowl-edgeable about this stuff. Also, someone said there'd be free wine and snacks.

I take a set of papers and pass the rest to Marie.

"I don't need these," she says, "I wrote them."

Marie, our Membership chair emeritus, hasn't been around this year, as her twins graduated from Carter Preschool last year. They now attend "Neighborhood School," a popular magnet. Marie has come to the meeting to tell us how she got them in. She is our suc-cess story, a mom who worked the system and hit the kindergarten jackpot.

"First," says Jerri, "I'd like to thank Marie for coming to the meeting and sharing her story about how she got the twins into a great kindergarten."

Jerri gestures to Marie, who stands. We all clap. Marie looks like she's dressed for the opera. A woman who is no stranger to surgical upkeep, her tennis-ball-shaped breasts look dangerously close to bouncing out of her dress.

"Thank you, everyone," Marie says. "The papers you have in your hand are your lifeline to finding a great school. Don't lose them."

She looks out at us gravely.

She seems ready to continue, but Jerri cuts in, "We'll be hear-ing from Marie soon."

Marie frowns, yanks up her bodice on one side, and sits.

"Let's all look at the first page," says Jerri.

Everyone shifts as attention turns to the papers. I look at mine—a sort of chart. What a pain in the ass. I hate charts. Although I am a reasonably bright woman, I can't understand charts or instruction booklets for anything. Hand me a manual and I simply shut down.

I look at the paper in my hand, a Rosetta stone of instructions for getting my son into kindergarten.

"This page shows the due dates for various applications. Now, everyone here has already filled out paperwork for their local school. That's the first thing you do."

What paperwork? I didn't know this. I thought that a couple of weeks before school started, you showed up with a birth certificate and that would be that. Is it possible that Spence won't get into any kindergarten at all? Is that legal? I can't imagine that Spence would be denied kindergarten simply because I missed a deadline. On the other hand, I should allow for the possibility that this kindergarten panic is born out of a very real Bureaucratic Threat. It is wise for me to pause long enough to consider that other parents know more than I do, since this has often been the case. My jaw begins to feel tight as I listen to Jerri with determined concentration.

"While you were at your school," Jerri continues, "you should have picked up one of these." She holds up a booklet. "It's a book called *Choices,* and it lists all the magnets in the city."

I scramble in my backpack for a pen. Why wasn't I better prepared? I fish around till I find an eyeliner. I slip off the cap and write "Choices" on the back of my papers in a crumbly black scrawl.

"Now, on the second page of the papers I gave you, you'll find a list of the magnets that are in the book."

Then why do I need the damn book? I think, tossing the eyeliner on the table and reaching for my glass of wine.

"Magnets are schools that you apply for. People with the highest number of points get in, then there's a lottery. You get points in various ways."

Points? I put down the glass and pick up the eyeliner again to scribble "Points."

"You get points if you're any race other than white."

I look around at all the disappointed white faces in the room. Our one Hispanic dad giggles as he writes something down.

"You get points if you're in a school district that's overcrowded."

I jot down "Overcrow—" before the tip of the eyeliner breaks off, splintering down to Jerri's carpet. I know I should pick up the shards rather than let them get ground into her carpet. But I'm afraid I'll miss a key point. I resolve to pick them up later.

"And you get 'waiting list' points," says Jerri.

Marie pounds the table with her fist. "Those are the points you're after, folks!"

The wine in my glass jiggles.

Jerri holds up her hand. "We'll get to you in a minute, Marie."

I look back at Marie, who appears to be chomping at the bit to get into this. She's been bobbing up and down in her chair since the meeting started. Last year Marie's passion for the Membership Committee at Carter Preschool shone in her eyes at every parent meeting. I imagine that coming back to the kindergarten meeting this year offers her an opportunity to relive her glory days.

I lean over and whisper to her, "Do you know if Darwin School is considered overcrowded?"

She rolls her eyes.

"Not technically," she whispers back. "You don't get any points for it, even though it's crowded enough that kids have to share textbooks."

I tense, imagining Spence sitting on a floor, sharing a tattered textbook with two unwashed children.

Jerri's voice gets louder. "You get four points each time you don't get into a magnet school. So apply to one this year. Even if you don't get in, you'll get four 'waiting list' points you can apply to the points you get the next year."

"The twins got into Neighborhood School with only four points!" says Marie.

A murmur ripples through the group. I'm not following this whole waiting list conversation too well. How do people "wait" if their child is supposed to go to kindergarten that year?

Jerri talks above the buzz. "Hold on, folks. We'll hear from Marie in a few seconds. Let's get through the chart first."

A mom stands up and asks Marie, "The twins got in with only four points?"

A father in the back yells, "No one gets in with just four points!"

Jerri watches the group turn toward Marie like a many-headed organism. It's clear that Jerri has lost whatever tenuous command she had over the meeting. Marie is the star, and the slump of Jerri's shoulders shows her resignation.

"All right," says Jerri, her voice weary. "Why don't we hear from Marie? She's already been through the process."

Jerri plops into an armchair. Someone hands her a glass of wine.

Marie jumps up.

The eyeliner is in my hand. At this point I, too, want to hear all about how the twins got in with only four points.

"I put the twins on the waiting list for Neighborhood School *two years* ago!" she says, her eyes shiny. "I put them on the list even though I knew I was going to keep them in preschool an extra year. That way they graduated with four points each in their pockets!"

"Let me get this straight," says a mom. "The twins got in with just four points?"

"I'm here to tell you," says Marie.

People start leaning over to each other, talking excitedly, flipping pages. Marie's twins getting in with only four points seems to be such miraculous news that the parents can barely comprehend it. Awed as shepherds the night of the Nativity, they whisper repeatedly, "Four points."

Someone yells, "I thought you had to have at least eight points to get into a magnet!"

I've never heard of these points until tonight, but the kinetic thrill in the room makes me want points. As many as I can get.

"I heard eight too. But it's a myth. You can do it with four," Marie says above the din. "Get on a waiting list and sit the year out!"

I screw the remaining tip of my eyeliner into position and write "Waiting list," circling it several times. The renewed tip cracks apart on the paper again, sending more minuscule shards to Jerri's carpet. I tuck my legs in.

"And Neighborhood School is fantastic," says Marie. "The twins are flourishing. They're working above grade level and they both play the flute already."

Two moms clap.

"I've brought some handouts on the school," says Marie.

She throws a stack of papers on the table. Parents get up from their seats, reaching across and over each other to grab one. I duck under the arms to snatch one before they disappear.

Marie's voice rises above the melee. "Neighborhood School works on a constructivist model. The school says that it's respect-based and completely child-centric."

I throw the eyeliner into my backpack, grab Marie's pen, and write down "Child-centric." Though I'm a tad confused. I imagine *all* schools would say that they're child-centric. What else would they say they center around? I can't imagine a school saying that they're "completely teacher-centric and shame-based."

A mom's hand shoots up.

Marie spots her, points at her, and yells to the group, "Here's a question."

The mother puts her hand down and mumbles something.

"I can't hear you," says Marie.

"Tell her to stand up," says Jerri, pouring herself another glass of wine. "Everyone has to stand up when they speak."

"Right," says Marie.

The mother stands and says a little louder, "I've heard that the kids at Neighborhood School squeeze their own juice for lunch."

Marie nods as the parents shift, emitting a low rumble.

Another hand pops up, Marie points.

The mother stands. "I heard that all the kids make quilts out of silk-screened pictures of their families!"

Another mom jumps up and blurts out, "A friend of mine's boy goes to Neighborhood School and she says that he can order from a menu in German, Japanese, and Spanish."

Jerri yells with a slight slur, "Wait for Marish to call on you!"

The offending mom's face falls.

"I'm sorry," she says, turning to Jerri. "It's just so exciting."

Marie raises her arms in the air like someone ordained. "Let's all calm down. I can answer all your questions."

The parents settle to a reluctant hush.

"It is true," says Marie, "that the kids squeeze their own juice on Wednesdays, if and *only* if their parents have remembered to send oranges with their kid that day. I can't tell you how many parents forget. Then the kids without oranges have to watch all the other kids squeeze. Parent participation at Neighborhood School is vital. This is not a school that you pack your kid off to and forget about till they fall in the door that afternoon."

I stare at my notes. See, Marie has just described the school I'm looking for. The one where you drop your kid off and assume that he's got a pretty groovy teacher who's going to teach him the basics in a way that's fun and engaging. I can see myself going on a few field trips and attending PTA meetings. But that's about it. I certainly don't want my kid being penalized because I forgot the oranges. I am the sort of parent who forgets oranges.

Marie goes on. "The twins did make quilts this year out of family photos. That's true. We have two of them hanging in our entryway."

"I want one of thosh," slurs Jerri, who's on her fourth glass of wine by my count.

Papers flutter from her lap to the floor.

"And the twins can name most foods in four languages, including 'sign,' " says Marie.

"But you can't even get in the door of Neighborhood School without points!" a voice from the back yells.

"Yes," says Marie, her voice triumphant. "You need points and you need to *convince* the school that you're the kind of parent who's going to be there every day, one hundred percent."

I slide my notes to the center of the table and reach for my wine. Having caught kindergarten fever for two minutes, I have made a full recovery. I'm not getting wrapped up in this point hysteria. I simply don't have room in my life for that kind of anxiety. I'm the sort of person who tenses when I see a list for a potluck event at the school. If I start going crazy for these points, Spence may get into a child-centric school, but his mommy will become one of those characters who never leave their bed, making him mix martinis for her, demanding that he rub her back while she calls her girlfriends and cries.

I flip through the rest of the papers, occasionally looking up, while questions about points and magnets fly.

I think of the chunks of eyeliner at my feet. Although I am tempted, I can't quite leave them there, waiting to become streaks of black at the first touch of someone's shoe. As the conversation rages, I drop to the floor and crawl under the table.

This is how I come to find myself picking specks of black out of a carpet, under a table, avoiding the dance of Marie's feet, at the Carter Preschool kindergarten strategy meeting.

And while I've got plenty of stories that end with me under a table, this is the first that doesn't involve a man, a vial, or olives.

✳ Friday

✳

✳

Everything sounds better on a Friday. A plan, a thought, an idea that might lie untended and shriveled in a corner, can spring to life under the careful consideration of friends. Throw in a few drinks and the shriveled idea expands and acquires brilliance. This is the only reason, I think later, that we spent a chunk of time discussing Lana's marriage to Enrico.

"It's fucking perfect," Katherine says to Lana. "He gets his green card and you get some cash, plus a guy who loves kids and will babysit for free."

Babysitting is becoming a huge issue for Lana, as Tony is often MIA. He sometimes sleeps at the house. But since separating from Lana, he often disappears for days like an errant cat.

"What more do you need?" I say, pushing my empty glass to the edge where Mack will see I need another. "It's an awesome idea. An award-winning idea. A solution so stunningly easy that we will marvel, for years to come, that we came up with it in just one afternoon."

"You're forgetting that we've had other truly brilliant ideas," says Michelle, pushing her empty Amstel bottle next to mine.

"This is only one of several remarkable ideas we've had on Fridays. Really. We're a think tank. An informal symposium of problem solvers."

"Remember our idea of starting a line of truly hip pants called Stretch-When-You-Sit?" says Katherine.

"Why didn't we do anything with that idea?" I ask, turning to Michelle. "Weren't you supposed to start the Web site?"

Michelle shrugs as Mack removes the empties.

"Yeah," Lana says to Michelle. "Didn't your dad have Stretch-When-You-Sit pants in the sixties?"

"Only we decided that these would be based on my dad's pants. But made for the woman who usually wears DKNY."

"Right," says Lana.

"That's the kind of idea that we're going to see cropping up a year from now and we're going to kick ourselves that we didn't do anything about it," I say.

"So let's not let the Enrico idea die," says Michelle.

She's right. You've got to get a jump on these things; otherwise someone else will do it and suddenly you're at Enrico's wedding—he's getting married to some other American woman, not Lana, and everyone there is wearing Stretch-When-You-Sit pants. While you're still sitting around with your mom pals on Fridays with nothing but memories and broken dreams.

"Right," I say. "Let's get practical. What do we have to do to get Lana married to Enrico?"

"First we have to ask him if he wants to do it," says Michelle.

"Right," says Katherine. "But that's pretty much a no-brainer. I mean, she's hot, she's smart, funny, and available."

"He's gay," I say. "He's not looking for a real wife."

Katherine looks down at her foamy black and tan. "Yeah, I guess I get so used to doing the big sell on my single friends."

Mack slides a red wine and an Amstel in front of us.

I straighten up. "So someone asks Enrico if he's interested in marrying her."

"We know he's looking for a green card," says Lana.

"Right," says Michelle. "I think he'll go for it. But we do need to ask him. The real question is, what are we looking for in return?"

"Three solid nights of babysitting and two early mornings," I say. "Plus a couple of pickups and drop-offs to day care. That would be for the first four years. Then you could go to two nights a week, one early morning, and one pickup/drop-off for the next eight years."

"Sounds like you've really thought this out," Michelle says to me.

"That sounds a bit steep," says Lana. "How about we go for your plan for the first four years, but trim back to only one night a week the next eight years. And no early morning. I don't want to get piggy."

"Whatever the deal," says Katherine, "it sounds great to me. It's almost worth me kicking Slim out and stealing Enrico right from under you."

"Slim doesn't stay with the kids some nights?" asks Michelle.

"Sure, sometimes. But he's got all these gigs and rehearsals. What am I supposed to do, stomp all over his dreams? I don't do voice-over jobs at night. So that leaves me sitting at home watching *Law & Order* five nights a week. Unless I spring for Enrico—who's now going to be living with Lana. "

"Shit, does he have to live with me?" asks Lana. "He never stops talking."

"Nah, he lives with Genius," I say.

"But they inspect these things. They have people who are like marriage police, who might come by some morning while I'm in bed with someone new. Daisy's watching toons. And my gay husband is nowhere in sight. How's that going to look?"

Michelle starts to peel the label off her Amstel. I tilt my wine-glass to see if the house red sticks.

We think.

"It's risky," says Katherine.

"I don't think so," I say.

"Now that I think about it, I wonder about all the other stuff you have to negotiate. Like what the guys you're dating think. Plus, you're basically living a lie," says Michelle.

We stare at ourselves in the mirror behind the bar.

"I'm just looking for something easy," Lana says to our reflections.

We mumble something like "yeah" back.

Jesus, I bet she's looking for something to be easy. I can't imagine being alone in this. If Pat's home ten minutes late, I start making phone calls to friends, talking in a hyperexcited tone that makes them worry. So they tell me later.

"I don't think that anything having to do with Enrico is easy," says Michelle. "Remember, he got banned from Target for screaming in Customer Service."

"Wait, I don't fault Enrico for that," I say. "They fucked up his friend's wedding registry. She got four Mizrahi lamps."

"Target messes everything up. It's Target," says Michelle. "You start losing it at Target and it's going to be a long, difficult life."

"*I* lose it at Target," says Lana. "I wanted to buy this Graco car seat and this salesgirl tells me that I can't have it because it's the last one in stock. How insane is that? The car seat is sitting right there. I have my hand on it and she says I can't buy it!"

Lana's face is red. And I think, There you have it. Maybe a marriage between Lana and Enrico would be a perfect matching of personalities and needs.

I doubt that it will happen, however. I suspect the idea will go the way of Stretch-When-You-Sit pants.

It simply requires too much effort.

Christmas in Mooresville

Pat's mother lives with her housemate, Eleanor, in a tiny farmhouse that's so idyllic it's like living inside a snow globe. When we visit her in Indiana, at Christmas, we can count on snowflakes drifting onto the fields and neighbors dropping by with nuts they caramelized themselves. Out back, Tiny the pig will snort and eat just about anything Spence offers her with his mittened hand.

At night Pat and I will snuggle under the blankets, listening to our two boys breathing, as they sleep inches away from us. Pat will curl around me, his hand finding my breast. I will brush it aside.

"The children," I'll say.

"They're completely out."

"Your mother."

"She won't hear," he'll say. Even though we could reach the knob of her bedroom door without leaving the pullout sofa.

"I can't relax," I'll say.

He'll pull his hand away and roll onto his back. After a moment of us lying there, I will hear him say in a voice that is both controlled and pouty, "You hate my mother."

This is not true and Pat knows it. But it's Christmastime and this conversation is as much a ritual as opening presents and eating ham.

Last year we had a reprieve. Murphy was born right before Christmas, so our families came to us. But this year, with Spence excited about Santa and snow, and Murph beginning to walk, we have to remount the Midwest tour of relatives. The tour usually involves picking up my father's minivan in Madison, Wisconsin, and driving ourselves to visit folks in Chicago and Indiana.

Pat's mom loves Mooresville. You can walk right into the candy shop on the square, plop your money on the counter, and help yourself to a bag of sweets, even if no one's at the register. Folks are hardworking and don't say much, which seems to be highly regarded. Pat's mom says things like, "That man doesn't talk much, but he works from sunup to sundown with no thoughts but the next day's work ahead of him." Mom Towne loves the country as much as I love cities. To her the country is a place where folks are honest and life uncomplicated. To me the country is where murderers hole up in shacks, boiling skin off the bones of the last old lady they eviscerated. Behind every farmer's smile, Mom Towne sees a stoic, private person. I see a man who keeps his family in a locked basement, requiring them to wear purple robes and call him Most High Prophet.

But every time I visit Mooresville, the murderers and crazies keep pretty much to themselves. Which is a shame. Since that leaves boredom—the silent killer.

*　　*　　*

My mother-in-law and Eleanor lie back in their matching La-Z-Boys, watching a rerun of *Murder, She Wrote*. Eleanor is a large woman who speaks with a strong Indiana twang. "That Jessica is smarter than any of 'em in the room," she says of Angela Lansbury's character.

Pat and I wrap the last of the presents for the boys, who have fallen asleep in Grandma's bed. It's late. It's Christmas Eve. And we are Santa.

I can tell by the robotlike precision of his wrapping that Pat is not entirely here. He has sunk deep into his own mind, a coping mechanism he employs as soon as we cross from Illinois into Indiana. My guess is that he is replaying a football game, thinking about the next series of coins he's going to buy for his collection, or having sex with a stranger.

I'm writing the tags from Santa, careful to misspell Spence's and Murphy's names. For some reason my mother characterized Santa as a bad speller and fellow who liked his glass of wine— which she left out for him next to some cookies. My mother created a Santa that was so real to us, so kind and flawed, that we children believed in him way past the age that it was appropriate. Her elaborate ritual of tracking snow through the living room, leaving reindeer hoofprints on the linoleum, and writing long letters from him had me believing until I was easily twelve. One year I found a few long white hairs caught in the nap of the sofa.

Pat's head pops up like he's coming to.

"I just remembered," he says, "the glass bottle of soda froze in the van and exploded in that back pocket."

"Things are always exploding in the cold," says Eleanor, rocking.

"Right," says Pat. "I've got to go out and get the glass out right now."

"Now?" says his mother. "It's eleven degrees below with the windchill."

She always knows the windchill.

"Yeah, but I don't want to forget and have someone cut their hand," Pat says, grabbing his hat that pulls down over his face, making him look like a rapist.

Something about his eagerness to get out to the car tells me that it's not about the exploded glass.

"I'll go with you," I say, pulling on my boots.

"Sure," says Pat, turning to the two old women in his rapist mask. "We'll get that glass out of there in no time."

I've got weed," says Pat.

We sit in the front of the van, the lights off, shivering.

"How are we going to smoke it?" I ask.

I'm not much of a smoker, to be honest. But back-to-back episodes of *Murder, She Wrote* require desperate measures.

Pat whips a Coke can out of his jacket, grabs a pen from the glove compartment, and punctures the can.

"Bobber gave it to me," he says, referring to a high school buddy of his, who we visited the day before.

"When?" I ask. I'm remembering us opening gifts, listening to Bobber and his wife talk at length about how their fourteen-year-old is driving them senseless dating black boys.

"When he showed me the garage," says Pat, flicking the lighter.

A short flame, then out.

"Oh, yeah," I say. Bobber had taken Pat out to the garage to show him how they were stopping up the holes where the squirrels were coming in.

"It's Bobber's homegrown," Pat says, shaking the lighter.

The flame catches the loose ball of weed settled in the dent Pat made in the can. Pat inhales and hands it to me.

"Do you think Mom and Eleanor can see the flame?" I ask, turning around to look at the farmhouse, Christmas-card-quaint in the sparkling snow.

"They'd have to get out of their La-Z-Boys," says Pat, taking the can back and firing up again.

A shift in mood sneaks up on me. I start to feel warm and silly. I inhale a few more times.

Huddled in the van, Pat and I are like teenagers putting off the end of our date. We giggle and hunch over, hiding from the adults in the house. I am filled with that youthful arrogance that comes from having time and possibilities. An arrogance that has mostly dissolved since having children.

"Do you think Eleanor's hair is a wig?" I ask.

"It just *looks* like a wig," says Pat. He goes on to explain that the wiglike appearance of Eleanor's hair is an aesthetic cultivated by women over sixty in Indiana. Immovable hair is an ideal that his mother has never attained, try as she might, with the pink rollers she takes out of her hair every morning. When we visit, she hands Spence each roller, which he slips into a bag till it's full, then Ziplocs shut.

I take another drag from the Coke can and am filled with love for the little pink rollers and for Eleanor's wig. I love the farmhouse and my mother-in-law and my sons and Christmas. I love Mooresville. I love Pat's face. I love the van and the cold and Tiny the pig.

★   ★   ★

Angela Lansbury is putting together the pieces of the crime as Pat and I stomp back into the house. Mom Towne and Eleanor are riveted. This is Jessica's best thing and she never disappoints.

Pat and I sink to the couch and assess the work ahead of us. Stockings lie only partially stuffed, on the coffee table. A pile of unwrapped toys waits next to the tree. We look at the scissors and tape and tags.

Pat picks up Spencer's stocking, reaches in, and pulls out a big plastic M&M, which contains several of the real things. He breaks the seal with his teeth and pops it open.

"I've seen that episode before," says Eleanor, "but it don't matter."

"It must be about the fourth time I've seen it," says Mom Towne. "And I only realize it when I'm half the way through. That tells you how good a show it is."

I pick up Murphy's stocking and plunge my hand in, hoping to find the other plastic M&M. My hand moves past the tangerine and the super-bouncy ball. *Where the hell is that damn plastic M&M?*

Pat crunches happily beside me.

My hand finds something smooth. I pull it out. It's a plastic egg of Silly Putty. I throw it into the corner of the couch.

Where the fuck is my M&M? I dump the contents of Murphy's stocking on the coffee table. The looked-for green sphere bounces onto the carpet.

"You folks have a bunch of wrapping to do," says Eleanor.

I slide to the floor and crawl around to retrieve the *M&M*. *Aha.* The plastic seal slides off and—pop—I grab the candies and put a fistful into my mouth.

"You sure like those M&M's," says Eleanor.

"Looks like you're going off your diet," says Mom Towne, looking down at me as I kneel on the carpet, gobbling up chocolate. There is pleasure in my mother-in-law's voice. An overeater herself, she encourages complicity.

I have only a few M&M's left and I look to the table to see what else I can pilfer from Murphy's stocking. Pat leans his head back and pours Gummi bears from the bag meant for Spence straight into his mouth. I grab a bag of sugared Gummi worms from the table and rip it open.

"I knew she wouldn't be able to stay on that diet," Mom Towne says to Eleanor. "You can't cut out bread for too long. It'll make you crazy."

I look at Pat slowly putting PEZ candies into a PEZ Spider-Man dispenser. Surely, he doesn't think there's some kind of rule that you have to load the PEZ candies before you can eat them? I watch him push each candy out of Spider-Man's neck. His fingers grab each cube carefully.

I love his fingers. I want them inside me.

Mom Towne pushes herself out of her chair and heads for the kitchen.

"I think I've got a Hershey bar out here somewhere," she says. "If you kids keep eating the boys' candy, they won't have any from Santa."

Santa? Jesus Christ, I'm Santa and I'm eating up all my sons' candy on Christmas Eve. What kind of monster of a mother am I?

"Here it is," says Mom Towne, bringing the chocolate bar into the living room.

I am a hungry monster mother.

I take the Hershey bar and tear it open. Pat crawls over to the wrapping paper, unrolls it, and places a big toy whale on top. As he cuts around the whale, I think of Spencer's recent obsession with deep-sea animals. I think about the nights he and I have pored over ocean books checking out the freaky creatures that live so far down that they have not evolved for millions of years. These creatures create their own light and feed off of bacteria they create themselves. They are sci-fi crablike beings climbing over the boiling-hot surface of underwater volcanoes, burning themselves white as they cling on.

I think about how hard I cling to my men. How painful it is to hold on and how impossible to let go. Someday it will be one of my boys outside in the van. I will be watching *Law & Order,* with Pat beside me. Will I be able to let that boy be? Will I *know* that I am now the grown-up inside the house?

I swallow the last bite of the Hershey bar and look at the whale, contemplating my evolution from baby to child to woman to mother to . . . what? I feel small as a whisper in the tiny farmhouse, in the tiny town, in the great white expanse of snow that goes on forever, under the winking Christmas heavens.

I tell myself that this is why I don't smoke pot. One should not have to think that much while eating chocolate.

✳ Friday

I talked to Katherine on the phone, but I haven't seen her since her mother died. She is the first of our band to lose a mother. Now she's an orphan—a forty-two-year-old orphan, having lost her father five years ago. Michelle, Lana, and I still have both parents. We can only guess at what it feels like to be a parentless child.

"You know that joke," she says, "about there are two kinds of people in the world, those who have children and those who don't?"

"Right," says Lana, "and those who don't, don't know that there are two kinds of people in the world."

"Yeah, well, it applies to having a dead mother too. You don't know what it's like until it happens. You're a different kind of person than you were before."

"I can't imagine life without my mother," I say. "Who will I blame?"

Katherine smiles and puts down her beer. "Oh, that part doesn't change. You can blame a dead mother. It's just a one-way conversation."

"I am not looking forward to the blaming," says Michelle.

"What on earth would Faith blame you for?" I ask.

Michelle cocks her head and says in a teenage voice, "Why am I the only kid in school with lezzie moms?"

"Maybe the other kids will think that lezzie moms are the coolest thing," says Lana. "What about me? Daisy's going to blame me for kicking her father out of the house."

"Not as an adult," I say. "When she's older, she'll know why you're not with Tony."

"Hey, being an adult doesn't mean you're not a child. You're always your mother's child," says Lana.

"Jesus. I know that's true," says Katherine. "But does everything that's true about being a mother have to sound like a line from a greeting card? Speaking of which, I've got a big complaint about sympathy cards."

"Which was your favorite?" I ask, then wonder if I'm being inappropriate.

"None of them. I kept looking for a card that said something like 'Even though your mom was a bitch, we know you miss her. It sucks being alone in the world.' "

"I bet that card would sell like mad," I say.

Lana downs a shot. "Or how about a card that says 'I know you're blaming yourself for every rotten thing you said about your mother. Stop it, now. She loved you anyway.' "

"That's great," says Michelle. "Or how about a card that says 'Even though your mother never accepted you as a Sex-Positive Feminist Dyke, she still loved you, especially when she could forget about that part.' "

I think about the card that would comfort me most after my mother's death. But my mind won't stay there long. I don't want to think about it. And when I do, all I can think about is the word "bereft." Which is an odd-sounding word when you say it over and over again.

The sympathy card conversation gets silly as I flash on my mother standing in our living room after she heard that her mother had died. She had her hand on a chair and she was looking out the window to our balcony. I stood in the doorway, not knowing what to do. We stood like that for a long time. My father also, a little apart from her—standing, waiting. After a while she shifted. Then came her voice. A deep and long wail, "Mamaaaaa."

". . . or a card that says 'Now that your mother's dead, you can stop lying to her,'" Katherine says, laughing, tears shining in her eyes.

We laugh back a release of a laugh. A bigger laugh than is warranted. A laugh that subsides into giggles and eventually sighs.

Then quiet—except for the noise of the bar.

"When my grandmother died," I say, "my mother told me that what she missed most was that she could no longer say to her mother, 'Look, Mom, look what I did. Look at me. Mom . . . look at me.'"

We think.

I wonder if the others are seeing their own children yelling out on a playground, "Look, Mom. Look at me."

I look at Katherine, now soft and teary.

"Yeah," she says. "That's it. I've got no mom to look at me."

* Murphy's Eye

The first time I see green in the corner of Murph's eye, I pick it out with a Kleenex. I don't think about it much, even though it reappears a couple more times that day.

At dinner Pat notices it and says it might be an infection.

This hasn't occurred to me.

He says, "His hands get covered in sticky food and then he rubs his eyes and gets an infection. We really have to keep his hands clean."

Pat says "we," but I hear "you," and my back stiffens.

Pat is the Felix Unger of parenting, wiping our children's chins raw after every drip. I am the casual parent. The one who doesn't mind if chocolate ice cream hardens in the creases of my child's chin. Childhood, I think, is a time when we can be free of care about stains on our shirts and dirt in our hair. Too soon it turns. Too soon we become ashamed of our very humanness—the flaky, smelly fact of ourselves. Live it up, I say. Be sticky.

"I bet it doesn't have anything to do with food on his hands," I say, working to keep my voice even.

Murphy slams his hand into a bowl of peas. Pat jumps up and runs to the kitchen, returning with a washcloth. Murph screams as Pat rubs his hands. Spence covers his ears and starts screaming too.

Lately, scenes like this are frequent. The children screeching, Pat and I snipping at each other.

I want to say, "No. This isn't it. This isn't what I wanted."

The second time I see the telltale green ooze, I'm sitting in a dorm room at Tulane University in New Orleans. Murph and Spence play with straws under the table when Murph looks up at me and there it is.

Pat has taken a job as a guest lecturer, and the children and I have joined him—my having had some romantic notion about being a faculty wife and going to all those parties where professors drink a lot, talk about literature, and fuck each other's wives.

If this faculty does indeed have parties like this, they are keeping it to themselves. It appears that it's not enough for me to feel isolated and purposeless at home; I must drag my children to New Orleans to experience it afresh—in a landscape inhabited by students so beautiful my loins ache with memory.

Days pass as I push Murphy in the stroller through the campus, Spence dragging behind. It's February, but damp heat is omnipresent. The children and I seek one air-conditioned building after another as we make our slow progress toward the Theater Building, where we hook up with Pat after class every day. Pat then takes the children, cranky from the pilgrimage, back to the cinder-block room we all share, while I go somewhere to read.

On this particular day Spence, Murph, and I take the elevator up to the second floor of the Theater Building. The doors slide open, air-conditioning hitting us like a welcome arctic blast. I push the stroller past offices where people glance up from their desks giving polite nods. An older professor moves his elbow— probably to hide the invitation to some literary orgy. I imagine the memo attached to the invitation: "Don't let the new couple know about the orgy. I've talked to the wife, who's intellectually dull and physically soft in all the wrong places."

Pat's office is at the end.

"What's that pus in his eye?" asks Pat, looking at Murph.

"It looks like an eye infection again."

"Dammit. We have to keep his hands clean."

"Kids get eye infections."

"Brett, he's getting food in his eye. We can't keep letting this happen."

"We?"

"I'm just saying we're going to have to pay more attention."

"Fine. *You* take care of them," I say, giving the stroller a shove into the office.

I catch Pat's look (anger? concern?) before striding past Spence toward the elevator. Even as the doors slide open and I step inside, I know I'm behaving badly.

Moments later I sit in a student bar across the street, one that advertises "Blackout Shots," sipping from a mini of white zinfandel. The bartender tells me that it's the only wine available: "Students don't drink wine."

So I sit drinking pink wine, watching young people lean into each other, firm not only in muscle tone but in their belief that they will never grow old.

I could chalk it up to the swampy heat or to the fact that I'm living in one room with three other people or to the fact that I have no one to spend time with outside my tiny family, but the truth is that my blues stem from the most banal of human conditions: I feel unimportant. I feel infinitesimal. I have no sense of where I belong in the universe.

I have to assume that this latest bout of sadness is connected to getting older. Because until recently, I've loved the shape of my life. Having two children feels right. I've been writing a lot. Pat's made a bunch of money on commercials. Until recently, I've thought, is it possible that I might get everything I always wanted?

But something has changed.

Lately, I am frightened. I want to do my life over again. I want to be able to say, "No. I don't want this. This isn't the life I pick. You know that man I said I'd stay true to? You know those children I said I'd raise? I've changed my mind."

I want to say, "No. Thanks, but no. I'm going to do something else."

I sit on the floor of the student clinic. Murph crawls over my knees as Spence flips the pages of a book about reptiles. A few blue-jeaned students stand in front of the counter. A roadblock of a nurse checks them in. Two she sends away.

When the students clear, I pick up Murphy and walk over, Spence following with his open book.

"My son," I say, "has something wrong with his eye."

"Are you a student?" she asks in a sugary Southern drawl.

I start to smile at this possible compliment but quickly realize that it's more condemnation than question. The tone being "Isn't it obvious that you're in the wrong place?"

"My husband is a guest lecturer here and I don't know where else to go."

I consider bursting into tears. I'm close enough to crying, to let loose. But I am dimly aware that as a faculty wife, I should be more together than the students who flop around the waiting room like it's their parents' living room.

The nurse shuffles some papers. "Do you have a med card?"

"A medical card? No. We're only here for a month."

I'm annoyed by the pleading tone in my voice. I try to readjust. I shift Murphy to the other hip.

"Obviously," I say, "this is an emergency. I didn't anticipate needing a med card."

"Mmm" she says, stapling. "We really can't help anyone without a med card."

"I'm not just anyone. My husband works here."

"But how do I know that?" she asks. "You could be anyone."

"I guess that's true," I say, trying my best not to see her as some divine messenger sent to confirm my worst fears that I don't matter. "You can call the Theater Department. I'm sure they'll tell you that my husband's on the faculty."

"Or you could go to the Theater Department yourself," she says, opening a file, "and ask them to apply for a med card."

I feel my face get hot. I pull Murphy further up on my hip.

"By then my son's eye might rot right out of its socket," I say in my meanest voice.

And I'm not sorry.

She lowers the file.

"Have a seat," she says like I'm someone to be managed.

Two hours later I sit on the edge of an examination table, Murph in my lap, while Spencer jumps on and off a chair adding up numbers. "One plus two equals three. Four plus six equals ten." The consideration Murph gets from the doctor has Spence shouting out his greatest talent in order to earn some attention for himself.

I understand this. I want the doctor's attention too. She's a maternal type, wearing practical sandals, a single salt-and-pepper braid fraying down her back.

"He's so cute," she says, leaning in to pull Murph's cheek down from his eye.

"Six plus five is eleven," shouts Spencer.

I wonder if she'd be impressed by the fact that I speak almost fluent German.

She takes a tissue and swipes it under Murphy's eye.

"Little Murphy," she coos.

"Ten plus four is fourteen."

I can ski down an advanced slope.

"It looks like there's an obstruction there," she says.

"Four plus eleven is fifteen."

I can blow concentric smoke rings.

She taps her finger on Murph's nose. "He's such a cooperative baby."

"Ten plus six plus two is eighteen."

I can roll a joint with one hand, keep a secret, and cum again.

She pulls up and walks over to her desk, where she tosses the tissue in the garbage can.

"I'm going to prescribe a topical antibiotic ointment," she says, reaching for a pen, and starting to write. "Also, I want you to put hot compresses on his eye for ten minutes at a time. Will he stand for that?"

"I don't think so," I say.

"Well, give it a try. We have to knock whatever's in there out."

I slide off the examination table with Murph. "Do you think what's in there is food?"

"Ten plus four plus two plus one is . . ."

"Could be," says the doctor.

Shame floods me. I haven't washed his hands enough. Pat was right.

Spence tugs my shirt. "How much is that?"

"What?"

"How much is that?"

"I don't know, Spence."

"Come back if you have any questions," says the doctor, handing me the prescription.

"Thanks," I say, wanting something more. Anything. A look. Forgiveness.

She gives her final "time's up" smile.

No, I think. I don't want to leave yet. But I do. I leave the cool air of the Student Health Center, the prescription already soggy in my hand.

I try a hot compress a couple of times that afternoon, while Pat is still teaching. Each time Murphy screams and shakes his head so that it's impossible to hold it there for any length of time. I remember that the doctor said "give it a try"—like the compress is a helpful thing but not necessary. I figure the ointment's the real solution.

The next morning Murph's eye is sealed shut with pus, the surrounding skin bruised. A bath softens the hardened pus and his eye opens, though he looks like he's been in one hell of a bar brawl.

Pat and I decide to return to the Student Health Center, past Bouncer Nurse to Mama Doctor's office.

"Did you do the hot compress?" she asks, pressing under Murph's eye. Pearly green stuff seeps out of it.

Spence looks on, concerned now.

"What compress?" asks Pat.

"Murph wouldn't let me," I say. "Every time I put a hot wash-cloth on his face he screamed like I was trying to kill him."

"We were supposed to do compresses?" asks Pat, looking for clarification.

Dr. Mom talks to Pat as though he's the only adult in the room. "I told your wife that she needed to do ten-minute compresses five times a day."

Not true! Not true! I want to scream as Pat and Dr. Liar stare at me. The doctor turns back to Pat, sighs like "There's your problem," and leaves the room.

We four wait while nothing much happens. Nothing is said. I know that Pat is wondering why he married me. He looks down unsure, I'm sure, of what to say. Spence flips a loose latch on the examination table. Murph sits on the floor, happily gurgling, sliding his hand across the linoleum.

"She didn't say that I *had* to do the compress, Pat."

"What did she say?"

"She said to try it. I don't remember anything about five times a day. She said a compress might help, but no big deal if Murphy put up a fuss. She didn't make it sound like it was this for-sure-do-this-thing thing."

"Are you sure? It sounded pretty for-sure-do-it to me."

"I don't remember exactly."

"You don't remember?"

"I was upset and Spence was adding and I was worried and I couldn't hear her exactly."

"You couldn't *hear* the doctor?" he says.

"I couldn't concentrate on what she was saying."

Pat stops. I hear the air conditioner. I see Spence flip the latch. I feel Murph's bottom against the edge of my sandals.

Looking at us, I think, Is this it? Four people in a room alone together?

No, I think. Don't let this be all there is.

"No" repeats in my head as it has for several days now. No, no, no.

The third time we see green we are back in Los Angeles. The infection Murphy had in New Orleans finally succumbed to the antibiotic cream and frequent massaging and draining of his eye. But here it is again. Our regular pediatrician sends us to Dr. Goode, a portrait of whom hangs in his waiting room. In it he is seated on a couch next to bespectacled girl triplets.

I sit in the waiting room without Pat, since he is at work. Spence trots off to the miniature kitchen set up along one wall and Murph crawls over to a pile of blocks. I flip through *Parents* magazine, occasionally looking up to scan the room.

Across from me a father reads to his son, who has a patch over one eye. To my left sits a mom with a two-year-old little girl. One of the girl's pupils lolls in the corner of her eye, her other eye looking straight ahead. Since I've had endless eye problems myself, the clinic feels familiar.

"What kind of food would you like to eat, Mommy?" asks Spencer, holding a spatula and a plastic plate.

"Um. Eggs."

I watch Murph toss a block into a bucket. Spence walks over to the kitchen and plops plastic eggs onto a plate. I expect to see him slip them into the plastic frying pan and hold them over the toy stove. Instead, he opens up a cabinet, slides the plate in, and shuts the door. He presses his finger next to the door, like there's a button there.

"*Ding,*" he says loudly, removing the plate from the cabinet.

He delivers the eggs to me and I pick them up, making munching sounds around the yellow plastic.

"Thank you," I say, dabbing the corners of my mouth with my fingers.

"What else would you like to eat?" he asks.

"Pancakes."

Spence trots off to throw a plastic pancake onto a plate, slide it into the cabinet, and push the button.

"*Ding.*"

He microwaves everything I order. Spaghetti. Soup. A sandwich.

I feel warm with embarrassment. Spence's routine is so obviously a reflection of what he sees me do. I bury my head in the magazine, praying that Spence won't come over with the yellow square of plastic cheese, tap it on the armrest, and offer me a cigarette.

If he starts shaking martinis, I'm going to have to reschedule.

Dr. Goode shines a light in Murphy's eye and nudges the raised bruise near his tear duct. Murph, now used to all this poking, sits patiently. Spence rolls around under the doctor's desk.

"Looks like a blocked tear duct," Dr. Goode says. "It's very common." He recommends a simple procedure in which he inserts a tube through the tear duct, perhaps piercing any organic obstruction, allowing Murphy's tears to drain. Right now his tears simply collect in the duct, causing repeated infections.

"I've never heard of that," I say.

"Very common. Very common," he says, pulling a book from the shelf.

He flips open to a picture of a boy with a fleshy mound obscuring half of his eye. I pull back.

"Ughhh."

Spence jumps up to see the picture. "Wow," he says before I can pull the book away.

"Obviously, this is a bad case," says Dr. Goode. "Nothing like Murphy's."

Then why the hell did you show it to me? I think. Just to scare me shitless?

"But we should nip this in the bud," he continues. "I recommend surgery this week."

"Surgery?"

"You can get a second opinion," he says, snapping the book closed. "But they'll only refer you back to me. See, I wrote the book."

He hands the book to me and I see that he did indeed write the book.

Dr. Goode tells me a little more about the tube he'll insert into the duct. "Most likely, it'll come out by itself."

"What do you mean?"

"Oh. You may see the tube poking out of his eye at some point. If that happens, just cut it off with a pair of scissors and give me a call."

Sure, I think, after I run around the house screaming, "HOLY FUCK, THERE'S A TUBE COMING OUT OF MY SON'S EYE!" After I pass out, come to, and crawl to the phone to call Pat and demand that he come home.

"All right," I say, my voice tight.

Then something occurs to me.

"Could the obstruction be caused by food? I mean, could Murphy have rubbed food into his eye?"

Dr. Goode shakes his head. "No. He's probably always had this."

Aha, I think. I want to call Pat right now and tell him that it's *not* because of the food on Murphy's hands. It's *not* because I don't clean my baby well enough. It's *not* because I'm negligent or lazy.

I stop there, realizing that Pat has never called me negligent and lazy. That accusation is all mine.

"Then what causes it?" I ask.

"Murph was probably born with a duct that didn't go all the way through. We're only just seeing evidence of that because he's started crying tears."

Murphy wiggles in my lap and I let him down. I reach in my backpack for my phone so I can call Pat.

Spence squats in front of Murphy and stares into his eye. He is all concern. I look at the two brothers nose-to-nose and feel a pull in my chest.

That night I lie next to Pat, feeling his skin against mine. I think about Murphy's tears and I think about his eye. I think about how you can know a lot about someone and still not know much. Today I found out that a tiny part of Murphy is made differently. I don't know how important this little biological kink is. It doesn't seem like a complicated thing. But it does make me think about the whole universe that's inside us.

I think about Murph's tears giving him an infection. Right now he cries over a lost toy. Later, when there's true heartbreak, could his tears quite literally cause an infection, coursing through his body? In centuries past, before tubes and sophisticated medical care, did children quite literally die, infected with grief?

Pat rolls toward me and flops his heavy arm over my stomach. Usually, the weight of his arm makes me uncomfortable. But right now I like it.

I dream of being shrunk down so small that I can commandeer a submarine through Murphy's veins, right up to the inside of his left eye.

I want to be there for the operation, which is scheduled for 6 a.m., but Pat and I decide that it might be upsetting for Spence to go. And I don't want to leave him with a babysitter, knowing that we're all at the hospital with Murphy. So I stay home, padding through the living room in the early morning. Glancing at my watch every two minutes. I look into the boys' room several times to see Spence still sleeping, one leg hanging off the bed.

I sit at the dining table, drinking a cup of tea. I think about Murph, but I don't want to think about him. So I think about my recent discontent.

Is it simply that I am mourning a carefree, careless youth? Do I really want to be young like that again? Do I really want to be single again? Childless?

Sometimes I do, I think. Sometimes. Well, often.

I clink the spoon against the teacup that I inherited from my grandmother. It's floral. Not a bit like the kind of teacup I would choose if I were choosing.

Something new occurs to me as I stare at the painted flowers. I know it's new because I rarely have a thought that cannot be traced to a former thought or one uttered by someone far wiser than myself.

It is this: The only difference between Now and Then (aside from the obvious tracks of time) is that Now I have something to lose.

Spence wakes up, and instead of making breakfast, I say we're going to go get a milk shake.

I lay my cell phone on the counter of the local coffee shop.

Why isn't it ringing? Pat must know I'm anxious. The surgery must be over by now.

"Why do you keep looking at the phone, Mommy?"

"I'm just wondering when Daddy's going to call."

"Is he with Murphy?"

"Yes. They're fixing Murphy's eye."

When the phone finally does ring, I pounce. "How's Murph?"

"He's fine, honey. We're on our way home. I couldn't get reception at the hospital, so I couldn't call. I knew you'd be worried."

"Murphy's fine?"

"He's fine."

But he's not fine.

The next time we see green, and the next time and the next, we follow a routine of draining Murph's eye and visiting Dr. Goode, who is stumped.

After four unsuccessful operations—four mornings of Pat driving off with Murph as Spence and I hang by the phone—Dr. Goode says that he thinks that Murph should get an MRI.

"Okay," says Pat.

We say okay to everything. Dr. Goode shows us more pictures in his book. Pictures of children with huge growths coming out of their eyes, abscesses oozing from their lids.

Pat and I talk very little about Murphy's eye. I think, but don't know, that he is thinking what I am thinking: If I follow the instructions, if I do everything the doctor tells me to do, if I am good and thorough and responsible and practical, it will be all right.

★   ★   ★

The night before the MRI, I lie in bed with Pat's arm across my stomach. I watch my thoughts go close to the thing I haven't said to Pat or anyone. I watch my thoughts go forward and pull back, go forward and pull back. "Don't think about it," I say to myself. "Don't ask. Don't say the word 'cancer.'"

I dream that I am hanging off a cliff . . .

I know that it's not real. It's not real because it's impossible for me to bear my own weight with just my hands digging into the grass of the precipice.

"God," I say. "God, keep me hanging on."

Dr. Goode looks at the results of the MRI.

"This doesn't really tell me why the eye isn't draining," he says.

"Let me ask a stupid mom question," I say, determined to say the unsayable.

I look to Pat, who turns from showing Spence and Murph the eye chart.

In a voice that sounds like it's hardly worth asking, I ask, "There isn't a chance that this could be cancerous?"

Dr. Goode clears his throat. "No. We don't think there's any malignancy. That was, of course, the first thing we looked for."

It was? Why didn't he tell us that?

"And you're saying there's no cancer?"

"I'm almost positive."

"Almost?"

"I'd say there's no cancer."

"Are you going to check again?"

"Yes. We'll be checking again."

Pat says, "But you have no reason to believe, right now, that there's any malignancy."

"Right."

I don't know why I don't feel better. I guess I'm looking for some signed statement from Mr. Guy-who-wrote-the-book-on-all-this that my son does not have and never will have cancer.

"I want you to take Murphy to see Dr. Braunstein," says Dr. Goode. "He's a friend of mine in Beverly Hills. He's a plastic surgeon."

"Why do we need a plastic surgeon?" asks Pat.

"I think I want him with me the next time I go in. He may have to reconstruct Murphy's tear duct."

Pat and I look at each other.

"Uh. Okay," says Pat.

The four of us cram into Dr. Braunstein's office for the usual eye poking. Dr. Braunstein talks fast, treating Pat's and my questions like annoyances that must be endured. The effect of which is that we don't ask many. We listen to him give his theory that perhaps the network near the eye is vastly different from one that functions normally. He might have to cut into the nose, he says. He might have to reconstruct passageways.

I put Murphy on the floor and square myself. I feel like I need to slow all of this down. How did we get from bothersome infections to slicing into my son's face?

"If we choose not to do anything about this," I say, "what would be the consequence? I mean, would we simply have a child who got occasional eye infections?"

Dr. Braunstein looks at me like I'm a remedial student who accidentally got funneled into honors class.

He sighs loudly. "I'm sure I don't have to tell you that everything's connected up there in his head. And you don't want any infections, especially repeated ones, happening that close to the brain."

My stomach takes a dive like I'm on a roller coaster. Pat's face goes soft.

Infections near the brain? No one told me this. Not in the four months that we've been hauling Murphy in and out of offices.

The roller coaster shuttles up the next rickety hill. My breathing gets tight as I approach the apex. I hear nothing but the pounding of my pulse. Then down I go, whizzing through the last terrifying loop. The car seems to careen out of control. I scream, *"Noooo,"* as I hang on, feeling it shudder. As the loop flattens out, I feel a drag, slowing me down. Up ahead, I see the end. I try to steady my breathing as I pull into the platform. The safety bar clangs over my head and I get out, my knees quivering, my heart thumping, my shirt soaking.

". . . avoid reconstruction, we will," Dr. Braunstein is saying.

I look down at Murphy tugging on my shoelace.

"I don't want him to have any more infections," I say.

The nurse smiles at Murphy as Pat and I check him in the next morning. Spence is still asleep at home, I hope, while my brother watches the *Today* show.

"Aww," she says. "Little Murph is back."

As Pat checks us in, various nurses and technicians smile or wave at Murph.

He's a regular.

I follow as Pat carries Murph through the familiar maze of swinging doors and polished floors. We follow arrows. We buzz buzzers. We walk past adult patients on gurneys. I try not to look at them. It seems invasive.

Curtains are shushed open by a nurse who also seems to know Murph. On a rolling bed is a small pair of pale green scrubs. Pat starts to take off Murphy's clothes.

"They make scrubs this small?" I ask, holding them up.

"I guess it's standard for anyone who's having an operation," says Pat.

He puts Murph's arms through the armholes of the scrubs and begins to tie up the back.

"I didn't imagine the tiny scrubs," I say. "You didn't tell me he wore these."

"I didn't think about it."

I've missed all this, I think. I haven't been here. It's true I've been home with Spence. But I think I was too afraid to come, before.

Pat finishes the tying and picks Murphy up as the nurse wheels a cart next to the bed. There are more forms this time, she says. Forms that give our permission for the doctors to do anything that they feel is required, once they're "inside."

His *head,* I think. Once they're inside his head.

Pat puts Murph on the bed and starts to sign. Murph grabs the edges of the papers as Pat flips through them.

The nurse hands me a Sharpie. "And just write the word 'yes' over the eye that's going to be operated on."

"Write 'yes'?"

"Over the eye. It's another sign of permission from the parents."

I pick Murph up and lay him down on the bed. He looks at me, unwavering, as I take the cap off the pen and write the word "yes" over his left eye.

The next hour is like a generic scene from a hospital movie. The doctors talk to us briefly before going into the OR. They wear scrubs that look similar to Murph's. I train my attention on what they are saying, calmed a bit at the thought that these highly moneyed, very important doctors are dressed in what looks like green pajamas.

Murph is given a sedative that makes him heavy in my arms. His head rolls off my shoulder every time I move.

When the time comes, I lay Murph on the gurney. He looks at me like he has a question he's unable to ask. Pat and I watch as he's wheeled into the OR, the doors swinging shut.

While Murph is gone, we wait. We pace. We drink Diet Coke from the machine. We pace. We look at our watches. We talk about other things. We look out the window. We flip through magazines. We go to the bathroom. We sip from the water fountain. We try not to look at the other patients through the break in their curtains.

Finally, the green doctor twosome appears and tells us that things went better than they could have imagined.

Pat and I melt with relief as Braunstein draws us a picture of what was done to Murph's eye on the back of a newspaper. He's happy to report that they did the whole procedure through the duct and didn't have to cut through the nose. I want to hug Braunstein, but I don't. He hands me the newspaper with the drawing on it and shakes my hand. He turns to shake Pat's, but Pat pulls him into his chest, enveloping him in a grateful embrace.

Murph arrives minutes later. Asleep on the gurney. A bit of dried blood in the corner of his eye. "Yes" still scrawled across the left side of his forehead.

Pat and I look down at him, our arms touching.

Pat reaches out and smooths Murph's curls.

I look at *Yes.*

Every mom writes YES on her child as soon as she claims him. She writes it with a prayer and with hope. Whenever she looks at her child, or thinks of him or dreams of him, she says YES you are mine and YES I'll let you go.

Pat takes my hand as I put my other hand on Murph's chest.

Yes, I say to myself. Yes, I take this man. Yes, I take these children.

Yes, I have. Yes, I will. Yes, I do.

Yes, I say over and over and over and over.

Yes, I say. Yes. Yes.

YES.

Acknowledgments

I owe everything always to my mother and father, Audrey and Fred Paesel, who give me the courage and blind faith to be a parent because they do it so well. I had such a happy upbringing, my only complaint is that I don't have any salacious material for a childhood memoir. Thanks, too, to my brothers, Erik and Keir, who are two of the funniest guys I know. They taught me the double take, the deadpan, the slow burn, and the value of telling a story in which you are the biggest idiot in the room.

And thank you to my mother-in-law, Patricia Towne, who is a great sport and a flawless grandma.

Many thanks to my manager, Adam Peck, who is a cheerleader, a workhorse, and a benevolent nudge. He introduced me to my agent, Erin Hosier, whose dogged devotion to this project has been moving and inspiring. My editor, Amy Einhorn, has been patient and wise and pregnant through the entire editing process— a true soldier. All three have given me invaluable counsel, both business and artistic. Emily Griffin has been my daily contact over at Warner. I appreciate her patience and good humor.

A huge thank-you to my teacher, mentor, and friend, Claudette Sutherland. She has literally shown me the way to realize my dreams. She read through many drafts of the book, providing expert advice. Her class has been one of the pivotal experiences of my life. And thank you to my fellow students around that table: Frank Sharp, Adrienne Barbeau, Andrea Goyan, Dani Klein, Justin Jorgensen, Brooks Almy, John Miranda, David O'Shea, and Moon Zappa.

Paula Killen is a valued friend, critic, and muse, as is Marcia Wilkie. They, along with Sarah Stanley, Doug Cooney, and Jill Soloway, read drafts of many chapters. Their feedback and encouragement had a profound effect on my writing and on the book.

Two writing groups helped me greatly. The first was the Thursday group that met in my living room, and the second was a group who called themselves "The Disclaimers."

Thanks to dear friends Stephanie Young and Kerry Haynie, who gave me a room of my own.

I want to thank all the women who meet for drinks on Fridays. That weekly happy hour is a highlight of any given week. The genesis of this book was really the desire to celebrate the love and laughter I experience in the midst of those friends. I have already thanked several of the joiners, but I am also deeply indebted to Bernadette Sullivan, Melanie Hutsell, Kelly Morris, and Josette Di Carlo.

Thank you to the women who have shaped my life from adolescence on: Milly Gallagher, Karen Hill, Cathy Mathews, and again, Stephanie Young.

My high school English teachers instilled in me a love of literature: Wilma Counts, Betty Kennedy, and Annie Schmidt.

Thanks to my agents at UTA: Sue Naegle, Marissa Devins, and Larry Salz; as well as Farsh Askari and Tim Phillips.

Thanks to Birds Restaurant, Christian Lebano, Jenny Bicks, Anne Etue, Tanya White, Dee Ryan, Kim Fitzgerald (for the iconic parenting joke), Judith Scott, Fabio Sehbe, and Mark Luther. And thanks to Edward Louis Luther, who could not be here today.

Thank you to James Joyce and John Lennon for inspiring me with their exaltation of the word "yes."

Thank you to my husband, Patrick Towne, who believes that I can do anything. And who is my one true love.

And thank you to my children, Spencer and Murphy, who are the answer to, and the reason for, everything.